THE JOHNS HOPKINS UNIVERSITY STUDIES IN HISTORICAL AND POLITICAL SCIENCE

Under the Direction of the Department of History,
Political Economy, and Political Science.

SERIES LXXXII
(1964)

NUMBER 2

UNITED STATES POLICY AND
THE PARTITION OF TURKEY, 1914–1924

UNITED STATES POLICY
AND THE PARTITION OF TURKEY,
1914–1924

By
LAURENCE EVANS

BALTIMORE
THE JOHNS HOPKINS PRESS

Printed in the United States of America

Library of Congress Catalog Card Number: 65-11660

This book has been brought to publication with the assistance of a
grant from the Ford Foundation.

To

A. M. E.

E. T. E.

C. A. E.

E. I. E.

PREFACE

The probable dissolution of the Ottoman Empire and its partition among the states of Europe was the central political fact in the Middle East from 1774 to the settlement of World War I. The object of this book is on the one hand to describe the significance of that political fact in the foreign policy of the United States during the War and its settlement, and on the other to describe the role which the United States assigned to itself in the settlement of the Eastern question.

This is a policy study, and it considers its subject primarily from the standpoint of the center looking outward, from the point of view of the President and the Secretary of State as the makers of American foreign policy. In relating the stages through which American Middle East policy passed, from complete non-involvement to intense concern and back to non-involvement, my aim has been to present, first, the problems facing the United States as they were seen through the eyes of American policy-makers; second, the information about these problems that was available to the policy-makers; third, their interpretation of the situation in terms of American interests; fourth, the process of determining policy; and fifth, the implementation of policy.

There are several limitations on the scope of this study, some imposed by the approach taken to the subject and others imposed by the availability of data. Since this is a study of policy, it treats such matters as the diplomatic, economic, and social relations between the United States and the Ottoman Empire—and the other states concerned with the Middle East—only as they affected the making of policy or reflect its implementation. The events with which American policy is concerned are not considered in their own right but as objects of that policy. In the same way, since this is a study of American policy, the policies of other powers are also considered as the raw material of American policy.

In the second category are the limitations which result from

9

the inability to subject the policies of foreign countries to the same scrutiny, in depth, as the policies of the United States. None of the archives of the foreign ministries of the European and Middle Eastern countries are open for the period covered, in contrast to the United States, where not only are the pertinent Department of State documents available to the public, but also the papers of the chief figures of the time, including President Wilson, Secretary of State Lansing, and Colonel House. However, as far as this study is concerned, the important thing is what the presidents and secretaries of state thought the policies of the powers were, rather than what they actually were.

In addition to the contribution this study may make to the understanding of American foreign policy and the history of the modern Middle East, it is hoped it will shed some light on the nature of international relations generally. American Middle East policy developed until recently in the absence of any significant direct political interest in the area and was thus the product of the political forces generated by the international situation itself, rather than the result of the need to advance or defend particular American interests. The United States had nothing to fear and little to gain from the Middle East. The reactions of the American government to the situation in the Middle East at any given time, therefore, reflect the political pressures brought to bear on the United States by its involvement in the international community of states, and the analysis of these reactions can throw into strong relief the nature of the community of states as a distinct political phenomenon. The opportunity to study international relations in its " pure " form, and to study a foreign policy almost divorced from domestic forces, occurs rarely; American Middle East policy during World War I is the only instance, to my knowledge, which offers the opportunity on such a level of significance and with all the relevant data available to the historian.

It is a pleasure to acknowledge the debt I owe to Professor Majid Khadduri for his assistance and encouragement during the writing of this book and, in fact, during the whole of my professional career from my days as a graduate student under him, to the present. Another long-standing debt is owed to Professor Harry N. Howard, who pioneered in the study of American Middle East policy. His comments on my manuscript were most helpful and were responsible for correcting several errors of fact. Professor Dankwart Rustow also read the manuscript, and my thanks are due to him for his suggestions and comments. I would also like to record here a special note of appreciation to Professor Zeine N. Zeine and Mr. Asad Khairullah of the American University of Beirut for their assistance in locating and translating source material in Arabic (though the responsibility for the selection and translations is mine). A book of this nature would be impossible to write without the assistance of those in charge of the archives and libraries where the source material is located, and for this assistance I am indebted to: Mrs. Carroll and Mr. Heise of the National Archives; Miss K. Brand, late of the Library of Congress; Mr. Frank Schork, formerly librarian of the School of Advanced International Studies; the librarians and staffs of the libraries of Yale University, the American University of Beirut, the British Foreign Office, and the British War Office; and the staff of the Public Records Office. The research and writing of this book were made possible by generous grants from the Joint Committee on Near and Middle East Studies of the American Council of Learned Societies and the Social Science Research Council, and the Rockefeller Foundation. The former enabled me to finish my research in the Middle East and Europe, and the latter to spend some fifteen months writing.

A note on the transliteration and spelling of Arabic and Turkish words: this has presented an almost insuperable problem. There were two main systems of translations, each with its variations, in use at the time of World War I—the French and British systems; the differences between them were due to the different values each language assigned to the same letter. Thus, in French, Djamal, Beyrouth; in English, Jamal, Beirut. In addition, there are variations within each system which can give five spellings to the same name in as many documents—Djamal, Djemel, Jamal, Jemel, and Gamal—according to the nationality and personal preference of the writer. Since there are so many direct quotations in this book, I have not found it practical to attempt to impose my own pattern on other peoples' spelling merely for the sake of consistency; where any ambiguity exists I have tried to clarify it. In the same way I have not attempted to modernize the spelling of Turkish names, nor the names of Turkish cities and towns. Angora remains Angora, not Ankara; Constantinople has not been changed to Istanbul; Djamal, not Cemal. I have kept the names used at the time, not only by the Europeans but by the Turks also, who used the French spellings of their names and their cities as a rule when writing in English and French.

Acknowledgment is gratefully made to the Yale University Library for permission to quote from the papers of Colonel Edward M. House, and to Houghton Mifflin Company for permission to quote from *The Intimate Papers of Colonel House*, by Charles Seymour.

Annotation of Documentary Sources

This study is based principally on material from five documentary sources: the files of the Department of State and the American Mission to Negotiate Peace, in the National Archives; the papers of President Wilson and the papers of Secretary of State Robert Lansing in the Library of Congress; and the papers of Edward M. House in the Sterling Library of Yale University.

The State Department uses a decimal file system, with each country being assigned a two digit number and the various categories of information about each country, its relations with the United States, and its relations with other countries being indicated by combinations of numbers. Thus the numbers for Austria and Serbia are 63 and 72 respectively; the 700 file relates to political relations; file 763.72 covers material on political relations between Austria and Serbia and is the file under which most of the material on the war is filed. State Department documents are cited under the file number together with the telegram or despatch number, date etc. (unless they have been published, when the published source is cited). For example, footnote 5, p. 4: Despatch 490 from Constantinople, March 24, 1913, 867.00/546; the file number is in the 800 series dealing with internal conditions, 67 is the number for Turkey, 00 after the point indicates political affairs; this is the file for internal political conditions in Turkey, and the number after the slash indicates the individual documents. The Peace Commission papers are filed separately under the same system; they are differentiated in the footnotes by the addition of " Peace Commission files " to the citation.

The Wilson papers are divided into two main groups, those papers accumulated by President Wilson during the Peace Conference and those accumulated during the rest of his term of office. At the time my research was undertaken the Peace Conference documents were designated series VIII A, and the others as series II. Each series is filed chronologically in numbered boxes, and citations are made to " Wilson Papers " with the series and box numbers. The Lansing papers and the House papers are filed chronologically, and citations to these sources are to " Lansing Papers " or " House Papers " with the individual documents identified.

In addition to the above sources, much use has been made of the official publications of the United States and Great Britain. *Papers Relating to the Foreign Relations of the United States*, including the regular annual series, the war supplements, the Paris Peace Conference series, and the published Lansing Papers, is cited as *Foreign Relations*. *Documents on British Foreign Policy 1919–1939* is cited as *British Documents*.

TABLE OF CONTENTS

UNITED STATES POLICY AND
THE PARTITION OF TURKEY, 1914–1924

PART I
THE WAR

CHAPTER I

TURKEY AND THE WAR AGAINST GERMANY

1.

In the summer of 1914 the Middle East was, politically speaking, the most remote of the regions of the world with which the United States maintained diplomatic relations. In Latin America, the Far East, and in Europe, American interests were direct. For ninety years the Monroe Doctrine had been a guidepost for the protection of American hemispheric interests and had been invoked with effect throughout that time. The Open Door policy and the maintenance of the integrity of the Chinese Empire were policies the advancement of which had been a major preoccupation of successive administrations in Washington. Even the fate of Tibet had occasioned considerable misgivings in the Department of State at the time of the Younghusband mission. The Russo-Japanese War had seen an American President assuming the role of peacemaker in the Far East, and most important, the United States possessed the Philippines. The principles of Washington's Farewell Address were based on the importance of European affairs to the United States, not their remoteness, and the tradition of isolation was a policy that had to be renewed constantly, being the other side of the Monroe Doctrine. But the countries of the Middle East, pawns in the international politics of Europe, were insulated from the United States by intervening layers of interests, ambitions, and fears of the European powers and by the lack of direct American political interests in the area.

Even the Ottoman Empire was no exception to this rule. It impinged on American awareness only when news of massacres of Armenians, Bulgarians, and other Christians came out of the Levant. Traditionally, the United States had avoided involvement

21

in the Eastern question. This was not difficult to do in view of the limited American interests in the Ottoman Empire; these in the main consisted of missionary endeavors and a small trade in currants, tobacco, and manufactured goods. On the Straits question, the United States was concerned with free passage for its ships in time of peace and left the great political question of the passage of ships of war through the Bosporus and Dardanelles in time of war to the European Powers.[1] Thus, in the Turco-Italian War and the Balkan wars, two great Eastern crises that immediately preceded the outbreak of the European war, the Department of State rejected suggestions that the United States undertake a limited role in the Eastern Question. In December, 1911, President Taft requested the opinion of Secretary of State Knox on the advisability of American diplomatic intervention in the Turco-Italian War. The Secretary replied that there was no mutually acceptable basis for an attempt by the United States to negotiate between the belligerents. Italy insisted on having Tripoli and the Turks refused absolutely to consider ceding it. In any event, other powers more intimately concerned should initiate steps to end the conflict. As for the internal problems of Turkey, continued the Secretary, American interference was even less feasible; there was no way for the United States to bring pressure on Turkey or even offer advice. He advised the President that American action should be confined to the protection of American interests, strictly defined.[2]

In February, 1913, during the Balkan wars, shortly after the C. U. P. (Committee of Union and Progress) had renewed the fighting between Turkey and the Balkan allies, Morgenthau, the American Ambassador in Turkey, reported to Washington

[1] On American policy on the Straits, see Harry N. Howard, " The United States and the Problem of the Turkish Straits," *Middle East Journal*, I (1947), No. 1, 59–72. Professor Howard has in preparation a book-length study of this subject. On other American interests in the Middle East at this time, see John DeNovo, *American Interests and Policies in the Middle East* (Minnesota, 1963), chaps. I and II.

[2] President Taft to the Secretary of State, letter, December 20, 1911, 867.00/357; reply sent December 27; correspondence sent to the Embassy in Constantinople as enclosure to Instruction 74 on December 28, all 867.00/357. The occasion of the President's inquiry was the visit of two American missionaries who had called on the President to impress on him the terrible conditions in Turkey due to the war and to beg him to intervene to stop the war and ameliorate the plight of all Turks, Christian and Muslim.

that outbreaks of violence against Christians and foreigners in Constantinople were likely and that the international fleet in Turkish waters was being increased to cope with the situation. He said that American citizens in Turkey would have to rely on foreign protection unless the United States sent ships to Constantinople. The Department replied that it was " loath " to become entangled in the politics of the Ottoman Empire, a situation which might attend the presence of an American vessel at Constantinople and its co-operation in action by the naval forces of other powers there, in view of the possibility that such action might assume a character other than that of mere precaution or the protection of the interests of foreign citizens. However, if the Ambassador apprehended actual danger to American citizens, he might take steps to obtain permission from the Porte for an American cruiser to enter the Straits.[3]

While the United States was not prepared to take an active part in the settlement of the problems of Turkey, it was not unconcerned with events in the Near and Middle East. American aloofness grew, not out of a lack of perspicacity on the part of the Department of State but out of the remoteness of these problems from the vital interests of the United States, and from its inability—without a revolution in American foreign policy and diplomacy—to affect significantly the course of events in the Middle East. But the United States was quite aware of the importance of the Eastern question to the Ottoman Empire itself and in the greater arena of European power politics. The Department of State received a constant stream of reports from its diplomatic and consular establishments in the Middle East describing, with varying degrees of accuracy and insight, the events and developments in the Ottoman Empire and in the diplomatic sphere. Morgenthau reported to the Department in February, 1913, that the " moral and material assistance " which the great powers had promised Turkey in its efforts to reform her finances and administration would lead to the " hypothecation " of Turkey's most valuable natural resources and to the establishment of international control.[4] In May he outlined in a despatch the various plans

---

[3] Telegram from Constantinople, February 17, 1913; Secretary of State to Secretary of the Navy, letter, February 20; Secretary of State to Constantinople, telegram, February 19, all 867.00/471.

[4] Despatch 407 from Constantinople, February 7, 1913, 867.51/63.

of the European powers and what they hoped to get out of this moral and material assistance. He said that the British hoped to get the opportunity to lend more money to Turkey, also an understanding on the Turco-Persian frontier, and greater influence in lower Mesopotamia; the Germans wanted more railroad concessions on easier terms than before and with a greater degree of control over their operation and exploitation; the Russians wanted an understanding on the eastern frontier; the French, more concessions and recognition of their interests in Syria.[5]

From Beirut the Consul-General sent back a series of despatches during 1912, 1913, and 1914,[6] describing the efforts being made by France to extend its influence in Syria through financial support for French educational establishments in Lebanon; numerous visits to Beirut by French warships; and " visits, tours, interference with the government, etc." by the French Consul-General. He also noted that the British seemed to have acknowledged French primacy in Syria, but that only ten per cent of the populace wanted a French protectorate, which was being openly discussed. He thought that ninety per cent would prefer a British protectorate since they had before them the example of Egypt and the great strides made there, whereas in Algeria and Tunis the French seemed intent on turning these countries into extensions of France, complete with French colonists. An American protectorate, he said, would be welcomed by the Syrians with open arms.[7] (On

[5] Despatch 490 from Constantinople, March 24, 1913, 867.00/546.

[6] Cf. despatch 247 from Beirut, May 14, 1912; despatch 341, November 16, 1912; despatch 350, November 29, 1912; despatch 610, December 9, 1913; despatch 718, June 19, 1914; all file 867.00, various enclosures. In despatch 350, the Consul-General said that French plans for Syria were being openly discussed; the Egyptian papers spoke openly of a French protectorate, but the Beirut press confined itself to occasional hints. In despatch 610, the Consul-General reported that a French fleet had visited Beirut, but a British fleet cruising in these waters had avoided the port; he had learned, he said (he did not say from what source), that this had been done deliberately by the British to give the French an opportunity to make as much political capital out of the visit as possible. He added that the events of the past year showed that the British no longer had any pretensions in Syria, and it might very well be that the Syrians had best start making plans to govern their actions, looking to the eventuality of a French protectorate, and other countries with interests in Syria had better do the same.

[7] In despatch 355 from Beirut, December 6, 1912, the Consul-General enclosed a despatch from the Consul at Aleppo describing a visit to the Consulate of a Mr. L. Woolley and a Mr. T. E. Lawrence of the British archeological expedition at Carcemish. They told him there were reports circulating that the Khedive of Egypt, the Sherif of Mecca, Izzat Pasha, the former secretary of Abdul Hamid,

the other hand, the consulate at Baghdad sent a despatch in March, 1913, reporting rumors of a secret movement for autonomy among the Arabs; the name of the society was " La Markazia.") [8]

2.

After the outbreak of war in Europe in August, 1914, American policy toward Turkey remained essentially unchanged. Turkey remained neutral for three months before joining the Central Powers under the terms of a secret treaty signed with Germany on August 2,[9] and though the United States was concerned to prevent the extension of hostilities, no attempt was made to dissuade Turkey on political grounds from entering the war. Ambassador Morgenthau reported, on August 7, that the Cabinet was divided on the question of war. (The secret treaty with Germany was known to very few men in the Turkish Cabinet.) He said that the Minister of War, Enver, under the influence of the German Military mission, favored an alliance with Germany, the Minister of Marine and Finance favored France, while the Minister of the Interior counseled moderation and neutrality. Sentiment was developing in favor of an invasion of the Caucasus, however,

---

and Abdul Rahman, Amir of the Hajj, were plotting to overthrow Turkish rule in Syria, Palestine, Mesopotamia, and Arabia. There was also talk, they said, of giving the caliphate to a member of the Kuraish of Mecca and removing it from politics. In despatch 361, December 11, a second report from Aleppo was enclosed giving details of further talks with Mr. Woolley and Mr. Lawrence on the threat to Aleppo by the Kurdish irregular cavalry that had concentrated near the city. The two visitors told the Consul that the Kurds planned to sack the city, and their organization of the attack was so far advanced that they had allotted individual houses to particular groups of men. The Kurdish irregulars had been recruited by the Ottoman government for service in the Balkan War. Constantinople reported in a telegram of January 10, 1913, 867.00/449, that 15,000 Kurds had reached Constantinople from the front and that to get them to return home peacefully would be difficult for the government since they had had no booty. There were a similar number near Aleppo, said the telegram, with the declared intention of sacking the city in revenge for the assassination of a Kurdish chief by the C. U. P. in 1909.

[8] Despatch 80 from Baghdad, March 17, 1913, 867.00/517.

[9] On August 8, 1914, the Ottoman Embassy delivered a note to the Secretary of State declaring that the Ottoman Empire would maintain strict neutrality in the war and that the present mobilization was for defense only. The text of the treaty is in J. C. Hurewitz, *Diplomacy in the Near and Middle East: A Documentary Record*, 1914–1956 (Princeton, 1956), II, 1.

he added.[10] On the 11th Morgenthau reported that the German cruisers *Goeben* and *Breslau*, sent to take the place of two cruisers then building in Britain for Turkey but appropriated by the Royal Navy on the outbreak of war, had passed the Dardanelles, and would, with the German admiral and all their personnel, join the Turkish service. Morgenthau thought that this completely changed the situation and that it was likely to precipitate Turkey into the general war.[11]

Later in the month Morgenthau asked whether, in view of the closely balanced sentiment in the Turkish Cabinet on the question of neutrality, he should urge the Minister of War and the Minister of the Interior to remain neutral. He had just been informed, he said, that his advice at the present stage of affairs might have considerable weight, and he believed that a strong representation to the two ministers, of Turkey's financial, commercial, and military unpreparedness and of the damaging consequences of their antagonizing the Entente Powers, who were in complete control of the Mediterranean and could, therefore, capture Smyrna, Beirut, and the other coastal towns, would convince them to remain neutral.[12] The State Department replied in categorical terms the following day. "Under no circumstances offer any suggestions officially or unofficially to the Turkish Government or to any Turkish official relative to the question of Turkish neutrality in the present war, . . ." the cable instructed the Ambassador, but, it went on, if the Turkish government on its own initiative should ask his opinion and advice, Morgenthau was to state that the United States government, solely in the interest of humanity and from no political consideration, was desirous that the war should not spread further and earnestly hoped that Turkey, inspired by the same motives, would find that her national interest did not prevent her from preserving neutrality.[13]

Shortly after the Allies had declared war on Turkey following

[10] Telegram from Constantinople, August 7, 1914 (received August 16), 763.72/439.

[11] Telegram from Constantinople August 11, 1914, 763.72/447; an earlier telegram of August 8 reported the great disappointment in Turkey over the expropriation of the cruisers by the British, 763.72/468.

[12] Telegram from Constantinople undated (received August 25, 1914), 763.72111/348.

[13] Telegram to Constantinople, August 26, 1914, 763.72111/348.

the bombardment of Odessa on October 28,[14] Morgenthau, in an interview with Enver on November 15, commented on the call to Jihad promulgated by the Sheikh-ul-Islam. He told the Minister of War that it might arouse the masses in Turkey to a wave of fanaticism. This might get out of hand, he said, and lead to attacks on all non-Muslims. He warned of the harmful effects if massacres occurred; Turkey would lose the friendship of the United States, and that might mean that the United States would side with the Entente Powers.[15] On receiving the Ambassador's report on this interview, the Department replied warning him against making any statement that the United States might take sides in the war and instructing him to maintain strict neutrality.[16]

The formal relations of the United States and Turkey during the period of American neutrality also reflected the determined effort of the United States to maintain strict impartiality in the Eastern War. The United States refused to recognize the unilateral abrogation of the Capitulations by Turkey[17] but, on the

[14] This was carried out by a German-Turkish fleet under German command; most of the Cabinet were completely ignorant of the attack until after it had taken place.

[15] Telegram 38 from Constantinople, November 15, 1914, 763.72/1238; Enver had made an official call at the Embassy to apologize for the search of the British and French embassies. In this telegram Morgenthau described the mounting violence in Turkey against foreigners and Christians and reported that he had told the German Ambassador Germany would share in the responsibility if massacres occurred. In despatch 137, November 28, 763.72/1357, Morgenthau gives a summary of Turkish violations of diplomatic premises, expropriation of schools, the "Turkification" of instruction and the expulsion of teachers of Allied nationality. He adds that all mob outbreaks were government inspired.

[16] Telegram 64 to Constantinople, November 24, 1914, 763.72/1238.

[17] For correspondence regarding the attempted abrogation of the capitulations by the Ottoman government, see *Foreign Relations*, 1914, pp. 1090–94, and *ibid.*, 1914, Supplement, pp. 767, 777. The Turkish government took the official position that the capitulations were privileges granted unilaterally by the Sublime Porte to the several powers for its own convenience and could, therefore, be terminated at any time by the action of the Porte. Historically this position had a solid foundation, but practically it had not been valid for over a century. The Turkish position is stated in a note, from the Minister for Foreign Affairs to the American Ambassador, of September 9, 1914, and sent to the Department of State as an enclosure to despatch 115 from Constantinople, September 11, 1914, 711.673/49; *Foreign Relations*, 1914, pp. 1091–93. The American position was put to the Ottoman government in a note of September 16, 1914, to the Turkish Ambassador, and by the American Ambassador to the Porte on instructions from the Secretary of State. The reply of the Turkish Ambassador to the Secretary of State bordered on the impertinent and did nothing to soothe the strained relations then existing between the Turkish Embassy and the United States government; see below. The text of the Turkish reply is in *ibid.*, p. 1094.

other hand, did not recognize the British declaration of a protectorate over Egypt and the assumption by the Khedive of the title of Sultan.[18] After an unfortunate beginning, when the Turkish Ambassador was asked to leave the country for publicly and volubly commenting on the general attitude of Americans toward his country, and more particularly for making invidious comparisons between Turkish treatment of minorities and American treatment of Philippine supporters of independence, commenting on American treatment of Negroes, and asking if the American people were advocating war on Turkey,[19] the wartime diplomatic relations between the two countries continued on the surface to be correct and without incident. Relations became actually cordial in the beginning of 1917 except for the very strong representations made by the United States in May, 1916, with respect to the commandeering of American missionary buildings by the Turkish military.[20]

[18] On August 7, 1914, the Diplomatic Agency and Consulate-General at Cairo reported, in despatch 57 (763.72/725), an official announcement by the Egyptian government that since the presence of the British Army in Egypt had rendered the country liable to attack by Britain's enemies, Britain had been entrusted with the defense of the country. (Egypt also made a declaration of belligerency against the German Empire, much to the anger of the Turks.) On November 2, Cairo reported by telegram it had been notified by the British Chargé that the British Army in Egypt had received orders from London to assume military control of Egypt, and responsibility for its protection, and that martial law would be proclaimed immediately; 763.72/1159. On November 7, Cairo cabled that the British General Officer Commanding in Egypt had issued a proclamation in the name of King George that Britain had assumed the sole burden of protecting Egypt against Turkey; 763.72/1180. When rumors began to circulate in Cairo that Prince Hussain, uncle of the deposed Khedive, was about to be proclaimed Sultan of Egypt, the Diplomatic Agent cabled for instructions whether he should attend any ceremonies that might be held, in view of the attitude of Turkey towards events in Egypt; telegram, December 11, 1914, 883.00/49. The Department replied on December 12 that when the Khedive assumed authority, the Diplomatic Agent was to deal with him as a *de facto* official but was not to attend any ceremonies. He could show the telegram to the British authorities and was to explain to them that the American attitude was taken " out of a scrupulous regard for neutrality "; telegram, December 12, 883.00/49.

[19] *Foreign Relations*, Lansing Papers, I, 68–75.

[20] Correspondence in *Foreign Relations*, 1916, pp. 829–46; on May 27, 1916, the Department of State instructed the Chargé in Turkey to inform the Turkish government that the United States had received " with great surprise and astonishment " the information that the Turkish authorities had seized missionary property, and considering this in relation to a series of other acts, namely, the breaking of American seals on foreign consular offices under American protection, the treatment of American consular mail, and the harassment of American consular officers and employees, " which have already occasioned grave concern," made it necessary

3.

Although the United States maintained a policy of careful neutrality towards Turkey, President Wilson's exhortations to his countrymen to be neutral in thought as well as in deed in the war, apparently were not meant to apply to the Turks. In the affair of the Turkish Ambassador mentioned above, the Ambassador's strong feeling on the subject of American attitudes toward his country had some justification, if his conduct did not. As he put it in an informal letter to the Secretary of State, when asked to explain his action in making a statement to the press containing much undiplomatic and unacceptable language, " The attitude of the press has poisoned public opinion in the United States in regard to the Turkish people to such an extent that a member of that race is seldom thought or spoken of in this country otherwise than as the ' unspeakable.' . . ." Nor was the government itself impartial in its opinion and attitude concerning the present or the future of the Ottoman state. The loss of large and populous segments of the Empire in 1908, in the Turco-Italian War, and in the Balkan wars, had seemed to indicate its rapid disintegration even before World War I broke out. When Woodrow Wilson was considering the appointment of ambassadors shortly after his election in 1912, Colonel House suggested Henry Morgenthau as Ambassador to Turkey; Wilson replied, " There ain't going to be no Turkey," to which House rejoined, " Then let him go look for it." [21] After August, 1914, Turkey seemed fated to disappear entirely; if the Central Powers won, it would at best become a German protectorate, and if the Allies were victorious it would be parceled out among the victors. Having regard for the record of the Ottoman government in mis-government, oppression, and the massacres of the Armenians, the United States government was not disposed to do anything to prevent the extinction of the Ottoman Empire—an attitude that was progressively reinforced during the war.

---

to request " without delay " a statement of the " attitude of the Turkish government towards the United States. . . ." The Turkish reply, sent on June 26, 1916, to the Chargé, was long and evasive and unresponsive to the American charges, but the matter was not pressed further.

[21] Charles Seymour (ed.), *The Intimate Papers of Colonel House* (Boston, 1926), I, 96.

The position of the government is shown clearly in the discussions of possible peace terms during the two missions of Colonel House to Europe, in 1915 and 1916, to explore the possibility of a negotiated peace. In February, 1915, House was told by the British Foreign Secretary, Sir Edward Grey, what France and Russia would expect in a final settlement—Alsace-Lorraine for France and control of Constantinople for Russia. Although House told Grey that the United States could not take part in negotiations on such territorial questions, he did not raise any objection in principle to Russian aims.[22] Again a year later, during his second mission, in discussing with Grey the entry of the United States into the war, House suggested that the United States could come in on the submarine issue, or, alternatively, the President might demand a peace conference, and if Germany refused " reasonable terms " the United States might enter the war to enforce them. The " reasonable terms " seem to have included Russian occupation or control of Constantinople.[23] House describes a meeting with members of the British War Cabinet, including Prime Minister Asquith, Grey, Lloyd George, A. J. Balfour, and Lord Reading, in which peace terms were discussed: " We all cheerfully divided up Turkey, both in Asia and Europe. The discussion hung for a long while around the fate of Constantinople." Lloyd George and Balfour were not enthusiastic about giving it to Russia, but Grey and Asquith thought that if it were not done material for another war would always be at hand. House suggested neutralization.[24]

The results of House's conversations with the British government were embodied in the Grey memorandum of February 22, 1916, in which the Foreign Secretary outlined the understanding of the Cabinet of House's statement of the American peace proposals. On the territorial settlement, the memorandum states: " Colonel House expressed an opinion decidedly favorable to the restoration of Belgium, the transfer of Alsace and Lorraine to

[22] *Ibid.*, pp. 362–64, 367–69.
[23] *Ibid.*, II, 170 (Diary, February 10, 1916). House had left the United States for Europe in December, and after a brief stay in England went to Germany in the middle of January; he discussed with the German authorities their war and peace aims and came away with the impression that the German government, pushed by the " military and naval men," would consider nothing less than a " victor's peace " as a satisfactory basis for negotiations with the Allies.
[24] *Ibid.*, p. 181 (Diary, February 14, 1916).

France, and the acquisition by Russia of an outlet to the sea. . . ."
For her territorial losses in Europe, Germany was to be compensated outside Europe, which in the discussions was understood to
be, in part at least, in Asia Minor. With a minor change, the
memorandum was accepted by Wilson.[25]

Due to the failure of the German attack on Verdun and the
great hopes of the Allies for the Somme offensive, nothing came
of these plans. The Allies hoped for better than "reasonable
terms" without American participation in the war. Later in the
year, in June, House wrote to Grey that the French Ambassador
in Washington had told him that he did not think the French
government would consider peace proposals of any kind at this
time since France would never again have such powerful allies.
House surmised that at the present time France could probably
get Alsace-Lorraine, with the status quo in other respects; Germany would be compensated in Asia Minor; Russia would get a
warm-water seaport; and Italy "what she is entitled to."[26]

From a passive acceptance of the extinction of the Ottoman
Empire by other powers, the United States progressed to the point
where the government was on the point of advocating it publicly.
Early in January, 1917, Wilson, in preparing the address he made
to the Senate on January 22—his "peace without victory" speech
—discussed the territorial terms of such a peace with House; the
two men agreed that Belgium and Serbia should be restored and
that Turkey in Europe should cease to exist. House urged on Wilson the right of Russia to a warm-water seaport, but Wilson was
not prepared to go so far. They considered jocularly what would
happen to the American Ambassador in Turkey after the speech
was made—whether he would be promptly executed or allowed
to leave the country. In a more serious vein they were concerned
with the fate of American educational institutions in Turkey and
the effect on missionary and relief activities.[27] Wilson, of course,
did not mention specific territorial terms in the address, as it was
finally given, in order not to blur its main point. The United
States declared war on Germany, uncommitted to any course of
action in Turkey.

[25] *Ibid.*, pp. 201–2.
[26] *Ibid.*, pp. 290–92 (letter, House to Grey, June 8, 1916).
[27] *Ibid.*, pp. 414–15 (Diary, January 3, 1917).

4.

The declaration of war on Germany by the United States on April 6, 1917, had little direct effect on American Middle East policy. The causes of the participation of the United States in the war were far removed from the limited American national interest in Turkey, even allowing for the fact that Turkey was allied to Germany, so much so that relations between the two countries actually improved after diplomatic relations between the United States and Germany were broken in February, 1917, and continued to be cordial after the outbreak of war and the consequent rupture of diplomatic relations with Turkey. On February 8, 1917, Ambassador Elkus and the new Turkish Minister of Foreign Affairs discussed the rupture between the United States and Germany; the Foreign Minister said that there was no reason why Turkey should sever relations with the United States, though if war were declared Turkey would have to consult with her ally. Elkus told the Department that he thought Turkey would do not as she wanted but as Germany told her to do.[28] A few days later Elkus reported again that the general feeling in government circles was that relations with the Americans remained normal and friendly, perhaps more so than for some time, and that Turkey, unless forced to do otherwise by Germany, wished to continue these relations. Relations between the Turks and Germans were not good, he said, and if Germany and the United States declared war, Turkey would not.[29] Even the Sultan participated in these attempts to improve relations. In November, 1916, at the presentation of the new United States military attaché, he had expressed his pleasure at American efforts to bring about peace and his great admiration for the humanitarian feelings of the American people.[30] After the German-American break, the Grand Vizier told the Ambassador that the Sultan had personally expressed to him his friendship for the United States and his desire to preserve friendly relations between the two countries.[31]

[28] Telegram 2475 from Constantinople, February 8, 1917, 763.72/3385.
[29] Telegram 2479 from Constantinople, February 11, 1917, 763.72/3333.
[30] Telegram 2288 from Constantinople (via Copenhagen), November 28, 1916, 867.48/476.
[31] Telegram 2479 from Constantinople (via Berne), February 16, 1917, 867.00/793.

While the United States was not impressed by the substance of these protestations of friendship, attributing them to the awareness of the Turks of their unpromising future which ever side won, and their hope-against-hope that the United States, as the only country with the means and disinterestedness to do it, would provide financial and moral support in the postwar period—nevertheless, it was a fact that Turkey wanted American good will. Even after the United States declared war on Germany the Turkish attitude remained unchanged. On April 2, the day President Wilson asked Congress to declare war on Germany, the Ambassador met the Foreign Minister, who showed great interest in learning what the Congress would do in response to the President's request. The Ambassador sounded him out on what Turkey would do should war break out between the United States and Germany. The Minister said that America and Turkey were friendly, more so than ever before, and he saw no reason why this should not continue—the Turkish government, therefore, had not taken into consideration a war with the United States. The Ambassador commented to the State Department that this in no way committed the Turkish government and that it was impossible to know beforehand what Turkey would do in case of war with Germany.[32] Turkey broke diplomatic relations on April 20, and American interests were confided to the Swedish Minister in Constantinople. The Turkish government behaved most courteously to the Embassy staff, and instructions were sent to the local authorities that American institutions were to be treated as they had been before the break, since the two countries remained at peace with each other.[33]

However, notwithstanding the absence of any direct conflict of interest between Turkey and the United States, the indirect consequences of the war with Germany—the increase in Germany's

[32] Telegram 2587 from Constantinople, April 2, 1917, 763.72/3680. For further correspondence on the effect of the American declaration of war on Germany on Turkish-American relations, see *Foreign Relations*, 1917, Supplement 2, I, 15 ff., *passim*.

[33] Telegram 2639 from Constantinople (via Berne), April 20, 1917, 763.72/3991; *Foreign Relations*, 1917, Supplement 2, I, 35. Details of the relations between the Embassy and the Turkish government after the break are given in several despatches: despatch 912 from Constantinople, April 23, 1917, 763.72/5428; despatch 939, May 19, 1917, 763.72/5598. This was Elkus' first report; he had been ill at the time of the break and was still recuperating when he arrived in Paris. The previous despatches had been sent by the First Secretary.

capacity to wage war on the United States afforded by Turkey's alliance with the Central Powers; and Allied war aims in the Middle East insofar as they would affect American participation in the peace conference—meant that the era of detachment in Turkish-American relations was over, though America's quarrel was with Germany and not with the Central Powers as such.

Turkey was, militarily and economically, an appendage of Germany, and, as far as the evidence indicated, might continue to be so after the war. This fact was fully appreciated in Washington. The information received from American embassies, and other sources abroad, before the United States entered the war had shown unmistakably that Germany exercised full control over Turkey (and to a lesser extent and mostly in the military sphere, over Austria-Hungary also). Germany had made extensive conquests in Russia and Russian Poland, and the whole mass of territory under the direct or indirect control of Germany stretched from the English Channel to the Caucasus and from the Baltic almost to Baghdad. This powerful German position was a present fact, and its future implications for the postwar era, if it were left intact, had become more ominous in the Allied countries and in the United States after the writings of the German proponents of the " Mittel-Europa " idea were publicized during 1916 and 1917 by the journals *The New Europe* and *Le Monde Slav* in Europe and, after April, 1917, by the American Committee on Public Information in the United States, all with official approval and encouragement.[34]

The theme of the immense strength achieved by Germany thus far in the war and the threat of a new German Empire erected across the lands acquired by conquest and intrigue was the subject of Wilson's first major foreign policy speech after the address to Congress on April 2. It was given on June 14, Flag Day, at Washington. After summarizing the reasons for the American declaration of war in Germany, the President continued:

The war was begun by the military masters of Germany, who proved to be also the masters of Austria-Hungary. These men have never regarded nations as peoples but merely as serviceable organizations which they could by force or intrigue bend or corrupt to their own purpose. . . .

---

[34] On the Mittel-Europa idea, and its effect on Allied and American thinking, see Henry Cord Meyer, *Mitteleuropa in German Thought and Action, 1815 to 1945* (The Hague, 1955).

Their purpose has long been avowed. The statesmen of other nations . . . regarded what German professors expounded in their classrooms and German writers set forth to the world as the goal of German policy as rather the dream of minds detached from practical affairs . . . than as the actual plans of responsible rulers; but the rulers of Germany themselves knew what concrete plans, what well advanced intrigues lay back of what the professors and writers were saying. . . . They filled the thrones of Balkan states with German princes, putting German officers at the service of Turkey to drill her armies and make interest with her government, developing plans of sedition and rebellion in India and Egypt, setting their fires in Persia. . . . Their plan was to throw a broad belt of German military power and political control across the very centre of Europe and beyond the Mediterranean into the heart of Asia. . . . And they have actually carried the greater part of that amazing plan into execution! . . . The Turkish armies, which Germans trained, are serving Germany, certainly not themselves, and the guns of German warships lying in the harbor at Constantinople remind Turkish statesmen every day that they have no choice but to take their orders from Berlin. From Hamburg to the Persian Gulf the net is spread. . . . If they can secure peace now with the immense advantages still in their hands which they have up to this point apparently gained, they will have justified themselves before the German people: they will have gained by force what they promised to gain by it: an immense expansion of German power, an immense enlargement of German and industrial opportunities.[35]

While this statement is exaggerated and oversimplified (and the reader will note that the junior Hohenzollern monarchy in Rumania was allied with the Entente and that Egypt was, until the outbreak of war, a part of the Ottoman Empire), its purpose being to emphasize the scope of the problem presented by Germany to the United States and to discourage the prevalent idea that a victory in France and Belgium by the Allies would solve the German problem, it does nevertheless represent the essence of American policy insofar as it illustrates the ultimate ends of Wilson's war policy.

5.

The Flag Day address stated the problem of American Middle East policy, but consideration of its solution was not taken up until the fall, though the possibility of negotiating a separate

[35] *Foreign Relations*, 1917, Supplement 2, I, 96–100.

peace with the Turks had received serious consideration in May and June, and former Ambassador Morgenthau was dispatched on an abortive mission to the Middle East to explore the ground (this topic, together with American policy toward the Zionist program, will be taken up below). Germany occupied almost all of the attention of the United States during the first months of the war, and it was not until the basic problems of organizing America's war and co-ordinating it with the war of the Allies had been settled, or at least analyzed and understood, that time and attention could be devoted to a serious consideration of the particular role of Turkey in the war and its significance in over-all strategy in the war against Germany. Turkey was a minor problem for the United States; when the Allied Missions were in Washington in April and May to discuss war problems, Colonel House in a conversation with Foreign Secretary A. J. Balfour, head of the British mission, had dismissed Turkey as a " sideshow." [36]

On October 10 the President and Colonel House conferred on the address the President was to make to the American Federation of Labor at Buffalo in November. The President outlined the main points of the speech to House. Its theme was that the United States must not be deceived by a German offer to give up Alsace-Lorraine and Belgium in return for a negotiated peace, for this would leave her impregnable in Austria and Turkey and her dream of Mittel-Europa would be realized. Evacuation of occupied territory was only a part of the American program—the rest was to restrict German power for evil in the future, and the American people must be made to realize this, said Wilson. The discussion then turned to the specific details of his plans for Germany and her satellites. Wilson told House that he was thinking of saying that Turkey should be " effaced " and her disposition left to the Peace Conference. House commented that if such a statement were made it should be added that Turkey must not be partitioned among the belligerents but constituted into autonomous regions along racial lines; the President accepted this.[37]

When the speech was given, on November 12, the President

[36] House Papers, Diary, April 22, 1917. See below, pp. 51–58.

[37] *Ibid.*, October 10, 1917; in this same conversation the President asked House if the American people would accept him as the sole American delegate to a peace conference. House said that such a question would have to be considered at a later date.

confined himself to generalities. The Bolsheviks, having seized power in Russia but a few days before, were calling for peace without annexations or indemnities, and Wilson wished to emphasize the main point of his address—that German power must be completely destroyed—without blurring it with details. "Look at the map of Europe, now," said the President,

. . . Germany in thrusting upon us again and again the discussion of peace, talks—about what? Talks about Belgium; talks about Northern France; talks about Alsace-Lorraine. Well, those are deeply interesting subjects to us and to them, but they are not the heart of the matter. Take the map and look at it. Germany has absolute control of Austria-Hungary, practical control of Turkey, control of Asia Minor. I saw a map in which was printed the whole thing in appropriate black the other day, and the black stretched all the way from Hamburg to Baghdad—the bulk of German power inserted into the heart of the world.[38]

Secretary of State Lansing's thoughts were running in the same channels. In a private memorandum of October 24, written for his own use, on "Certain Essentials of a Stable Peace," he analyzed the problem presented to the United States by German power. The first essential for the United States was to break Germany by war; then, to insure that she could not recuperate her military strength, she must be surrounded by strong states able to hold their own, either alone or in combination, against future German aggression. And where this was not possible, for instance to the north, her strategic position must be weakened by depriving her of such aids to her military power as the Kiel Canal.[39]

The possibility that Turkey might, under the pressure of further military reverses, be forced to abandon the Central Powers and ask for peace, gave rise to the serious consideration by the United States at this time of the advisability of sending the main American force to the Turkish Front rather than to France; with the overwhelming military superiority thus opposed to the Turkish armies in Palestine and Mesopotamia, the war in the East could be ended quickly, thus offsetting to a degree the effects of the Russian withdrawal from the war, and creating a new Eastern

[38] James Brown Scott, *President Wilson's Foreign Policy* (New York, 1918), pp. 326–36.

[39] Lansing Papers, Private memorandum on certain essentials of a stable peace, October 24, 1917.

front for the German armies to face.[40] This plan did not go
beyond the memorandum stage, but one result of these studies
and the development of strategic thinking about Turkey in the
Administration, for example Lansing's memorandum of October
24, was the decision that Turkey must be deprived of control of
the Straits.

In reply to a cable from the Ambassador in London reporting
that certain elements in the British government were considering
the question of a negotiated peace with Turkey,[41] Lansing told
the Ambassador that the "conclusion of a separate peace with
Turkey is regarded as chimerical and of questionable advantage.
. . ." He said that "arrangements" with regard to Constantinople must be made at the peace conference which could not be
made if peace were concluded with Turkey at the present time,
for this would preclude any radical changes of control over Constantinople and the Straits. "It appears, therefore, to this Government," continued the Secretary, "that the only advantage to
be gained by separate peace with Turkey now would be to prevent the bargains of the Allies with regard to Asia Minor from
being carried out at the end of the war." [42]

The question of declaring war on Turkey was again considered
when, in early December, war was declared on Austria. Why
leave any of the Central Powers untouched by American war
power when the two senior members were the declared enemies of
the United States? In his address to the Congress recommending
a declaration of war on Austria-Hungary, Wilson stated the logic
behind this action:

The Government of Austria-Hungary is not acting upon its own initiative or in response to the wishes and feelings of its own peoples but as
the instrument of another nation. We must meet its force with our own
and regard the Central Powers as but one. The war can be conducted in
no other way. The same logic would lead to a declaration of war against
Turkey and Bulgaria. They also are the tools of Germany. But they are
mere tools and do not yet stand in the direct path of our necessary action.
We shall go wherever the necessities of this war carry us, but it seems

---

[40] Wilson Papers, Series II, Box 129.

[41] Telegram 7782 from London, November 23, 1917, 763.72119/953.

[42] Telegram 5930 to London, November 30, 1917, 763.72119/953. On Allied
war aims, see below, pp. 51–58, 109–13.

to me that we should go only where immediate and practical considerations lead us and not heed any others.[43]

The Senate Foreign Relations Committee was dissatisfied with this brief exposé of Wilson's reasons for not declaring war on the two minor members of the Central Powers and the Chairman asked Secretary Lansing for a fuller statement of the Administration's position. Lansing replied with a lengthy memorandum on the inadvisability of a declaration of war on Turkey and Bulgaria. He noted that the Allies had not requested the United States to declare war on Bulgaria and Turkey, and, in any case, the United States could not, at this time, provide a significant military force to fight on the Eastern Front. The question had, therefore, to be considered, first, from the standpoint of the moral effect of a declaration, and, second, from the point of view of the indirect damage the United States and Turkey could inflict on each other. It was well known that there was much friction between the Turks and the Germans, and a declaration of war would isolate the Turks and throw them even further under the domination of Germany. They had no troops on the Western Front and direct conflict between troops of the two countries was most unlikely. Turkey had few interests in the United States, whereas the United States had many in Turkey, mainly educational institutions worth millions of dollars; these would be closed and confiscated. The schools were now open and operating and were attended by many Turks; this very valuable influence would be lost. The United States had nothing to fear from the activities of Turkish subjects in this country; they were, in fact, mostly Syrians, Christians, and Armenians and very few of them were real Turks. Finally, if we declared war on Turkey, Turkey would reply by new massacres of Christians and Jews in Turkey. As for Bulgaria, its people were very friendly to the United States and it was in the war for local reasons—to fight its old enemy Serbia; it was not interested in German grand strategy but, on the contrary, was beginning to

[43] *Foreign Relations*, 1917, Supplement 2, I, 446. On November 20, Lansing sent to the President a memorandum prepared by Woolsey, the Counselor of the Department, on American grounds of complaint against Austria. In the covering letter, Lansing said, "We have not a very strong case against Austria so far as hostile acts are concerned. It seems to me that it comes down very largely to a matter of national safety in having at large and free to act a very considerable body of Austrian subjects in this country." The case against Turkey was immeasurably weaker; 763.72/7796a.

worry about the dangers of German domination after the war. Nothing would be gained by war with Bulgaria and it would add nothing to the achievement of victory by the Allies and the United States.[44]

Though this reply by the Secretary of State ended any immediate plans in the Congress for a declaration of war, the feeling there continued and, indeed, grew throughout the following spring. A resolution was introduced into the Senate calling for a declaration of war against the two countries and on its consideration by the Committee on Foreign Relations, the Secretary of State was called by the committee to testify. Lansing took the position that it was the responsibility of the Congress to declare war and that neither he nor the President could do more than lay the situation before the committee. He pointed out that the question was whether such a declaration would help or hinder the winning of the war, and he agreed, at the request of the committee, to obtain the views of the Allied governments on the advisability of declaring war on Turkey and Bulgaria.[45] Accordingly, instructions were sent to the ambassadors at London, Paris, and Rome to sound out the governments to which they were respectively accredited on the advisability of such a step. " You will perceive," said the Secretary, " that the action of the United States is based essentially on expediency. I desire therefore to know the judgment of the Government as to whether it will be of material aid in defeating the Central Powers." A similar instruction was sent to General Bliss, the American Military Representative on the Supreme Council, to obtain the opinions of his colleagues.[46]

Within a few days, replies were received from the three ambassadors and from General Bliss, all indicating that the Allied governments and the military representatives of the Supreme Council would welcome a declaration of war on Turkey, though there was a difference of opinion on the juestion of Bulgaria. Bliss reported that his colleagues believed a declaration against Turkey was desirable, but an attempt to detach Bulgaria from the Central

[44] Secretary of State to the Chairman of the Senate Foreign Relations Committee, letter, December 6, 1917, 763.72/8475b.

[45] *Foreign Relations*, Lansing Papers, II, 121–22. Secretary of State to the President, letter, May 2, 1918, 763.72/10115b.

[46] Telegram 7556 to London, telegram 3830 to Paris; telegram 1248 to Rome, May 3, 1918, 763.72/9799a. The telegram to Paris was repeated to General Bliss.

Powers by diplomatic means should be attempted first and, if this was unsuccessful, war should be declared. However, no troops should be detached from the American forces on the Western Front. They believed that the military advantages of a declaration were that, by showing the real unity of the Allied countries and the United States, it would lower the morale of the peoples of Turkey and Bulgaria, and those elements in the Middle East who were waiting for a clearer indication of the outcome of the war than the present situation offered them before declaring for the Allies would, with the overwhelming strength of the United States thrown into the scales against the Ottoman government, be encouraged to throw in their lot with the Allies. In addition, should the military situation warrant it, the United States could, in the future, participate in the Eastern war, which she could not do if she remained at peace with Turkey. The British, French, and Italian governments delayed for some weeks acknowledging formal answers to the American query but indicated informally that they would welcome a declaration of war.[47]

Lansing wrote to the President on May 8 informing him of these responses. It could be assumed, he said, that all the Entente Powers favored a declaration against Turkey, but that the British thought that a declaration against Bulgaria should be delayed. The point of view of the Allies was based on purely military considerations chiefly concerned with the encouragement of resistance by the Georgians and Caucasians and others to the Turkish ad-

[47] Telegram 3835 from Paris, May 8, 1918, 763.72/9904; the Ambassador reported that he had also seen Clemenceau to obtain an elaboration of the views of the French government. Clemenceau had commented that there was nothing more to add to Foreign Minister Pichon's statement that a declaration of war would give "great satisfaction" to the French government, except to emphasize that the declaration should be made as soon as possible. The British answer was handed to the Ambassador at London, by the Foreign Office, on May 17. After reciting the military and political benefits that would follow a declaration of war by the United States on Turkey and Bulgaria, the note submitted an additional factor for the consideration of the American government—the participation of the United States in the peace conference. The part the United States would play would be of "decisive" importance, said the note, and nowhere more so than in the Near and Middle East. If the United States did not declare war on the two allies of Germany, the world would draw the inference that the United States was not concerned with the peace in those areas; His Majesty's government would regard this as a great misfortune. Ambassador at London to the Secretary of State, telegram 10116, May 17, 1918; the substance of the British Note was cabled to Lord Reading by A. J. Balfour, and was handed to Lansing by Reading on May 18. The London telegram was sent to the President on May 20.

vance in the Caucasus and the Upper Euphrates since the Russian collapse. But, said the Secretary, the United States should also consider the humanitarian side, which the Allies had failed to do. Thousands of Syrians and Armenians were being kept alive in Turkey by funds sent to American missionaries in Turkey to the amount of over a million dollars a month. As for Bulgaria, his impression was that the chief value of a declaration against her would be its effect on Greece and Serbia. He noted also that one argument against a declaration against the two countries was that neither had committed any act of war against the United States since the declaration of war on Austria, and, in view of this fact, there were no reasons which could be put forward in support of a change of policy at this time. It would be said by Germany that we had so far not declared war on Bulgaria and Turkey in the hope of detaching them from Germany, and now that we knew this was impossible we had declared war in order to coerce them into an acceptance of our demands; this would create an extremely bad impression in both countries. The United States had three courses open to her: she could refrain from a declaration of war against either country on the grounds that it was not possible to declare war on Bulgaria and not Turkey and that to declare war on Turkey would remove the protection and relief which the United States had furnished to thousands of refugees in Turkey; she could declare war on Turkey alone on the grounds that this would encourage resistance in the Caucasus and would, at the same time, constitute a threat to Bulgaria which would bring her to terms; or she could declare war against both countries on the grounds that every nation which was an ally of Germany should be treated as a foe.[48] The President decided against advocating war on Bulgaria and Turkey, and the Committee on Foreign Relations, noting the President's opinion, reported against the resolution, which was not passed.[49]

[48] Secretary of State to the President, letter, May 8, 1918, 763.72/9893.

[49] The general position of the United States on sending American troops to war theaters other than the Western Front was put to the Allies in an *aide-memoire* handed to the British, French, and Italian ambassadors on July 17, 1918, which stated that the controlling purpose of the American government was to do everything necessary and effective to win the war, which it believed could only be won by common council and intimate concert of action. If it was obliged to decline to participate in any course of action, it did so only from imperative considerations either of policy or fact. As long as the situation on the Western Front remained critical, it could not consent to slacken its efforts there by diverting

6.

There were two exceptions to the general rule of non-involvement governing American policy toward Turkey. These were the Morgenthau mission and President Wilson's policy on the Balfour Declaration. After the declaration of war on Germany, former Ambassador Morgenthau called on Secretary of State Lansing and told him that he believed " the time was ripe to make secret overtures to Turkey for he was sure that by this time the Turkish leaders were heartily sick of their German Masters." He suggested that he be authorized to get in touch with certain disaffected Turks to negotiate a separate peace. Lansing was persuaded and wrote to Wilson supporting Morgenthau's proposals, though he was careful to point out that there was only a slight chance of success. Wilson agreed to the sending of a mission to put out feelers but not to negotiate; it was to go to Palestine, under Morgenthau, ostensibly to investigate conditions among the Jews there.[50]

American troops to other areas. The *aide-memoire* added that the American government considered the Italian Front to be part of the Western Front and if the Supreme Council considered it advisable, American troops would be sent there. The *aide-memoire* then went on to comment on suggestions that the United States take part in intervention in Russia; this, rather than the question of war with Turkey, was the main reason for this statement of the American position. The United States believed, it said, that intervention in Russia could only add to the existing confusion and would be of no advantage in winning the war. The United States could not take part in or sanction intervention except to help the Czechs consolidate their forces, co-operate with their Slavic kinsmen, and help Russia to achieve self-determination. The American position was not in any sense a criticism of the Allied policy, but the United States proposed to ask all the Allies to state that they had no intention of interfering in the right of the Russian people to self-determination. Secretary of State to Embassy at London, telegram 298, July 18, 1918, 763.72/13370a.

[50] *Foreign Relations*, Lansing Papers, II, 17–19. Secretary of State to the President, letter, May 17, 1917, 867.00/804 1/2a. The original is in the Wilson Papers, Series II, Box 118; it bears the notation in the President's handwriting, " Answered orally, W. W." Lansing's desk diary has the entry for May 16, " Alsberg, Morgenthau's secretary, on desperate situation in Turkey. Morgenthau with plan to win over Turks." Among the items of information that came into the Department at about this time on the chances of a separate peace with Turkey is a telegram from Constantinople, 2558, March 17, 763.72/3572, which reported a rumor that the German officers on the Turkish General Staff had advised the Turks to pull back on the Caucasus front to Sivas and in the south to the Taurus Mountains. The Turks were very reluctant to do this. Enver had left for Berlin the day before, it was said, to reassure the Germans who were afraid that Turkey was ready to negotiate a separate peace. The Embassy said that no foundation for the rumor

The scheme called for the participation of the British Zionist leaders in the mission, and the Embassy at London was instructed to obtain permission from the British government for Dr. Chaim Weizmann to join Morgenthau and Felix Frankfurter, the other American delegate, at Gibraltar en route to Palestine. The British Foreign Secretary was very happy to oblige. The British government was already in contact with Talaat and other Turkish leaders and wanted no intrusions by the Americans to complicate the issue or to dilute their offers by providing an alternate purchaser for what the Turkish leaders were willing to sell. Weizmann was instructed by Balfour " to talk to Mr. Morgenthau and to keep on talking till I had talked him out of this mission," wrote Weizmann in his autobiography.[51] The Zionists were also opposed to the mission, since their claims to Palestine depended on the defeat of Turkey, and were thus quite ready to co-operate with the British in subverting the Morgenthau mission. Weizmann did talk it to death in Gibraltar, and the mission was abandoned.[52] It is questionable whether it would have been successful if it had continued. Morgenthau went far beyond his instructions in talking to Weizmann and was sharply reprimanded by the State Department for discussing American aims in the Middle East without authorization. In any case, news of the mission was leaked to the

---

could be found and it should not be relied on. On June 10, 1917, the British Embassy sent a memorandum to the Department of State with the information that the British Minister in Switzerland had reported a former Albanian official in touch with the Germans saying that when Talaat was in Berlin recently he had told the Germans that Turkey could not carry on the war any longer in view of the military, financial, and economic situation. The Germans told him to hold out to the end of July when the submarines would have brought Britain to her knees and the Central Powers could conclude an honorable peace. These are fair examples of the material available for the determination of American policy at this time. The President called on Lansing at the latter's house on May 21 to discuss the possibility of a separate peace with Turkey and on June 1 the two men decided that before making a final decision they would ask Elkus for his opinion. Morgenthau called on the Secretary on May 28 and May 30 to discuss his going to Palestine " to look after the Jews."

[51] Chaim Weizmann, *Trial and Error* (New York, 1949), p. 196.

[52] Telegram 670 from Madrid, July 8, 1917, 763.72/5815. The full report of the Conference, signed on July 6 by Weizmann for Great Britain, E. Weyl for France, and Morgenthau and Felix Frankfurter for the United States (763.72119/703 1/2), was sent to Washington on July 10 in a letter from Frankfurter to Leland Harrison, Assistant Secretary of State, 763.72/5815.

press and the Ottoman government was aware of Morgenthau's real mission.[53]

On September 14, 1917, House wrote to Wilson that he had been asked by Lord Robert Cecil, on behalf of the British government, to " ascertain unofficially if the President favored a declaration of sympathy with the Zionist movement." [54] In a further letter, three days later, House warned Wilson of the dangers involved in giving his unqualified support to the British declaration. " There are many dangers lurking in it, and if I were the British, I would be chary about going too definitely into that question," he said.[55] Wilson, too, apparently, was chary of the declaration and instructed House to inform the British government that " the time was not opportune for any definite statement further, perhaps, than one of sympathy, provided it can be made without conveying any real commitment." [56]

The Zionist leaders in England were told by the British government of this response by Wilson to the proposed declaration and at once telegraphed to Justice Brandeis to persuade the President to support the declaration. Brandeis saw House on September 23 and, on the next day, wrote to him " pursuant to yesterday's conference," enclosing a copy of a telegram he had sent the same day to Weizmann which read: " From talks I have had with the President and from expressions of opinion given to closest advisors I feel that I can answer that he is in entire sympathy with declaration quoted in yours of 19th as approved by Foreign Office and

[53] Leonard Stein, *The Balfour Declaration* (London, 1961), pp. 352–60, gives the details of the British and Zionist points of view on the Morgenthau mission. According to Lord Beaverbrook, the British emissary in the negotiations with the Turks was Sir Basil Zaharoff. The German Foreign Office Archives mention in two reports from Berne of May 18 and May 24, 1917, that British agents were putting out feelers to the Turks; cited in Stein, *Balfour Declaration*, p. 354. The " delegations of Armenians and Jews " who were said to have protested to the Foreign Office the sending of the Morgenthau mission were actually Weizmann and James Malcolm, a leader of the Armenian National movement. With both the Foreign Office and the leader of the British Zionists actively engaged in sabotaging the mission while purporting to support it, it is fortunate that the United States escaped so lightly from the affair. See also William Yale, " Ambassador Henry Morgenthau's Special Mission of 1917," *World Politics*, I, No. 3 (1949), 308–20; Frank E. Manuel, *The Realities of American-Palestine Relations* (Washington, 1949), pp. 155–59; Weizmann, *Trial and Error*, chap. XVII. Stein's account is the best documented and, in my opinion, the best balanced.

[54] Wilson Papers, Series II, Box 100.

[55] *Ibid.*

[56] Cited in Stein, *Balfour Declaration*, p. 505.

Prime Minister." [57] (The reference was to a draft declaration drawn up by the Zionists that referred to Palestine being reconstituted " as the National Home of the Jewish people," a far stronger statement than that actually used in the Balfour Declaration.)

In the meantime, active consideration of the declaration had been dropped by the British Cabinet after the receipt of Wilson's reply but was taken up again early in October after the Turks, with German prompting, seemed to be about to forestall the British with a Zionist program of their own. Again, the British government approached Wilson through House, and on October 13 the President sent a note to House: " I find in my pocket the memorandum you gave me on the Zionist movement. I am afraid I did not say to you that I concurred in the formula suggested by the other side. I do and would be obliged if you would let them know it." [57a]

The Department of State was not informed of all of the President's activities relating to the Zionist declaration, and a month after the Balfour Declaration had been published in *The Times*, a telegram was sent to Ambassador Page in London requesting him to " investigate discreetly and report fully and promptly to Department reasons for Balfour's recent statement relative Jewish state in Palestine." [58] Page saw Lord Robert Cecil, who was in charge of the Foreign Office while Mr. Balfour was ill. He told the Ambassador that the British government had an understanding with the French government that Palestine was to be internationalized. Mr. Balfour's letter to Lord Rothschild merely stated that the British government pledged itself to put the Jews of Palestine on the same footing as other nationalities there, and that no discrimination be made against them; this was as far as his government had gone.[59]

[57] *Ibid.*, pp. 506–7, citing the Brandeis Papers, University of Louisville.
[57a] House Papers.
[58] Secretary of State to Embassy at London, telegram 6041, December 15, 1917, 867 n.01/2a.
[59] Telegram 8033 from London, December 21, 1917, 867 n.01/2. In an informal discussion of Palestine at this interview, Cecil said that Palestine must be under the control of a Great Power; speaking for himself, he feared that the Continental powers would not be able to agree on any one of them holding the protectorate and that some of them would object to Britain holding it, and it was his hope that the United States would take the protectorate.

It was one thing for the President to inform the British government that he " concurred " in the Balfour Declaration; it was a very different thing for the United States government to indorse publicly the Declaration. In the first instance Wilson's concurrence merely committed the American government not to object to the actions of the British government in the matter; in the second instance, the United States would have been committed to support the intent and principles of the declaration. No commitment of this nature was made by the United States government until the Joint Resolution of the Congress in 1922, but this was at a time when the United States had disengaged itself from active participation in the politics of Europe and the Middle East. In 1917 and 1918 such a commitment would have profoundly affected the position of the United States in the proposed settlement of Eastern questions by the Allies. A public commitment to one of the Allied plans for the partition of the Ottoman Empire would have been, by implication, a commitment to them all, and this was one of the principal pitfalls in the way of American Middle East policy that the Administration was careful to avoid.

The capstone of the Zionist program would have fallen into place had its supporters been able to persuade the United States to match the British action by a similar declaration, and this the Zionist movement in the United States made strenuous efforts to bring about. On December 13 Secretary Lansing wrote to the President saying that considerable pressure was being brought by the Zionist element of the Jews to have the American government issue a declaration of its policy on the disposition of Palestine. It was his judgment, he told Wilson, that the United States should proceed very slowly in announcing a policy, for three reasons: The United States was not at war with Turkey and, therefore, should avoid any appearance of favoring taking territory from that Empire by force; the Jews were by no means united on the Zionist question; and many Christian sects and individuals would resent turning over the Holy Land to the absolute control of the race credited with the death of Christ. " For practical purposes," he said, " I do not think that we need go further than the first reason given, since that is ample ground for declining to announce any policy in regard to the final disposition of Palestine." [60]   Lans-

---

[60] Secretary of State to the President, letter, December 13, 1917, 867.01/13 1/2a.

ing saw the President at a Cabinet meeting the next day; Wilson told him that "very unwillingly" he was forced to agree with him, but that he had the impression that the Administration had assented to the British declaration regarding returning Palestine to the Jews.[61]

Ten months later, on August 31, 1918, after continuous efforts by the American Zionists, Wilson was persuaded to give the Balfour Declaration his personal indorsement, after he had been assured by the leader of the American Zionists, Rabbi Wise, that it involved "no challenge to the present suzerainty and leaves that for determination at the peace table." [62] On this basis—that the implementation of the declaration did not necessarily require the alienation of any part of Ottoman territory—Wilson was prepared to state publicly, but informally and in a private communication, his personal opinion of the Zionist program. It would seem that Wilson had no objection in principle to the idea of handing over Palestine to the Zionists; however, he was not willing to associate the United States with any project that was based on the acquisition of Turkish territory by conquest, again not on principle, but because to have done so would have had the effect of associatiing the United States with all of the Allied schemes for the partition of Turkey.

[61] Note by Lansing attached to 867 n.01/13 1/2a; 867 n. 01/11 1/2a.
[62] Cf. Stein, *Balfour Declaration*, pp. 594–95.

CHAPTER II

WAR AIMS AND PEACE AIMS:
THE SECRET TREATIES AND THE FOURTEEN POINTS

1.

The determination of American policy toward Turkey itself was relatively straightforward, and was based on the answers to the questions: Could Turkey endanger the national interest? and, Could the United States, by changing its traditional policy of non-involvement in the Middle East, enhance its ability to destroy German power to endanger the national interest? The answer to the first question was, no; and to the second, that the United States could do little if anything in the Middle East that could not be done more effectively in Europe. In short, Turkey was, as Colonel House put it, a side show. Of far greater importance to the United States was, paradoxically, the problem of Allied policy toward Turkey. On the general question of Allied war aims, Wilson's attitude was colored by his disillusionment of a year before when the Allies had rejected his peace proposals, generous to the Allies though they were, in favor of continuing the war.[1] The achievement of Allied war aims, except insofar as they implied the defeat of Germany, would contribute nothing to the security of the United States; in fact Wilson was concerned whether the elimination of Germany as a factor in European politics might, in the future, itself constitute a threat as great as the establishment of German hegemony in Europe. On the night before he asked Congress to declare war on Germany Wilson sent for his old friend Frank Cobb, editor of the New York

[1] See above, p. 31. On the President's attitude towards the Allied rejection of his peace moves in 1916, see Seymour, *Intimate Papers*, II, 292 ff., and Edward Buehrig, *Woodrow Wilson and the Balance of Power* (Bloomington, 1955), chaps. **VI** and **VII**.

49

World; he apparently wanted his companionship as he wrestled with the great decision. Cobb found the President full of doubts, "worn down" with the weight of the problem facing him. He told Cobb that the entry of the United States into the war against Germany "would mean that Germany would be beaten and so badly beaten that there would be a dictated peace. . . . The President said that such a basis was what the Allies thought they wanted, and that they would have their way in the very thing America had hoped against and struggled against."[2]

On the other hand, these war aims were what kept the Allies in the war. Events in Europe had reached a stage where only the prospect of great acquisitions of territory and economic opportunity, and vastly enhanced military and political security, could supply the incentive to continue the bloody struggle. Any diminution of the hoped-for rewards for the sacrifices then being made in France and on the other war fronts would inevitably mean a diminution of effort by the Allies, and a corresponding increase of the burden on the United States.

Thirdly, there was the problem of the reconciliation of the war aims with American participation in the peace settlement. This was both a political problem and a psychological one. The United States, unlike the Allies, entered the war absolutely uncommitted to its cobelligerents, either as to its continuation in the war, its contribution to the common effort, or to the political outcome of the war. Presumably there would be a single peace conference and a single peace treaty (though there was no reason why the United States, if it so chose, should not conclude a separate peace with Germany). The Allies were already committed to each other on certain aspects of the nature of the settlement; the United States was not. What, then, was the place of Allied war aims in the settlement when Allied and American war aims were far from being identical and had not already been reconciled, as had the differences between the war aims of the individual Allies? The answer lay in determining whether their inclusion would advance or injure the American national interest, and if they could not be excluded entirely, on what terms would they be admitted. The psychological aspect of the problem concerned the attitude of the American people to the war and to the Allies. Few of them would

---

[2] J. W. Heaton, *Cobb of the "World"* (New York, 1924); cited in Buehrig, *Woodrow Wilson*, pp. 264–65.

accept either the prospect of sacrificing American lives and money for the furtherance of any other country's political ambitions, or the prospect of their country sitting at the peace conference and participating in a political act that contradicted the basic principles on which the United States was founded and which they considered to be America's chief contribution to the world.

2.

The problem of Allied ambitions in the Middle East was presented to the United States in concrete form at the very outset of its participation in the war, when, in the latter part of April, missions from the Entente Powers arrived in Washington to concert with the United States measures for the more effective prosecution of the war.[3] The British mission, headed by the Foreign Secretary, A. J. Balfour, came to the United States via Halifax, passing through New York on the way to Washington, and while the train was in Pennsylvania Station Colonel House visited the Foreign Secretary to discuss privately, and without publicity, the questions which would be taken up in Washington by the Administration and the mission. Apart from questions concerning the most effective methods of utilizing American resources and easing the pressing financial and material needs of the Allies, the most important topic discussed by the two men was the place of peace terms in the coming conferences in Washington. " I urged him not to talk peace terms," House wrote in his diary:

and to advise the President not to discuss peace terms with any of the other Allies. If he did, differences would be certain to arise and the problem now was to beat Germany and not discuss peace. Balfour agreed to this in full, and said he would not talk to the President about peace terms unless the President himself initiated it. Balfour asked what I thought of negotiation with Austria, Turkey and Bulgaria for separate peace. I thought well of Austria and Bulgaria. . . .

House commented that Turkey should be put on the " scrap-heap " with Germany and that no attempt should be made to negotiate a separate peace with her. Balfour agreed.[4]

---

[3] For correspondence relating to the Allied missions, see *Foreign Relations*, 1917, Supplement 2, I, 149, *passim*.

[4] House Papers, Diary, April 22, 1917; part of this entry is in Seymour, *Intimate*

House wrote to Wilson, giving an account of his talk with Balfour:

I hope you will agree with me that the best policy now is to avoid a discussion of peace settlements. Balfour concurs in this. If the Allies begin to discuss terms among themselves, they will soon hate one another worse than they do Germany and a situation will arise similar to that in the Balkan States after the Turkish War. It seems to me that the only thing to be considered at present is how to beat Germany in the quickest way. . . . If you have a tacit understanding with him not to discuss peace terms with the other allies, later this country and England will be able to dictate broad and generous terms—terms that will mean permanent peace.[5]

In the phrase " peace terms," House included the terms of the secret treaties between the Allies. The broad outlines of the most important of the treaties were known to Wilson and House before the United States entered the war. The general terms of the Treaty of London, under which the conditions of Italian entry into the war on the Allied side had been laid down, had been reported to Washington by the London and Paris embassies;[6] and that the Allies planned to extinguish the Ottoman Empire was not only known but approved by Wilson and House, though they were far from approving its partition among the putative victors. Not that there was any great secret about the general outlines of Allied ambitions. Lenin, writing in March, 1917, from

---

Papers, III, 38–39. House also suggested to Balfour that he minimize his visit to dampen talk of alliances between the Allies and the United States.

[5] Wilson Papers, Series II, Box 117; House to the President, letter, April 22, 1917. In this letter House again refers to the necessity of quieting fears that the British mission had come to the United States to obtain a secret alliance. He said that Walter Lippmann, among others, believed that this was the purpose of the mission.

[6] Paris cabled on May 1, 1915, "on authority which I believe reliable" that Italy had signed an agreement with the Allies on April 27; the terms were not yet known but were supposed to give "territorial extensions" to Italy in return for military support; 763.72/1722. On May 8, London cabled that the Foreign Editor of " The Times," who was well-informed and trustworthy, had told Ambassador Page " in strictest confidence" that England, France, and Russia had made a bargain with Italy ceding to it Austrian territory, some of which was Slavic, and that Serbia had not been consulted; *Foreign Relations*, 1915, Supplement, pp. 31–33. On January 27, 1915, London reported that the Italian Military Attaché had told a member of the Embassy unofficially that Italy would enter the war on the Allied side about March 1, being by then fully armed. He said also that if Turkey attacked Egypt, Italy would enter the war by declaring war on Turkey.

Zurich to *Pravda*—where this, his first *Letter from Afar*, was published on April 3—said, referring to the ease with which the dynasty had been overthrown, that it had been the work of a:

conspiracy of the Anglo-French imperialists who were pushing Miliukov Guchkov and Co. to seize power in order to prolong the imperialist war, in order to wage it more ferociously and tenaciously, in order to slay fresh millions of Russian workers and peasants, so as to obtain possession of Constantinople for Guchkov, Syria for the French, and Mesopotamia . . . for the British capitalists, et cetera.

In its comment on Wilson's note to Russia on May 22, 1917, the *Norddeutsche Allgemeine Zeitung* said:

Most especially however we would like to recommend to President Wilson that he . . . look into the agreements of his allies in which the members of the Entente Cordiale assure to each other their respective war winnings. He will find that—Monsieur Briand has been forced to admit this recently in a secret session of the French House—France, and with France, England, has promised Constantinople to Russia and as a return Russia had promised to France not only Alsace-Lorraine, but the left bank of the Rhine as well. He will further find that the Entente Cordiale has formulated a complete plan for the division of Asia Minor, the detailed settlement of which (though made behind Russia's back) is still causing difficulties.[7]

If the United States discussed the treaties at the Washington conferences, it would have been necessary to have come to a decision on her policy toward them, there and then, and to either approve of their terms (and silence would amount to acceptance once they were officially discussed) thus committing herself to their being a significant factor in the peace settlement, or reject them, in which case, as Charles Seymour points out, if the Allies had refused to renounce the treaties, the United States could not say she would not continue the war against Germany, for she had her own quarrel with that country; and it would be futile for the United States to announce that because she disapproved of Allied war aims she would make war on Germany on her own. If the United States had said to the Allies that, disapproving of the treaties, she would neverthless fight Germany as a cobelligerent but reserved the right to dispute the treaties at the peace confer-

[7] Text in *ibid.*, 1917, Supplement 2, I, pp. 104–6. On the background of the Secret Treaties, see below, pp. 109–13.

ence, this would only have caused irritation and uncertainty.[8] On the other hand, by not raising the question at all the United States would retain complete freedom of action to adapt her policy on the postwar settlement to circumstances as they arose, and either reject the treaties, accept them in part or whole, or offer substitutes. And last, but by no means least, the policy advocated by House was not an innovation but merely the continuation of a policy already well established on the basis of experience and a careful judgment as to the American interest in the territories covered by the treaties.

On April 26 House was in Washington for the conferences with the mission,[9] and as usual conferred with the President, returning again to the question of the discussion of peace terms. " I argued against discussing peace terms with the Allies," he wrote in his diary, of his talk with the President, " just as I did in my first conversation with Mr. Balfour and in my letter to the President. The President thought it would be a pity to have Balfour go home without a discussion of the subject. My thought was that there was no harm in discussing it between themselves if it was distinctly understood and could be said, that there was no *official* discussion of the subject. . . ." [10]

The President, feeling that his formal meetings with Balfour had been unsatisfactory, asked House to invite Balfour privately for dinner at the White House, where the three of them could talk in an atmosphere of informality.[11] House was to discuss the general question of war aims with Balfour before the dinner; this was done on April 28. House and Balfour spoke at first in general terms of the desirable features of a peace based on the supposition that Germany and the Central Powers were decisively defeated. House then asked " what treaties were out between the

---

[8] Seymour, *Intimate Papers*, III, 40.

[9] The mission arrived in Washington on April 22, and was met at the station by Secretary of State Lansing and a reception committee of distinguished Americans; there were great crowds waiting to greet them on their arrival. The next day Balfour went to the Department of State and conferred with Lansing for half-an-hour or so, then with the Secretary went across to the White House and talked with Wilson for fifty minutes. In the evening the President gave a dinner to the Foreign Secretary. On April 24 Lansing entertained Balfour at a dinner at which there were twenty-four guests, of which four were ex-Secretaries of State, Foster, Day, Root, and Knox; Lansing Papers, Desk Diary, dates as indicated.

[10] House Papers, Diary, April 26, 1917; in Seymour, *Intimate Papers*, III, 41.

[11] *Ibid.*, p. 41.

Allies as to the division of spoils after the war?" Balfour mentioned Italy, and the fact that Britain and France had promised Italy "when she came in . . . pretty much what she had demanded." The House Diary records:

I said to him what I once said to Grey, that if we are to justify our being in the war, we should free ourselves entirely from petty, selfish thoughts and look at the thing broadly and from a world viewpoint. Balfour agreed to this with enthusiasm. Constantinople was our next point. We agreed that it should be internationalized. Crossing the Bosporus we came to Anatolia. It is here that the secret treaties between the Allies come in most prominently. They have agreed to give Russia a sphere of influence in Armenia and the northern part. The British take in Mesopotamia (and the region) which is contiguous to Egypt. France and Italy each have their spheres, embracing the balance of Anatolia up to the Straits. It is all bad and I told Balfour so. They are making it a breeding ground for future war.[12]

The meeting with Wilson took place on April 30. After dinner at the White House, at which the only others present were Mrs. Wilson and a family friend, the three men retired to the President's study for the conference.

The ground we covered was exactly the same as Balfour and I had covered in our conference Saturday. . . .   When we touched upon the internationalization of Constantinople, I suggested that it might lead to trouble . . . I thoroughly agreed with the general idea, but desired to point out that it would inevitably lead to an attempt to internationalize the Straits between Sweden and Norway and Continental Europe, and the Suez and Panama Canals. They did not agree with me that the two questions had much in common . . . I asked Balfour again about the Allies' treaties with each other and the desirability of giving copies to the President. He again agreed to do so. When the conference broke up I walked downstairs with Mr. Balfour and asked if he felt that his mind and the mind of the President had touched at all points. He was quite enthusiastic. . . . Before I left, the President had returned and we had a few minutes further conversation. He was delighted at Balfour's comments, and seemed happy over the result of the evening's work.[13]

---

[12] House Papers, Diary, April 28, 1917; in Seymour, *Intimate Papers*, III, 42–46.
[13] House Papers, Diary, April 30, 1917; Seymour, *Intimate Papers*, III, 47–49. House notes that the President did most of the talking. After the meeting, the President and Balfour went to a reception, at the Pan-American Building, given by Lansing to the French mission. In considering House's reports of his own and

Copies of the treaties were sent to the President by Balfour on May 18 with the comment, in the covering letter, " I do not think that they will add much to the knowledge which you already possess." Included were the Pact of London, pledging each signatory not to conclude a separate peace (with the adhesions of Japan and Italy); the Treaty of London of April 26, 1915, under which Italy entered the war; the Sykes-Picot agreement and the Sazanow-Paleologue agreement, covering the disposition of the Ottoman Empire; the Treaty of Bucharest; and the exchange of notes between Britain and Russia with reference to British interests in South Persia and Russian control of Constantinople. Not included were the Togoland agreement, the Shantung and Pacific Islands agreement with Japan, the Franco-Russian agreement on the postwar frontiers of Germany, and the St. Jean de Maurienne agreement on Italian interests in Anatolia, recently concluded.[14] Some of these gaps in the series of treaties were later filled. While the Allied missions were arriving in Washington in April, the Ambassador in Italy, T. N. Page, reported that the Allies had recently held a secret meeting at St. Jean de Maurienne. On being queried about the meeting, Sonnino, the Italian Foreign Minister, had been vague, Page said, but he suspected that it had something to do with the Eastern Mediterranean and the settlement of Allied ambitions there.[15] The British Ambassador, Spring-Rice, gave Secre-

---

the President's satisfaction with the rapport established with Balfour, the following comment on Balfour is of interest: " He possessed and practised the art of always appearing interested in any subject that was raised, or in any person with whom he was talking . . . yet often himself speaking very little. All who met him came away feeling that *they* had been at their very best, and that they had found someone who, whether he agreed or differed, understood their point of view. Very often they remembered the things they had said to him, which he had welcomed or seemed to agree with, better than what he had said to them. . . . But underneath all this there was a cool ruthlessness where public affairs were concerned. . . . Had his life been cast amid the labyrinthine intrigues of the Italian Renaissance, he would not have required to study the words of Machiavelli. Had he lived in the French Revolution, he would, when it was found absolutely necessary, have consigned a dangerous enemy of his Government or party or even an erring colleague to the guillotine with much complacency. But he would have done it in a thoroughly polite and completely impersonal manner." Winston S. Churchill, *Great Contemporaries* (Fontana ed. [London] 1959), pp. 195–96.

[14] Wilson Papers, Series II, Box 119; A. J. Balfour to the President, letter with enclosures, May 18, 1917.

[15] *Ibid.*, Box 117; Ambassador in Italy T. N. Page to the President, letter, April 25, 1917.

tary of State Lansing details of the Pacific Islands agreement in August.[16]

Wilson and House were not the only Americans who were informed of the treaties. Lansing discussed them several times with Balfour and with members of the French mission, and received from Balfour a copy of the minutes of a meeting of the Imperial War Cabinet at which Balfour made a statement of British foreign policy which included details of the treaties.[17] Henry White, a prominent Republican and later a Commissioner at the Peace Conference, was host at his Washington residence to the leaders of the French mission, Joffre and Viviani, who discussed with him the secret treaties, particularly the proposed division of Mesopotamia and Syria between France and Britain.[18]

During the conferences, House's advice was followed and peace aims and the treaties did not appear on the formal agenda of any of the meetings, but were discussed only in the informal and personal way described above. Until the opening of the Peace Conference in Paris, the United States exercised great care, either directly by an open acknowledgment of the existence of the treaties, or indirectly by participating in discussions or negotiations relating to them, not to admit officially the existence of the treaties or their validity as a solution of the territorial problems that would arise out of the defeat of the Central Powers. By so doing, the Allies were placed under the burden of establishing the place of the treaties in the peace settlement, rather than the United States being forced to protest their application to the terms of peace. The United States never denied that a territorial settlement

[16] Lansing Papers, Desk Diary, August 12, 1917; Memorandum on the President's address of January 8, " Points Open to Debate," January 10, 1918.

[17] On April 25, 1917, Lansing headed the official reception of the French mission at the Navy Yard in Washington, and for the next three days he attended all of the official receptions and dinners given by and for the mission. He had his first real discussions with the mission on May 2, when Viviani and the French Ambassador called at the State Department and discussed peace terms, including Balkan affairs, with the Secretary for an hour and a quarter. Between May 5 and 7, Lansing entertained Balfour and Sir Eric Drummond at Gunston Hall. On May 6 Lansing and Balfour went over " nearly every phase of the International situation," discussing Austria, Bulgaria, Russia, China, inter-Allied relations, and Turkey. Balfour promised to send to the Secretary a copy of a statement he had made to the Imperial War Council on foreign policy and British war aims. This he did on May 18. Lansing Papers, Desk Diary, dates as indicated. The Foreign Secretary's statement is printed in *Foreign Relations*, Lansing Papers, II, 19–32.

[18] Allan Nevins, *Henry White* (New York, 1930), p. 341, fn.

would be an important part of the peace terms; but it was made plain that any settlement in which the interests of the United States were not represented would not be binding on the United States, and would not be admitted as a matter of right to a place in any negotiations or settlement in which the United States was a participant.[19]

3.

A few weeks after the Allied missions returned home, an inter-Allied conference on Balkan problems was called and an informal inquiry was made by the British government as to whether the President would attend. Page, the Ambassador in London, was asked by the Foreign Office to bring unofficially to the attention of the President the importance of American representation at the Conference; it was to consider matters of the highest importance to the prosecution of the war and would be attended by the prime ministers of the participating countries. The Foreign Office acknowledged the difficulties of distance and the fact that the President was the Head of State as well as Prime Minister, but asked that the President consider how these difficulties might be overcome.[20] The President declined either to attend the conference or to be represented there.

[19] The question of the knowledge the President had of the secret treaties has been hotly debated for many years. The debate had as its starting point the testimony of the President before the Senate Foreign Relations Committee, in 1919, during the hearings on the Versailles Treaty. Wilson said that he had learned of the " whole series " of the treaties only during the Peace Conference. Assuming that the President said what he believed was the truth, this raises many questions about the President's memory and his understanding of the nature of international politics. This is discussed in a note at the end of chapter II, Seymour, *Intimate Papers*, III. But if it is assumed that Wilson was not entirely veracious in his testimony, these questions do not arise. There is no evidence that Wilson did not know what he was doing, and a great deal of evidence that it would have been political suicide and the end, there and then, of the Treaty of Versailles and the League if Wilson had told all he knew. Lansing did not tell the truth about his knowledge of the treaties when he appeared before the Committee. In a private memorandum on the Hearings, August 17, 1919, he says that the reason why he did not tell the truth was that it was a public hearing and, under the Chairmanship of Senator Lodge, was aimed at purely political purposes. It is not unreasonable to suppose that Wilson was moved by similar considerations.

[20] The Department of State was directly informed by the British Embassy in an informal note of June 21, 1917, that the President was being approached through

The British government then suggested to the Ambassador that he ask Washington if, since the President did not wish the United States to be represented at the Conference, General Pershing and Admiral Sims might attend as visitors in order that the United States be kept informed on military matters as they came up at the Conference. The Ambassador so informed the State Department on July 18,[21] and on the 20th the Department replied that the suggestion had been submitted to the President, who felt that the presence of Pershing and Sims, even as visitors, might be misconstrued; in any case, all the necessary information could be obtained after the Conference.

For your confidential information [the telegram went on], the President [is] unwilling to be represented at [a] conference of all powers engaged in the war as we are not at war with Austria, Bulgaria, or Turkey. Attendance at the conference might also give the impression to this country that this Government was discussing not only the conduct of the campaign but the ultimate purposes having to do with peace terms.[22]

On learning of the President's position, Cambon, the French Foreign Minister, asked Ambassador Sharp whether, in lieu of American attendance at the Conference, the United States would give its opinion on certain questions not concerned with the Conference. These were: the Russian proposal for a re-examination of war aims, a separate peace with Austria, the magnitude of the American war effort, American loans to the Allies, and Asia Minor, "which has been the object of agreements between the Allies." The Allied governments would be very happy to know the sentiments of the United States government on these matters, Cambon said.[23] The response of the Department of State was to instruct the Embassy to state to Cambon that the Department had no information on the Allied agreements on Asia Minor and

---

the Embassy at London; 763.72/6128; *Foreign Relations*, 1917, Supplement 2, I, 142.

[21] Ambassador in Great Britain to the Secretary of State, personal telegram, 6767, July 18, 1917; 763.72/5896; *Foreign Relations*, 1917, Supplement 2, I, 131.

[22] Telegram 5177 to London, July 20, 1917; 763.72/5896; *Foreign Relations*, 1917, Supplement 2, I, 138.

[23] Telegram 2321 from Paris, July 23, 1917; 763.72119/685; *Foreign Relations*, 1917, Supplement 2, I, 144–46.

wished to be informed of their nature so that it might form an answer.[24]

Sharp gave this reply to Cambon, and, in the ensuing discussion, Sharp reported on August 2:

I learned a most interesting and complicated situation as it bears upon the question of Allied future interests in Asia Minor. It develops that prior to the entrance of Italy into the war, England, France and Russia had entered into an alliance or at least an understanding as to their respective interests in that country. The interests of England in the valley of the Euphrates were tentatively defined also those of Russia and Armenia and those of France in Syria where she has valuable properties and many people of French nationality or allegiance. Besides, she had for several centuries protected Christianity in that country. . . . Then however Italy joined the Allies. She at once manifested a desire to assert her rights in the . . . future exercise of power and possible acquisition of territory in the Eastern Mediterranean, which has not been well received by Britain and France. . . .

(Sharp added that the Italian Prime Minister had, since the end of the Conference, been talking with Lloyd George on these questions.) Cambon said that he was submitting the information on Asia Minor affairs so that the United States would be aware of the questions which confronted the Allies and would have to be dealt with sooner or later, and added that he was glad that the United States was not represented at the Conference, for she was thus not involved in " these enormous subjects of contention." [25]

In the meantime, however, the President, already knowing in detail the " interesting and complicated situation," had himself, on July 23, drawn up the reply to be sent to Cambon.[26] " It would be exceedingly difficult," said the President, " to conclude peace on any terms which would mean arrangements in Asia Minor for the benefit of particular nations rather than for the benefit and protection of the peoples of that part of the world. The sentiment of the world is now aggressively democratic and will have

[24] Telegram 2501 to Paris, July 31, 1917; 763.72119/685; *Foreign Relations*, 1917, Supplement 2, I, 151.

[25] Telegram 2353 from Paris, August 2, 1917; 763,72/6168; *Foreign Relations*, 1917, Supplement 2, I, 155–56.

[26] Wilson Papers, Series II, Box 122; shorthand notes by the President transcribed by Katherine Brand, late of the Manuscripts Division of the Library of Congress.

to be met half way. . . ." Since the United States had no official knowledge of the treaties, however, this reply was not sent until August 3, aftcr the August 2 telegram had been received.[27]

While this exchange was taking place, Secretary of the Treasury MacAdoo wrote to Wilson on July 17 suggesting that a communication be sent to all the countries receiving loans under the Liberty Loan Act, stating that the " rendering of financial assistance to your government under the provisions of the Act should not be construed as approval or disapproval of any particular national objectives which your government may now have in view." Wilson referred the letter to the Department of State for reply, and it was answered by Under Secretary Polk on behalf of Secretary Lansing. Polk said that Lansing thought it would be a mistake to send such a communication at that time, that it might raise awkward questions of policy and that " it would be better not to have anything on record or have any discussion at this time." MacAdoo wrote again on August 14, urging his point with further arguments. Lansing replied that he was " more firmly convinced than ever that it would be a grave mistake." He said that MacAdoo's arguments could be used in regard to the embargo, the presence of an American Army in Europe, and so forth, and that he did not think that the silence of the United States could be interpreted as acquiescence in the ambitions of the Allies. Statements such as those proposed might be misconstrued and it would be wisest to avoid them.[28]

The Administration's silence was maintained even in the face of a direct query on the treaties from a congressman. On March 12, 1918, after the treaties had been published by the Bolsheviks, Representative J. T. Heflin wrote to the Department of State asking if it had any information on the treaties. The Department replied that the United States was not concerned with the treaties and the government knew of them only through press reports. Heflin was apparently not satisfied with this reply. He wrote again on March 20 and this time received a letter from Lansing

[27] The telegram of August 3, to Paris, transmitting the President's reply was not found in the Department's files; on August 8, the Ambassador at Paris cabled to the Department an acknowledgment of the August 3 telegram and conveying the thanks of M. Cambon for the President's answers; 763.72/6252.

[28] U. S. Senate, 74th Congress, 2nd Session; Hearings, Special Committee Investigating the Munitions Industry, pp. 899–901; Lansing's letter to McAdoo is printed in *Foreign Relations*, Lansing Papers, II, 45–46.

himself, who wrote that the State Department had no proof of
their existence and knew of them only through rumors and press
reports. He added, perhaps to give a touch of authenticity to his
answer, that it was as very difficult, " at this time," to get information on them from the British and French ambassadors.[29]

4.

The point-blank refusal of the United States to attend the
Balkan Conference and, perhaps more to the point, the inability
of the Allies to do more than swallow the refusal, illustrated the
great diplomatic strength of the United States and the corresponding weakness of the Allies, which derived from American freedom from the mutual commitments of the Allies as well as from
the geographical position of the United States and from its enormous wealth. The United States possessed the most important
political asset a state can hope for—freedom of action—and,
unless steps were taken by the Allies, would continue to possess it
at an even more critical time—at the peace conference. Added to
this, no one knew or had been permitted to discover precisely what
the United States' policy would be at the close of hostilities. Many
attempts were made, therefore, to find out what American policy
would be and to commit the United States, before the peace conference opened, to a certain line of action and to as much of the
Allied program as was possible. They were all unsuccessful;
Wilson was aware of the danger and took great care to preserve
the American position.

These attempts continued throughout the course of the war
and up to the opening of the Peace Conference. While the Allies
were attempting to persuade the United States to attend the inter-
Allied Conference on the Balkans, Jusserand, the French Ambassador, wrote to the Secretary of State giving the substance of a
telegram he had received from M. Ribot, which referred to the
President's desire for a league of nations as one of the motives
for the United States joining the war against Germany, and asked
for the views of Wilson and the American government on the
league; M. Ribot was studying with great interest this proposal
of the President, said Jusserand, and before coming to any de-

[29] *Foreign Relations*, 1917, Supplement 2, I, 493, fn.

cision on it, would be glad to have the views of the American government and President Wilson, in particular. He said that M. Ribot had told him that he would attach great value to receiving positive information on the matter.[30] The President himself prepared the answer to this message at the same time he wrote the answer to Cambon's questions; it was sent on August 3 over the signature of Acting Secretary Polk. Jusserand was informed that the President thought it premature "at this time" to consider formally the constitution of a society of nations; it might produce jealousies and difficulties which need not be faced now.[31]

The best known occasion of the President's refusal to commit himself was that concerning the proposals for the organization of the Peace Conference made by Jusserand on behalf of the French government on November 29, 1918. This program, and other formulae presented by the French, constituted a concise but complete outline of the organization of affairs and of the subjects to be discussed. Of some note were the sections relating to Allied treaties and the fate of the Ottoman Empire; " all previous special agreements arrived at by some of the Allies only (are to be suspended) with a view to the fullest of freedom of the [sic] examination by the Congress. . . ." Turkey was to be entirely reorganized and the fate of the subject nationalities left to the Congress; a specific reference to Point XII of the Fourteen Points was made in connection with the Eastern Question.[32] Even this tempting offer was rejected by the President.

While the French approach to the problem of American freedom of action concerned itself with general questions, the British characteristically concentrated on specific and concrete situations. Their chief efforts were concentrated in attempting to get American participation in the Supreme War Council and, by associating it with the Council's essentially political activities, bring down the United States to equal political status with the Allied countries. Again Wilson refused to relinquish American freedom of

[30] French Ambassador to the Secretary of State, July 20, 1917; 763.72119/684; *Foreign Relations*, 1917, Supplement 2, I, 140.

[31] Acting Secretary of State to French Ambassador, August 3, 1917; 763.72119/684; *Foreign Relations*, 1917, Supplement 2, I, 153.

[32] *Foreign Relations*, The Paris Peace Conference, I, 344 ff. It may be noted that while the French proposals suggested that previous engagements be suspended, there was no assurance that any new engagements which might take their place would be responsive to American interests. Jusserand's proposal is on p. 365.

action; he did go so far as to appoint General Tasker Bliss to be the American member of the Military Representatives Committee of the Council but was extremely careful to ensure that it did not imply American membership in the Council itself. On one occasion the Department of State repudiated a statement by the Supreme Council that by inference, in mentioning the presence of General Bliss and an American observer at a Council meeting, sought to associate the United States with a political decision of the Council.[33]

There were frequent suggestions that the United States undertake the administration of Palestine. These came from several quarters, including Lord Robert Cecil[34] and Sir Reginald Wingate, Governor-General of the Sudan.[35] Lloyd George suggested to Colonel House during the discussion of armistice terms in October, 1918, that the United States take German East Africa under a trusteeship. House's opinion of this, as he told Wilson, was that the British would like the United States to take something so that they could take what they wanted more freely.[36] On December 16 Lansing wrote to General Bliss, one of his fellow peace commissioners:

We are peculiarly strong because we have no territorial cravings, no selfish interests to serve. If they [Britain and France] could succeed in tarring us with that stick, they would gain a decided advantage. I believe it will be attempted by tempting us with an African colony or starting a controversy in regard to the Pacific Islands. Possibly a protectorate over Armenia or Palestine will be the bait.[37]

---

[33] Telegram 3149 to Paris, February 5, 1918; 763.7250/176.

[34] P. 46 above, footnote.

[35] E. g., despatch 400 from Cairo, 867.00/808; Gary, the Agent, reported that it was his belief that Britain wanted the United States to undertake the protection of Palestine. He said that Sir Reginald Wingate had "made some very pointed remarks in this vein." In a letter dated April 25, 1918, to the Department, Gary said that Wingate had several times endeavored to draw his attention to the Palestine situation and had pointedly raised the question of the United States "taking a hand there." Wingate said that it would be fortunate for Palestine if the United States was the "guiding power," and he believed that it would be acceptable to all the powers. This was only his personal opinion, he said, and he was not speaking officially. Gary commented that he had the impression, however, that this was the view of the British government.

[36] Foreign Relations, Supplement 1, pt. 1, p. 424; Special Representative House to the Secretary of State for the President, telegram 10, October 30, 1918; 763.72119/8984.

[37] Foreign Relations, Paris Peace Conference, I, 296–97; Secretary of State to General T. H. Bliss, letter, December 16, 1918.

5.

The problem of war aims was not merely a problem for the United States on the intergovernmental (and intragovernmental) level, however. One of the chief failures of the Allies in the field of psychological warfare had been their failure to meet the challenge to state their peace aims, the ultimate reasons why they were fighting the war and why the war should be continued in spite of the enormous losses in men and treasure—a challenge presented them by the Central Powers' vague and indeed unacceptable terms for peace which had been started from time to time, by the " no annexations—no indemnities " peace terms of the new Russian government, and by the various statements of the President, particularly the April 2 address to Congress. The people of the Allied countries were no longer willing, so it seemed in the summer of 1917, to continue to pay with the lives of their best men and the future of their children for such war aims as the security of the Channel and the Low Countries, or for Alsace-Lorraine, or the Brenner frontier. Many were asking themselves: Why not go back to July, 1914, and start again from there? This situation presented two problems to the United States. First, what should the public attitude of the United States be toward the aims of the Allies; and, second, should the United States itself announce the specific aims it was fighting for, over and above general statements about the destruction of German power to dominate Europe and the making of the world safe for democracy?

Although Wilson rejected any idea of associating the United States with the secret war aims of the Allies and firmly intended to do what he could to see that they played as small a part as possible in the peace-making, he was nevertheless extremely cautious not to say or do anything that would seem to indicate an American policy of rejecting the war aims while the war was still in progress. To have done so would have made the continuation of the war on the part of the Allies of even more doubtful value than it was already, and the United States might have found herself fighting the Germans alone. This was not probable but it was possible, and it had to be taken into consideration in determining American policy.

The first major development in the war aims issue after the

United States entered the war was the appeal of the Pope, on August 1, for peace based on a return to the *status quo ante bellum*.[38] The weakness of the Allies' position on war aims was made apparent when no effective reply was forthcoming from them, whereas in the Reichstag resolution of July 19 a call for peace on the basis of "understanding and the permanent reconciliation of peoples" and rejecting "forced acquisitions of territory and political, economic, or financial oppressions" had been passed by a vote of 212 to 126.[39] This did not commit the German Imperial government, but it created a certain effect, particularly when contrasted with the silence of the Allies.

After debating with himself for some weeks whether or not to respond at all to the Pope's peace call, Wilson replied to it on August 27. He disavowed, as "inexpedient" and "worse than futile" as bases for peace, "punitive damages, the dismemberment of empires, the establishment of selfish and exclusive economic leagues"—these would form no part of the American purposes in the war; but the present rulers of Germany were completely untrustworthy, and no peace that was not based on firm effective guarantees of the good faith of Germany could endure.[40] This statement marked the first step of the United States along the path from non-involvement to leadership in the determination of the public peace aims of the states at war with the Central Powers. But though it contained an implicit rejection of the Allied war aims as set forth in the secret treaties, Wilson was careful not to make his statement an explicit rejection of them. He told Colonel House that he had been forced to be vague for the sake of sparing Allied feelings. "I have not thought it wise to . . . be more specific because it might provoke dissenting voices from France and Italy if I should—if I should say, for example, that their territorial claims did not interest us."[41]

The deteriorating military and political position of the Allies in the fall of 1917 made the problem even more acute, reaching its crisis during the first two weeks in November with the Bol-

[38] For correspondence relating to the Pope's appeal for peace see *Foreign Relations*, 1917, Supplement 2, I, 161 ff., *passim*; the text of the appeal is on pp. 162–64.
[39] *Ibid.*, pp. 139–40; text of the Resolution transmitted in telegram 1252 from the Legation at Berne.
[40] *Ibid.*, pp. 177–79; telegram 5348 to London, August 27, 1917; 763,72119/726.
[41] Seymour, *Intimate Papers*, III, p. 107.

shevik coup in Russia, the collapse of the Italian front on the Piave, and the fall of the French Cabinet. As it happened, House was in Europe attending the inter-Allied Conference on the conduct of the war as the President's representative. The principal problems to be discussed were the co-ordination of the military efforts of the Allies, the embargo, and shipping. The growing necessity of integrating American and Allied war efforts occasioned the presence of House, though, while he was willing enough to talk about joint action, normally the President was reluctant to associate the United States in joint discussions of policy with the Allies. Allied policy discussions usually were concerned with the difficulties arising from reconciling the various political aims of the Allies with the co-ordination of military strategy on the several fronts. Wilson was extremely careful not to become embroiled in these disputes, partly to retain the political freedom of action of the United States and partly because the political sacrifices that would have to be made by each ally to obtain a rational direction of the common war against Germany could only be decided on by the parties concerned. Thus while Wilson was willing to discuss particular problems with the Allies, he refused to have the United States permanently represented on Allied war councils. House was sent to Europe as head of a mission to discuss individual problems of co-ordination, but not to represent the United States in a conference on the conduct of the war as a whole.[42]

House arrived in England on November 7, 1917. Two days after House arrived news came from Petrograd that the Bolsheviks had seized power and had called for an armistice of all the bel-

---

[42] In the entry for September 16, 1917, House mentions in his Diary an inter-Allied conference to be held in October or November, to which Lloyd George wanted the President to send representatives to further the idea of a separate peace with Austria and Turkey. He wanted House to attend, he said, as the British had "no secrets from Colonel House." Lloyd George had written to House on September 4 saying that he thought it essential that the United States have a representative in Europe to take part in the deliberations of the Allies on future war plans, and that he hoped it would be Colonel House who was appointed. House discussed the matter with the President at lunch on September 16 on board the Presidential yacht, "Mayflower." The President commented that "he could not go much further towards meeting Lloyd George's wishes than to express the feeling that something different should be done in the conduct of the war than had been done, and to say that the American people would not be willing to continue an indefinite trench warfare. He thought it would be inadvisable to commit himself further. . . ." House Papers.

ligerent powers. A day later the remnants of the Italian Second
Army, fleeing from the disaster of Caporetto, were behind the
Piave, having lost three-quarters of a million men. Then, on the
13th, the French Cabinet fell.[43] House spent part of the first
week of his mission in attempting to persuade the British to revise
their war aims, at least to the extent of issuing a liberal statement
on their purpose in continuing the war; he also planned to take
the same question up with the French when he got to France,
where the conference was to be held. The people of the Allied
countries were tired, he wrote to the President on November 11,
and needed something more than, for example, the return of
Alsace-Lorraine, to stir them up; what was wanted was a statement of war aims that could rouse them to continue the fight.[44]
The Conference was postponed on November 15 until the Italian
situation became clearer and the new French Cabinet had settled
down; everyone was waiting to see if Italy would fall, House
cabled Wilson.[45]

House used the delay to continue his talks with British leaders
on war aims. On November 16 he dined with Lloyd George at
Lord Reading's and tried to sound him out on British terms for a
peace settlement, but found it impossible to pin him down to anything concrete.[46] On November 20, however, he talked with the

[43] For correspondence relating to the House mission and to the events in Russia,
France, and Italy, see *Foreign Relations*, 1917, Supplement 2, II, 276–345; *ibid.*,
Lansing Papers, II, 48 ff., *passim*, especially 56–57; and Seymour, *Intimate Papers*,
III, 187–286.

[44] Wilson Papers, Series II, Box 129; House to the President, letter, November
11, 1917. On November 9, House cabled to the President that the mission had
come at a very advantageous time to put new life into the Allies; the Russian
and Italian situations were very depressing. He sent on the same day, by mail, a
memorandum by Buckler of the Embassy of a conversation he had had with Lord
Milner on November 3. Milner was pessimistic about the war and expected it to
last two or three years longer. The situation in the Balkans was bad, he said; the
Serbs would never achieve their ambitions for a Greater Serbia because the collapse
of Austria was very unlikely. Britain had made too many promises in the Balkans
and couldn't keep them all. He thought that Britain should pay more attention
to German peace offers. The two also discussed the possibility of international
commissions to rule Palestine and Albania. Milner said it might be feasible in
Palestine, but very difficult to work properly.

[45] *Ibid.*, House to the President, telegram, November 15, 1917.

[46] House Papers, Diary, November 16, 1917; Seymour, *Intimate Papers*, III,
233. ". . . I find it will be useless to try to get either the French or British to
designate terms. Great Britain cannot meet the new Russian terms of ' no indemnities and no aggression ' [sic] and neither can France. Great Britain at once would

Prime Minister again on war aims, and was this time able to do so. Britain, he was told, wanted Germany's African colonies, an independent Arabia under British suzerainty, an independent Armenia, and the internationalization of the Turkish Straits; Palestine was to go to the Zionists under Britain or the United States.[47] House reported this to Wilson by letter and added that he was to go into the question more fully the next day; he would give him the details of the talks when he returned to Washington, for the mails were not safe.[48]

The talks continued at 10 Downing Street, where Lloyd George, Balfour and House went over the territorial arrangements envisioned in the British war aims, with Balfour outlining them on maps. House said that it was impossible to be so certain of definite ends at the present stage of events, and that it was worse than useless to discuss territorial aims. What was necessary and pertinent at the present time was a statement of general war aims, to put new life into the Allied peoples, and the announcement of an association for the prevention of future wars. The Prime Minister and Foreign Minister were noncommittal.[49]

The inter-Allied Conference finally opened in Paris on November 29. As the consideration of problems arising from the prosecution of the war permitted, House persisted in his attempts to persuade the Allies to adopt a program of liberal war aims, while refusing to be drawn into controversies about territorial questions and maintaining his policy of holding to broad principles. He found the atmosphere hardly conducive to such a radical departure from previous concepts of the function of war.[50] The Allies could not, even in the midst of military disaster, agree to a unified military command because their respective political objectives might be neglected by a Supreme Commander of another nationality. They were far from adopting a program of self-denial for the abstractions that the United States seemed to be motivated by.

House cabled to Wilson, for his approval, the text of a mild resolution he proposed to submit to the Conference:

---

come in sharp conflict with her colonies and they might cease fighting, and France would have to relinquish her dream of Alsace and Lorraine. . . ."

[47] House Papers, Diary, November 20, 1917; Seymour, *Intimate Papers*, III, 235.

[48] Wilson Papers, Series II, Box 130; House to the President, letter, November 21, 1917.

[49] *Ibid.*, November 21, 1917.

[50] Seymour, *Intimate Papers*, III, 280–82.

The Allies and the United States declare that they are not waging war for the purposes of aggression or indemnity. The sacrifices they are making are in order that militarism shall not continue to cast its shadow over the World and that nations shall have the right to lead their own lives in the way that seems to them best for the development of their general welfare.[51]

The President replied immediately:

The resolution you suggest is entirely in line with my thought and has my approbation [the cable read.] You will realize how desirable it is for the Conference to discuss terms of peace in a spirit conforming with my January address to the Senate. Our people and Congress will not fight for any selfish aims on the part of any belligerent, with the possible exception of Alsace-Lorraine. Territorial decisions must be left for the decision of all at the Peace Conference, especially plans for the division of territory such as have been contemplated for Asia Minor. I think it would be obvious to all that it would be a fatal mistake to cool the ardor in America.[52]

This resolution was not adopted by the Conference. House thereupon cabled to Wilson suggesting that, as the Conference could not seem to bring itself to enunciate a statement of liberal war aims, the President should take it on himself to do so. There was as urgent a need for diplomatic co-ordination as there was in military matters, he said; what the Allies needed was a " world appealing policy," one which would " shake Germany behind the lines." He wanted the President to defer mentioning foreign affairs publicly until his return from Europe, so that he could confer with him and give him full details of what he had learned in London and Paris of the Allied attitude to war aims.[53] Wilson replied that he could not wait until House returned, for he was to make an address to Congress on December 4 and, since it was expected, it might do harm if he omitted from it foreign affairs.[54]

---

[51] *Foreign Relations*, 1917, Supplement 2, I, 328; House to the President, telegram, November 30, 1917.

[52] *Ibid.*, p. 331; President to House, telegram, December 1, 1917; 763.72119/ 967 1/2.

[53] House to the President, telegram, December 2, 1917; Seymour, *Intimate Papers*, III, 286.

[54] Wilson Papers, Series II, Box 131; President to House, telegram, December 3, 1917. The address to Congress was devoted to asking Congress to declare war on Austria, hence the rather misleading reference to the necessity of mentioning foreign affairs.

6.

House returned from the inter-Allied Conference in the middle of December. He went immediately to Washington, where he saw the President on December 18 [55] and made his personal report on the proceedings in London and Paris and the failure of the Allies to agree to a new peace program. He also saw Lansing briefly and gave him the gist of his report.[56] After his conference with House, Wilson decided to make a definitive statement of American peace terms as soon as feasible, partly because the need was urgent [57] but also because he was afraid either Clemenceau or Lloyd George would forestall him and issue their own peace terms.[58] Lloyd George did in fact anticipate the President when, in an address to the Trades Union Congress on January 5, 1918, he announced the peace aims of the British government; they were almost identical with those announced by the President three days later.[59] Wilson asked House to have the Inquiry draw up a memorandum on questions that would appear at the Peace Conference, for guidance in preparing his statement.

The Inquiry was a group of experts that had been set up under the supervision of Colonel House to study the problems that would be faced by the United States at the Peace Conference. The formation of such a group had been suggested by the Department of State, in August, 1917, to fill the gaps in the information available to the government on questions likely to appear at

[55] *House Papers*, Diary, December 18, 1917; see also Seymour, *Intimate Papers*, III, 317–18.

[56] Lansing Papers, Desk Diary, December 18, 1917. Lansing had already seen House's report on his mission; Desk Diary, December 16.

[57] According to House, Wilson had three special purposes in mind when he made the Fourteen Points Address: to answer the Bolsheviks' call for peace on the basis of no annexations and no indemnities, to appeal to the German socialists, and to give notice to the Allied governments that there must be a revision in a liberal sense of the war aims as exemplified by the secret treaties. The President was particularly disturbed by the Treaty of London and the plans for the partition of Turkey, House states.

[58] House Papers, Diary, January 1, 1918; see also Seymour, *Intimate Papers*, III, 338–41, for correspondence between Balfour and House on the two addresses.

[59] Shortly after his January 5 address, Lloyd George sent a message to the President excusing himself for "stealing his thunder" but that the labor situation demanded it. Sir William Wiseman told House on January 19 that Lord Robert Cecil was the real author of the address; House Papers, Diary, January 19, 1918. Text of the address in *Foreign Relations*, 1918, Supplement 1, part 1, pp. 4–12.

the Peace Conference.[60] The Secretary of State passed the suggestion on to the President, who asked House to set up the necessary
organization.[61] In September, therefore—with S. E. Mezes, President of The City College of New York, as Director and Walter
Lippmann, the well-known young liberal journalist, as Secretary—
the Inquiry began its work.[62] Throughout the fall of 1917 it had
been selecting experts and gathering basic information on every
conceivable aspect of the peace.[63] When the President asked
House to have the Inquiry prepare the memorandum on peace
terms, it had already prepared several studies on the basic work of
the Inquiry that included, in outline form, the problems on which
work would be concentrated; [64] and a preliminary memorandum
was completed on December 22 and delivered to the President
the next day.[65]

The study on which the presidential memorandum was based
was a memorandum on the context of the Inquiry prepared during
the early part of December by Walter Lippmann; it was a statement of the current strategic and military situation and its implica-

[60] The Third Assistant Secretary of State, Breckinridge Long, wrote to Lansing
on August 4, 1917, proposing a bureau for the study and preparation of the
questions likely to be proposed at the Peace Conference; *Foreign Relations*, Paris
Peace Conference, I, 9. On the organization and work of the Inquiry, see Lawrence E. Gelfand, *The Inquiry* (New Haven, 1963).

[61] The President to House, letter, September 2, 1917; Seymour, *Intimate Papers*,
III, 169.

[62] *Ibid.*, pp. 169–70.

[63] On November 9, 1917, Dr. Mezes wrote to the President giving him a
rough outline of the work of the Inquiry. Wilson replied on November 12
approving of the plan of operation and the areas being studied, but suggested
one omission, the just claims of the great powers—even including Germany. The
American aim, he said, was a fair peace for all which would not plant the seeds
of future wars. Mezes to the President, letter, November 9, 1917; President to
Mezes, letter, November 12, 1917; Wilson Papers, Series II, Box 129. In a letter
to the Secretary of State of October 1, 1917, Ambassador Page in England wrote
that press comment in England on Colonel House's " quest for peace data " showed
a great deal of concern—" peace is not a popular word here "—despite Lansing's
statement that the program had no reference to making peace but only to collect-
ing information for a peace conference. Page thought that while the program
should be carried out, it should be done without publicity. He added that the
United States was getting all the information it asked for from the British government. For correspondence on the organization and work of the Inquiry, see *Foreign Relations*, Paris Peace Conference, I, 9–118.

[64] *Ibid.*, pp. 27–34, Inquiry Document No. 885; undated, *circa* December 15,
1917.

[65] *Ibid.*, pp. 41–53, Inquiry Document No. 887, submitted December 22, 1917.

tions for the termination of the war and for the Peace Conference. The basic theme was that which the President had reiterated in all his public statements on the war since April, 1917—German control of Mittel-Europa, and the necessity of nullifying this overwhelming position of power by war and then insuring that it would not be a factor in the postwar world; with the addition of an acknowledgment of the complexity of internal German politics that would have been out of place in a public address, and an analysis of the conflict between the two schools of German strategic thinking—that which looked to the world arena and that which saw the future of Germany in the East. In the section devoted to the methods of achieving control of German ambitions after the war, it was suggested that to seal off the German thrust to the East through Turkey it would be necessary to establish " strong allied control over the essential parts of Turkey—Armenia, Palestine, Mesopotamia."

The December 22 memorandum was basically an application of these principles to specific military and political situations, together with detailed suggestions for peace terms that would accomplish American political objectives at the Peace Conference. The strategic position of the Central Powers was fundamentally the control of the Berlin-Baghdad axis. The Allies, in addition to the frontal assault on the German position in France, had made many attempts, all unsuccessful, to break this axis on the Russian, Italian, and Salonika fronts, but the only success achieved so far in holding and containing the Central Powers had been on the Middle Eastern fronts—in Mesopotamia and Palestine—where the British held the terminal points of the drive of Mittel-Europa to Suez and the Persian Gulf. Mittel-Europa was bound together by certain common interests; in the case of Turkey, though to a great extent its adhesion to the Central Powers had been in part bought and in part coerced, this was in some measure due to the fact that in the alliance alone lay the possibility of even a nominal integrity for the Ottoman Empire. The broad goals to be aimed at " in order to render Middle Europe safe " included, for the Ottoman Empire, the neutralization and internationalization of Constantinople and the Straits, and control of the eastern terminals of the Berlin-Baghdad axis by an administration friendly to the Western nations. To accomplish this, and as a matter of

justice and humanity, a " guaranteed autonomy" for the Armenians must be secured.

The memorandum then gave a suggested statement of peace
terms which would serve both as the " bases of an ultimate just
peace and as a program of war aims which would cause the
maximum disunity in the enemy and the maximum unity among
our associates." For Turkey this meant the following:

It is necessary to free the subject races of the Turkish Empire from
oppression and misrule. This implies at the very least autonomy for
Armenia and the protection of Palestine, Syria, Mesopotamia, and Arabia
by the civilized nations. It is necessary also to establish free intercourse
through and across the Straits. Turkey proper must be justly treated and
freed from economic and political bondage. Her war debts to Germany
must be cancelled. None of the money involved was spent in the interests
of Turkey, and none of it should be regarded as a Turkish obligation. . . .
This will appear on the surface to be a drastic solution of the Turkish
problem, but it is one which the military situation enables us to accomplish, and it can hardly be doubted that no principle of justice requires
the return of occupied portions of Turkey to the German-Turkish alliance. . . . Turkey can be given a new start, considerably reduced in
size, without power to misgovern alien races, and therefore free to concentrate upon the needs of her own population. . . .

The Inquiry, of course, was a research organization, not a
policy-making body. Its suggestions were merely suggestions and
do not represent the official position of the American government
on any of these matters. Neverthless, the Inquiry's close association with Colonel House, and the use to which its work was put
by the President, make its memoranda of more significance in the
development of American Middle East policy than their character
and their provenance would at first indicate, and while when they
were written they were unofficial and illustrative, they gained
official status, as it were, by assimilation.

House returned to Washington on December 23, and delivered
the memorandum to the President. After reading it, Wilson asked
House to have the Inquiry clarify the suggested peace terms and
explain in more detail the reasoning behind their thinking.[66] The
revision was sent to Wilson on January 2, 1918,[67] and a final

---

[66] House Papers, Diary, December 23, 1917.
[67] Wilson Papers, Series II, Box 133; A Suggested Statement of Peace Terms,
January 2, 1917 (18); this was taken to Paris by Wilson.

version, used by Wilson in the preparation of his Fourteen Points address, was completed two days later.[68] Commenting on the suggested peace terms for Turkey, an explanatory memorandum said that these terms were "very tentative"; the dominant idea was breaking the Berlin-Baghdad axis by freeing oppressed peoples, but the precise method of doing this was a "very puzzling" problem—one method would be the establishment of national or international protectorates over these freed peoples. Wilson went over these papers carefully, making changes and annotations. The only major change in the Turkish section was the alteration of "protectorates" over the freed peoples of the Ottoman Empire to "protection" of them.

With these memoranda and a mass of other material also supplied by Colonel House, Wilson began the work of drafting his address. On the evening of January 4 House came down to Washington from New York to work with the President on the proposed address. "I did not reach the White House until nine o'clock," wrote House in his Diary. "They had saved dinner for me, but I touched it lightly and went into immediate conference with the President concerning the proposed message to Congress on our war aims. . . . We were in conference until half-past eleven, discussing the general terms to be used, and looking over data and maps. . . ."[69] The actual drafting began the next morning; the President and House "got down to work at half-past ten and finished remaking the map of the world, as we would have it, at half-past twelve o'clock."[70]

Wilson had little difficulty in deciding on the terms for Turkey and "the oppressed nationalities." On the Inquiry memorandum he had written a marginal note translating the words of the suggested peace terms for the Ottoman Empire into a brief statement: "The Turkish portions of the present Turkish Empire must be assured a secure sovereignty and the other nationalities which are now under Turkish rule must be assured full opportunity of autonomous development." This was a great advance from the "effacement" of Turkey. In the version written on January 5 Wilson changed "full opportunity of autonomous

[68] *Ibid.*, Box 134. The changes mentioned in the text were made directly on the memorandum by Wilson.
[69] House Papers, Diary, January 4, 1918; Seymour, *Intimate Papers*, III, 322.
[70] *Ibid.*, p. 235.

development" to "absolutely unmolested opportunity" and added a clause on the free passage of the Straits. Apparently the only discussion of the Turkish terms between House and Wilson on January 5 was that mentioned in House's Diary: "After the Turkish paragraph had been written, the President thought it might be made more specific, and that Armenia, Mesopotamia, Syria, and other parts be mentioned by name. I disagreed with this, believing that what was said was sufficient to indicate this, and it finally stood as originally framed." [71]

As it was given in the address to the Congress on January 8, the section dealing with Turkey, the Twelfth of the Fourteen Points, read:

The Turkish portions of the present Ottoman Empire should be assured a secure sovereignty, but the other nationalities which are now under Turkish rule should be assured an undoubted security of life and an absolutely unmolested opportunity of autonomous development, and the Dardanelles should be permanently opened as a free passage to the ships and commerce of all nations under international guarantees.[72]

It will be noted that in this final version there is an additional change from Wilson's original note which said that the Turkish terms "must" be carried out; now it reads that they "should" be carried out. This change was also made in all the other Points except those dealing with Belgium and the League of Nations. In a late draft of the address "must" was used throughout but, after discussing the matter with House, Wilson changed all the territorial clauses, except that relating to Belgium, to read "should." According to House, it was decided that:

where there was no difference as to the justice of the question the word "must" ought to be used, and where there was controversy the word "should" was correct. He went through the entire message and corrected it in this way. . . . My argument was this: The American people might not consent to fight for the readjustment of European territory, therefore in suggesting these readjustments, with the exception of Belgium, the word "should" ought to be used.[73]

---

[71] House Papers, Diary, January 5, 1918; portions of the entry are in Seymour, *Intimate Papers*, III, 325–29.

[72] Text in *Foreign Relations*, 1918, Supplement 1, part 1, pp. 12–17.

[73] Seymour, *Intimate Papers*, III, 329–30.

It may be noted that the change in wording also removed any possibility of the territorial clauses of the Fourteen Points being interpreted as an American commitment on the terms of the peace settlement. The United States was still free to conclude peace on terms of her own choosing.

7.

The Fourteen Points address was a public statement of policy; it cannot, therefore, be taken as it stands as a definitive expression of Wilson's foreign policy. The territorial terms outlined in the address were based on strategic considerations which were not explained to the public. It is necessary to look behind what was said publicly to the application of the Fourteen Points to specific political situations, in order to arrive at their significance in the formulation of American foreign policy and in its implementation.

The first concrete political situation in which the Fourteen Points were a factor arose almost immediately after the address was given. On January 26, 1918, the Ambassador at Rome reported to the State Department that the Italian Prime Minister, Orlando, had gone to London to get the Treaty of London reaffirmed in view of the recent speeches by Lloyd George and the President. It was rumored that the Prime Minister and his Foreign Minister, Sonnino, had had a " stiff quarrel " about the trip, as Sonnino maintained that he had the Allies' promise in writing and did not want the subject discussed.[74] Two days later the Ambassador cabled that Sonnino had gone to Paris to join Orlando in demanding that the French reaffirm the Treaty.[75] Page wrote privately to the President and to Lansing on the reasons for the Italian concern about the Treaty of London. He said that the references to Italy and her claims in the speeches of the President and Lloyd George " fall far short of what Italy desires and what her Government and Press have led her people to expect." There had been a tremendous stir, he said, and much

---

[74] Telegram 1362 from Rome, January 26, 1918; 763.72/8648.

[75] Telegram 1368 from Rome, January 28, 1918; 763.72/8682. The Ambassador also informed the Department that he had heard the Pope intended to publish all the Allied secret treaties; it was improbable, he said, but he had it on good authority that the Pope had said the Allies were as imperialistic as the Central Powers.

critical feeling against Britain and the United States.[76] (When this information on Italian dissatisfaction first reached Wilson, he asked Balfour to let him know his thoughts on the Treaty of London and the Italian territorial claims under it. Balfour replied that the Treaty bore proof that the Allies were anxious to get Italy into the war and that the Italians made good use of this anxiety. "But a treaty is a treaty; and we—I mean England and France [of Russia I say nothing]—are bound to uphold it in letter and spirit.") [77]

In a letter to Lansing, Wilson described his attempt to explain his position to the Italian Ambassador. "This is a very delicate matter," wrote the President,

but while you were away from your office I took occasion to say to the Italian Ambassador . . . that I had limited my statement about Italian rights as I did because I was taking my program as a whole, including the League of Nations through which mutually defensive pledges were to be given and taken which would render strategic considerations such as those affecting the Adriatic much less important. I told him that failing a League of Nations my mind would be open upon all such matters to new judgments. . . .[78]

The second occasion when the Fourteen Points were subjected to a political interpretation was during the armistic discussion in October, 1918. The Allied leaders and Colonel House were considering their joint response to the German overtures for peace negotiations based on the Fourteen Points, and it became neces-

[76] Ambassador in Italy to Secretary of State, private letter, January 29, 1918; 763.72/8706 1/2. He added that those Italians who remained pro-American urged that steps be taken to counter anti-American propaganda. He had made such suggestions, he said, but they had fallen on deaf ears. The Italian people had suffered a great deal and needed some demonstration of American interest in them and in their aspirations. Page suggested that a small detachment of American troops on the Italian Front would work wonders. He asked the Department to provide him with the means of carrying on "some small propaganda effort" on what the United States had done for Italy. Lansing sent a copy to the President, suggesting that a military mission might be sent to Italy. He commented that he agreed with Page that trouble lay ahead in Italy.

[77] Wilson Papers, Series II, Box 135; Balfour to President, letter, January 31, 1918.

[78] *Foreign Relations*, Lansing Papers, II, 94; President to Secretary of State, letter, January 29, 1918; 763.72119/1266 1/2. For additional correspondence relating to Italian reactions to the Fourteen Points, see *Foreign Relations*, 1918, Supplement 1, part 1, pp. 18 ff., *passim*.

sary to decide exactly what the Fourteen Points meant in terms of the German proposals and the military and political conditions then existing. House asked Frank I. Cobb, editor of the New York *World*, and Walter Lippmann, Secretary of the Inquiry, who were attached to House's mission, to draw up an interpretation of the Fourteen Points for use in his talks with the Allies; this was sent to the President for his approval.

The memorandum compiled by Cobb and Lippmann went over each of the Points, briefly analyzing the current political situation affecting each and giving their view of the appropriate interpretation of the President's statement for the individual cases comprising the over-all situation with which each Point was concerned. For Point Twelve, dealing with the Ottoman Empire, the memorandum stated:

The same difficulty arises here as in the case of Austria-Hungary concerning the word "autonomous."

It is clear that the Straits and Constantinople, while they may remain nominally Turkish, should be under international control. This control may be collective or be in the hands of one power as mandatory of the League.

Anatolia should be reserved for the Turks. The coast lands, where Greeks predominate, should be under special international control, perhaps with Greece as mandatory.

Armenia must be (given) a port on the Mediterranean, and a protecting power established. France may claim it, but the Armenians would prefer Great Britain.

Syria has already been allotted to France by agreement with Great Britain.

Great Britain is clearly the best mandatory for Palestine, Mesopotamia and Arabia.

A general code of guarantees binding upon all mandatories in Asia Minor should be written into the treaty of peace.

This should contain provisions for minorities and the "open door." The trunk railroad lines should be internationalized.[79]

Wilson cabled back his reaction: "Analysis of fourteen points satisfactory interpretation of principles involved but details of

---

[79] *Ibid.*, pp. 405–13; Special Representative House to Secretary of State for the President, telegram 5 from London, October 29, 1918; 763.72119/8979.

application mentioned should be regarded as merely illustrative suggestions and reserved for peace conference. . . ." [80]

The wording of Point Twelve was vague and was, as we have seen, subject to interpretation according to the political situation as it existed at any given time; notwithstanding that he had said that the oppressed nationalities under Turkish rule should be assured " an absolutely unmolested opportunity of autonomous development," Wilson accepted as a " satisfactory interpretation " of this principle the allotment of Syria to France. The significance of the Fourteen Points in American Middle East policy, however, lies chiefly not in the expression of a qualified belief in self-determination for the peoples of the Middle East but simply in the fact that the President of the United States had, in the name of his country, expressed an opinion on the settlement of the Eastern Question. Up to that point the United States over a period of many years had declined to become involved in Middle East politics, had stated this position both to the other governments concerned with Middle East affairs and to the public, and had recently publicly explained that it was not necessary for the security of the United States to declare war on Turkey. Now, with the deliberate intent of influencing postwar settlement of political problems in the Middle East, the President broke with tradition and, on his own initiative and without even a semblance of deference to those powers whose interests in the Middle East were well established and recognized and, most important, whose interests were a major cause of the war, intruded the United States into this closed preserve. Wilson had not committed the United States to any particular course of action, but he had made known in unmistakable terms that the United States considered the Middle East to be within the sphere of American interests and that the solution of its problems would not be left to the determination of the powers that had, up to now, considered the Middle East to be their exclusive concern. The implications of this revolution in American foreign policy were not understood by the other powers concerned for some time; it has been mentioned that they were most favorable to an American declaration of war on Turkey and the subsequent participation of the United States in the peace settlement with Turkey. It may

[80] *Foreign Relations*, 1918, Supplement 1, part 1, p. 421; President to Special Representative House, telegram, October 30, 1918.

be that they did not think that the United States might claim, on the basis of a public statement of a general principle, an equal voice in this settlement—what country, a neutral in the Eastern war at that, would have the audacity?

8.

As the war ended, the United States had, to say the least, an indefinite position in a future settlement of Eastern problems. In the Fourteen Points, Wilson had deliberately refrained from committing the United States to a definite course of action. But the United States had, for all practical purposes, complete freedom of action coupled with great diplomatic strength; these two factors made it possible for Wilson to choose the course he would take at the Peace Conference—and if he chose to make the United States a partner with the Allies in settling the Eastern Question, there was very little the Allies could do to stop him.

At the same time, the United States exercised great caution in its relations with the Allied Powers in Eastern matters, particularly when, in the late summer of 1918, the Turkish and Bulgarian fronts were crumbling and Allied success in these theaters seemed assured. Typical of Wilson's attitude was his response to a scheme put forward by General Pershing at the end of August, 1918. On August 30 General Bliss sent a cable to the Secretary of State and Colonel House outlining a discussion he had had, at Pershing's request, on an idea the latter had had " ruminating " for several days. Pershing told Bliss that the successful advance of the Allies and Americans on the Western Front would continue, and while the Germans were not yet beaten, he was satisfied that their morale was bad. He thought, therefore, that united action should be taken to end the war before 1919, and if the President urged the Allies to attack on the Italian Front, in Salonika and in Mesopotamia; if he encouraged the pro-Ally sections of the Russian people; if he was to intimate to Austria-Hungary, Bulgaria, and Turkey that the time had come for them to yield; and if pressure were brought to bear on the neutrals, especially Spain, the defeat of the Germans, which he considered to be certain, would be hastened.[81] This cable was sent to the President,[82] and on September 2 he sent his reactions to the Secretary of State. " Such a message as this from General Pershing surprises me very much," he wrote. " It is the first time he has undertaken to give advice, political as well as military, in this way." It was out of the question for us to urge such a course without the at least intimated concurrence of the Supreme Council and it was clear, said the President, that events, not any suggestions from the United States, would determine the actions of Bulgaria and Turkey. " You know the advances that have been made to us from Bulgaria and Turkey and how unwise it would be for us to use the only channels that are open," he added.[83]

On the other hand, the United States had no intention of being frozen out of the settlement of Eastern affairs and kept a close watch on the progress of the movement for peace in Turkey and Bulgaria and on Allied reactions to it. On September 24 a cable was sent to the Embassy in London, stating that the American government was " gratified " at the success of the British Army in Palestine, which might be the occasion of an attempt by the Turks to arrange a separate peace. It was noted that a London newspaper had urged diplomatic efforts be made to detach Turkey from its allies. The Embassy was instructed to keep the Department informed and to report immediately if there was any possibility that the British government would consider favorably such an approach from Turkey.[84] The Embassy replied the next day, saying that it had no knowledge and could obtain none that would indicate that the British would consider such a proposition.[85]

[81] General Bliss to Secretary of State and Colonel House, special telegram from Paris, August 30, 1918; 763.72/13369.

[82] Secretary of State to President, letter, August 31, 1918; 763.72/13369.

[83] President to Secretary of State, letter, September 2, 1918; 763.72/13378 1/2. The United States did not break relations with Bulgaria and at this time had a Consul-General at Sofia, but I have not been able to trace the reference to the advances to the United States referred to by the President. Though this is an interesting matter, it cannot have been very important or the persons involved of great significance, since nothing came of it. Referring again to Pershing's suggestions for speeding victory, his better known suggestion that unconditional surrender be demanded of Germany and failing its acceptance that the Allies march to Berlin got very much the same reception as his earlier idea. Lansing mentions in his Desk Diary the receipt of Pershing's " extraordinary " advice; Lansing Papers, Desk Diary, October 31, 1918.

[84] Telegram 1569 to London, September 24, 1918; 763.72119/1951a.

[85] Telegram 2206 from London, September 25, 1918; 763.72119/1952.

A further cable was sent from London on October 1, stating that
in view of events in the Balkans, the Councelor of the Embassy
had inquired at the Foreign Office and had been assured that the
British government had no information on Turkish attempts to
obtain a separate peace, but that it would occasion no surprise
if the Turks made a move in this direction soon; the Embassy
would be informed as soon as anything happened.[86] Peace feelers
were put out by the Turks shortly after this, and the United States
was kept informed. On October 9 the Chargé in Greece cabled
that the British Minister, through whom the Turkish approaches
had been made, had just told him that a reply had been received
from Lloyd George stating that the British government could not
negotiate with any group unless it was sure that such a group
represented the Turkish government. They apparently did not
negotiate.[87]

The American position was put formally before the Allies when
the Bulgarians asked for an armistice. On October 2 the Embassy
at London was instructed to inform the British government that
the United States was " gratified " that Bulgaria had severed her
alliance with Germany and Austria-Hungary, but felt it should
state frankly that it regarded every question which concerned the
Balkan States as an essential part of a general peace settlement,
since the Balkans were a seedbed of war. The United States
believed that the peace with Bulgaria could not be separated from
a general peace without embarrassing the consideration of such
subjects as the treaties of Brest-Litovsk and Bucharest, and without making very difficult the consideration of matters which
should be left for the final settlement. The Embassy was to
stress that the government of the United States desired to register
the opinion that it would be very hazardous to treat separately
any part of the whole question of general settlement, which
would have to be dealt with in the final treaty of peace.[88] The

[86] Telegram 2380 to London, October 1, 1918; 763.72119/1990.
[87] Telegram 578 from Athens, October 9, 1918; 763.72/11687; it was probably
such a group of Turks as those that approached the British on this occasion that
the President referred to in his letter of September 2 mentioned above.
[88] This instruction was based almost word for word on a memorandum drawn
up by the President in response to a letter from Lansing of September 30, 1918,
drawing his attention to the situation in Bulgaria and the dangers of permitting
peace to be made by the Allies acting alone. The memorandum is undated, but

Foreign Office replied in a note of November 6 to the Embassy that the President's views had always been shared by the British government.[89]

Nevertheless, the United States did not make any attempt to capitalize on the fact that the formal Turkish request for an armistice was made to the United States. The Spanish Ambassador, who had charge of Turkish interests in the United States, sent to the President on October 14 a copy of a note from the Turkish Chargé in Spain to the Spanish Foreign Minister requesting, on instructions from the Ottoman government, that the Spanish government ask the President of the United States " to take upon himself the task of the reestablishment of peace," and inform him that the Imperial government accepted the Fourteen Points and his subsequent messages as a basis for peace negotiations.[90] Before any reply was made, the Allied ambassadors in Washington were asked to obtain the views of their respective governments as to the reply that should be made to the Turks. By October 26 only the Italian Ambassador had received a reply from his government, which reply suggested that the President tell the Turks to get in touch with the Allied military authorities; the French Ambassador told the Department that while he had not received any positive instructions, he thought it would be the opinion of his government that the Turks should apply to the military; the British Embassy had received no word at all from London.[91] This delay was due to the fact that the Turks were already engaged in *pourparlers* with the Allied military authorities in the East. On the day that Secretary Lansing sent his reply to the Turks through the Spanish Embassy, October 30, 1918, stating that he would bring the message of the Imperial government to the attention of the Allies,[92] the Turks signed an armis-

bears the notation "Handed me at Cabinet Oct 1/18 R L"; *Foreign Relations, Lansing Papers*, II, 157–58. Text of the telegram to London is at *ibid.*, 1918, Supplement 1, part 1, p. 334; 763.72119/2004a.

[89] Telegram 3473 from London, November 6, 1918; 763.72119/2498; *Foreign Relations*, 1918, Supplement 1, part 1, p. 474.

[90] Spanish Ambassador to the President, October 14, 1918; 763.72119/2532.

[91] Secretary of State to President, letter, October 26, 1918; 763.72119/2370 1/2; *Foreign Relations, Lansing Papers*, II, 167.

[92] Secretary of State to Spanish Ambassador, Note 984, October 31, 1918; 763.72119/2532; *Foreign Relations*, 1918, Supplement 1, part 1, p. 428.

tice on board a British warship anchored off the island of Mudros.[93]

[93] Special Representative House to President, from Paris, telegram 32, undated, received November 1, 1918; 763.72119/9044; *Foreign Relations*, 1918, Supplement 1, part 1, pp. 441–43. This telegram gives the full text of the armistice conditions. The Embassy at the Hague cabled on October 29 (telegram 4904, 763.72119/2393) that the Turkish Ambassador, through an entirely reliable spokesman, informed the Embassy that he had been instructed by his government to see the representative of the United States and to say that the Turkish government was very desirous of renewing diplomatic relations with the United States.

PART II

THE PEACE CONFERENCE

CHAPTER III

ESTABLISHING THE MANDATE SYSTEM

1.

From the time the United States entered the war in April, 1917, up to the Armistice in November, 1918, American concern with the future of the Ottoman Empire had been primarily based on the necessity of limiting the military, political, and economic power of Germany by denying to it the control of strategic areas through which this power could be directed against the Allies and the United States. This had given rise to a secondary consideration, the question of the nature and extent of American participation in a general peace settlement which included matters affecting the disposition of the Ottoman Empire. The problem here touched not only on the question of the degree of American involvement in the affairs of a country where American interests were minimal and with which the United States was at peace but also the larger question of whether the United States would associate itself with the Allied plans for the partition of Turkey, or would oppose them and provide an effective substitute. To this there was no easy answer. It was not merely a choice between morality and imperialism, between self-determination and the secret treaties. Blocking the Central Powers from South Asia and the Indian Ocean was the goal of American as well as Allied policy toward the Ottoman Empire. The implementation of the secret treaties would accomplish this without a doubt. What alternative solution could the United States offer that would do as much? The Fourteen Points had not laid down a concrete American peace program, for apart from the establishment of a league of nations and the restoration of Belgium the President had been careful not to commit the United States to anything. But he had set down a foundation on which an American program could be constructed, if the opportunity arose, while at the same time leaving the door open, should the United States not be in a position to offer a plan that would effectively seal off the Central Powers from Asia, for the establishment of European control over the Ottoman Empire under conditions acceptable to the United States government and the American people.

This was the situation when, on October 6, 1918, the Swiss Chargé d'Affaires in Washington communicated to the President a note from the German government requesting him " to take steps for the restoration of peace " on the basis of the Fourteen Points and the subsequent addresses of the President.[1] Germany had been defeated in war. But did this mean that it could not recover? There was at this point no reason to suppose that Germany and Mittel-Europa would not, if the future permitted, regroup their forces and strike again.[2] Only two weeks before the German peace overtures, Secretary Lansing had drawn up a private memorandum on territorial arrangements after the war in which Germany and Mittel-Europa, even though defeated, were treated as still constituting a continuing threat in the postwar world, drawing much strength from the control of southern Russia with its rich lands and oil, and from there threatening the route to India. In order to nullify this control, certain essential territorial terms must be written into the peace. Turkey was to retain Anatolia but was to be deprived of its European possessions. Constantinople was to be constituted an international protectorate, and the Straits were to be internationalized. Armenia and Syria were to become protectorates with self-government as soon as possible and provisions for the " Open Door." Palestine was to be autonomous under international control or a mandatory designated by the Powers. Arabia was to " receive careful consideration as to the full or partial sovereignty of the State or States established." Britain was to have sovereignty, or a full protectorate, over Egypt. The German colonies were to be disposed of by an international commission.[3] The same interpreta-

---

[1] *Foreign Relations*, 1918, Supplement 1, I, 337–38.

[2] Cf., Analysis of the Military Situation by the Permanent Military Representatives of the Supreme War Council, September 14, 1919; 763.7256/138½; originally written July 4, 1918 and reissued. *Foreign Relations*, Lansing Papers, II, 146.

[3] Lansing Papers, Private Memorandum, " The Essentials of Peace," September 21, 1918.

tion of German strength underlay the Cobb-Lippmann analysis of of the Fourteen Points described in the preceding chapter.

But even as the armistice negotiations were proceeding, the political situation changed completely. The Central Powers were disintegrating. Austria-Hungary was disappearing; not only had the subject nationalities torn themselves away from the fabric of the state, the Austro-Hungarian state itself was dissolving. The Ottoman Empire had crumbled into ruins and was under the complete domination of the Allies. Between Germany and the East a barrier of new nations was forming, from Poland in the north to Yugoslavia in the south. And with the collapse of Mittel-Europa the *raison d'être* of American Middle East policy disappeared.

The threat to the United States of a German-dominated Europe no longer existed. There was now no necessity for the United States to participate in a general settlement of the war, for the immediate aims of American foreign policy had been realized. Of what concern to the United States were French national sentiments about the lost provinces of Alsace and Lorraine; the British routes to India; European commercial and financial opportunities in the Ottoman Empire; the right of Belgrade to rule in Slovenia and Croatia? Taken individually, none. To the European powers these matters were the ultimate ends of foreign policy; to the United States they were merely parts of a pattern of behavior and attitudes that had brought upon Europe a devastating war which, with the aid of modern technology and science, had reached across the Atlantic and threatened the security of the United States.

But this was the whole point as Wilson saw it. The conflicts of the European powers had started one world war, and they could also start another. The rivalries of states could no longer be taken individually; the world was too small for international problems to be dealt with piecemeal, and some method had to be introduced to solve them collectively. The war had demonstrated that the United States was, willy-nilly, involved in world politics. Hence, to protect American interests, the United States must participate in the peace settlement. Wilson determined that only through the establishment of a league of nations competent and able to influence, in its own name and not merely as the agent of the several powers constituting it, the political relations of states, could the United States exercise its full influence in international affairs. Such a league would prevent America from being dragged into the treaty system of Europe and being used as a tool by one or another grouping of European states, and it would present an opportunity for American participation in the political life of the great powers that corresponded with the domestic political system of the United States, making international relations less of a strain on American political institutions and more acceptable to the American people.[4]

The acceptance of the Fourteen Points by the Allies and Germany as the basis of peace put the seal on Wilson's policy, for the creation of a league of nations was one of the two American war aims set down in the Fourteen Points that can be considered as American commitments. The adoption of the league as an essential part of the terms of peace also provided a new means of settling territorial problems, particularly those relating to the Ottoman Empire, and the inclusion of these problems within the framework of the league became the new basis for American Middle East policy.

2.

On December 10, discussing the problems facing the United States at the Peace Conference with the experts of the American Commission to Negotiate Peace, then proceeding to Europe on the U. S. S. *George Washington,* the President said that his solution for the problem of the ownership of conquered German colonies would be to have them " declared the common property of the League of Nations and administered by small nations." " Nothing stabilizes an institution so well," he said, " as the possession of property." [5] Five days later General Smuts of South Africa, one of the British Commonwealth leaders, published a pamphlet, " The League of Nations, a Practical Suggestion." In referring to the problem of conquered colonies in this pamphlet, Smuts advocated outright annexation for the German colonies because of their extreme backwardness and manifest inability to

---

[4] See, Seymour, *Intimate Papers*, IV, chaps. I, II. Also Wilson's speech at the Metropolitan Opera House in New York, September 27, 1918, where he called for a League formed under " efficacious covenants." *Foreign Relations*, 1918, Supplement 1, I, 316–21.

[5] *Ibid.*, pp. 281–82, 285.

govern themselves. The other newly won lands and the remains of the Austrian and Turkish empires should be disposed of by the League: ". . . any authority, control or administration which may be necessary in respect to these territories and peoples, other than their own self-determined autonomy, shall be the exclusive function of and shall be vested in the League of Nations and exercised by or on behalf of it." While both Smuts and Wilson advocated League ownership of conquered territory, they were at this point far from agreement, for Wilson so far had only mentioned in this respect the German colonies,[6] while Smuts had specifically excluded them. The idea had been put forth, however, and the two men, when they met in Paris, found their ideas close enough so that a compromise plan was worked out.[7]

During the first days of January, 1919, while waiting in Paris for the Peace Conference to open, Wilson was primarily engaged in drawing up a draft covenant for the League of Nations. He was very much impressed with Smuts's plan for the League and with the scheme to place conquered territory under the ownership of the League. To his two so-called " Paris Drafts " of the covenant, he appended a " Supplementary Agreement " for the League ownership of the debris of the three empires. The League was to enjoy the right of ultimate disposal and administration of all of the territories in question, thus excluding annexation. Any authority of control other than that deriving from self-determination was to be vested in the League; this authority might be delegated to individual powers. Further provisions dealt with the degree of control of the states who might be the agents of the League, trade policy, international relations of the territories, labor, and racial equality. The second draft added to these provisions sections dealing with the right of eventual self-government, the right

[6] The United States, as a co-belligerent, had certain rights in the disposal of conquered German territories. Not being at war with Turkey, however, the American role in the territorial settlement in the East was obscure at this stage of the peace settlement. When Wilson saw Lloyd George at London in December, 1918, they discussed the German colonies but not the future of Turkish territory.

[7] On the origins of the mandate idea see Quincy Wright, *Mandates under the League of Nations* (Chicago, 1930), chap. I. H. D. Hall, *Mandates, Dependencies and Trusteeships* (Washington, 1948), chap. VIII. League of Nations, *The Mandate System, Origins—Principles—Application* (1945), VI A. I. For the official position of the American government on the mandates see Marjorie M. Whiteman, *Digest of International Law* (Department of State publication 7403, 1963), I, 598–730.

of the League to dismiss the mandatory, and the rights of the inhabitants to petition for dismissal. Religious equality was also to be assured. In these " Supplementary Agreements " no distinction was made between the various territories on the basis of the stage of political and social development they had reached.[8]

Wilson's plan for a unified system of dealing with territorial questions would, if adopted, accomplish several things for the United States. It would go a long way toward the solving of the problem of the secret treaties, and the American people would not see themselves as partners in the imperialistic designs of the European powers. More important, it would give Wilson the legal right to a voice in the settlement of territorial questions from the points of view of international law and constitutional law—a right that would have been open to question without the mandate system. Above this, in Wilson's view, the mandate system was far more politically realistic than annexation. The world was growing " aggressively democratic," as he put it, and the future held little promise for the permanency of imperialistic rule under the rising tide of nationalism.

3.

The creation of the League of Nations had ostensibly been accepted by all the powers concerned with the peace settlement as an essential part of the settlement, but Wilson was not satisfied merely to have a paper organization result from the Peace Conference—a form without substance. To give the League meaning, Wilson wanted as much as possible of the peace settlement itself accomplished under the aegis of the League, as well as the League made an integral part of the Treaty of Peace with Germany, at least, and if possible of the peace treaties with the other Central Powers. In this way the United States could participate in all phases of the negotiations, whether American interests were directly involved or not, and could thus insure that the complete settlement was acceptable to the United States. Moreover, the League provided alternative bases for the settlement of issues on which the Allies had reached agreement among themselves on principles unacceptable to the United States. The disposition of

[8] D. H. Miller, *Drafting the Covenant* (New York, 1926), II, 87, 103–4.

conquered territory was a case in point. The German colonies and the non-Turkish portion of the Ottoman Empire were not, it was agreed, to be restored to their former owners. It was also agreed that they were not ready to stand alone as independent states. The Allies' solution was simple, well established in practice, and legal—the transference of ownership from the losing states to the victors; it was also an effective way of limiting the ability of the Central Powers to attempt again that in which they had just failed. Without the League the United States had no alternative but to accept this solution, attempting to modify, where possible, the terms of ownership; with the League in existence, an entirely new principle for the disposition of Allied conquests could be introduced.

Wilson's first task, then, when the Peace Conference opened, was to draw up the charter of the League and have it accepted by the Conference before any final decisions were reached. This he succeeded in doing; but not without a chorus of complaints being raised by the members of his own delegation, as well as the delegations of the other powers, who objected to the delays and waste of time which could have been devoted to the consideration of what to them was the real business of the Conference—to wind up the war and make secure the benefits they had gained by victory. But even after the creation of the League, Wilson was to give his colleagues further cause for complaint as he strove to bring the individual problems of the settlement under the League and thus within the compass of American influence.

The first of these problems to appear before the Conference was the disposition of the German colonies. The techniques used by Wilson in this opening phase of his policy at Paris are both informative and instructive. It will be noted how careful he was to conduct his campaign on ground of his own choosing, and keep it there; how quickly and positively he established the American position and made the Allies apply to him for concessions rather than, as one would have expected and no doubt the Allied Premiers expected, the reverse; how he used his strength, without bluster or even undue emphasis but leaving no question as to its existence or of his own awareness of it. By succeeding at the very beginning of the Conference, he not only achieved his immediate object but also made quite clear who the senior member of the Conference was. From the firm base he constructed, he developed all of his Middle East policy at the Conference, both in substance and in its diplomatic aspects vis-a-vis the Allied Premiers; for this reason Wilson's handling of this phase of the Peace Conference is worthy of close attention, containing as it does the key to the complicated maneuverings, in and out of the Conference, of the claimants to the Sultan's heritage.

On January 24, 1919, the Prime Ministers of the British dominions presented to the Council of Ten their case for the annexation of the colonies conquered by them. The Council was composed of the chief delegates and Foreign Ministers of the five great powers—the United States, Britain, France, Italy, and Japan; it was the policy-making and decision-making body of the Peace Conference. The Commonwealth Prime Ministers, supported by the British Prime Minister, Lloyd George, rejected control by the League as impractical, and asked the Conference to recognize their claims to the colonies on the basis of national security, since the territories in question were all contiguous or lay near to their respective countries. There was no discussion at this meeting.[9] On January 27 Wilson proposed that Japan present its case for the annexation of certain German possessions in the Pacific so that the whole question of German Far Eastern territory could be considered at the same time and a decision reached as to whether the mandate system should be applied to these territories; [10] and in the afternoon the Japanese annexation of Kiauchow and the German islands north of the equator was taken up.

The case for annexation, as opposed to the mandate system, had been put before the court, and now Wilson rose to rebut it and to state the case for the new system. " The basis of this idea of the League of Nations," he said,

was the feeling which had sprung up all over the world against further annexation. Yet, if the Colonies were not to be returned to Germany (as all were agreed), some other basis must be found to develop them and to take care of the natives of these backward territories. It was with this object that the idea of administration through mandatories acting on behalf of the League of Nations arose. . . . The purpose was to serve the people in undeveloped parts, to safeguard them against abuses such as had occurred under German administration and such as might be found under other administrations . . . the world [would be] acting as

---

[9] *Foreign Relations*, The Paris Peace Conference, III, 716–28.
[10] *Ibid.*, pp. 729–37.

trustee through a mandatory until the day when the wishes of the inhabitants could be ascertained. . . . If the process of annexation went on, the League of Nations would be discredited from the beginning. Many false rumors had been set about regarding the Peace Conference. Those who were hostile to it said that its purpose was merely to divide up the spoils. If they justified that statement in any degree, that would discredit the Conference. . . . Assuming the League of Nations existed (and it was born on Saturday), was it necessary, from the point of view of protection, to have annexation? If not, what was there in the principle of a mandatory that would make its adoption objectionable? "

The Dominion prime ministers were not impressed by Wilson's arguments. They were not in Paris primarily to establish a League of Nations, but to wind up a war that had almost been lost and to provide for the future safety of their countries. They claimed that all the benefits of the mandate system would be obtained under direct control. Lloyd George raised the question of the large expenditures that would be laid upon the mandatory power. He asked for time for further study to clarify " the practical application of the principles of the mandatory power as laid down by President Wilson in his speech." [11] The question was again postponed until the next day's session, when Lloyd George accepted the mandate system as being applicable to those territories conquered by troops of the United Kingdom, distinguished from those conquered by dominion troops. He again referred to the dominions' case as one that could be excepted from the mandate system, and Massey of New Zealand reiterated the strategic importance of the territories involved to his country. Clemenceau brought up the secret treaties and asked if these conventions should be produced before the Council. It was agreed by the three other prime ministers concerned that this should not be done and when Wilson asked that " no sense of finality should be attached [to them]," Lloyd George " entirely agreed." [12]

In the afternoon meeting the lines of battle began to clear and the opposing views of the nature of the mandates met head-on. Simon, French Minister for the Colonies, addressed the Council in behalf of the French claim for the Cameroons and Togoland. After noting French historical claims to the territories, he analyzed the three possible solutions to the question of the governments to

[11] *Ibid.*, pp. 738–48.
[12] *Ibid.*, pp. 749–57.

be given to them since they had now become ownerless. These were: internationalization, a League mandate, and annexation. The first of these was, as had been shown by experience, impractical. To the second, the dominions had made very strong objections " and these objections were supported by France also," because a revocable mandate would not permit the development of the sense of security necessary to the development of the country and because of the lack of political security in the international sphere should the mandatory be, for instance, a large powerful state. He asked the Council to recognize the right of France to sovereignty in the areas under discussion, under guarantees to the other powers of the application of a liberal system of government with full protection of the rights of the natives and other states.

Wilson now took a firm stand on his policy and served notice on the French that they were treading on dangerous ground. The discussion so far had been, he said, a negation in detail, one case at a time, of the whole principle of mandatories. The discussion had been brought to a point where it looked as if their roads diverged. He thought it would be wise to discontinue the discussion for a few hours, say until the next day, as he thought it might lead to a point where it would appear that the powers had reached a serious disagreement—and this he particularly wished to avoid.

Balfour and Lloyd George hastened to smooth over the disagreement. The former stated that though the dominions had claims to annex territory, the United Kingdom government was very much in favor of the mandate system. He also pointed out that there was as yet no carefully worked out system of mandates, and hence it was difficult to discuss them profitably. The Prime Minister was encouraging. He thought that the difficulties were more imaginary than real. He had been greatly struck by the fact that M. Simon had in the beginning of his speech appeared to be bitterly opposed to the whole idea but in the end had accepted the whole list of conditions proposed for a mandatory, except the name.

Wilson was not to be put off, however. He wished that he could agree with Mr. Lloyd George that there was no great difference between the mandatory system and M. Simon's plan, he said. The former assumed trusteeship on the part of the

League of Nations; the latter implied definite sovereignty. The two ideas were radically different, and he was bound to assume that the French Colonial Office could not see its way to accept the idea of the mandatory. Here they were at this stage, when the only acceptance had been on the part of the Imperial British government with respect to the area taken from Germany by troops under the direct authority of the government in London. They would have to consider how this treaty would look to the world; for as it looked to the world it would be, since the world would not wait for explanations. The world would say that the great powers first portioned out the helpless parts of the world, Wilson went on, and then formed a League of Nations. The crude fact would be that each of these parts of the world had been assigned to one of the great powers. The world would not accept such action; it would make the League of Nations impossible and they would have to return to the system of competitive armaments. There must be a League of Nations and they could not return to the *status quo ante*. The League of Nations would be a laughingstock if it were not invested with this quality of trusteeship. He regarded the acceptance of the genuine idea of trusteeship as a test of their labors and he thought that the world would so consider it, he concluded. Clemenceau was conciliatory and told the President that the French were still open to concession and, though he did not himself approve of the trusteeship idea, " he would be guided by his colleagues." [13]

While the Big Ten had been discussing annexation and mandates in the Council, the second-echelon delegates had been conferring on the same subjects. On January 27 House, Cecil, Miller and Wiseman met in House's hotel room where they discussed the German colonies. The difference between the American and British points of view turned upon the basis upon which Australia, New Zealand and South Africa should acquire the former German possessions which they claimed, but not whether they should have them. House agreed that the dominions should have the territories they had conquered, but that possession should not be on the basis of conquest but should be assigned to them by the League of Nations.[14] House at this time was ill and confined to his bed; after the Council of Ten meeting on the 28th, the

[13] *Ibid.*, pp. 758–71.
[14] House Papers, Diary, January 27, 1919.

President telephoned House and told him what had transpired that afternoon. (" He is much disturbed—" noted House in his Diary). House advised the President to bring the matter up before the whole Conference.[15]

The next day Smuts called to confer with House on the colonial question, to see if a compromise could be reached. He produced a draft agreement on mandates, that he had drawn up, saying that Lloyd George and some of the Empire delegates approved it but that Hughes and Massey had not yet seen it. House sent it to the President for his comment, adding in the covering note that it " seemed a fair compromise." [16]

This draft was the basis of Article Twenty-two of the Covenant. It included not only the German colonies but also Syria, Armenia, Mesopotamia, Palestine, and Arabia as areas where the mandate system would be applicable. It divided these territories into three classes according to their development and geographical position, to meet the demands of Wilson on the one hand and the French and the Colonials on the other. It recognized both the principle of trusteeship under the League and the close control demanded by the dominion leaders. Smuts told House that his colleagues did not want to press the scheme on Hughes and Massey until they had the President's approval. House told him that he thought that Wilson would find it satisfactory.[17] Lloyd George had not attended the Big Ten meeting that day, but had waited for Smuts's return from seeing House so as to be immediately available to attend an Imperial conference when the President's views were known. The conference then took place and, after much discussion, Massey and Hughes were persuaded to accept the Smuts plan.

On January 30, Lloyd George introduced the Smuts draft to the Council of Ten. Wilson said that he considered it to be a " very gratifying paper [that had] made a long stride towards the composition of their differences." However, he added, he did not think that a decision should be reached immediately but should wait on the creation of the League of Nations as a functioning organ, for the nature of the mandate system would depend on the nature of the League. Lloyd George answered that

[15] *Ibid.*, January 28, 1919.
[16] *Ibid.*, letter, House to Wilson, January 28, 1919.
[17] *Ibid.*, Diary, January 28, 1919.

the President's statement " filled him with despair " for the delay would mean that the United Kingdom would be forced to keep, indefinitely, over a million men in the areas covered by the mandates, and he would have to answer for this at home. Moreover, the dominions had accepted this compromise unwillingly, solely to further the work of the Conference. He asked his colleagues to accept the draft, subject to reconsideration. Hughes made the comment that he, too, had to answer to his people and that so far he had nothing to tell the people of Australia. He pointed out that if the mandates had to wait for a League of Nations, the League was then sitting in that room. He urged that the Council of Ten appoint mandatories immediately.[18]

After an adjournment for lunch the Council met again, and Massey opened the session with New Zealand's reaction to Wilson's request that the assignation of mandatories be postponed. The sections of the Smuts plan dealing with the territories claimed by New Zealand were " a matter of life and death " to the people of New Zealand and he had, he said, expected a " clear and definite statement" from the President in regard to them. In that expectation he had been disappointed. They (he and his dominion colleagues) were prepared to accept the conditions laid down in the Smuts plan right away, but they had not any definite opinion from the President that he would accept them. He himself still believed that annexation was the best solution, but he also believed in the proposal for a League of Nations. However, as far as he was concerned, he was responsible to his constituents, and he was prepared to shoulder that responsibility.

Wilson reacted immediately and with some heat. Was he to understand, he asked, that New Zealand and Australia had presented an ultimatum to the Conference? They had come here and presented their cases for annexation of New Guinea and Samoa. After discussion among themselves they agreed to present to the Conference the new mandate proposal. Was he now to understand that that was the minimum of their concession and that if they could not get that definitely, now, they proposed to do what they could to stop the whole agreement? Massey said that was not the case but after the question was repeated to Hughes, who was deaf and had not heard it the first time, the latter

[18] *Foreign Relations*, Paris Peace Conference, III, 785–96.

told the President that he had "put it fairly well." The President was furious and Botha stepped into the breach with healing words, calling for sacrifice of small matters to achieve the larger aims of the Conference. He discounted the idea that anyone was presenting the Conference with threats and in this was backed up by Massey, who said that if the President had imagined that any threat was intended by Mr. Hughes or himself, he had quite misunderstood the matter; he and Mr. Hughes had instructions from their respective governments and were merely acting on them. This exchange cleared the air and the Conference resumed. It was agreed that the Smuts resolution should be accepted as a provisional settlement subject to reconsideration by the Conference. Wilson had made his point—that the mandates must not be distributed by a mere act of the assembled powers—but the dominions still held out for the immediate distribution of the German colonies.

At this point Pichon raised a question that was to be the source of much friction later in the year. This was the right of raising troops in the mandated territories. "It is absolutely necessary for the future security of France," he said. Clemenceau explained to the Conference why this was so, and Lloyd George assured him that the phrase in the Smuts draft—that recruiting was not permitted "for other than police purposes and the defense of territory"—would permit the French to do "exactly the same thing as they had done before" in raising native troops. Wilson agreed that this was a correct interpretation. What the French were thinking of was the defense of metropolitan France, not the mandated territory; Wilson, apparently, did not catch this and assumed the contrary. On the face of the discussion the French interpretation was valid, and in subsequent disputes on this point with the Americans the French had the material at hand for a sound case.

Orlando then asked if the Conference was now proposing a system of provisional mandates and, if so, whether the Conference would distribute them by resolution. Wilson suggested that, in view of the difficulties in maintaining the status quo mentioned by the Prime Minister, it might be better to rearrange the military control in the Turkish Empire, since most of the troops were stationed there. He said he made this suggestion because the United States had no troops of her own in Turkey since she had not declared war on her. Lloyd George wanted something drastic done at once, however. The United Kingdom was maintaining over a million troops in Turkey and this could not go on indefinitely, he said; unless the Conference was prepared to relieve them of this responsibility, he would have to press very hard for a definite appointment of mandatories.

Wilson replied that if the United States were to assume part of the burden of Asian mandates this would take time to accomplish, since he would have to persuade the Americans to shoulder what to them would be a very unwelcome task. The question was largely a military one and he suggested that the military advisers be asked to make recommendations as to the redistribution of the burden of occupation. This was accepted and the Military Representatives to the Supreme War Council were directed " to meet at once and to present a report on the most equitable and economical distribution among these Powers of the burden of supplying military forces for the purpose of maintaining order in the Turkish Empire pending the decisions of the Peace Conference." [19]

During the next few days Wilson had several conversations with the British during which, by dint of much argument and compromise, the objections of the dominions were overcome. The Class " C " Mandates were a close approximation of the degree of control they desired and the task of distributing the mandates was taken from the League and placed in the hands of the principal powers, who would be certain to distribute the conquered territories correctly. On the other hand, the system would now be incorporated in the Covenant as Wilson had originally planned, instead of being implemented as an act of the Big Ten.

On February 8 the Smuts plan, as amended, was proposed as an article of the Covenant, to the League of Nations Commission. Orlando objected to the wording as being " too limiting" but Wilson replied that it was based on a decision of the " Big Five," as he put it, and could not be lightly dismissed. Leon Bourgeois supported the Italian delegate and proposed an amendment striking out the list of specific countries enumerated in the original. This, of course, would mean that there would be no guarantee in the Covenant that any particular country should be under the mandate system and the way was left open for other, more attrac-

[19] *Ibid.*, pp. 799–817.

tive, arrangements.[20] Wilson, however, agreed to the amendment and it stood when the Smuts draft was adopted in the next meeting, on the 10th.[21]

The Military Representatives gave their reply to the request for information on the distribution of occupation forces in Turkey by requesting further advice on three subjects—the territories to be occupied, since certain parts of the Ottoman Empire were not then occupied; the estimates of local commanders as to the number of troops necessary in each district; and whether a joint occupation was intended or whether individual zones were to be allocated to each power. Lloyd George commented, in the Council of Ten on February 1, that only the third question should be answered by the Council since the other two were military questions and had been included in those asked by the Council of the Military. Wilson added that individual zones would be allocated and, after further discussion, a statement was sent to the Military Representatives that there would be no joint occupation and that, unless the Military thought it desirable, there would be no further occupation of territory. They were told to obtain the troop estimates themselves. A copy of the minutes of the January 30 meeting was sent with this message to give the context of the questions.[22]

The report of the Military Representatives was finished and made available to the Council of Ten on February 8. They had recommended not only the number of troops required but also what their nationality in particular areas should be; in Syria they advised that the French should garrison that country " on the grounds of military convenience" until a mandatory had been appointed or some other settlement had been arranged by the League of Nations.[23] When this report became known among the delegations, it created uneasiness. The American Near East experts went to Wilson to express their concern. Amir Faisal, the Arab leader, they told Wilson, maintained that these new military policies would lead to war; they agreed with him. They suggested that Wilson press Faisal's idea of an inter-Allied com-

[20] League of Nations Commission, minutes, sixth session; Department of State files 181.1101/6.
[21] *Ibid.*, seventh session, annex #1; 181.1101/7.
[22] *Foreign Relations*, Paris Peace Conference, III, 835–55.
[23] Wilson Papers, VIIIA, Box 19.

mission to investigate conditions in Syria, in the hope that this might lead to a solution.[24]

The situation seemed to call for more direct action and the President cabled the same day to Secretary of War Baker, asking his opinion of the legality of sending American troops to Turkey since the United States was not at war with her; what public opinion at home and in the Army would be about such a move; and what public policy indicated to be the best action. He suggested that it might be possible to use American troops in Constantinople and Armenia since the United States was interested in those areas, but it might be more difficult in Syria and Arabia.[25] Baker replied on the 11th, advising against using American troops in Turkey. He thought it would be legal in American law, but demands for the return of the army were growing at home.[26]

Meanwhile, on February 10, the report was laid before the Council where Lord Milner, speaking for Britain, said that the report's recommendation on the nationality of troops was a " big political question " and that " very large issues had . . . been raised " which should be dealt with by the Peace Conference. The President agreed with him that military occupation tied in so closely with the future of the countries concerned that the Peace Conference should settle the matter.[27] The question was adjourned until the following day; but Lord Milner required a further postponement. The subject was not taken up again in the Council of Ten, but was discussed privately among the leaders of the Powers.

4.

The mandate system has often been characterized as a compromise, and so it was. What is usually meant is not that it was a political compromise between the conflicting policies of the powers, but that it was a compromise between the imperialist designs of the Allies and Wilsonian self-determination. From this point of view, Wilson suffered a setback, for the mandated states did not gain full freedom but were mortgaged to the Allies

---

[24] *Ibid.*, memorandum (unsigned) Feb. 8, 1919.
[25] *Ibid.*, telegram, Wilson to Baker, Feb. 8, 1919.
[26] *Ibid.*, telegram, Baker to Wilson, Feb. 11, 1918.
[27] *Foreign Relations*, Paris Peace Conference, III, 945–69.

in lieu of outright annexation. From the point of view of his political problems, however, the President won a resounding victory.[28]

When the Conference opened, the American position in territorial questions was vague and, in some cases, nonexistent, due, not to any failure on Wilson's part, but to the political conditions existing at the time. The United States had been at war with Germany and so had acquired certain rights in the disposal of her colonies which, however, had been conquered and were now occupied by French, British, and Dominion troops; the Fourteen Points, studiously noncommittal in regard to the colonial question, did not, though they had been accepted as a basis of the peace, guarantee American participation in territorial matters. As for Turkey and the Arab lands, the United States had not been at war with the Ottoman Empire and had no standing in the Near Eastern settlement. Now with the mandate system accepted, Wilson could speak in territorial questions with authority equal to that of the representatives of any of the powers.

Wilson, naturally enough, had to give up something of his original plan for the disposal of conquered territory in return for the Allies' renunciation of their rights of annexation (very real rights in international law), but the essential features were maintained. The point was summed up by Henry White in a letter he sent to Senator Lodge, who had criticized the mandate system in a Senate speech. White agreed with the Republican leader that the mandated territories would be given to the states who had had imperialist designs on them in the first place but, White pointed out, the mandate system would establish the principle that mere conquest would not of itself give a right to territory.[29]

Sovereignty in the mandated territories, clearly stated in Wilson's original plan to reside in the League, was now left undefined, and its location has been the subject of much thought by jurists since 1919.[30] Lansing was the first to draw attention to this anomaly, in his memorandum on the mandates written not

[28] Cf. Paul Birdsall, *Versailles Twenty Years After* (New York, 1941), p. 47; the author cites Wilson's " surprisingly extensive diplomatic victory " in achieving acceptance of the mandate system.
[29] Nevins, *Henry White*, p. 375.
[30] See Wright, *Mandates*, pp. 314–44 for a discussion of this question.

long after the system was approved.[31] The question for the Class "A" Mandates was resolved as questions on the location of sovereignty usually are solved, by political methods; during World War II, Syria and Lebanon, with the help of Britain and the United States, established in two minor wars the validity of the theory that sovereignty resided in the mandated territories themselves.

On February 14 a Plenary Session of the Preliminary Peace Conference was held at which the League Covenant, as formulated by the League Commission, was presented to the delegates of all the powers for their decision. The provisions relating to mandates were protested by Ali Haidar Pasha, a delegate from the Hejaz, who reserved the right to discuss them later and refused to recognize any arrangement concluded without the consent and knowledge of the state he represented.[32] In the fifth Plenary Session, held on April 28, the provisions of the Article were changed to provide for the consent of the territory in the choice of the mandatory power.[33]

---

[31] Robert Lansing, *The Peace Negotiations: A Personal Narrative* (Boston, 1921), pp. 151–53.

[32] *Foreign Relations*, Paris Peace Conference, III, 208–30.

[33] *Ibid.*, pp. 285–332.

CHAPTER IV

SELF-DETERMINATION: THE CLAIMANTS

1.

The issues raised by Wilson's introduction of the mandate system into the settlement of territorial questions and by the presentation of indigenous national claims to the Peace Conference, brought to the surface problems that were to be of great importance not only to the settlement of questions relating to the Middle East but also to the character of the entire postwar settlement and the success or failure of American policy at the Peace Conference. The most important of these problems was the Syrian question. Its significance was not due to the intrinsic importance of Syria, which was but one region (though an important one) of the Arab areas of the Ottoman Empire, but because it brought to a focus centuries of conflicting ambitions; because it represented a major stage in the clash of the new Asian nationalism with European imperialism; and because Wilson believed that the application of the secret treaties to its settlement could mean the failure of American policy during the war and at Paris, and a return to the old system of international relations.[1] The Syrian

---

[1] The official position of the United States on the place of the secret treaties in the formal negotiation of the peace settlement was stated by the peace commissioners (the American Commission to Negotiate Peace consisted of Wilson, House, Lansing, Henry White, and General Tasker Bliss; the Commission held regular meetings throughout the Peace Conference, though Wilson almost never attended them) in reply to a query by W. L. Westermann, the American expert on Western Asia, asking for the attitude of the United States towards the London agreement of 1915 and the Sykes-Picot agreement. The commissioners replied that the United States did not recognize either of these agreements as having any bearing on the final settlement, and that the United States intended to ignore them in any discussions in the Conference unless they contained provisions which were in accordance with declared American policy. *Foreign Relations*, Paris Peace Conference, XI, 49–53. This of course bound only the experts.

question had an additional significance for the United States. It was the first direct contact with Eastern affairs. Up to this point, American policy had been conducted on the basis of general principles and large concepts of strategy. Now the United States was in the thick of Middle East power politics.[2]

2.

Two events had been the immediate cause of the secret treaties—the naval attack on the Turkish Straits by the French and British in February, 1915, and the entry of Italy into the war on the Allied side a few weeks later. The Anglo-French attempts to force the Straits, while it was designed to ease Turkish pressure on the Caucasus Front and to ensure a continuous flow of war supplies to Russia, occasioned considerable misgivings in Petrograd. Constantinople had been for centuries one of the ultimate goals of Russian foreign policy, and the Czar's government could not view with any satisfaction the prospect of the Straits coming under the control of any European power—enemy or ally. Accordingly, two weeks after the initial bombardment of the forts of the Dardanelles, the Russian government announced to Britain and France its firm intention of incorporating Constantinople, the Straits, and sufficient territory on the European and Asiatic hinterlands for its effective defense, into the Russian Empire; hitherto it had required from its Allies only the control of these areas. At this stage in the war Britain and France could not afford to risk the possibility of Russia's signing a separate peace with the Central Powers, a risk which existed even without depriving Russia of the principal goal of its foreign policy. The two countries therefore reluctantly agreed to the Russian demands, on condition of the war being won by the Allies and " the desiderata of Great Britain and France in the Ottoman Empire and elsewhere being realized." [3]

[2] For Lloyd George's interpretation of the Syrian question, see his *Memoirs of the Peace Conference* (New Haven, 1939), II, 659–720.

[3] The best summary of the Allied treaties dealing with the Ottoman Empire is in Stein, *Balfour Declaration*, chap. XVI. Mr. Stein's account is based on official material from the British, French and Russian archives, viz., *British Documents*, Series I, Vol. IV; Vol. VI of the volumes of the Russian Foreign Office Archives published by the Soviet government in 1924 and translated into German under the

Once Russia had gained her objective in the Ottoman Empire, it became necessary for Britain and France to put their own desiderata into concrete terms; not only because of the desirability of defining and reconciling their respective territorial claims in the Ottoman Empire but also because with Russian control of Constantinople and the Straits the Ottoman Empire would become a Russian satellite. Neither country could afford to permit this; the logical consequence was the complete partition of the Ottoman Empire and its division between the Allies. During the latter half of 1915 and the first half of 1916, tripartite negotiations were carried on among the three powers resulting in an agreement by which Russia received large areas of eastern Turkey as well as Constantinople and the Straits; under the Sykes-Picot agreement, signed on May 9, 1916, France received all of present-day Syria, the vilayet of Mosul, Cilicia, Adana, and part of Central Anatolia up to Sivas; Britain received all of Iraq, except Mosul, together with the territory between the French area and the Hejaz and Nejd stretching from the Persian frontier to Aqaba on the Red Sea and the southern boundary of Palestine; Palestine was to be an international area. The French and British zones were each divided into two areas, one where direct control was to be established and one where an Arab government was to be formed under the auspices of the respective powers. The area of direct control in the French zone was the coastal region of Syria north from Palestine to Alexandretta, including Mount Lebanon, and all of the French area of Anatolia; the area of French primary influence included all of interior Syria and Mosul. The British area of direct control consisted of the vilayets of Basra and Baghdad; the rest was under British influence.

While these negotiations were in progress, Britain had been conducting the correspondence with the Sherif of Mecca, Hussain, looking to the participation of the Sherif in the war against Turkey. In the course of the exchange of letters, an agreement was formed on the terms under which Hussain would throw in his lot

title *Die Europäische Mächte Wahrend die Weltkrieges—Die Aufteilung des Asiatischen Turkei* (ed. E. Adamov; Dresden, 1932); and A. Pingaud, *Histoire Diplomatique de la France pendant le Grande Guerre* (Paris, n. d. [1939]), which was based on official material. On the Constantinople agreement, see also H. W. V. Temperley, *History of the Peace Conference at Paris* (London, 1924), VI, 4–9.

with the British. These terms have ever since been the subject of controversy, but, briefly, they included the following: Hussain was to bring all the military and political power at his command into the war against the Turks, and Britain would supplement his resources with men, money, and arms; the Sherif committed himself to proclaim an Arab revolt and denounce the Ottoman government as an enemy of Islam; Britain was to recognize the independence of the Arabs within an area to be agreed on and was also to recognize the re-establishment of an Arab caliphate should one be proclaimed. The problem lay in defining precisely what area was meant to comprise the independent Arab state. In the agreement the British had excluded the areas " lying to the west of the districts of Damascus, Homs, Hama and Aleppo," southern Mesopotamia, and, the British claimed later, Palestine, from the Arab zone, which otherwise was to include all Arab-speaking areas south of the Taurus. The Arabs claimed that Palestine was included within the Arab area. Hussain apparently had not agreed outright to the exclusion of these areas, but agreed to postpone his claims until after the war. All of the excluded area had, of course, already been allotted either to France or Britain, but this was not made clear to the Arabs; the matter was hinted at, but ambiguously.[4]

Up to the appearance of the Syrian question before the Peace Conference, several modifications were introduced into these agreements. They were: the renunciation of Russian claims in Turkey by the revolutionary government of Prince Lvov in March, 1917, and the publication of the secret treaties by the Bolsheviks; the Balfour Declaration; the Anglo-French Declaration of November 7, 1918, which promised the Arabs independence under governments of their own choosing;[5] and the mandate system; in addition there was the moral force of the Fourteen Points, knowledge of which was widespread in the Middle East[6] and

---

[4] On the British undertakings to the Arabs, see *Correspondence between Sir Henry MacMahon, His Majesty's High Commissioner at Cairo and the Sherif Hussein of Mecca July 1915—March 1916*, cmd. 5957, H.M.S.O., 1939; for narrative accounts see George Antonius, *The Arab Awakening* (London, 1938), chap. IX; and Zeine N. Zeine, *Arab Independence* (Beirut, 1960), chap. I.

[5] Text in Hansard, *Parliamentary Debates*, House of Commons, fifth series, vol. 145, col. 36. See also Lloyd George, *Memoirs*, II, 671–72.

[6] Knowledge of the Fourteen Points was widespread in the Middle East, and they often were taken seriously. According to Hafiz Wahbah, " Certain of (the

the general application of which the Allies had seemed to endorse in the armistice negotiations with Germany, particularly when coupled with Lloyd George's statement of January 5, 1918, and the Anglo-French Declaration.

The Arabs were well aware of the existence of the Sykes-Picot agreement. After the publication of the secret treaties by the Bolsheviks in November, 1917, Jamal Pasha, Governor of Syria, had sent copies of them to Faisal and invited him to return to his allegiance to the Sultan.[7] Faisal informed his father of Jamal's overtures, but it was decided not to act precipitously. The offer was refused, but Faisal kept up a correspondence with Jamal almost up to the Armistice. The Allies might lose, after all, or the peace might be a stalemate, and, in any case, it would do no harm after the war, when the Turks and Arabs would be neighbors, to have the groundwork laid for amicable relations. He had no illusions on the nature of international affairs and was perfectly well aware that the postwar settlement in the Middle East would reflect the ability of the several parties involved to get as much as they could, not less than it would reflect their solemn mutual undertakings. As Faisal himself put it in a conversation with a French liaison officer shortly before he left Syria for the Peace Conference: "England, France and I are now like merchants in front of a merchandise which has no owner. Is it not logical that each one of us should try to appropriate it before the others?"[8]

Shortly after the Russian *démarche* of February, 1915, Italy entered the war on the Allied side, under the terms of the Treaty

---

Arabs) did not acknowledge the applicability (of the understandings and agreements between the British and the French) because they contradicted the principles of President Wilson, which the Allies had made the basis of the Armistice and of the peace settlement." *Jazirat al-Arab fi-l-Qarn al-Ishrin* (Cairo, 1935), p. 192. Sir Ronald Wingate records a telegram sent by the Sultan of Egypt to Wilson on November 12, 1918, congratulating him on the victory over the Germans, which referred to "l'expansion irresistible des principes de liberte et le droit qui grace a votre action s'imposent desormais dans le reglement des affaires des nations." The Sirdar, Sir Reginald Wingate, warned London that Wilson's "self-determination ideas" had "taken a strong hold on the Sultan." *Wingate of the Sudan; the Life and Times of General Sir Reginald Wingate, Maker of the Anglo-Egyptian Sudan* (London, 1955), pp. 232–33.

[7] See Antonius, *Arab Awakening*, p. 257; T. E. Lawrence, *The Seven Pillars of Wisdom* (London, 1935), pp. 555–56.

[8] Edouard Brémond, *Le Hedjaz dans la guerre mondiale* (Paris, 1931), pp. 307–8.

of London. Italy was promised an " equitable " share of Turkish territory in the region of Adalia. Attempts to reconcile the French and Italian claims in this region (Italy claimed part of the coastal area allotted to France in the Sykes-Picot agreement) were unsuccessful until April, 1917, when Britain, France, and Italy met at St. Jean de Maurienne and, while recognizing that Italy had claims in the Middle East, agreed to postpone without prejudice the final settlement of these claims until the Peace Conference.

3.

The distribution of occupation troops in the Ottoman Empire by nationality was indeed a " big political question." [9] The French and the British had been having trouble on this point ever since the latter had begun their drive northward into Palestine and Syria, bringing the Arabs under Amir Faisal into the conflict, with promises of independence, to harry the eastern flank of the Turks; and the French were not particularly happy to see an army almost entirely British conquering from the Turks territory that they considered to be their own preserve, even though the two countries had an understanding on its future. The good relations of the British with the Arabs, developed over the past three years during the common effort, boded no good for the French, and the tension mounted as Allenby advanced further into Syria during the summer of 1918.

The Americans were not unaware of this situation. William Yale, special agent of the United States in the Middle East, sent back to the State Department reports of the growing bitterness between the two allies and by December of 1918 Walter Lippmann was writing, in a list of the most pressing territorial questions, that: " The most acute immediate problem in Asia Minor turns on Franco-British relations in Syria." [10] The military representatives could advise, on the grounds of " military convenience," that France garrison Syria until a final disposition was made by the Peace Conference, but if it had been that simple the French would have been there already.

[9] See above, p. 105.
[10] *Foreign Relations*, Paris Peace Conference, I, 287–88.

Anglo-French differences on Syria had a long history. From Napoleon's invasion of Egypt and throughout the nineteenth century, France had been attempting to obtain a foothold in the eastern Mediterranean; and each attempt had been frustrated by Britain, except for the brief French occupation of Mount Lebanon and French pre-eminence among the Maronites. The suppression of Muhammed Ali, the purchase of the Suez Canal shares by the British government, the failure in Egypt, Fashoda, all rankled still. In 1912 Britain had acknowledged French priority in Syria, however, and in the secret treaties France had received a written commitment from Russia, as well as Britain, that France would have Syria and adjacent southern Anatolia as its share of the Ottoman Empire. But even this solemn commitment by Britain (Russia, of course, was no longer a factor) was, or so it seemed to many Frenchmen, being gradually and deliberately undermined and the area to which it applied being chipped away little by little. First, Syria had been conquered from the Turks by a British Army, which was still in possession; second, the Balfour Declaration had implied to suspicious minds that Britain claimed pre-eminence in Palestine, which had been detached in the Sykes-Picot agreement from what many Frenchmen considered to be Syria proper and constituted an international zone—this was bad enough, but now it seemed as though Britain was to claim Palestine herself; third, the British had installed Amir Faisal, the son of King Hussain of the Hejaz and leader of the Arab forces in the Syrian campaign, as military governor of interior Syria, where he was busy in establishing a purely Arab administration;[11] fourth, Clemenceau had been persuaded by Lloyd George in December, 1918, to give up Mosul, originally allotted to the French sphere of influence; and now, the final blow, the mandate system threatened the whole French policy in the Middle East with its talk of self-determination, trusteeship for the benefit of the inhabitants, and other serious departures from what had been envisioned in the Sykes-Picot agreement.

This sequence of events was not of equal significance to all

[11] Georges Picot, the French High Commissioner in Syria and Armenia at the time, cabled Paris on November 14, 1918, that the only way to save the French position in Syria was to send 20,000 troops there and ask Britain to leave to France the responsibility of organizing the country, otherwise the presence of the British Army in Syria would encourage anti-French elements. Brémond, *Le Hedjaz*, p. 308.

members of the French government. Clemenceau was not of the Colonial party, and in fact had been one of the bitterest opponents of French imperialism. He had been chiefly responsible for the withdrawal from Egypt in 1882 and only barely failed to stop the occupation of Indo-China. However, within his government, and among certain sections of the public, there was an extremely influential group politically committed to the extension of French influence overseas and in particular in the Mediterranean, where the acquisition of Syria in the east would complement the possession of Morocco, Algeria, and Tunisia and make France predominant in the Mediterranean. The "colonials" could not be expected to stand idle while their policies were brushed aside. A strong statement of French claims in Syria had been made on December 29, 1918, when M. Pichon, the French Foreign Minister, stated in the Chamber of Deputies: "We have in [the Ottoman Empire] incontestable rights to safeguard; we have them in Syria, Lebanon, Cilicia and Palestine. They are based on historical title, on agreements, and on contracts." [12] These claims were never abandoned, the mandate system notwithstanding; the French position was, throughout the Peace Conference, not that their claims should be reconciled with the mandates but that the mandates should be reconciled with them. The first step in French policy toward the mandates was to get the list of specific countries removed from the Covenant article implementing the mandate system.

Up to a point, the British apparently meant what they said when they disclaimed any interest in Syria, as they had both to the French and to Faisal. They already had the territory they wanted. The security of the route to India and the East was strengthened by the protectorate over Egypt, the buffer state of Palestine was in the process of formation, and the approach to the Persian Gulf was under their control. Of equal importance, all of the oil of the Middle East was in their hands. But in 1912 the British had made a strategic decision that reversed a policy dating from the Battle of Aboukir. This decision was the Anglo-French understanding on the disposition of their respective fleets to meet the maritime threat of the Central Powers whereby Britain assumed primary responsibility for the North Sea and the Atlan-

[12] *Journal Officiel: Chambres des Deputes,* Debats Parlimentaires, 2me seance, 29 Dec. 1918, IV, 3716, col. 1.

tic, and France for the Mediterranean. This, together with the agreement on Syria of that year, was in fact an acquiescence by Britain to French parity in the Mediterranean. This threat to the British routes to the East had been accepted as the necessary price for containing the greater threat of the German fleet. But now the German threat had vanished and the French threat remained. Undertakings had been given to France and the letter of these agreements would be kept, but it was far from the intention of the British to let the French remain in a position to exploit freely their new position of strength. In the meantime, Syria was a very valuable asset.[13] Britain controlled it in fact and a price could be exacted for relinquishing this control in the form of concessions in Tangier, perhaps, and Morocco, or wherever the occasion arose during the Conference. And after France gained control of Syria it would not harm British interests to have as its ruler one who was under an obligation to Britain, hence the support of Faisal. Nor would these interests suffer if French control were made less firm than might be desired by France. To the British—or, more exactly, to Lloyd George—the United States was a convenient instrument to achieve a certain weakness of the French case for Syria in the Conference, hence the continual stress, in meetings where an American representative was present, of Syrian opposition to French rule, in the hope that American misgivings on the score of self-determination might be strengthened

[13] There is an interesting parallel between the policy of Britain toward France in Syria and its policy toward Italy in Libya. While Britain was negotiating a settlement with Italy on questions affecting relations between Egypt and Libya, Allenby, High Commissioner in Egypt, signed an agreement with Muhammad Idris (the present king of Libya) the leader of the Sanussi and the main focus of native Libyan opposition to Italian rule. Under this agreement Muhammad Idris was to support King Hussain's claim to the caliphate and to engage in pro-British propaganda among the Muslims; in return Britain was to supply the Sanussi in Libya with arms and munitions to fight the Italians. Muhammad Idris had been pro-British during the war and had been of considerable value to the British in repelling attacks on Egypt by the Libyans under the direction of the Turks. His uncle, Ahmad Sherif al-Sanussi, whose secretary told Admiral Bristol about the agreement in June, 1924, had been pro-Turk during the war and had actually led the Libyan attack on Egypt. He claimed the leadership of the Sanussi and had repudiated his nephew's agreement. Despatch 1255 from Constantinople, June 17, 1924; 867.00/1801. The maintenance of the balance of power in the Mediterranean is a thread which runs through all British policy in the Middle East in this period, and helps to explain many puzzling developments, from the apparent contradictions in British war-time policy in the Middle East to British policy toward Mussolini.

and the French forced to make concessions to Arab demands to meet these misgivings.

4.

The Arab position on Syria was undefined except that certain Syrians and Lebanese wanted European control and the majority of Arabs, that is to say the majority of those Arabs in a position to have an opinion on the matter, wanted independence, when they did not desire to return to the rule of the Sultan Caliph. Beyond these ultimate goals, however, Arab opinion had not progressed to the point where it could be said that a given policy represented the wishes of most, or even a plurality, of the Arab peoples. There was no general agreement on the organization of an Arab state; whether there should be a single government of all the Arab peoples or one for each of the main geographical divisions of the Arab areas, Syria, Mesopotamia, Hejaz, and Nejd, not to mention the lesser subdivisions. There was no agreement on the form of government, nor on who was to rule. But in fact the Arab position at the Peace Conference was to all intents and purposes the position of the Amir Faisal, partly because of the existing political confusion among the Arabs and partly because, simply, he was the head of the only Arab delegation at the Conference.

Faisal was the Chief Delegate of the delegation of the Hejaz, appointed by his father, the King of the Hejaz, and sent to Europe with strict instructions to follow the British line in everything.[14]

---

[14] Telegram (undated, but sometime in November, 1918) " King Hussain to the Amir Faisal: Our loyal ally Great Britain has invited you to attend the Conference which will be held at Paris on the 24th of this month, November, in the capacity of Delegate of the Arab people and to represent them in questions pertaining to their general interests and in the vital question of the boundaries and form of government [of the Arab state] which are of great significance to the future of the Arabs. The details of these matters are well known to you. In execution of the wishes of Great Britain you will immediately proceed to Paris, after having discussed with the General Officer Commanding [i. e., General Allenby] the route and means of transportation of your journey, and after having provided for the welfare and administration of the country [i. e. Syria] in your absence, which will not exceed one month. Since our fundamental policy is based on an exclusive relationship with Great Britain, and since we have thus no connections with any other country, you should discuss all your ideas and opinions with the British Delegates and other prominent personalities at the Conference, and also with their public men, if they choose to take you into their confidence.

But Faisal had greater ambitions than to be the son of his father. He wanted Syria for himself, and stood a good chance of becoming its ruler; his policy in Paris was primarily directed toward this aim. The principal obstacles to be overcome by Faisal were French claims to Syria and French objections to him, personally. The French objected to Faisal for two main reasons. First, he had close relations with the British and owed his present position largely to them, for they had instigated the Arab revolt and it had been conducted under their auspices, as it were.[15] Second, Faisal's position among the Syrians owed nothing to the French, but was based on the prestige he had acquired as the Commander of the successful Arab Northern Army in the Syrian campaign and on his present position as the *de facto* ruler of Syria in the capacity of commander of the Allied occupation forces in eastern Syria, that is to say, all of Syria east of the coastal areas. If a native administration was to be set up in Syria, the French wanted it and its head to receive their authority from themselves. On this count, Faisal was the least acceptable of any of the Arab notables suitable for the position of titular head of a French protectorate.

Faisal's objections to the French were twofold. Compared to the British system, French colonialism offered far less opportunity for national development and less opportunity to control local affairs. The Arabs had constantly before them the example of Algeria; what apparently were the two principles of French colonial policy—immigration of French nationals and integration into

---

You will also carry out all their instructions with respect to your actions and your public statements, whether in the Conference or elsewhere. The foregoing is the extent of the authority we grant to you at the Conference. . . ." Wahbah, *Jazirat al-Arab*, p. 307. (The Department of State was notified of Faisal's appointment in a Memorandum from the British Embassy, November 22, 1918, at the request of King Hussain; 763.72119/2757.) This telegram was sent through British facilities, and it may have been worded with this in mind; however there are other records of Hussain's commitment to the British. On August 28, 1918, he wrote to the High Commissioner in Egypt explaining his expectations from the Arab revolt and his complete reliance on British power and influence, rather than the Peace Conference, in obtaining the desiderata of the Arabs. What he wanted was: The protection of Islam no matter what happened to Turkey and the Caliph, and the protection of his own position. In return he would do all in his power to protect British interests in the Middle East. Wahbah, *Jazirat al-Arab*, pp. 364–66. In the summer of 1919 he forbade Faisal to obtain tanks and other military equipment from France, because of the Arabs' "exclusive" relations with Britain.

[15] Cf. Clemenceau's comment in the Council of Four, "Faisal was practically a soldier of England. That was a fact all the world knew . . ."; below, p. 137.

metropolitan France—had there produced a society dominated by the immigrants with the indigenous population reduced to second class citizens, where every attempt was made to suppress indigenous culture and tradition and to supplant them with those of France. They could see this policy being introduced into Tunisia and Morocco, and they could see no reason why France would refrain from continuing it in Syria. A second objection was that, even if France modified her policy in Syria and established a political system more in tune with Arab wishes, there was still little that it could contribute either to the security of Syria or its economic development. The Arabs believed that France had been bled white in the war, that she was no longer able to hold her own in the world, and that she did not have the economic resources at her disposal for its own needs, to say nothing of repairing centuries of neglect and exploitation in Syria. If they were to have a protector, the Arabs wanted one that could protect them and offer a *quid pro quo* for their lack of freedom.

Faisal's campaign against French aspirations in Syria began many months before the Peace Conference opened. His two main allies in this campaign would likely be the United States, if the Fourteen Points meant anything, and the Zionists, whose own aspirations in Palestine (or, to the French, southern Syria) ran counter to those of the French. With the Americans Faisal had no contacts and no experience. The Zionists had had a great deal of both. The British, while far from being antagonistic to Faisal, had made it clear to him that in any conflict between him and the French they would support the French if the situation reached a point where it was necessary to choose whose friendship they would retain. Faisal's first step, therefore, was to come to an understanding with the Zionists. He was not afraid of their program, for their leaders had stated publicly to the Arabs and to him personally that the Balfour Declaration did not mean the establishment of a Jewish state in Palestine, and Faisal apparently thought that the help he received to achieve Arab independence was worth what he had been given to understand was the aim of the Zionist movement—the free right of Jews to immigrate to Palestine, to acquire land there, and to manage the affairs of the Jewish community. In June, 1918, Chaim Weizmann met Faisal at the latter's headquarters at Guwaira (Quwaira), north of Aqaba. Weizmann said, according to the report of the meeting in the Arab Bulletin of the British Arab Bureau in Cairo, that " the Jews do not propose to set up any government of their own but wish to work under British protection to colonise and develop Palestine, with all consideration for legitimate vested interests." Faisal did not endorse this program—he felt that it would be most dangerous to make any public statement because of the use to which it might be put by Turkish and German propaganda; the most he could do, he told Weizmann, was to express his personal opinion that the Zionist program was not incapable of realization.[16]

Discussions between Faisal and the Zionists continued in London in December. Lord Rothschild gave a dinner in Faisal's honor which was attended by several Zionist leaders, including Weizmann, and later in the month he was given a luncheon by the Lord Mayor of London, when the guests included Lord Rothschild and Sir Henry MacMahon.[17] Pressure was put on both Faisal [18] and Weizmann by the British to come to an agreement. Weizmann, in discussing the Palestine question with A. J. Balfour on December 4, stated the Zionist program in terms very different from those on which the Guwaira Conference had been conducted in June. He talked of the " free and unfettered development of the Jewish National Home in Palestine . . . so that we should be able to settle in Palestine about four to five million Jews within a generation and so make Palestine a Jewish country." Balfour questioned whether this could be reconciled with the provision in the Balfour Declaration providing for the safeguarding of non-Jewish interests in the country. Weizmann replied that non-Jewish citizens in the Jewish Commonwealth would enjoy all the privileges of citizenship. Balfour said that the Arabs would not be a serious problem to the Zionist program, but that he thought it would be very helpful indeed if the Zionists and Faisal would act unitedly.[19]

In his London talks with Faisal, Weizmann still maintained the interpretation of Zionism he had put forward at Guwaira. On the basis of these assurances, and Zionist promises to assist the

---

[16] Cited in Stein, *Balfour Declaration*, p. 638; see also Weizmann, *Trial and Error*, pp. 232–36.

[17] Zeine, *Arab Independence*, pp. 62–64.

[18] Temperley, *Peace Conference at Paris*, VI, 142.

[19] Cited in Stein, *Balfour Declaration*, pp. 637–38.

Arabs in getting their case before the Conference and combatting French policy, Faisal signed an agreement on January 3, 1919, in which he, on behalf of the Kingdom of Hejaz, and Weizmann, on behalf of the Zionist organization, recognized the creation of a state of Palestine which would implement the provisions of the Balfour Declaration and encourage Jewish immigration and settlement while protecting the Arab population. There was to be no discrimination on religious ground with respect to political and civil rights or the exercise of religion. In return, the Zionist organization was to make available to the Arab state a commission of experts to survey economic possibilities and to use their best efforts to assist the Arab state in obtaining the means of developing its natural resources and economic potential. This was an important provision for the Arabs, for it freed them from dependence on the European powers for capital development funds, and removed a powerful lever from the hands of the French. To this agreement Faisal appended a rider which made the agreement effective only if the Arabs obtained their independence.[20]

One of the principal services the Zionists were to perform on behalf of Faisal in getting the Arab case before the Conference was to introduce Faisal to the leaders of the American delegation in Paris. Shortly after the agreement was signed, the American Zionist leader, Stephen S. Wise, asked President Wilson for an interview for Faisal. Wilson suggested that Wise write him a note on the matter so that it would be on record and not lost sight of in the press of work. Wise accordingly wrote, on January 15, reminding the President to send word to Faisal and T. E. Lawrence about their interview; in the letter he referred to the fine work of the Prince's people in the freeing of their lands from the Turks. On January 21 the President's secretary sent the invitation to Faisal via Lawrence.[21]

[20] Antonius, *Arab Awakening*, pp. 437–39; see also Stein, *Balfour Declaration*, pp. 641–44.

[21] Wilson Papers, Series VIII A, Box 11. T. E. Lawrence wrote to Close on Faisal's behalf on January 23 accepting the invitation; *ibid.*, Box 13. I have not been able to find a record of the interview, but since Faisal wrote to the President on February 11 asking for "another" interview (see below), it is possible to assume that a previous interview had taken place. Lawrence was not unknown to the Americans. He first came to the Department's attention in 1912, as related above, p. 24, fn. Yale had met him in Palestine in 1913, and, of course, during his work as Special Agent in Cairo.

On February 4 Faisal had an interview with Colonel House; the latter records in his Diary that Faisal told him of the " sorrows of Arabia " and of his difficulties with the French over Syria. House soothed his visitor and told him that he knew all about his troubles. He noted in the diary entry that he had " a kindly feeling for the Arabs and my influence will be thrown in their direction whenever they are right." [22] Faisal wrote to Wilson on February 12 asking for another interview; he had heard that the President was leaving for America, he said, and wanted his advice.[23] Wilson replied on February 14 regretting that, as he was leaving immediately for the United States, he would be unable to see him; the President suggested that he see the other American peace commissioners, but said that he himself hoped to see him on his return to the Conference; he was " deeply interested " in the Arabs, he added.[24]

Faisal also met several of the advisors and experts on the staff of the American delegation. The Zionists were not responsible for these contacts, however. On January 20 he discussed Arab affairs with W. L. Westermann, the expert on Western Asia. Lawrence was present and acted as interpreter. Faisal related the background of the Arab revolt and the rise of the Arab national movement and the secret societies. He said he did not know of the Sykes-Picot agreement when he entered the war. It was not realistic; for example, the boundaries between the British and French spheres bore no relations to conditions in the countries concerned. He rejected French and British control of the Arabs, but said if it had to come to that, the British were better than the French. His main program, he said, was to get an inter-Allied commission to Syria.[25] On February 13 he told William Yale that he wanted the United States, as " the most disinterested " nation, to accept a mandate for the whole Arab area, but that Britain would be " acceptable," if necessary. Yale commented in the memorandum he prepared of the conversation that Faisal was not very clear in his mind just what a mandate was.[26] Faisal made

[22] House Papers, Diary, February 4, 1919.
[23] Wilson Papers, Series VIII A, Box 19.
[24] *Ibid.*, Box 20.
[25] Yale Papers, memorandum of conversation, January 20, 1919.
[26] Yale Papers, Notes of a Conversation between Amir Feisal and William Yale, February 13, 1919; also in Peace Conference files, 867s.00/25.

an excellent impression on the Americans, and the experts and advisers were generally in support of Arab claims at Paris. They were particularly responsive to suggestions that the President's principles were being violated; an example is their reaction to the suggestions of the military men for the redistribution of occupation troops in Turkey.

5.

On January 1, 1919, Faisal opened the Arab case before the Peace Conference by submitting to it a memorandum on Arab aspirations. He asked for the fundamental unity of the Arabs, while recognizing that different forms of government would be needed for different areas since they varied in natural resources and social development; thus, Syria would be granted its independence and any foreign advice and technical assistance necessary would be paid for in cash—the Arabs would not sacrifice for this help any of the freedom they had just won, Faisal stated. The Jezira (i. e., the northwestern plains of what is now Iraq, with the most eastern parts of present-day Syria) and Iraq were mostly desert inhabited by Bedouins; these needed training in self-government, and the resources of this area needed a great deal of development, therefore, an Arab government buttressed by men and material aid furnished by one of the great powers should be established. Palestine was mostly Arab, but there was no fundamental conflict with the Jews since they were close in race; the Arabs could not take the responsibility of holding the balance between the two, so a Great Power should be the trustee. Faisal ended the memorandum by asking the Powers not to consider the problem from the point of view of European material interests and spheres of influence, but to put the Arabs in the way of eventual unity and progress.[27] On January 29 Faisal expanded this memorandum with another giving the area to which the Arabs laid claim; it ran from Alexandretta to Diabekir, south to the Indian Ocean. He based his claim on the second point of Wilson's Mount Vernon address of July 4, 1918.[28]

[27] D. H. Miller, *My Diary at the Peace Conference*, IV, doc. 250, 297–99; copies were sent to President Wilson and to the American Peace Commission, and are filed, respectively, in *Wilson Papers*, Series VIII A, Box 7, and Peace Conference files, 185.5138/2.

[28] Peace Conference files 185.5138/3.

Faisal appeared before the Council of Ten on February 6 to make the formal statement of the Arab case before the policy-making body of the Conference. He again asked for the independence and unity of all the Arabic-speaking peoples in Asia. (This limitation, it will be noted, excluded Egypt, French North Africa, and Libya, where the European powers were already well established.) Referring to his January 29 memorandum, he said he based his case on several points: The area was once the home of important civilizations and its inhabitants still had the capacity to play their part in the world; they were linguistically and racially a unit; their homeland had natural frontiers and economic and social unity. The Arabs had fought on the side of the Allies in the war, and kept all their promises; now it was the time for the Allies to keep their promises of independence. The Arabs thought themselves entitled to and worthy of independence, in accordance with the principles laid down by President Wilson and accepted by all the Allies. If the Peace Conference had any doubts about the wishes of the people of a particular area for independence or for a certain mandatory power, said Faisal, an international inquiry made in the area concerned might be a " quick, easy, sure and just way of determining their wishes." He recognized the necessity of foreign advice and help, but, he said, " the Arabs will not sacrifice for this any of the independence for which they had fought . . . [He] hoped no power imagined that it had the right to limit the independence of a people because it had material interests in the country." He added that he excluded Palestine because of its universal character.

Thus far his statement was a repetition of his two memoranda, but under questioning by President Wilson he was able to expand his ideas on the settlement of Arab questions. Wilson asked him whether, seeing that the mandate system had been adopted by the Conference, he would prefer one mandatory or several for the Arabs. Faisal replied that he could not assume the responsibility for answering the question; it must be decided by the Arab people themselves. Wilson said that he understood perfectly, but wished to know the Amir's personal opinion. Faisal said that he was afraid of partition and that his principle was Arab unity; it was for this that the Arabs had fought. They asked for freedom only and would take nothing less. For four hundred years the Arabs had suffered under a violent military oppression and, as long as life remained in them, they meant never to return to it.[29] Secretary Lansing, who was present as the second American delegate, commented in his Diary that Faisal had made "a very dignified and interesting presentation." [30]

One of the strongest, and most effective, supporters of the Arab case was President H. A. Bliss of the Syrian Protestant College in Beirut, an American institution. Bliss was an American but had been born and raised in Lebanon. He was well known to President Wilson, and it was from this fact that his effectiveness was mainly due, for Wilson invited him to speak before the Council of Ten; he was the only person, apart from Faisal, to put the Arab case for independence formally before the Conference. Bliss wrote to Wilson on February 7, supporting Faisal's statement; he said that the Syrians were relying on Point Twelve and placed their hopes in the Americans. He warned that the American delegates should be cautious of a delegation of Syrians that had recently come to Paris to speak before the Conference. They had been sent by the French, said Bliss, and were not representative of Syrian opinion and national feeling. Wilson replied on February 11, saying that he had hoped that Bliss would be present when Faisal appeared before the Ten, but that "somehow" the invitation was not sent. (It might be mentioned that, according to protocol, the French administered the secretariat of the Conference, since France was host to the Conference.) However, he wanted him to address the Conference before he returned to the United States.[31]

Bliss appeared before the Ten on February 13. He asked the Conference to send an inter-Allied commission to ascertain the wishes of the inhabitants of Syria, basing his request on Point Twelve and the Anglo-French Declaration of the previous November. After he had spoken, the pro-French Syrian delegation addressed the Ten, requesting a French mandate and rejecting control by "the desert Arabs" under Faisal. They made a poor impression on the Americans. One of the American advisers

[29] *Foreign Relations*, Paris Peace Conference, III, 889 ff.
[30] Lansing Papers, Desk Diary, February 6, 1919.
[31] Wilson Papers, Series VIII A, Box 20; Bliss saw Lansing on January 28, 1919, and gave him a brief outline of his proposals for the Syrian settlement, including the sending of a commission of inquiry to the country; Peace Conference files 185.5137/54.

present at the meeting passed Wilson a note informing him that the leader had not been in Syria for thirty-five years, and the delegation had been brought to Paris by the French for the specific purpose of bolstering their case for control of Syria.[32] Bliss was interviewed by the American peace commissioners at one of their regular meetings on February 26. Again he urged that an inter-Allied commission be sent to Syria; the Syrians were relying on Point Twelve, he said, and this involved the honor of the United States. Lansing told him that he had already proposed such a commission, but it had been refused by M. Pichon on Clemenceau's orders. However, he said, he intended to press the matter if he got British backing, but the time for a protest would be when definite action on the Syrian question was proposed.[33]

6.

Greece, in the person of Venizelos, was actually the first country to make its claim to a share of the Ottoman Empire before the Council of Ten. On February 3 and 4 Venizelos, in a lengthy exposition, put the case for the reconstitution of Hellas and the unification of all Greek-speaking peoples under one flag. This, according to Venizelos, basing his claim on Point Twelve and on the right of self-determination, called for the cession to Greece of Northern Epirus, the islands of the Aegean, Thrace, and Western Anatolia.[34] Such vast ambitions could not be evaluated in detail by the Council, and the matter was put into the hands of a Commission on Greek Claims, composed of representatives of Britain, France, Italy and the United States, with instructions to examine the Greek claims and report to the Council. A month later, on March 6, the Commission completed its work. It accepted the basic principles of the Greek case with modifications, but with important reservations on individual points by certain members. All four countries accepted Greek claims to Thrace with minor changes, though Italy recommended that Bulgaria be left Dedeagatch. In Asia Minor there was a good deal of difficulty due to the prior commitments of the Allies in the secret treaties; Italy

---

[32] *Foreign Relations*, Paris Peace Conference, III, 1013 ff.
[33] *Ibid.*, Vol. XI, pp. 76–77.
[34] *Ibid.*, pp. 856–75.

would make no recommendations at all on the grounds that the question was too involved in the general solution of the Anatolian question as a whole.[35] Westermann, the American representative, was opposed to the cession of western Asia Minor to the Greeks on general principles and also, as he stated to the Commission, because the United States was not bound by the secret treaties and could not take them into consideration in the settlement of the question. Neither France nor Britain would make any recommendations on the Dodecanese; Westermann supported the Greeks. On the Epirus, Britain, France and the United States accepted a modified version of the Greek claim, but it was opposed by Italy. When the report was presented to the Central Committee on Territorial Questions, on March 7, both the American and Italian members were opposed to its acceptance.[36]

Notwithstanding the opposition of the American experts, the Commission report was accepted by the peace commissioners. The feeling this aroused among the experts is reflected in a memorandum sent by Westermann to Sidney Mezes on March 25; it also throws some light on the background of the switch in policy. The memorandum was a formal statement for the record of Westermann's position. He said that he had been asked by Mezes to work on the boundary of the Greek sphere in Asia Minor. He himself disagreed with the Greek claims, and was under the impression that the decision to support them was made either by the President and House or by House alone. He had gathered this from the use of the phrase " higher-ups " by Mezes when he asked him to undertake the work. This decision overrode the decision taken by the American members of the Commission on Greek Claims. He also understood from a conversation with Mezes that the change was due to the " necessities of the international situation." However, there were two sides to the Greek question, and it was possible that the peace commissioners believed more strongly in the Greek case. In agreeing to work on the boundaries, Westermann emphasized, he was going against his own judgment and therefore wished to put his position in writing, hence the present memorandum. Since it seemed that House " was the father of this business," he added, he was send-

---

[35] Peace Conference files 185.1; see also Miller, *Diary*, pp. 156–57.
[36] *Ibid.*, 185.1/36; and Miller, *Diary*, Documents 470 and 471.

ing a copy of the memorandum to him also.[37] The Greek question simmered in the Territorial Committee for some weeks after the Greek Commission reported, and it was not until the early part of May that it began to assume any significance in the Conference beyond that of principle or the respective interests of the Greeks and the Turks. This phase is dealt with in Chapter VI.

7.

Two minor claimants, minor in the sense that their claims did not have the political significance to the peace settlement and to American policy of those of the Arabs and Greeks, also presented their respective cases for a share of the Ottoman Empire to the Council of Ten. They were the Armenians and the Zionists. The Armenians appeared before the Council on February 26 and asked for the recognition of an independent Armenia including Caucasian or Russian Armenia, Turkish Armenia comprising the six vilayets, and Cilicia.[38] There was a good deal of sentiment for the United States to take the mandate for Armenia—not only among a significant portion of the American people, who had been aroused by the massacres of Armenians over the past thirty years, but also among the Powers. Britain in particular was anxious to put under American control this strategically important but economically barren area, which would then form a convenient buffer against attack from the north against Mesopotamia. Wilson would not commit the United States to accepting the mandate until he had a clear expression from the Senate. He was not interested in extending American control in the Middle East and was willing to consider an American mandate only as the necessary price for the mandate system as a whole.[39]

On February 27 the Zionists presented their case. They asked that the historic title of the Jewish people to Palestine and their right to reconstitute there their national home be recognized. With the sovereign possession of the country vested in the League of Nations and the government entrusted to Great Britain, the

[37] Peace Conference files, 185.5122/13.
[38] *Foreign Relations*, Paris Peace Conference, IV, 138 ff.
[39] On American policy toward Armenia see J. B. Gidney, "An American Mandate for Armenia." (Doctoral dissertation, Western Reserve University, 1963.)

boundaries were to run from a point south of Sidon, along the slopes of Mount Herman including the watershed of the foothills of Mount Lebanon, and then eastward to a point close to and west of the Hejaz railway, then south, following the line of the railway but still close to and west of it to Aqaba. The boundary with Egypt was to be negotiated with the Egyptian government. Palestine was to be administered so as to secure the establishment there of the Jewish National Home and ultimately an autonomous commonwealth without prejudice to the rights of the existing inhabitants of Palestine. Following the statement of Chaim Weizmann (who was one of the Zionist delegation) Secretary Lansing asked him " to clear up some confusion in his mind as to the correct meaning of the words ' Jewish National Home.' Did that mean an autonomous Jewish Government? " Weizmann replied that it did not. The Zionists merely wanted to set up in Palestine, under a mandatory, an administration not necessarily Jewish which would render it possible to send there 70,000 to 80,000 Jews annually, and also permission to take steps to develop a Jewish nationality. Later when the Jews formed the majority, they would be ripe to establish such a government as would answer to the state of the development of the country.[40]

The American position on Palestine was vague. Wilson had agreed to the issuance of the Balfour Declaration; this committed the United States not to object to British policy, but it did not commit the United States to the support of British policy, nor to the support of the Zionist position. When Wilson had expressed his good wishes for the success of the Zionist program in the letter to Stephen Wise on August 31, 1918, he had merely expressed a personal opinion and then only on the assurance that Zionism did not necessarily imply the alienation of Turkish territory; but that was before the creation of the Mandate System and the decision of the Council of Ten that all non-Turkish territory should be detached from the Empire, a decision in which Wilson had participated. Since the opening of the Peace Conference he had written to Lord Rothschild that he was " greatly interested in the development of the plans for Palestine. I hope with all my heart that they can be given satisfactory form and permanency." But he had not made any definite statement about what

[40] *Foreign Relations*, Paris Peace Conference, IV, 159 ff.

the United States was prepared to do to see that the Zionist program was implemented. This was in line with his general policy on Middle Eastern matters not to commit himself before the definitive settlement.

There was one occasion when Wilson was asked by his staff for a statement of his position on Palestine, but he would not commit himself even to his own delegation. In March a Cairo newspaper printed a story which it had picked up from an American paper to the effect that President Wilson had stated to a delegation of American Zionists, shortly before he returned to the Peace Conference from the United States: " I am persuaded that the Allied nations, with the fullest concurrence of our Government and people, are agreed that in Palestine shall be layed the foundations of a Jewish Commonwealth." The Cairo story had been picked up by the American Diplomatic Agency there and sent to Paris in the course of the normal information service. In Paris it was noted by Westermann who brought it to the attention of the peace commissioners, asking if the statement was authentic; it might cause repercussions among the Arabs both in the Middle East and in Paris, he thought, and wanted to be prepared to meet any representations by them.[41] The commissioners took up the matter at one of their regular meetings, on April 12. They decided that it was very doubtful that the President ever made such a statement, but sent the statement to Wilson asking whether the quotation were correct and if not, recommending that it be denied at once.[42] Wilson replied in a letter to Lansing on April 16. " My Dear Lansing," he wrote:

Of course I did not use any of the words quoted in the enclosed and they do not indeed purport to be my words. But I did in substance say what is quoted, though the expression " foundation of a Jewish Commonwealth " goes a little further than my idea at the time. All that I meant was to corroborate our expressed acquiescence in the position of the British Government with regard to the future of Palestine.[43]

This answer was considered by the commissioners on April 18, when it was decided that, in view of the " rather ambiguous

[41] Peace Conference files, 185.5137/103; Memorandum, Westermann to Bullitt enclosing a copy of the news report.
[42] Peace Conference files 867 n.00/64; also in Wilson Papers, Series VIII A, Box 37; also *Foreign Relations*, Paris Peace Conference, XI, 150–51.
[43] Peace Conference files, 867 n.00/69; Wilson Papers, Series VIII A, Box 37.

phrasing " of the President's reply, it would be " safer " not to make any official denial of the news story.[44]

8.

Wilson's policy on the Syrian question, and on Turkish territorial questions generally, was governed by two considerations. First, that any decisions taken by the Peace Conference on former Turkish territory should be taken within the framework of the mandate system and should not under any circumstances be of such a nature as to weaken or nullify it. This would both strengthen the mandate idea and also strengthen the American position in the Conference generally. Second, Wilson had to make sure that no decisions were taken by the other Powers that would prejudice the terms of the Treaty of Peace with the Ottoman Empire, and, as the American role in the Turkish treaty would depend on the League of Nations, he had to force the postponement of the discussion of the treaty terms until the treaty with Germany was signed and ratified by the United States and the other Powers. Precisely what part the United States would play in the Turkish settlement was not yet determined. The United States had not been at war with Turkey but if the League of Nations was to be a part of the settlement then American interests would be involved, yet the standing of the United States in the negotiation of the Turkish treaty and its right to a voice in the determination of its terms was indefinite. Wilson had to construct the American position in the Turkish treaty from nothing, for the Turks had not been granted an armistice on the basis of the Fourteen Points as had the Germans.

As Wilson had pointed out in the Council of Ten, the political future of occupied Turkish territory was very closely connected with the nationality of the troops selected to occupy the area in question. It was necessary therefore, from the British and French points of view, to come to a definite understanding on Syria before British troops could be withdrawn and replaced by French troops. The Sykes-Picot agreement had laid down the extent of direct French control in former Turkish territory, but the man-

---

[44] Peace Conference files, 185.5137/104; *Foreign Relations*, Paris Peace Conference, XI, 155.

date system excluded direct control. If only indirect control was to be permitted in Syria, therefore, the French wanted indirect control of all of Syria rather than merely the sphere of influence envisioned in the Sykes-Picot agreement. Unfortunately for the American position in the Syrian question, Wilson returned to the United States on February 14 for a flying visit to attend to domestic matters before continuing with the work of the Conference. It was just at this time that negotiations between the British and French on Syria began, and they were conducted in a spirit far removed from Wilson's. During the absence of the President, Colonel House became the actual, though not the official, leader of the American delegation. While House supported the President's general policy on the League of Nations, he had during the preceding month grown increasingly critical of Wilson's emphasis on the League and the failure, as he thought, of the Conference in coming to grips with the real issues of the peace, because of Wilson's insistence on intruding the League into issues where it only confused the issue. Even before Wilson had returned to Washington, House had discussed the " delays " with Balfour, and the two men had decided that when the President and Prime Minister left Paris they would inaugurate a new program of work in the Conference; this apparently meant that more time would be spent on arriving at concrete solutions to the problems of peace-making and less on principle.[45] House did not seem to grasp what Wilson was accomplishing by his insistence on " principles "—which was to establish the right of the United States to participate in the settlement of questions hitherto considered to be solely the concern of European powers.

9.

On February 15 the French presented to the British their solution to the Syrian question.[46] Recognizing her historic, cultural, and economic interests, France was to receive a mandate for all of Syria. The British rejected this plan as confining too greatly the Arab state promised in the correspondence with Hussain (now

[45] House Papers, Diary, February 9.
[46] In the Council of Four Meeting of March 20 (see below, pp. 135–37) the French gave an account of the development of the dispute.

the King of the Hejaz), and submitted a counterproposal which limited the mandate to the coastal areas. This was in turn rejected and the British made a second offer somewhat more generous to the French, but the latter insisted on their original proposal of a mandate for all of Syria. The negotiations had thus far been conducted by the junior members of the British and French delegations, but having reached an impasse at this level, the question was taken up by the heads of the delegations on March 7, at one of the informal meetings of the leaders of the British, French, Italian, and American delegations—Lloyd George, Clemenceau, Orlando, and House—who had begun to meet togther to discuss privately matters which they considered too delicate for the Council of Ten with its large number of experts, advisers, and stenographers in attendance. Clemenceau put the French case for a mandate for all of Syria and Cilicia. Both Lloyd George and House rejected French claims to Cilicia, since it comprised the richest parts of the projected state of Armenia, and the United States might, as House stated, take a mandate for it. The discussion then turned to Syria proper. Lloyd George warned Clemenceau that if the French "went in" without coming to an agreement with Faisal, no matter what claims they had there, "there would be a long and bloody war." [47] On the following day, Lord Milner, who had been conducting the negotiations with the French, saw Clemenceau and warned him of the dangers he was courting if a regime on the pattern of Algiers were imposed on Faisal. The French should be satisfied with Lebanon and the coast regions. In Syria proper, a mandate of the "mildest form" with, for example, French advisers, French priority in loans and railroad construction, and so forth, would be acceptable to Faisal.[48] This scheme was discussed at a further meeting of the Four on March 10. Clemenceau insisted on the original French proposals, however, with, as an absolute minimum, French control of the North-South railway which ran through the four principal towns of the interior—Damascus, Homs, Hama, and Aleppo.[49] No agreement was reached at this meeting or at the meeting of March 12, when Lloyd George warned Clemenceau that the French were

[47] House Papers, Diary, March 7.
[48] Lloyd George's version of the history of the Syrian question is given in his *Memoirs*, II, 678–80.
[49] House Papers, Diary, March 10; also Miller, *Diary*, pp. 316–17.

making trouble for themselves and that war would come in Syria
if they continued in their present course. Clemenceau came to
see House privately after the meeting; House noted in his Diary
that he was very distressed at the turn of events and complained
to House that the British were breaking their word, for Syria
had been promised to France.[50]

Throughout these discussions House had remained on the side-
lines, letting the British and French leaders fight it out between
themselves and intervening only to soothe ruffled feelings. He
did not press the American point of view, that the settlement of
the Syrian problem should be under the mandate system. He felt,
in fact, that the injection of the League of Nations into the dispute would serve only to complicate and extend the problem.
Wilson had succeeded in drawing the highly controversial subject
of the disposal of conquered territory under the aegis of the
League and thus within the reach of the United States. But House
had so conducted himself in the Conference that territorial disputes were being openly discussed in terms of the secret treaties,
and Clemenceau was appealing to House to help him with the
British in Syria because they were not keeping the promises they
had made in the Sykes-Picot agreement.[51] When Wilson returned
to Paris on March 14, "very militant," he was faced with the
problem of re-establishing American control over territorial questions. Syrian problems were shelved for a week as matters concerning the German settlement, which House had also dealt with
after his own policy, were considered by the chief delegates, but
on March 20, at the first regularly constituted Council of Four
meeting, the Syrian question was the chief topic.

[50] House Papers, Diary March 12.
[51] For House's side of this question, see Charles Seymour, "End of a Friendship," *American Heritage,* XIV, 5 (August, 1963), pp. 5–9, 78–80, which cites
a House memorandum on the conduct of the negotiations. House pressed Wilson
to compromise on these controversial issues, stating that America had been built
on compromise. He seemed to forget that the United States, then engaged in the
settlement of a great war—the antithesis of compromise—had been created by a
war, and had been maintained by one of the greatest wars ever fought up to the
time, the Civil War.

CHAPTER V

FAISAL AND THE POWERS: THE KING-CRANE COMMISSION

1.

The Council of Four was an outgrowth of the informal meetings of the chief delegates of Britain, France, Italy, and the United States mentioned in the last chapter. They had been so successful, or rather the Council of Ten had been so inefficient, in the dispatch of business that control of the work of the Peace Conference was transferred to the smaller body on the initiative of President Wilson, though it kept its informal character so as to give to the delegates full freedom of discussion. It was understood that proposals and suggestions would not be binding on the person making them unless he chose to make them so, and would not be construed as constituting statements of policy of the country concerned.[1]

On March 20 then, the Syrian question was given a full airing. M. Pichon opened the discussion by tracing the development of Anglo-French relations on Syria, which, he said, originated in the agreement of May, 1916. Its purpose had been, first, to detach the Arabs from the Turks, and second, to decide the claims of Britain and France. This arrangement had been complicated by the disparity between the numbers of French and British troops engaged in the Syrian campaign. Pichon then went into the development of the dispute on Syria since the end of the war and wound up by demanding a French mandate for all of Syria. Lloyd George returned that the question did not lay between the

[1] *Foreign Relations*, Paris Peace Conference, VI, 752–55. On the creation of the Council of Four, see also Lord Hankey, *The Supreme Control* (London, 1963), chap. XII.

French and the British, who had no interests in Syria, but between the French and the agreements entered into with King Hussain. Pichon pointed out that the French had no agreement with Hussain, but Lloyd George said M. Pichon's predecessors had accepted the agreements with Hussain when they signed the 1916 agreement, which specifically mentioned the creation of an Arab state in interior Syria. Pichon said this was not the same as a French commitment to Hussain or the Hejaz. In any case, in the Sykes-Picot agreement France had been promised direct control over a certain area of Syria; under the new French proposals, no direct control would be exercised, but if the League of Nations granted a mandate over Syria, all he asked was that France should be given the mandate.

At this point, Wilson entered the discussion. He carefully disassociated himself from the previous argument between the British and the French, deriving as it did from the secret treaties, and based his intervention on the fact that the dispute had been brought before the Conference. He said that he

would now seek to establish his place in the Conference. Up to the present he had none. He could only be here, like his colleague Mr. Orlando, as one of the representatives assembled to establish the peace of the world. This was his only interest, though he was a friend of both parties to the controversy. He was not indifferent to the understanding (between) the British and French Governments. . . . The point of view of the United States of America was, however, indifferent to the claims both of Great Britain and France over peoples unless those people wanted them. . . . (The) only idea from the United States of America point of view was as to whether France would be agreeable to the Syrians. . . . It might not be his business, but if the question was made his business owing to the fact that it was brought before the Conference, the only way to deal with it was to discover the desires of the population of these regions.

He went on to point out that one of the elements of the mandates as adopted by the Council of Ten had been the consent of the governed and that this controversy was one that might develop into a situation where the peace of the world was threatened. He posed a formal question to General Allenby, who was present, " If before we arrive at a permanent settlement under the League of Nations we ask France to occupy the region of Syria, even as narrowly defined, what would the results be? " Allenby said that

" there would be the strongest possible opposition by the whole
of the Moslems, and especially by the Arabs." He recounted
some of his experiences with the French and Arabs in the military administrations of Syria. The Arabs and Faisal had objected
strongly from the very beginning to French administration, even
under the over-all Allied control in which Faisal, as the Commander of an Allied force, had a part. " If the French were
given a mandate in Syria," he said, " there would be serious
trouble and probably war."

After an adjournment Wilson proposed the sending of an inter-
Allied commission to Syria " to elucidate the state of opinion
and the soil to be worked on by any mandatory." Clemenceau said
that he " adhered in principle to an inquiry " but that it should
not confine itself to Syria. He did not place any great stock in
the idea that there would automatically be war if the French took
the mandate for Syria, he added. Faisal only represented one side
of the Arab race. " Moreover, Faisal was practically a soldier of
England. That was a fact that all the world knew. . . . The
members of the Commission must be very carefully selected, and
they must inquire into every Turkish mandate. Subject to those
provisions he was prepared to accept President Wilson's proposal
in principle." [2]

Lloyd George raised no objections to this and Wilson was given
the task of drafting the terms of reference to the Commission.
The commissioners were instructed that they were " to visit these
regions (in question) to acquaint yourselves as fully as possible
with the state of opinion there in regard to (the future administration of their affairs), with the social, racial, and economic conditions, a knowledge of which might serve to guide the judgment
of the Conference, and to form as definite an opinion as possible
on the division of territory and the assignment of Mandates."
These instructions were agreed to by the Four on March 25.[3]
Two days later occurred the first attempt to block the sending

[2] *Foreign Relations*, Paris Peace Conference, V, 1 ff.

[3] Text of the Commission's instructions in *Foreign Relations*, Paris Peace Conference, XII, 745–47. The instructions contained the texts of the Council of Ten
decisions on mandates of January 30 (see above, pp. 100–3) and the Anglo-French
Declaration of November 9, 1918 (see above, p. 111). For a complete study
of the King-Crane Commission see Harry N. Howard, *The King-Crane Commission*
(Beirut, 1963).

of the Commission of Inquiry. At the meeting of the Four on that day, Lloyd George said that he had been informed by one of the British administrators in Mesopotamia that it would be better not to send the Commission to the Middle East as it would create trouble there; moreover, it could not get adequate information to come to a conclusion because of the character of the Arabs. Wilson said that nevertheless he would prefer that the Commission go. If it were feared that it would delay the definitive establishment of peace in the Ottoman Empire by a too lengthy inquiry, it would be possible to give it instructions which would set specific limits to their task. Lloyd George went on to say that some of the inhabitants of Iraq had refused a British offer to set up a government under an Arab Prince, stating that they preferred a European administration. Wilson continued to insist on maintaining the decision on a commission of inquiry. Dr. Bliss, he said, who had lived with the Arabs for many years and had, so to speak, identified himself with them, had told him that the inquiry would make a good impression in the Middle East. Clemenceau said that he agreed with the President that the inquiry should be made without loss of time.[4]

2.

The acceptance of the mandate system by the Powers had established the nature of the control to be exercised over the territories conquered from the Central Powers, and had at the same time made it possible for the United States to participate in the territorial settlement by providing her not only with political rights of participation but also with a settlement acceptable to the American people. What the mandate system did not provide in itself, however, was a method of distributing the mandates. Here the United States was on weak ground for she had neither political nor military influence in the Middle East nor could she make any definite commitment, beyond her participation in the League, of direct participation in the affairs of that part of the world.

House had permitted France and Britain to set their own terms on the allocation of the Syrian mandate. Wilson disagreed sharply with his colleague; the United States was directly involved in the

[4] Paul Mantoux, *Les Deliberations de Conseil des Quatres* (Paris, 1955), p. 49.

Syrian question and had a position to maintain. But how was it
to be maintained? Not by merely refusing to permit France and
Britain to settle the Syrian question on the basis of the secret treaties; this would have brought forth the unanswerable response
that if the President did not like the Allies' solution, he should
provide a better one. Wilson could not promise that the United
States would take any Near Eastern mandate; Britain did not want
Syria; Italy and Greece, who had made some dubious claims to
Syria, were simply not possible as mandatories. France was the
only state able and willing to take the Syrian mandate.

It would, moreover, be politically impossible to exclude the
French from the distribution of Ottoman territory. France would
not stand by and see her neighbors enriched in the East while her
interests were sacrificed for the ideals of President Wilson. If
France did eventually receive the Syrian mandate, in the face of
Syrian opposition, it would be fatal to Wilson if this denial of the
principle of self-determination could be shown to be based on
the secret treaties; he could not even permit the treaties to be
discussed in the Council and remain silent, for this would have
been tantamount to an acceptance of them. In addition, any stand
the President might take must be consistent with his over-all
League policy.

Up to this point in the development of American Middle East
policy, Wilson had been able to operate in the sphere of principle; the problems that had arisen so far had been questions
touching the basic nature of American involvement in international politics or related to war strategy, or were concerned with
the place of the United States in the Peace Conference. In dealing with the Allies on these problems, Wilson had been able to
keep aloof from the rivalries, maneuvering, and ambitions of the
powers. In fact he had deliberately made sure that he would not
be involved in them, in order not to dilute the strength of the
American position or to fritter it away in internecine squabbling.
The diplomatic strength of the United States, unparalleled in
modern times, matched by its economic strength, had enabled
Wilson to impose the United States' will on the Conference while
it was concerned with important questions. But now began the
period of the application of these basic principles to specific situations, of making ideas work, of insuring that the American position was not eroded piecemeal among the complexities of a hun-

dred different political struggles. House's conduct of affairs during the President's absence from Paris had demonstrated the dangers. From now on the United States was in the thick of European power politics. In sustaining and advancing American interests amid the standard methods of European diplomacy, Wilson still had the weapons he had used to achieve the League and the mandate system, but it is difficult to negotiate on details such as the superiority of one nation's rights over another's to a hundred square kilometers of territory, or the degree of control appropriate to the exercise of one of the three grades of mandates, using as one's bargaining points the ability of the United States to withdraw from the settlement or to cut off all credit to Europe. These were strategic weapons; Wilson was now dealing with tactical situations and their use would make every dispute a major crisis. In any event, Wilson had determined that the United States' interest would be advanced by participating in the settlement if it could be done on American terms. What was needed were bargaining counters of less value, and Wilson had few of these; hence the difficulties he often found himself in. Wilson made good use of moral principle here as a type of negative veto in small cases, on other occasions he fell back perforce on standard practices of accommodation and compromise; occasionally he was forced to use his big guns. In Middle Eastern matters, his main tactic was to force the moral issue as part of his policy of postponing decisions until the American position on the Turkish treaty was clarified and the actual negotiations begun.

In the light of the situation facing the President, his proposal to send an inter-Allied commission to Syria can best be described as a delaying action. It did not settle the problem of the ultimate disposal of Syria. A French mandate was not excluded—that would have been impossible at this stage—for the Council of Four did not bind itself to accept the commission's recommendations, which would undoubtedly reflect the strong feeling in Syria against French control. What Wilson's maneuver did accomplish was to bring the problem of the distribution of the Turkish mandates within the reach of the United States and keep it there for the time being. It had been officially established that this problem was the concern of the Council as a whole, notwithstanding the vague position of the United States in Eastern affairs, and that its solution was attainable by the application of the principles upon which the League had been founded. What was equally important, France and Britain had in effect agreed to the suspension of their mutual agreements, which, though without official status in the Council, had yet considerable authority in matters affecting the two states alone. Now, should the secret treaties again appear in the discussions of the Four, Wilson would not be forced to base its objections on anything so fundamental as the inimicability of the treaties to the United States' interests; it would suffice to remind the Council of the existence of the Commission. Looking to the future, when the Turkish treaty was negotiated, the report of the Commission would provide the United States with a negotiating position of considerable strength. It was the necessity of maintaining this strong position that was Wilson's motive for insisting, as we shall see, on keeping the Commission in existence and finally sending the American section to Syria alone, in the face of French hostility, British indifference, and the advice of the American experts.

3.

The President's proposal to send a Commission of inquiry to Syria met with a mixed reception. The Arabs were delighted. Faisal wrote to Wilson on March 24 expressing his gratitude for the formation of the Commission. It would " enable the Arabs to make their voices heard above the cries of success raised by the victors in this War," he said, and asked for an interview.[5] Wilson was far too busy at this time to see the Arab leader, but five days later House held a conversation with him at the Crillon, T. E. Lawrence acting as interpreter. Faisal said that he had come to say good bye as he was leaving for Syria soon. House asked him what he thought of the Commission to Syria; Faisal replied that it was " the best thing he had ever head of," and went on to say that, though he liked the British, since there was friction between them and the French was there any possibility of the United States becoming the mandatory? House expressed doubt and Faisal added that the Arabs would die rather than accept a French mandate; Lawrence pointed out that the British could not take on the task, but House remained unencouraging. Faisal then

[5] Wilson Papers, Series VIII A, Box 27; in Arabic with translation.

asked about American plans for the Armenian mandate and was told that it was not possible to make a statement on that point.[6]

Meanwhile, French and British Middle East experts held an informal meeting on March 25 to attempt to reach a common understanding on the Syrian problem. Lawrence and Gertrude Bell were the principal British experts, De Caix and Phillipe Millet the French. The Commission of Inquiry on Turkish mandates was a prominent topic. There was general agreement that it would unsettle the country, make it appear that the Peace Conference could not reach a decision, and open the door to " intrigues and manifestations " of all kinds. It was Lawrence's opinion that the sending of the Commission had been prompted by the failure of the French to approach Faisal in a conciliatory way. It would be better, he said, if the Commission stayed in Paris and came to a general agreement before going to Syria to clear up details.

After considerable discussion, all present agreed that if some prominent official of the French government approached Faisal, a settlement might be quickly reached along the following lines: France would receive the mandate for Syria, and the Syrians would then elect their own prince in a convention to be held in Damascus. The prince would undoubtedly be Faisal. The pattern of control would be similar to that followed by Britain in Egypt and the Indian states. Lawrence took pains to impress on the group that Arab unity had no serious political value for the present or for the near future; there should be no connection between Faisal and Mecca. The political organization of the Arabs should not be based on the Sykes-Picot agreement, however, but on the dependence of particular areas on certain towns; for example, Damascus is the center not only for northeastern Syria but also for an area stretching to the far southeast of the Jordan. This point should be considered in determining the individual mandated areas. The French agreed to this analysis and the meeting adjourned with both sides coming to an agreement at last.[7]

Westermann sent a copy of the minutes of this meeting to House, together with a memorandum he had written giving his

---

[6] House Papers, " Notes of a Conversation with Amir Faisal, Colonel Lawrence acting as interpretor," March 29, 1919; also, House Diary.

[7] Peace Conference files, 185.513/94; also House Papers; Miller, *Diary*, has the text of the memorandum of the meeting, doc. 608.

own views. House was covering the minor problems of the Conference while the President was involved in the discussions on the German treaty in the Big Four meeting. Westermann analyzed the problem as a conflict between three elements—British imperial interests and the secret treaties; traditional French interests recognized by these treaties; and Arab interests, represented by Faisal, which had been acknowledged by official correspondence between Faisal and the Sherif of Mecca on the one hand and the British Foreign Office and military authorities on the other. " It is entirely fitting," said Westermann, " that these interests get together without reference to the United States. The solution proposed in the meeting should be backed by the United States if it is acceptable to the Foreign Office." [8] There was no mention of the fourth element, American policy and the League, and the resultant American commitment in the Syrian settlement. Apparently Wilson was still the only American in Paris who was aware of the implications of American policy; at least, he was the only one whose actions reflected this awareness.

The American experts in general were opposed to the sending of the inter-Allied Commission to Syria because they were afraid of the disturbing effect it would have in the area, and because they thought that all the information needed to arrive at a rational solution was already in Paris.[9] Their opposition to the Commission was confirmed after the curious episode of the De Caix memorandum. De Caix visited the headquarters of the American experts on April 18 and left there " accidentally " a " secret " memorandum on conditions in Syria as they related to the Commission and on French policy in the matter. In summary, the contents of the memorandum were: (1) Britain wants France to come to an agreement with Faisal quickly because she fears the results of the findings of the commission. (2) The intrusion of the United States into the Syrian problem has altered the situation in Syria so that it is no longer entirely in the control of the British. (3) The British must allow French troops to replace theirs. (4) France and Britain must agree that the mandate will follow the Sykes-Picot agreement; Faisal will be forced to agree with France when the latter agrees with England as he needs our help in ruling. From this document, the American

[8] House Papers, Memorandum, March 28, 1919.
[9] *Foreign Relations*, Paris Peace Conference, XI, 154–55.

intelligence experts, who took it at its face value, arrived at the following analysis and recommendations: (1) The French are afraid of the Commission. (2) The French know that the British are afraid of the Commission's findings in Mesopotamia and this is the reason why they insisted on a unified inquiry. (3) The French expect to be able to influence the American commissioners in their favor as the mandatory. (4) The mandates will probably follow the Commission's recommendations anyway. The analysis concluded that if the Commission went to Syria it would " find the cards stacked against it." All the information necessary to the performance of its task was in Paris; any delay would only add to present difficulties. The Near East was the " great loot of the war," and the fight on mandates must be made in Paris—the sooner the better. The document created something of a stir among the experts and shortly after the analysis was made the chief among them, and also Messrs. King and Crane, the American members of the Mandates Commission, sent a memorandum to the American peace commissioners stating that in their opinion it would be best to give up the idea of sending a purely American mission since it could not furnish sufficient data in such a short time.[10] This also is an excellent demonstration of how much in the dark the rest of the American delegation was about the basis of Wilson's policies.

The Zionists in Paris were also opposed to the sending of a commission of inquiry since, as they were aware, the inhabitants of Palestine had been vociferously proclaiming their opposition to the establishment of a Jewish National Home in their own homeland. If, as was assumed, the political settlement in the area was to be based on the findings of the Commission, and the Commission was to be guided by the wishes of the inhabitants, there was very little likelihood of the Zionist cause coming to fruition. Frankfurter sent increasingly anxious letters to House and Wilson on the composition of the Commission and the competence of their field of study. House eventually grew tired of these importunities and suggested that Frankfurter himself go along with the Commission if he wished.[11]

[10] Text of the De Caix memorandum in Wilson Papers, Series VIII A, Box 37; conclusions of the experts at *ibid.*; also in Peace Conference files, 185.5137/111.

[11] *British Documents*, Series I, IV, 260–62, for the letters to and from Wilson; the letters to House are in House Papers.

4.

The selection of delegates and the dispatch of the Commission on its journey held its own problems. The task of organizing its American section was placed in the hands of the peace commissioners and after a good deal of confusion, because of the lack of communications among the delegates and staff, this was finally accomplished. There was already in existence when the President proposed the inter-Allied commission an American mission of inquiry to Syria that had been formed on the pattern of the Central European mission. Lansing obtained Wilson's permission to send such a mission on January 30,[12] and since then it had been slowly getting underway.[13] By March 13 it had finally been decided by the peace commissioners in one of their regular meetings that four or five observers would be sent to Syria in the guise of " food inspectors " so as not to raise false hopes of American plans for the future.[14] Wilson did not inform his colleagues of his new inter-Allied Commission, but the news trickled down that the President had proposed some plan in the Council of Four and on March 27 White told the other commissioners that he had been informed that the President wished to send King and Crane to Syria as " field observers " and that the President felt that the two men were particularly well qualified to go to Syria because they knew nothing about the place.[15] (Lansing's private comment on this " penchant of the President's " for appointing inexperienced men was " amazing, amazing! ") [16]

The commissioners were still in the dark as to what the Presi-

[12] Peace Conference files 184.017/5.

[13] See *Foreign Relations,* Paris Peace Conference, XI, *passim*; indexed under Turkish Territories; Commissions and Committees concerning; American, proposed.

[14] *Ibid.,* pp. 115–19.

[15] *Ibid.,* p. 133.

[16] *Lansing Papers,* private memorandum, " Peculiar Prejudices of the President," March 20, 1919. This comment was not directed at the appointment of King and Crane—he had not heard of it at this time—but at Wilson's general tendency to act so. Lansing's Desk Diary is full of comments on the lack of communication with the President, e. g., on March 18 Lansing discussed with Auchincloss " these secret interviews of the President with Lloyd George and Clemenceau," and told him it was having a bad effect, and the other commissioners were beginning to resent it. On March 22 the Diary records that House told Henry White, who told Bliss and Lansing, that he hadn't had a private talk with the President for a week and was " very disturbed at the drift."

dent actually had in mind, and in their meeting four days later it was noted that the whole question had been held up until further information was available. There was a rumor going around that King and Crane had been appointed to " some kind of Mission " to the Near East and it had been impossible to find out just what the President planned to do.[17] In a day or so, however, the commissioners were informed of Wilson's project and the funds and organization of the American mission were turned over to the new group.[18]

Wilson had appointed the American commissioners immediately after the Commission had been agreed upon, but the French lagged and the British, though they appointed commissioners, would not move until the French did. Repeatedly in the meetings of the Four, the French were asked to name their commissioners but for over two months they dallied.[19] Clemenceau told dire tales of a coming massacre of Christians he had heard about and advised against sending the Commission. The De Caix document served its purpose and the French continued their efforts to persuade their American colleagues of the dangers of the President's scheme.

On April 21, on the eve of his departure for Syria, Faisal saw House and insisted that the Commission go at once or war would be probable.[20] Another month passed and still the Commission was incomplete. House received a letter from the Hejaz delegation on May 20 asking him to help the Commission to get started, since they had heard that it had been canceled.[21] On the same day House advised the President to tell Clemenceau and Lloyd George that the American section would leave " next Monday," and the next day Wilson announced in the Council of Four that his men were leaving for Syria.[22] For the next two days the subject formed one of the topics discussed in the Council, and

[17] *Foreign Relations*, Paris Peace Conference, XI, 140.

[18] *Ibid.*, pp. 145–46.

[19] See below, pp. 168–70.

[20] House Papers, Diary, April 21, 1919; the same entry records that House had written to Wilson about King, who was on the point of returning to the United States; House wanted Wilson's permission to persuade him to stay. Wilson approved.

[21] Wilson Papers, Series VIII A, Box 50; the Delegation wrote in a similar vein to House on May 19; House Papers.

[22] House Papers, Diary.

on each occasion the argument followed the same pattern—Wilson would insist that the Commission leave at once, Lloyd George would agree, and Clemenceau would refuse to name the French commissioners until French troops replaced the British in Syria; whereupon Lloyd George would say that he could not send the British commissioners until the French did.[23] The American section eventually went on alone.

On May 31 in the Council of Four, Lloyd George read a telegram from Allenby indicating that there would be serious trouble if the Commission did not go to Syria. It contained the texts of two telegrams that Faisal had sent to the British Commander-in-Chief. The first concerned a rumor current in Beirut that no commission would be sent and that a big French army was arriving to take control. Faisal informed Allenby that if the French were reinforced by a single soldier he would not be responsible for the consequences. The other telegram gave the contents of a cable from the Hejaz delegation in Paris to Faisal reporting that the future of Turkey was being considered by the Conference, that no commission was to be sent, and that the British were about to withdraw from Syria. Faisal told Allenby that if this was true, a great upheaval must be expected and asked for " any authentic news." He went on to say that he could not accept any decision not based on the Commission's findings and that the responsibility of shedding innocent blood must rest with the Peace Conference. Lloyd George then said that the time had come to decide whether the Commission should be sent or not. He preferred that it should leave at once. The Americans had already left but he could not act until the French did. Clemenceau replied that his position remained the same—he would not send French commissioners until the British troops in Syria had been replaced by French. Orlando added that he would not send Italian commissioners to Syria until the British and French sent theirs. There the matter was dropped.[24]

[23] See below, pp. 168–70.
[24] *Foreign Relations*, Paris Peace Conference, VI, 130–33.

5.

During this period consideration of the Anglo-French dispute on Syria continued in the Conference as more important issues permitted. On April 4 House attended a meeting of the prime ministers at the Ministry of War, the President being ill at this time. The French Premier and House discussed questions concerning France and her security. Lloyd George then injected into the conversation the Syrian problem and the French failure to come to an agreement with Faisal. " He (Lloyd George) is determined to get this settled before he lets the French get what they want," noted House in his Diary. " He has told me many times of this and this is a good example." [25]

On April 14 Clemenceau saw House and told him of a conversation he had had with Faisal " yesterday or the day before." Faisal had come to the interview accompanied by Lawrence as his interpreter. According to the French leader, he and Faisal had come to an agreement on the terms of the mandate. France was to pay Faisal the same subsidy as the British were then doing. Only the army was to use the French flag; for all other purposes the Arab standard was to be used. Loans and technical advisers were to be supplied by the French. After talking this offer over with Lawrence, however, Faisal had backed out. Clemenceau asked House to tell Wilson of this example of British politics, and also that he would give up Cilicia except for Alexandria and its river valley if the United States took the Armenian mandate.[26]

Notwithstanding Clemenceau's complaint to House of Lawrence's interference in the negotiations between the French and Arab leaders, Faisal had continued the talks, now with De Caix. It was agreed that the bases of a France-Arab understanding on

[25] House Papers, Diary, April 4, 1919; this is the only record of this meeting of the Council of Four.

[26] *Ibid.*, April 14, 1919; though this entry is dated April 14, there is a letter from House to Wilson dated April 16 (Wilson Papers, Series VIII A, Box 37; and *Foreign Relations*, Paris Peace Conference, XI, 550) referring to a conversation with Clemenceau on Syria and Armenia he had had " yesterday." I have found no record of a second conversation, and I am assuming that either the Diary or the letter to the President is mistaken. Clemenceau's remarks are no help. He refers to a meeting with Faisal " yesterday or the day before"; the meeting took place on April 13, and Clemenceau could thus have talked with House on either the fourteenth or the fifteenth. See below.

Syria should be laid down in an official exchange of letters. On April 17 Clemenceau wrote to Faisal " to confirm what I said to you in our conversation of Sunday, April 13." " The French Government," the letter continues,

desirous of assuring to Syria . . . a regime of liberty and progress in conformity with the principles by which it has always been inspired and which are the basis of the deliberations of the Peace Conference, declares that it recognizes the right of Syria to independence . . . France is prepared to give material and moral assistance to this emancipation of Syria. . . . In referring to the needs of the country and the interests of its people as well as to the historic role which France has played, Your Highness recognizes that France is the Power qualified to give Syria the assistance of the various advisers necessary to establish order and bring about the progress which the people of Syria desire.[27]

Faisal replied with a very frank statement of what the Syrians wanted from the French. This was rejected by De Caix, who did not even show it to Clemenceau. Another letter was sent by Faisal on April 20 couched in vague, formal language and asking for someone to be sent to Syria to continue the conversations, as he was returning to the East shortly. This was rejected by Clemenceau as inadequate to the purpose of the exchange of letters.[28] Faisal left for Syria shortly thereafter and the " agreement " languished until the fall.[29]

[27] English text in *Foreign Relations*, Paris Peace Conference, V, 115; original French text in *British Documents*, Series I, IV, 252.

[28] *Ibid.*, pp. 252–53.

[29] The American Delegation was well informed on the Faisal-Clemenceau talks. William Yale discussed them with Georges Picot on April 17. Picot said that the differences between Faisal and his father, King Hussain, had been settled temporarily, but Faisal realized that if he was to remain in Syria as its ruler, he would have to break with him again. Picot said he was sure France and Faisal could agree but a settlement between them would have to be accomplished soon as the situation in Syria might get out of hand—the Pan-Islam movement was growing and the northern Syrians were increasing their contacts with the Young Turks [sic]. Yale asked Picot about the French attitude on an American mandate for Armenia. Picot answered that his government would not like it if the Americans insisted on Cilicia. Peace Conference files, 867S.00/42. On April 20 Yale wrote a memorandum on the situation in the Middle East for William Bullitt for the use of the American Delegation. He told him of Faisal's talks with the French; he was now treating with De Caix, he said, in close association with Clemenceau, on French-Arab control of Syria. By Syria the French meant the area of the Sykes-Picot treaty and the discussions with Faisal were sure to have two results, (1) that by coming to an agreement with Faisal, the French would get British support for their claims to Cilicia and Diabekir " (a euphemism for the Arghana-Maden

Lloyd George lunched with House on April 18 and discussed Syria with him. He was " still disturbed " about relations between the French and Faisal; " They will surely clash," he said. He had been talking about it that morning with the President, he added, and Wilson had suggested that he take it up with his colleague. Would, then, the Colonel take it up with the French and try to get them to see the light? What he wanted, he went on, was to have the United States take the Syrian mandate and to let the French have Constantinople. Later in the day he spoke again with Wilson, who told House what had transpired. The Prime Minister had at that time suggested that France have the Syrian mandate. It would be the best solution since the League could keep an eye on her there.[30] George was probably merely fishing for reactions, but both the Americans kept their council. On the following Monday, April 21, Faisal had his last interview with House, insisting again that the Commission go to Syria at once or war would be probable.[31]

6.

Faisal arrived in Syria at the beginning of May. He had four tasks ahead of him: to calm the fears of the Arabs, who had been hearing nothing good from Paris, and organize Arab opinion for the arrival of the King-Crane Commission; to maintain and stimulate, if possible, American opposition to the application of the Sykes-Picot agreement in the Syrian settlement; to prevent the British from abandoning him; and to hold off a French occupation as long as possible. The British had made it plain to him that they would not quarrel with France over Syria. On the other hand, Britain was in actual possession of the country and would stay there as long as some political advantage might be gained in doing so, if the cost were not too great. It was a race against time for Faisal, to weaken the French claim to Syria and strengthen the Arab case to a point where the French could not maintain their claims, under the Sykes-Picot agreement, against American

copper mines)," (2) there would be a French proposal for a Franco-American mandate for Armenia. *Ibid.*, 867s.00/41.

[30] House Papers, Diary, April 18, 1919.

[31] *Ibid.*, April 21, 1919.

opposition when the Turkish treaty was negotiated. This had to be done before the French were in actual control of the country. To this end Faisal employed every means of delay, fighting every concession to the French to the last minute, conceding when necessary but no more than absolutely necessary, husbanding every advantage—anything to avoid a showdown, anything to keep French troops out of Syria. In doing this he had at the same time to maintain his position among the Arabs, many of whom could not appreciate the subtleties of his policy or the necessity of conceding anything to the French to buy time, and many of whom would see no advantage in supporting a leader who might fail.

Immediately after he arrived in Damascus, Faisal made an address to a meeting of Syrian notables in the Town Hall of the city. He gave them an encouraging version of what had passed in Paris and his part in the negotiations with the great powers. His policy, he said, had been based on two principles—that the Arab countries should not be partitioned among the European countries and that the Hejaz, Mesopotamia, and Syria should have, for the time being, separate identities as the time was not yet ripe for a single Arab government, though the Arab nation, the Ummah, was one. He said that the European nations had agreed to accept Arab wishes, and he asked for the approval of the meeting for his policy. It was freely given.[32] Arab national feeling being thus reassured, Faisal turned next to the organization of Arab opinion in a form that would have meaning at the Peace Conference, and particularly to the Americans. He encouraged a movement for the formation of a National Assembly that had been gaining popular support under the auspices of the Arab Independence party, formed by the Arab secret society, al-Fatat, to carry on its program now that the need for secrecy no longer existed. Elections were hurriedly held[33] and on July 2 the Assembly, under the name of the General Syrian Congress, opened its sessions in Damascus with delegates in attendance not only from the Arab-administered areas but also from the British and French

[32] Sati al-Husri, *Yawm Maisalun* (Beirut, 1947), pp. 202–13.

[33] This is true in the strict sense, but in fact no new popular elections were held; the delegates to the Congress were selected by the electors appointed at the time of the last elections for the Turkish Parliament, held before the war, under the two-stage system of the Constitution.

zones. Difficulties had in fact been put in the way of the delegates from the French zone and not all of them succeeded in attending the Congress, but enough arrived in Damascus to support the claim that the Congress did represent the entire Syrian people.

The most important accomplishment of the Congress was the adoption of ten resolutions demanding recognition of an independent Syria (including Palestine and Lebanon) with Faisal as King; repudiation of the Sykes-Picot agreement and the Balfour Declaration; rejection of any system of tutelage implied in the mandate system, though foreign assistance for a limited period was accepted, preference being given first to the United States and second to Britain; and absolute rejection of French assistance in any form. The demands for full independence and the rejection of any scheme for the " dismemberment " of Syria or the establishment of the Zionist program in " Southern Syria " were based on the

principles proclaimed by President Wilson in condemnation of secret treaties. . . . The lofty principles proclaimed by President Wilson encourage us to believe that the determining consideration in the settlement of our own future will be the real desires of our people; and that we may look to President Wilson and the liberal American nation, who are known for their sincere and generous sympathy with the aspirations of weak nations, for help in the fulfillment of our hopes.[34]

While the elections were being held and the Syrian Congress organized, a concerted effort to make the people aware of the importance of the King-Crane Commission was undertaken and the notables of the various districts were instructed to prepare their people and themselves to represent the Arab case to the Commission. Petitions were circulated and signed, committees established, the recalcitrant subdued.[35] Little persuasion was needed in Syria and Palestine to whip up public feeling against European rule.

[34] *Foreign Relations*, Paris Peace Conference, XII, 779–81.

[35] The Consulate at Aleppo reported in July that a number of Aneiza sheikhs, who had favored a French mandate before the King-Crane Commission, had been seized from a train on which they were being taken to Beirut by the French, publicly threatened by the local Arab authorities, and sent to Aleppo where they were now in jail. Despatch 384, July 21, 1919; 763.72119/6320. Despatch 385, July 25, 763.72119/6321.

7.

The King-Crane Commission or, to give it the official title, the American Section of the Inter-Allied Commission on Turkish Mandates, arrived at Jaffa on June 10.[36] For the next several weeks the commissioners traveled throughout Syria, Palestine, and Lebanon, hearing delegations, receiving petitions and talking to Arab leaders. On July 10, the Commission cabled a preliminary report to the President and a similar report was sent the same day to the American Peace Delegation in Paris. The gist of these two messages was that Faisal, the Syrian Congress and the Syrian people combined in opposition to the French and, except for the Maronites and Latin sects, the people absolutely rejected French control. War would be probable if the French received the mandate, the reports warned. All were united in their opposition to the Zionists. There was a strong feeling for the unity of Syria and for independence; Faisal was the man to support to achieve this. The people were relying on Wilson and his pronouncements, and there was a very strong movement to have the United States take the mandate. The commissioners suggested that the United States consider the problem on its own merits apart from the Anglo-French dispute on territorial allotments in the Near East.[37] Such advice was of as little help to the President as was the attitude that prompted it.

The King-Crane Commission returned to Paris in the middle of August after continuing its inquiry in Turkey in the area occupied by the French. The Commission had also been instructed to investigate opinion in Mesopotamia but, according to the report, it was not found possible to visit the country, and the recommendations submitted were based on the Commission's private judgment based on reports and the statements of various delegations who claimed the right to speak for Mesopotamia. The Commission's report was submitted on August 28 to the then head of the American delegation, Frank L. Polk. It was to be held until the Turkish treaty was negotiated and then presented to the Con-

[36] For correspondence regarding the Commission's journey, and its Report, see *Foreign Relations*, Paris Peace Conference, XII, 745–863.

[37] *Ibid.*; also Wilson Papers, Series VIII A, Box 159, for a report of the same date by Crane on the Commission's work, enclosing a statement by Faisal, the Resolutions of the Syrian Congress, and other material.

ference by the American delegation. This, of course, was not done, as the United States withdrew from the Conference before consideration of the Turkish treaty. It remained in the hands of President Wilson until he permitted it to be published in 1922. No copies were circulated to the other delegations, though the British were permitted to read it. They requested a copy but Polk refused; "I don't doubt they have made very copious notes," he commented. The report's recommendations for Syria followed very closely those of the preliminary report cabled on July 10; those for Mesopotamia followed those for Syria, and again America was indicated as the first choice of the people for mandatory, with Britain second if the United States did not take it. For Turkey the report recommended the establishment of three separate states of Constantinople, Armenia, and the rest of Turkey, all under mandate. A single mandatory should be appointed for all the states, and that mandatory should be the United States. The Greeks should be excluded from Anatolia and no separate state set up for the Greek-speaking areas, though some local autonomy might be permitted. Cilicia should not be attached to Armenia. A confidential appendix "for the use of Americans only" was attached to the report; it consisted of comments and observations which the Commission did not feel to be appropriate to a document intended for the use of the Peace Conference as a whole. It was chiefly concerned with obstacles put in the way of Arabs wishing to approach the Commission, and the various propaganda efforts of the British, French, and Arabs to gain support for their own programs; summaries of arguments presented to the Commission, with the Commission's comment on them; and with French feelings towards the British, French "rights," the Greater Lebanon scheme of the French, and Faisal's position in Syria.[38]

[38] *Foreign Relations*, Paris Peace Conference, XI, 427–34. The question is often raised why the Commission's report was "kept secret" by Wilson until 1922, and was then published unofficially. In the first place, the King-Crane Commission was not a purely American project; it was the American section of an inter-Allied Commission of Inquiry acting for the Conference as a whole. In the second place, the report was made for the enlightenment of the Conference, not the public. The United States did not make the report fully available to the Allies when the Commission returned to Europe for the reasons stated in the text. For the United States to have issued it officially after the withdrawal from the Conference would have been justifiably considered by the French to be a gratuitous attempt by the American government to increase their difficulties in Syria and

8.

While Faisal and the Arabs had been making every effort during the tour of the King-Crane Commission to impress upon it their abhorrence of French rule and their admiration for American principles of government, they did not neglect, in their program of building up American opinion against the French, the President or the local American representatives. Faisal cabled to Wilson on June 22 informing him that Picot, the French representative in Syria, had told him that the King-Crane Commission had been sent out privately by Dr. Wilson and that " its findings would carry no weight with the Conference," contrary to what he had been told by the Commission itself. " I and all my nation," said Faisal, " are convinced you are the outstanding figure in the world and that you will not allow the Syrian nation to voice its opinion and then see them punished for it revengefully if it is true that the future of this country is already settled as the spreaders of these rumors wish. . . ." [39] This telegram was sent via British channels, through Allenby to Balfour. On July 9 Faisal cabled again; this time he had available to him the facilities of the American consulate at Damascus: " There is no doubt that after the arrival of your honorable commission and the statements made to it expressing unreservedly the true desires and aspirations, the people and particularly myself have incurred as a matter of course the risk of a terrible strong current against us. I earnestly beg you not to leave me between the paws of the devourers. . . ." [40]

As the Commission finished its work in Syria the Consuls in the Arab countries continued to report on the political situation in the Middle East, in terms almost without exception that were pro-Faisal and anti-French. The Consul in Beirut sent, on July 31, a lengthy despatch giving an analysis of the situation in Syria and

---

might have had serious repercussions. Wilson probably made the report public in the manner he did for the same reasons that he made his private file available to R. S. Baker—to answer the criticisms of some of his former colleagues in the Conference who were finding in him a convenient scapegoat for their own mistakes.

[39] *British Documents*, Series I, IV, 279, fn.

[40] Telegram from Damascus via Cairo, July 9, 1919; 763.72119/5622(?). Sent to the President August 8; the delay was due to a further exchange of telegrams between the Department and the Consulate to clarify the text of Faisal's message. It had been translated from the Arabic. Wilson made no response as he was fully occupied.

Lebanon. A united Syria was the only solution for the present unrest and uncertainty, he said. Except for a small number of Lebanese, the Syrians did not want French control; they believed that France would make of their country another colony like Algiers and that they would never achieve independence. Another objection was that France did not have the financial resources to develop the country. A great deal of dissatisfaction had been aroused by French administrative policy since the occupation; the Christians had been openly favored over the Muslims and, moreover, the French were assuming all the important administrative functions of the local government to the exclusion of the Arabs.[41] On August 27 Beirut cabled that the French were persecuting anti-French elements throughout the French zone; anti-French feeling was on the increase, making more certain that there would be an uprising if France received the mandate. Even some of those who gave evidence before the King-Crane Commission were being jailed. The French, the cable reported, had been " by pernicious intrigue and propaganda " attempting to supplant Faisal by the Amir Zaid, second son of Abdul Kader, the Algerian, but he had been deported to Egypt by the British.[42] The Consul at Damascus cabled on August 30 that the great aim of Faisal was an undivided Syria, administered as a whole with one mandatory, and with full religious liberty for all sects and faiths; he had stated definitely that he did not want France as the mandatory power. The Consul commented that he had always been impressed with the " sincerity, conscientiousness and ability of Amir Faisal." [43]

9.

Faisal's approach to the British was to insist on and reiterate his claims on them, and his and the Arabs' undying opposition to the French; the British must be given no opportunity to believe that they could slough him off and turn him over to the French without the most strenuous opposition on his part (including incitement to revolt and even military operations) not only in Syria, where Faisal's agents were already at work stirring up the

[41] Despatch 3 from Beirut, July 31, 1919; 763.72119/6602.
[42] Telegram from Beirut via Paris, August 27, 1919; 763.72119/6476.
[43] Telegram from Damascus, August 30, 1919; 763.72119/6470.

people against France and whence they could move out into Palestine and Iraq and stir up the people against Britain (as they were to do six months later), but at the Peace Conference also where the United States would, he hoped, take up his cause in the name of self-determination under the aegis of the King-Crane Commission's report.

On May 20 and 21 Faisal had a series of discussions with General Clayton, principal British representative in Syria. He told him that while he had, on Lawrence's advice, agreed with Clemenceau to use his efforts in support of a French mandate for Syria, he never had any intention of doing this. He would accept a British or American mandate or a joint mandate under Britain, France, and the United States, but never France alone. Clayton commented in his cabled report of the interviews: "Faisal was obviously nervous as to the result of such an underhanded policy towards the French and asked for my advice. I told him that in my opinion a policy of intrigue and deception would only recoil on himself and might easily endanger Franco-British relations and as a consequence relations between Great Britain and the Arabs." [44] Faisal continued to press the British to accept the mandate for Syria. After a series of exchanges on the subject, the British informed Faisal on June 12 that they held to their announced policy of not accepting the Syrian mandate, though they would give fullest weight to the advice of the commission of inquiry.[45] Faisal replied, noting the British expression of unwillingness to take the mandate; however, he said, the intention to give the fullest weight to the advice of the commission " is cheerfully accepted by us all "—the Syrians would unanimously express to the Commission their preference for Great Britain " and no other." [46] This reply seemed not to appreciate the firmness with which Britain held to her intention not to take the mandate, notwithstanding anything the Commission might recommend. Balfour cabled British headquarters in Cairo on June 26, emphasizing it: " You can reply to Faisal that His Majesty's Government is determined not to take a Mandate for Syria." [47]

At this time, Clayton sent a summary of his estimate of the situation in Syria. He said that Faisal found the British attitude " extraordinary." After liberating the Arab countries at immense

[44] *British Documents*, Series I, IV, 265, fn.
[45] *Ibid.*, p. 276.
[46] *Ibid.*, p. 277.
[47] *Ibid.*, pp. 298–99.

cost in blood and treasure and after four years of unbroken friendship, England refused to say whether she would help the Arabs any longer, and was going to sacrifice the Arabs to suit the exigencies of European politics. France was entirely reliant on Britain and the United States, and Faisal could not understand why Britain was afraid of doing anything to offend France. Clayton then went on:

A French Mandate is regarded as National death. It will bring French colonists, French citizenship and French hegemony. The Emir and his Arabs did not make their revolution to see the fairest part of their country handed over to the French, whom they regard as nothing less than an enemy, and whom they fully intend to resist by force of arms should she attempt to exercise a protectorate over Syria. . . . If England is determined to avoid further responsibilities in Syria . . . then Syria wants complete independence. . . . These are the Emir's views and the views of all the best Moslem Arabs as well.[48]

During August the news reaching Syria from Europe became increasingly disquieting and at the end of the month Faisal made a last appeal to his British allies in a letter to Lloyd George and in a formal statement to the two chief British military representatives in Syria. To Lloyd George, after warning him of the dangers brewing in the Middle East, he said, quite accurately as it happened: " The future Government of the Arab provinces will be the last lesson to be given by Europe to the East. If it does not turn out to be in accordance with the wishes of the people, confidence will be lost in every future official treatment, and a wide channel opened for intrigues and troubles. . . ." [49] On August 31, in his statement to the Chief of the General Staff of the Egyptian Expeditionary Force and the political officers attached to his Command, Faisal gave an explicit warning of what he himself was prepared to do if the British government did not give independence to his people. He said that the Muslim peoples would not tolerate the establishment of alien rule over the Holy Places and would feel bound to establish a Muslim government. This would meet with the opposition of the Powers and fighting would break out. " We, the Arabs," he said, " were formally with the Turks and fought against them, not with the intention of dividing our country by giving a share to the French and a portion to the

[48] *Ibid.*, pp. 289–92.   [49] *Ibid.*, pp. 385–88.

British. We cannot possibly brook that insult in the pages of history and in the eyes of the Mohammedan world. I . . . will take part in the defence of our principle, knowing that this is certain by any way or means and in its right time. . . ." He also said, however, that the Arabs would never fire on the British, at least in Arabia; it was the French who were the enemies of the Arabs and who would be attacked.[50] Unfortunately for Faisal, steps were already underway in Paris and London that would bring French troops into Syria and with them French political control, while the ability of the United States to resist these moves was at the same time seriously weakened.

[50] *Ibid.*, pp. 388–90.

CHAPTER VI

THE POWERS AND TURKEY: THE SMYRNA LANDINGS

1.

The inter-Allied Commission on Turkish Mandates had temporarily put an end in the Council of Four to discussions of Turkish territorial questions based on the Sykes-Picot agreement, but President Wilson was soon faced with a far more serious threat to American policy on the Ottoman Empire. During the first weeks in April, Italian claims to former Austro-Hungarian territory in the Adriatic, over and above that which had been promised in the Treaty of London, had given rise to an increasingly dangerous situation in the Council. The Italians had extended their claims as an offset to the position of the new Yugoslav state; Italy's original claims had been predicated on the continuing existence of the Austro-Hungarian Empire in some form acting as a check on Serbian strength in the Adriatic. The Austrian naval forces in the Adriatic had demonstrated the threat to Italy of the facilities offered to naval operations by the islands and harbors of the Dalmatian coast, particularly in comparison to the almost harborless Italian coast. Most of the territory claimed was inhabited by Slavs and could only be given to Italy at the expense of Serbian national aspirations.[1]

On April 19 Orlando presented to the Council of Four a statement of the Italian case for the annexation by Italy of certain Slav-speaking areas at the head of the Adriatic, for Fiume, and for certain of the islands off the Dalmatian coast as well as the coastal regions of Dalmatia itself. Wilson had been deputed by the other premiers to answer the Italian case. He said he could

[1] For British material on the Adriatic question, see *British Documents*, Series I, IV, 1–240.

not accept Italian strategic problems as a basis for a settlement; such considerations had governed European international thinking since 1815 and had led to most of the wars of the past hundred years and to World War I. He said he could not submit such a settlement to the people of the United States; they simply would not accept it. Clemenceau and Lloyd George supported Wilson, though they agreed that they were bound by the Treaty of London if Italy insisted on it; the present Italian claims went far beyond the Treaty, however. The Italian leader said he could not go back to Italy with less than could have been obtained from the Austrians for remaining neutral, and could not therefore accept his colleagues' position and the decision of the Conference. However, if the Conference were to take as the basis of its decision the Treaty of London, with Fiume left to be settled later, then he was prepared to discuss it with the Italian delegation and inform the Council of their decision. Wilson refused to accept this. He said he could not answer for Britain and France, but for himself he did not consider the Treaty to be consistent with the principles on which the Treaty of Peace was being based. He did not wish to criticize the Treaty, but he could not see his way to making peace with Austria on different principles from that with Germany. He was bound to say to the world that the Conference was establishing a new order in which secret treaties would take no part, and to suggest that a secret treaty, the Treaty of London, would form the basis of the decision on the Italian claims would be to place the United States in an impossible situation. He was willing to state, and might have to state, to the world the grounds of his objections.[2]

On the following day, Orlando told the Council that the minimum for Italy was Fiume, and if Italy did not get it the whole population would react violently and with hatred against those responsible. Nevertheless, since the Allied Powers had said that they would not go any further than the Treaty of London and would not release Italy from her obligations under it, and since the peace of the world was at stake, he would formally state

<hr />

[2] *Foreign Relations*, Paris Peace Conference, V, 80–94. Lansing noted in his Diary on April 19 that Wilson had discussed with him the proceedings in the Council and told him the Italians would never get Fiume; he was thinking, he said, of making a public statement that they would never get it. (Lansing Papers.)

that if the Conference committed itself to the whole of the Treaty he would accept its decision.

There was a pause after this announcement, then Wilson answered. He said it was incredible that the representatives of Italy should take up this position. He said that the principles of the Fourteen Points represented the feeling of the whole world, not his feelings alone nor even of the United States alone. The Fourteen Points, based on the principles on which the United States had entered the war (and the United States had played an important part in winning the war) had made definite statements on the territorial settlement in the Balkans and Italy. If the Council accepted M. Orlando's position, it would be creating antagonisms that never would be stamped out. What M. Orlando was saying was that if the Treaty of London was not carried out, Italy would stand in the way of peace. The United States was not bound by the Treaty and in any case regarded it as unsuited to present circumstances. If Austria-Hungary existed his attitude would be entirely different for Italy would need every outpost of security, but this dangerous circumstance did not exist. Orlando replied that he had raised the issue of the Treaty only with reluctance, because Lloyd George and Clemenceau had raised it in saying that he had no right to break an alliance with those who were ready to honor their commitments. Wilson again warned that the United States could not in any circumstances associate itself with a decision based on the Treaty. The discussion continued on these points until the meeting ended, when it was decided to postpone the matter until the next day.[3]

The next morning Lloyd George proposed that the Italians be given the islands without Fiume and the coast of Dalmatia, as meeting their strategic requirements. He said that he had been told that the Yugoslavs were not too concerned about the islands and would probably accept this proposal. Wilson replied that he had been told by a Serb that the Italians would make a great deal of trouble for the Serbs if they held the islands.[4] When the Council met in the afternoon, without Orlando, Lloyd George produced an alternative scheme, with the approval of Clemenceau. This was to give Italy a share in the mandates for Turkey covering most of Anatolia except the Greek mandate in the

[3] *Foreign Relations*, Paris Peace Conference, V, 95–101.
[4] *Ibid.*, p. 106.

Smyrna region, the Constantinople mandate, and Armenia. Wilson said everybody seemed to dread the Italians as neighbors and this was the trouble with the scheme. He thought that great care would have to be exercised in the matter, since the Conference was supposed to be securing the peace of the world, and could not enter into arrangements that might threaten the peace. Lloyd George then suggested that perhaps Italy could be given a sphere of influence instead of a mandate, but Wilson again expressed his doubts. He said the Italians had no experience in such matters and had no ethnological claims such as had the Greeks. Lloyd George said that they would have no authority over the people of the region, merely commercial rights, and again Wilson declined to be persuaded. That left the whole point of Turkish mandates untouched, he said, for the entire scheme was based on the inability of the Turks to govern themselves. In any case he did not like the idea of paying the Italians for something they had no right to in the first place.[5]

It was finally agreed that Lloyd George's suggestion, of giving the islands to Italy, but with the mainland ports desired by Italy being constituted free cities, be put to the Italian delegation. It was refused by Orlando. Lloyd George attempted to persuade him privately to accept, warning him that he would be in a serious situation if he persisted in his threat to withdraw from the Conference. Wilson was " immovable," he told the Italian leader, and while France and Britain were willing to stand by the Treaty of London, if the United States did not sign the German treaty " it meant disaster." It was only with considerable difficulty that the President had agreed to give Italy the islands. The President moreover planned to make a public appeal to the Italian people; once that was done there would be no turning back and no chance of reconciliation. Orlando still insisted on getting ports on the mainland, however.[6] When Lloyd George reported this exchange to the Council on April 22, Wilson commented that Italy would never get anything on the mainland.[7]

The crisis had by now reached such proportions that Wilson called in his fellow peace commissioners for a conference on the Italians' demands and the public statement he planned to make to the Italian people (the President had not consulted his col-

[5] *Ibid.*, p. 106–9.   [6] *Ibid.*, p. 135.   [7] *Ibid.*, pp. 135–36.

leagues on anything for many weeks). He outlined what had occurred during the recent sessions of the Council of Four. He said that the Italians would never get his consent to Fiume and the Dalmatian Coast. He then read his statement. There was little comment.[8] After the meeting, General Bliss wrote to the President urging him to publish the statement immediately, before the Italians left the Conference rather than waiting until after the break. Wilson replied, thanking Bliss for his letter and saying, " I find my colleagues, Mr. Lloyd George and M. Clemenceau, opposed to its immediate publication because they believe that it would end the possibility of agreement with Italy, but I am standing out for my rights and shall not hold it back too long." [9] On April 23 Wilson had a conversation with House. The latter suggested that he release his statement, after conferring with Clemenceau and Lloyd George, in order to forestall Orlando, who had a statement of his own ready.[10] Wilson made his statement to the Italian people on the same day.[11] It had been agreed that Lloyd George and Clemenceau would follow this up with a similar statement supporting the President as far as their commitment to the Treaty of London would allow, but there was such an outburst in Italy following the President's statement that his colleagues thought better of their promise; and in fact Lloyd George not only declined to publish his statement but publicly criticized the President for making his, though there had been full agreement among the Three that it should be done.[12] The Franco-British statement was sent privately to Orlando. It again reiterated the dangers being courted by Italy in withdrawing from the Conference, and begged the Italian delegation to reconsider its position.[13] On April 24 the Italians once more appeared in the Council to explain their decision to return to Italy. Discussion of the problem yielded no result, though Wilson took the opportunity to make plain to his colleagues that his agreement to have Lloyd George's offer of the islands put to the Italians as a compromise was in no sense a commitment by him. All he had done, he said,

[8] Lansing Papers, Desk Diary, April 21, 1919.

[9] Wilson Papers, Series VIII A, Box 40.

[10] House Papers, Diary.

[11] Text in Ray Stannard Baker, *Woodrow Wilson and World Settlement* (Garden City, 1922), III, 287.

[12] House Papers, Diary, April 26, 1919.

[13] Text in *Foreign Relations*, Paris Peace Conference, V, 223–27.

was to ask Lloyd George to ascertain if the Italians would be ready to discuss the matter on this basis, and the reply he had received was that they were not; he had reserved his judgment in every case.[14]

2.

The Italians returned home and the Council turned to other matters. On May 2, however, it was learned that the Italians had sent a warship to Fiume and a squadron to Smyrna. When this was discussed in the Council, Wilson commented that it confirmed what Orlando had said to the American Ambassador at Rome, that Italy would not enter the League unless it got what it wanted. The President suggested that the three powers send ships of their own to the two ports.[15] This was agreed to; the battleship *Arizona* and a squadron of destroyers were ordered to Smyrna and destroyers to Fiume,[16] and British and French warships were also sent to watch the Italians. Shortly after this, news reached the Council that the Italians were expanding their zone of occupation in southern Anatolia and were landing fresh troops; it was rumored that they intended to occupy Smyrna and had forces ready to land there. On May 5 General Wilson reported on these new Italian moves to the Council. Lloyd George wanted Allied occupation policy reconsidered in the light of this activity. " Any day it might be found that Italy had captured Anatolia and it would be difficult to get them out of there once they had occupied it. The mandates for Turkey could not be settled then owing to the decision to send out a Commission. He thought, therefore, that we should fall back on his original proposal of a redistribution of the forces of occupation." The United States should go to Constantinople and garrison Armenia, the British should pull out of the Caucasus, the French should garrison Syria, and the Greeks occupy Smyrna. Wilson did not rise to this and expressed doubts as to the availability of American forces. It was finally

[14] *Ibid.*, pp. 210–22.

[15] *Ibid.*, pp. 407–14.

[16] Wilson Papers, Series VIII A, Box 44; instruction from Admiral Benson to U. S. S. *Arizona* to proceed to Smyrna to observe the naval activities of the other powers and to report all information obtained on them, particularly those of the Italians. " The President personally ordered this movement and it should not be disclosed to anyone."

agreed that General Bliss should confer with General Wilson so that he could then bring the President up to date on the military situation in Turkey.[17]

The next day Lloyd George suggested that the Greeks be permitted to land troops in Smyrna in order to forestall the Italians, who had seven battleships in the harbor and evidently intended to land troops. Wilson agreed to this, particularly since the Greek Commission was in favor of giving the area to Greece.[18] The Italians returned to the Council on May 7, but a decision had already been made and Greek troops were authorized to land on Turkish soil. A break in the deadlock between the Italians and the Council came on the twelfth when Lloyd George proposed that the Italians be invited to participate in the mandate system for Turkey. This plan was endorsed by Clemenceau and Wilson. The principal reason for the move was ostensibly that the Italians had had all along many talents, as a race, that qualified them for the task of assisting the Turks to achieve stability and progress.[19] On the fourteenth a comprehensive mandate scheme was worked out for Anatolia, defining the area to be left under Turkish sovereignty with Greece, Italy, and France sharing the burden of mandates in Turkish Anatolia and the United States provisionally accepting mandates over Constantinople and Armenia.[20]

The Italians had not waited for the formal conciliar stamp on this division of the land of the Turks, however. As the Greeks were landing at Smyrna on May 15, and while the Council was debating the precise lines of demarcation between the zones to be allotted to each country, the Italian landed secretly on the southern Anatolian coast with fresh troops and proceeded to widen the territory they had already pre-empted.[21] Then, on the afternoon of the same day that this became known to the Three, May 17, a delegation of prominent Indians appeared before the Council to plead for the integrity of the homeland of the Turkish race and for the retention of the Sultan as the spiritual leader not only of the Turks but also of the whole Muslim world. They appealed specifically to Point Twelve and to Lloyd George's state-

---

[17] *Foreign Relations*, Paris Peace Conference, V, 465–68; Wilson told his colleagues in the Council on May 6 that he had consulted his advisers, who had told him he had no authority to send troops to Turkey; *ibid.*, p. 482.

[18] *Ibid.*, pp. 483–85.   [20] *Ibid.*, pp. 614–15.
[19] *Ibid.*, pp. 579–87.   [21] *Ibid.*, pp. 668–69.

ments on the future of Turkey made three days before Wilson's speech.[22]

These two events completely reversed the plans for Anatolian mandates, and two days later Lloyd George announced in the Council his new policy. He told his colleagues that he had talked with Orlando and the latter had said that if he got Fiume, he would " drop Asia Minor." " The more [I think] of the problem of the presence of the Italians in Asia Minor," said the Prime Minister, " the more full of mischief the scheme seems." The Muslim delegation had been very much opposed to the partition of Turkey proper, particularly to that part of the plan which placed Turks under Italians, since the latter were despised by the Turks. " At the risk of appearing to vacillate, [I would like to reconsider the provisional decision already taken . . . my] present attitude is that it would be best to get the Italians out of Asia Minor altogether."

Wilson said that he had been impressed by what the Muslim delegation had said about Turkish sovereignty. He himself had forgotten that he had used the word in the Fourteen Points until he had been reminded of it by the delegation. He offered a tentative suggestion that the Sultan be left in Constantinople, retaining sovereignty over Anatolia but not in the city itself, where his position might be similar to the Pope's in Rome. He would be required to accept advice on certain matters such as financial and economic affairs and foreign relations. The President mentioned that he had noted the reaction of the Indian delegation when the word " mandate " was mentioned. The Turks would have difficulty in distinguishing between one type of mandate and another and he suggested to give, in effect, a mandate to France without calling it a mandate, with France not responsible to the League but advising the Turkish government under treaty stipulations.

Lloyd George took this up at once. He said that if France took a position of this kind toward the whole of Asia Minor, which would be a very important trust, he would have to ask for a re-examination of the whole question of mandates in the Turkish Empire.[23] True to his word, he appeared at the Council on the twenty-first with a new mandate plan and offered it as a settlement of the Turkish problem. Its main points covered the

[22] *Ibid.*, pp. 690–701.   [23] *Ibid.*, pp. 707–11.

American participation in Turkish mandates, Greek sovereignty over Aidin, and the provisional mandates over Syria, Mesopotamia, and Palestine that Britain and France were to exercise until the inter-Allied Commission reported. The United States was to exercise a " full " mandate over Constantinople and the Straits and over Armenia or alternately a " light " mandate over all of Anatolia.

After some discussion of this project, Wilson brought up the delay in getting the Commission of Inquiry to Syria and said that he was instructing the American delegates to leave in a few days. Lloyd George said that he would do the same. Clemenceau was not to be pressured, however, He said that in that case he must drop out. The British had not kept their promises; they had agreed in several instances to consult on a compromise in Syria, but they had not done so. France had given up Mosul and Palestine to Great Britain and a part of Cilicia to President Wilson and he " thought she had a right to compensation." No promises had been made, but only the day before it had been suggested that France have a mandate over the whole of Anatolia. Now Lloyd George had come along with " fresh combinations " which excluded France; while the plan was designed to eliminate Italian claims in Anatolia, " was it a good thing, though, that France should be excluded from Asia Minor because of the susceptibilities of the Italians? " He considered it dangerous to introduce the United States into Asia Minor and that it would not produce a " good opinion in France."

Lloyd George rejected these criticisms and Wilson took pains to point out that it was extremely unlikely that the United States would take a mandate for Anatolia. As for the commissioners, they were men of such standing that he would have to send them to Syria or back to the United States, but he could not keep them waiting in Paris indefinitely; he was not trying to coerce the French into sending their section. Clemenceau rejoined that he would be ready to do so as soon as French troops replaced British forces in Syria. These delaying tactics may be explained by Clemenceau's reluctance to further any kind of settlement until the French were in *de facto* control of Syria.[24]

In the afternoon session on the nineteenth, Wilson, Clemenceau

[24] *Ibid.*, pp. 756–66.

and Lloyd George met with Sonnino, the new Italian representative to the Council, and questioned him about the new Italian
landings. Sonnino handed to his colleagues a memorandum on
the Italian case which justified the landings on the basis of the
undertakings of the Allies in the Treaty of London and the St.
Jean agreement. This led to a great deal of discussion between
Lloyd George, Clemenceau, and Sonnino on just what Italy was
entitled to in Asia Minor. Wilson stepped in at once. He said
he must respectfully remind M. Sonnino that the meeting was
not a conversation merely among allies. The United States had a
right to a place in the Conference, and further had a right to ask
questions regardless of the Treaty of London. That Treaty, he
said, did not provide an effective reason why troops should be
disembarked on the mainland of Anatolia, nor why the regions in
question should be occupied by Italy. Sonnino replied that there
were disorders in the region, and the Italian action did not prejudice the final settlement. Wilson said that might not be the intention, but in fact the settlement was being prejudiced. There was
then another round of discussion on Italian rights; Wilson once
again reminded the others of his freedom of action. He said he
was sure that his British and French colleagues would understand
it when he said that the United States did not recognize their
right to hand over Turkish populations to Italy; this was a world
settlement and they were all partners in it. Sonnino once again
asked for the agreement of the Council to the maintenance of
Italian troops in Southern Anatolia, but Wilson ended the discussion by saying that, as far as he was concerned, the Italian government must take the whole responsibility for the retention of
their troops in Turkey. Lloyd George and Clemenceau supported
him.

Negotiations on the King-Crane Commission continued and in
the next day's session Clemenceau brought up the subject again,
going over the old grounds of the dispute. He and Lloyd George
repeated the argument they had had two months before—the
Sykes-Picot agreement, troops, oil, and territory. The resumption
of the argument on Turkish mandates on the basis of the Sykes-
Picot agreement and the subsequent negotiations between France
and Britain brought forth the same reaction from Wilson that
it had on March 20. He inquired "what part he was asked to
play in this affair? He himself had never been able to see by what

right France and Great Britain gave this country away to anyone."
The Prime Minister replied that he was quite willing to abide by
the decision of the inhabitants as interpreted by the Commission.
Wilson returned that " that was necessarily his own point of view.
He had no other means on which to form judgment. He did not
think that these peoples could be left entirely to themselves. They
required guidance and some intimate superintendence, but this
should be conducted in their interests and not in the interest of
the mandatory." Lloyd George asked that the question be treated
together with the Italian question. The French were not willing
to make any concessions to Italy in Africa, yet the British had
done so and had also made them to France in that region. This
should be considered together with the Syrian question. Wilson
merely rejoined that, as far as he was concerned, the Italians could
have a mandate over any area where the inhabitants asked for an
Italian mandate. This attitude ended, as it was intended to end,
all discussion of the Syrian question in the Council of Four based
on previous Anglo-French agreements.[25] At this point, too, the
German Treaty had resumed its position as the focus of attention
of the Conference. The scene of Middle Eastern matters shifted
to the Middle East itself.

3.

The decisions of the Council relating to Turkey had been
predicated on the assumption that Turkey was completely at the
disposal of the Allies. Superficially, the Council had good reason
to suppose this to be true. Turkey had been badly defeated in the
field and the Sultan and his government were completely subservient to the Armistice Commission in Constantinople. But the
Allied occupation forces controlled very little of Anatolia; almost
the whole of the interior of this region had never seen an Allied
soldier, and few of the people had any concept of the magnitude
of the defeat of the Ottoman Empire. Before the end of 1918
groups to defend the Turkish homeland were already being organized, notably in Smyrna and Thrace, and throughout the winter
more were established, particularly in the eastern provinces. The
Commander of the Turkish forces in the east refused to de-

[25] *Ibid.*, pp. 807–12.

mobilize his troops and, on March 3, 1919, the several " Societies for the Defense of Rights " in the eastern provinces, with the active support of the eastern army, combined to form the Association for the Defense of the Rights of Eastern Anatolia, with headquarters in Erzurum.

Shortly after the establishment of the American Commission at Constantinople, Lewis Heck, the American Commissioner, reported on conditions in the interior to the American delegation at the Peace Conference, on January 20, 1919. He said that the Turks of the interior were as arrogant as ever towards the Christians, particularly to the Greeks and Armenians returning to their homes after deportation; courts martial of Turkish officials responsible for massacres of Christians were a farce, he added, and suggested that the Allies extend the area of occupation to bring about a better state of affairs in Turkey.[26] During March reports of increasing disorder in Anatolia reached Paris and, on March 23, the American Commission at Constantinople, replying to a request from the American delegation for information, cabled that only very limited news about conditions in the interior was available due to the lack of military and consular agents there. However, such information as was coming into Constantinople indicated that there was considerable disorder in almost all of Turkey outside the cities and larger towns. The central government was weak and could not maintain order in case of serious trouble, such as might occur if the decisions of the Peace Conference displeased the local people. It was suggested that consuls should return to their former posts; at least consulates should be reopened at Smyrna, Sivas, Adana, and Aleppo.[27]

A month later, Constantinople reported that the Sultan had sent delegations into the interior to allay party and racial strife. Again it was emphasized that the government had little control in Anatolia; the Committee of Union and Progress was the principal political force there, and the country was full of armed men, demobilized soldiers who had been sent home with their rifles and ammunition. More men and munitions were needed in Turkey if the Allies and Associated Powers were to maintain control there,

[26] Despatch 42 from Constantinople to Peace Mission, January 20, 1919; Peace Conference files, 867.00/59.

[27] Telegram 39A from Constantinople to Peace Mission, March 23, 1919; Peace Conference files, 867.00/126.

the cable went on, and if Turkey were partitioned by the Peace Conference, critical times were ahead; the most serious defect in Allied organization was lack of unity and jealousy.[28] The State Department asked for more information on the Sultan's delegation and on Allied jealousies.[29] On May 8 Constantinople replied that the delegations were sent by the Grand Vizier in response to Allied complaints of the " intolerable " situation in the interior. As for relations between the Allies, they were in such a state as to encourage the disorders of which they complained. The inter-Allied council of control was quite ineffective; what was needed was a supreme Allied head appointed by the Peace Conference, a man of the calibre of General Allenby. The French and the British were at loggerheads. The British actually conquered Turkey and were thus the first in the field and assumed control of affairs. The French General D'Esperey was appointed Allied Commander in the Constantinople region; he was supposed to confine his activities to military matters but had tried to assert himself in political and other affairs. The British ignored him as much as possible and went ahead with their own plans. They were interested principally in trade advantages in Turkey and hoped to persuade the United States to take over political control. France on the other hand hoped to get the mandate for Turkey. Distrust between the two had been increased by events in southern Russia. The Italians were not active in Constantinople but were " perniciously so " in Southern Anatolia; the Greeks were active in the capitol and at Smyrna. The United States had so far been unaffected by these international jealousies, though the French had tried to impose French officers on American relief parties working in the interior so as to give the impression they were working under French auspices; they had not succeeded. In short, the cable concluded, the situation in Turkey was sufficiently unsatisfactory to warrant its full discussion by the Big Four in Paris.[30]

It is not clear how much of this information on conditions in Turkey reached the President; the record indicates that it was very little, if any. Wilson had isolated himself from his colleagues more and more since his return from the United States. The diaries of Lansing and House are full of complaints that Wilson is ignoring them and that they are not getting any information on what is going on in the Council of Four. General Bliss made arrangements with his British colleague General Sackville-West to receive reports on the Council of Four; House got his information from Sir William Wiseman. The American experts on Turkish affairs complained bitterly that their recommendations were being brushed aside. A few days after the Greeks landed at Smyrna, the experts, Magie and Westermann, wrote to Wilson warning him against taking the advice of the Commission on Greek Claims in Asia Minor; the American members were completely ignored, they said, and the recommendations of the Commission reflected almost exclusively the opinions of Premier Venizelos and the British experts.[31] The feeling among all the American delegation against giving Smyrna to the Greeks was so strong that Wilson agreed to discuss Turkish affairs with Westermann and Magie. On May 22, he called them in and went over the discussions in the Council of Four relating to Turkey with them.[32] Whether or not they succeeded in persuading the President to reverse his policy on giving Smyrna to the Greeks is not known, but in any case it was too late; the Greeks had already landed.

4.

On the night of May 14–15, 1919, Greek troops were disembarked at Smyrna under the protection of British, French, and Greek warships; the American squadron which had been sent to observe the Italians was still in the port, but took no part in the operations. The Greek forces occupied the city and immediately began to advance as far into Anatolia as they found possible. Thus was begun more than three years of bitter warfare and thus were laid the foundations of the Turkish Republic. For some days after the landings at Smyrna there was an ominous quiet in Turkey. Then the American Commission in Turkey reported receiving numerous telegrams from the interior protesting

[31] Memorandum, May 22, 1919; Peace Conference files, 185.5136/31. Magie and Westermann sent a memorandum to Wilson, elaborating on their remarks, on May 28; 185.5136/31.
[32] Wilson Papers, Series VIII A, Box 50; letter, May 21, 1919.

against the occupation of Smyrna. Many of them referred to the
Fourteen Points and the principles laid down by President Wilson;
others warned that Smyrna was Turkish and that everything would
be done to keep it so. Some threatened war to the death rather
than submission to Greek or Italian rule.

During the next week the chorus of protests rose. The Cabinet
resigned. Indignation meetings were held in the major cities and
particularly in Constantinople, where the government took vigorous measures, under the prompting of the Allied control commission, to suppress them; the methods used did nothing to increase
the popularity of the government.[33] Prominent Turks sent ap-
peals to President Wilson to preserve Smyrna.[34] On May 25 a
delegation of three members of the Cabinet, including the President of the Council, called at the American Commission and asked
that President Wilson and the American Peace Commission at
Paris personally see to it that Allied officers be detailed to accom-
pany the Greek forces on the Smyrna front to observe their conduct and to make sure that Greek " brigands " with the Greek
Army (presumably Greek irregulars operating with the army)
be sent to the rear.[35] At a special conference at the American
Commission on May 31, Djavid Pasha, Chief of Staff; Mahmud
Pasha an ex-general; and Izzet Pasha, who had been Grand Vizier
at the time of the armistice, asked for an American mandate for
all of Turkey, and assured the Commissioner that the United
States could rely on the support of the Turkish Army.[36]

The information on events in Turkey sent by the American
Commission at Constantinople did not reflect all that was happening in Anatolia; it had few sources there and the news that
did come through was confusing and full of wild rumors. It
bore, to be sure, evidence that Anatolia was in turmoil, but the
most important fact of the time escaped American notice for
some six weeks. It was not until July 1 that Constantinople reported the emergence of Mustafa Kemal as the leader of what

[33] Telegram 410 from Constantinople, May 18, 1919; 763.72119/5049. Telegram 70 from Constantinople via Paris, May 18; telegram 75, May 20; telegram
78, May 21; 867.00/876, 867.00/877, 867.00/878, etc.

[34] Telegram 474 from Constantinople to Peace Mission, May 20, 1919; Peace
Conference files, 867.00/198.

[35] Telegram 83 from Constantinople, May 25, 1919; 763.72119/5135.

[36] Telegram 611 from Constantinople to Peace Mission, May 31, 1919; Peace
Conference files, 867.01/39.

it had been calling the C. U. P. agitation in Anatolia. Four days after the Smyrna landings, Mustafa Kemal Pasha had landed at Samsun to take up his position as Inspector-General of the Ninth Army; he had been given this appointment by the Sultan as a means of getting him out of the capital, where his presence as the only Turkish General to come out of the war undefeated might serve as a rallying point for those Turks who felt that the present government went too far in co-operating with the victors.[37]

No sooner had he landed, however, than he began to prepare the ground for the organization of the Turkish people against the dismemberment of their homeland. He organized the defense societies into a co-ordinated whole and, together with Kazim Karabekir, Commander of the Turkish force at Erzurum (who had told Mustafa in April of his intention to use the army in the eastern provinces as a focus of national resistance) soon had the civil and military authorities of Eastern Anatolia organized into an effective nationalist government. In June he sent a circular telegram to certain civil and military authorities in Anatolia, who he knew were in sympathy with his program, stating the aims of his movement; these were the rousing of the Turkish people to protect the independence and integrity of the nation which was in danger from the Allies and from the incapacity of the central government to protect the nation; the only hope for the nation was the will and resolution of the people to resist. That the voice of the people might be heard a national congress must be called, free from the influence the Allies exercised in Constantinople, to state to the world the rights of Turkey. The congress was to be held in Sivas, "the safest place in Turkey for this purpose," whither each district was to send delegates secretly. A similar telegram was sent to the army commander at Adrianople, with the addition of encouraging words of the unity of Anatolia in

---

[37] The best account of the history of Turkey in these times is *A Speech Delivered by Ghazi Mustapha Kemal* (Leipzig, 1929). While it is certainly one sided, it is not inaccurate and gives the flavor of the time as no other source can. The most complete of western sources is the chronology compiled by G. Jäschke and published originally in *Die Welt des Islams*, vol. 10; a condensed version, prepared by E. Pritsch, was published as *Die Türkei seit dem Weltkriege; Geschichtskalender, 1918–1928* (Berlin, 1929). Arnold J. Toynbee, *The Western Question in Greece and Turkey* (2nd ed.; London, 1923), is a vivid personal account. A good modern summary is Bernard Lewis, *The Emergence of Modern Turkey* (London, 1961), chap. VIII. Correspondence between London and British officials in Turkey is printed in *British Documents*, Series I, IV, 654 ff., *passim*; and vol. XIII.

facing the threat to the existence of Turkey. A preliminary congress of delegates from the eastern provinces assembled at Erzurum on the invitation of Kazim Karabekir. It convened on July 23 under the chairmanship of Mustafa Kemal. While the congress was in session Kazim received orders to arrest Mustafa; they were not carried out.

Gradually the pattern of the Turkish reaction to the Smyrna landings became less obscure as the violence of the national feeling expressed itself in unmistakable terms. In the latter part of May the Commission reported that it was not at all certain that the " national bloc " could not organize a plot to overthrow the government in spite of the presence of Allied warships at Constantinople; the " Unionists " had ample arms stolen from government depots while the government had no funds to support an adequate military operation, and thus control over the Nationalists depended entirely on Allied strength in Turkey. In early June the Commission cabled that conditions in the interior were grave and preparations for armed conflict with the Greeks were proceeding rapidly; the government was unable to control these manifestations since its influence did not reach into the interior. Moreover, the Nationalists were not only better organized than the government but to some extent at least truly represented the country. On June 10 Paris was informed that a serious situation had arisen in the Marsovan-Sivas district, where Turkish and Kurdish troops were openly assembling and were being drilled by Turkish officers; a similar situation existed between Trebizond and Erzurum.[38] (Later in the month the government sent instructions, which were ignored, to all provincial authorities to cease the organization of volunteer militia groups.)

By the end of June the pattern of events had clarified itself considerably to the American Commission. On July 1 it reported that it was " fairly well established " that Mustafa Kemal Pasha and Raouf Bey had surrounded themselves with an army and established a military government at Amasia in the heart of Anatolia; they did not recognize the present government but were loyal to the Sultan and claimed that their only aim was to fight Greek infiltration. Both men were popular, noted the Commission, Mustafa Kemal being famous as the Turkish commander at the

[38] See Peace Conference file 867.00.

Dardanelles and Raouf as the captain of the cruiser *Hamadieh* during the Balkan wars. The government was "lamentably weak" against this new development.[39] Throughout July the cables came in to the State Department and the Peace Commission describing the rapid increase in the strength of Mustafa Kemal and his "insurgent" movement. On July 3 Constantinople cabled that the British High Commissioner had demanded the recall of Mustafa Kemal, but, said the Commission, it was doubtful that the government had the power to enforce any such order.[40] On July 7 it reported that Mustafa Kemal had been summoned to Constantinople but that he was unlikely to go as he had defied the government too often. He was rumored to be arranging a so-called National Assembly at Sivas. The Commission said that one question was troubling the Turks—was it true that France, Britain, and Italy had asked the United States to accept a mandate in Turkey; if the latter were true, the Sivas assembly would ask that the United States take the mandate for all of Turkey. Would the Department therefore send information on American mandate plans.[41]

The State Department replied that it was not in a position to furnish the Commission with this information, and added a note of caution that while the Commission was expected to report all significant developments, "you should scrupulously avoid advising [the] Turks relative to their political plans or expressing to them any opinion in regard to mandates." [42] The Commission, in acknowledging this on July 21, added the information that the Allied high commissioners were urging the government to "extirpate" the Nationalist movement, but there was little chance that it could be done. Mustafa Kemal had already resigned from the army and was cutting himself off more and more from Constantinople. The conference at Sivas would probably meet on July 23 and would in all likelihood demand elections and a new cabinet.[43] (It actually met at Erzurum.) A week later it was reported that the call for elections had become so widespread that the Grand Vizier had been forced to order them in order to hold his Cabinet

[39] Telegram 111 from Constantinople, July 1, 1919; 867.00/892.
[40] Telegram 112 from Constantinople, July 3, 1919; 763.72/13181.
[41] Telegram 119 from Constantinople, July 7, 1919; 867.00/895.
[42] Telegram 159 to Constantinople, July 18, 1919; 867.00/895.
[43] Telegram 125 from Constantinople, July 21, 1919; 867.00/896.

together. However, to gain time, the old election law was to be reinstated so that no results would be published for four months, and in the meantime it was hoped that the Nationalist movement could be brought under control by increasing the stringency of martial law and apprehending Mustafa Kemal and Raouf.[44]

On August 1 the Turkish Cabinet held a prolonged meeting which resulted in an order being issued to the Valis of all the provinces where the Nationalist movement was active for the arrest of Mustafa and Raouf. The Commission told Washington it was done under British pressure, and it was rumored the Cabinet had decided to ask for Allied assistance in case the Nationalist movement grew into a full-fledged insurrection in Anatolia. However, the Commission said, it was of the opinion that the warrant for the arrest of the two Nationalist leaders would be a dead letter since they enjoyed the full support of all of the local officials charged with the execution of the warrant. In any case, said the cable, Mustafa was a favorite of the Sultan whom he always excluded from his criticisms of the government, placing the blame exclusively on the Cabinet for " handing over the country to the foreigners." [45]

Thus far the Commission had been content to report on events and conditions in Turkey, rather than attempt to evaluate and analyze them; this was not due to lack of initiative on its part but because at the time a new head of the mission in Turkey had been appointed. This was Admiral Bristol, Commander of American Naval Forces in the Levant. His appointment had been urged by the American community in Turkey, and by the American Commissioner, Ravndal, who had succeeded Heck, in order that the United States might be represented by an official equal in status to the Allied high commissioners. They out-ranked by a considerable degree the American Commissioner and Bristol would be in a better position to maintain American interests.[46] Bristol's first analysis was sent in a cable on July 23. Its main point was that the United States was running great danger of becoming a tool in the hands of the Allies and that if the United States took a mandate for Armenia it would in effect be condon-

---

[44] Telegram 134 from Constantinople, July 31, 1919; 867.00/904.

[45] Telegrams 1171 and 1174 from Constantinople to Peace Mission, August 2, 1919; Peace Conference files, 867.00/342 and 343.

[46] On Bristol's appointment, see *Foreign Relations*, 1919, II, 810–13.

ing the partition of Turkey among the Allies. This telegram was expanded in a despatch sent to Paris at about the same time. He " beseeched " that all the facts be studied before the United States involved itself more deeply in Allied plans for Turkey. He said that Britain intended to take all of Mesopotamia, Arabia, and Palestine; the oil fields in Mesopotamia were perhaps the richest in the world and Britain was willing to give up Baku to the Italians in order to concentrate on them; the British, he said, were taking every possible step to monopolize Mesopotamian oil and to keep out all other countries. They believed that Russia would come out of the Revolution a great deal stronger than before the war and would constitute a correspondingly greater threat to the British position in the Middle East; they were therefore taking great care to make friends in the Caucasus and were even interfering with American relief operations in order that their influence there might not be " diluted." British policy with respect to the United States was to encourage it to take a mandate in the Caucasus and over Armenia to provide a buffer against Russia, in place of Turkey. He said if an American mandate were established in Turkey it would mean American agreement to the partition of Turkey and would destroy American objections to the imperialist designs of the Allies; Britain would then be able to take Mesopotamia and France, Syria, without a voice being raised in protest. The only possible solution to the Turkish problem was for all of the former Ottoman Empire to be constituted a single mandate and, after a period of tutelage, the several areas that wished for independence should have an opportunity for self-determination; at the moment they were incapable of making a choice as they were too ignorant and uneducated.[47] Subsequent reports by the Admiral were in much the same vein. They contributed not a little to the atmosphere of suspicion and rivalry that was to grow between the American and Allied representatives in Turkey, even though they were not always taken at their face value in Washington.

5.

Immediately after the Greeks landed at Smyrna, reports began to come in to Constantinople not only of the normal anti-Christian

[47] Telegram 3361 from Paris, July 28, 1919; 763.72119/5860.

attacks of the Turks but also of the misbehavior and cruelty of the Greek troops. The Commission reported on May 18 that there had been looting in the city by the Greeks; they were making many arrests and had killed some Turks in street fighting.[48] As the army moved inland, Greek atrocities continued and the evidence of them increased in credibility and authenticity. As already mentioned, a delegation of three members of the Turkish Cabinet, including the President of the Council, called at the American mission and begged that President Wilson personally see to it that Allied officers be detailed to the Greek forces as observers. By the middle of June, Westermann was recording in a memorandum that according to reports from senior officials, such as the commanders of American warships at Smyrna and the Swedish Consul there, as well as prominent American residents of the city, the Greek Army and Greek officials in Smyrna had been acting in such a manner there as to place them in the same class of " semibarbarity " as the Turks.[49] A month later the French, British, and Italian delegates at Smyrna sent identical notes to their respective high commissioners in Constantinople on the gravity of the situation caused by the Greek occupation of the Aidin vilayet. The Allied delegates stated that the Greeks were not following the orders of the Allied Commander at Smyrna, who, as Allied Commander-in-Chief of the Smyrna operation, was technically in command of the Greek forces; in fact, Greek field officers ignored the orders of their own commanders and acted completely independently. As a result there had been almost no control exercised over the troops in the field and none at all over the irregular forces operating in the front and flanks of the army. They had perpetrated massacres of the Turkish population, engaged in simple banditry, and looted whenever possible. It was recommended that the whole Greek force be recalled to the Smyrna district. In reporting this to Washington, the American Commission stated that it concurred in the report of events and in the recommendations.[50]

The receipt of a letter of protest against the Greek atrocities

[48] Telegram 435 from Constantinople to Peace Mission, May 18, 1919; Peace Conference files, 867.00/192.

[49] Memorandum, Westermann to C. A. Herter, June 10, 1919; Peace Conference files, 867.01/41.

[50] Telegram from Smyrna, July 12, 1919; 763.72/13206.

sent by the Shaikh-ul-Islam to the Peace Conference, together with
the report of the Allied delegates at Smyrna, brought the matter
to the attention of the Council of the Heads of Delegations, which
had replaced the Council of Four as the chief body of the Peace
Conference after the Treaty of Versailles had been signed. On
July 18 Clemenceau proposed the formation of a Commission of
Inquiry to investigate the charges against the Greek forces. Henry
White, the American delegate, stated that, while he approved in
principle of the Commission, he would have to refer to Washington for a decision on the inclusion of an American member.[51]
Constantinople was not informed, however, and when the Allied
high commissioners asked the American Commission there to
join them in sending a note to the Turkish government informing
it that a Commission of Inquiry had been appointed, the American
Commissioner had to tell them that he had no instructions and
would have to decline, though he had been told that the Commission of Inquiry was to include an American officer. After some
further confusion in the Department of State (all of the officers
of which had not been informed of the President's appointment
of Bristol to the Commission of Inquiry), Bristol himself was
told of his appointment and his instructions and commission were
duly sent to him.

After an investigation lasting several months, the Commission
of Inquiry reported to the Council on October 14, though the report did not reach the Council until November 8. The report
confirmed the Greek atrocities and also took note of certain acts
of reprisal taken by the Turks. The main cause of the outbreaks
had been religious hatred, the Commission found; the initial disorders had been due to the actions of the Greek High Command,
and this had been in fact acknowledged by the Greek government
by its punishment of the Greek officers responsible. The Turkish
authorities in Smyrna were also to some degree responsible. The
events in the interior following the extension of the occupation
were the responsibility of the Greek government because it did
not follow the instructions of the Supreme Council in settling the
limits of the occupation and communicating these limits to the
army in the field; because it permitted armed civilians to accom-
pany the army; and because Greek officers failed to prevent out-

---

[51] *Foreign Relations*, Paris Peace Conference, VII, 191–92. The text of the letter
of the Shaikh-ul-Islam is on p. 200.

rages and massacres, and the government did nothing to see that these officers obeyed orders. The report noted that what had originated as a plan for the maintenance of order had turned into an apparent annexation of the area. The Greeks were incapable of performing the task allotted them and should be withdrawn and replaced by an Allied force with some Greek detachments (if it were felt necessary to save the face of the Greeks); but Greek forces should not be permitted to come into contact with Turkish national forces operating in the region. The Commission recommended that as soon as this new occupation policy came into effect, Turkey should reorganize its *gendarmerie* under Allied officers and at the same time re-establish civil administration in place of martial law.[52] In cabling a summary of the report to the Department of State, Polk commented that it constituted " a weighty and damaging indictment" of the Venizelos Government.[53]

6.

On August 5 Constantinople reported that rumors of the increasingly threatening attitude of Mustafa Kemal were spreading; these "alleged patriots," said the High Commission, were said to be planning new massacres of Armenians in the eastern districts as a prelude to a drive to the Caspian where Muslim control was to be re-established. On the other hand, the friends of the Nationalists in Constantinople, who included most of the politicians outside the Cabinet and most of the journalists, maintained that the movement was not directed against Christians, nor even primarily against the Greeks, but against the weak and reactionary government.[54] On August 14 the High Commission cabled that the situation was reaching a crisis. All Anatolia not occupied by the Allies appeared to be in open rebellion against the government, whose authority was confined to a limited area around the capital. In some districts the "rebels" were installing their own local officials. The Allied high commissioners in Turkey might find themselves in the "very difficult" position of either defending a

[52] *Ibid.*, IX, 36–44. The Commission's Report is on p. 44.
[53] Telegram 5066 from Paris, November 7, 1919; 763.72119/7662.
[54] Telegram 142 from Constantinople, August 5, 1919; 867.00/907.

government discredited by its own people or of treating with Mustafa Kemal, added the Commission.[55]

Coupled with the news that the British were planning to withdraw their troops from the Caucasus, thus leaving the Armenians to the mercies of the Muslims, the increasing violence in Anatolia caused great concern among Americans for the fate of the Armenians. On August 16 a telegram was sent to Admiral Bristol stating that the " President desires [the] Turkish authorities to be warned " that if they did not take " immediate and efficacious measures " to prevent massacres of Armenians in the Caucasus and elsewhere, all support for the maintenance of Turkish sovereignty over the Turkish portions of the Ottoman Empire promised in the Fourteen Points would be withdrawn, and the " absolute dissolution " of the Ottoman Empire with the " complete alteration of the terms of peace " might result. Bristol was to say to the Turks, if they claimed they could not control the situation, that if they expected to exercise sovereignty over any part of the Empire, they should demonstrate that they could and would prevent atrocities by their co-nationals and co-religionists; therefore, no excuse would be accepted.[56]

Bristol reported, on August 24, that the President's message had been given informally to the Grand Vizier, and the formal transmission made through the Swedish Embassy. The Grand Vizier had said that the government had very few troops, and as the Allies would not allow more to be recruited it was very difficult to restore order. He also said that he realized that a fresh outbreak of anti-Christian violence would be a " calamity " for Turkey, and instructions had been sent on these lines to all provincial governors.[57] In the formal Turkish reply to the President, it was stated that the Imperial government was fully aware of its duty to protect its citizens, but that Turkey had just been through a devastating war which had completely disrupted the administrative machinery of the government, and with the Turkish Army disbanded by the Allies there were far too few troops left to

[55] Telegram 152 from Constantinople, August 14, 1919; 867.00/908.

[56] Telegram, unnumbered, to Paris, August 16, 1919; 763.72119/6130; on conditions in the Caucasus and British policy there, see *British Documents*, Series I, III, 406 ff., *passim*.

[57] Telegram, unnumbered, from Constantinople, undated, received August 24, 1919; 763.72119/6341.

maintain order. Everything that could be done was being done, however. The message noted that the present difficulties had been the result of the Greek landings at Smyrna; as for the Caucasus, the Imperial government was not responsible for events there as it was not in control of the region. The message closed by asking the President to help the Imperial government accomplish its task by permitting it to recruit more troops and by ending the Greek occupation of Smyrna.[58]

In the meantime, however, the Grand Vizier had communicated the President's message to the British and French high commissioners, carefully drawing their attention to the fact that the United States had acted unilaterally. He could not help remarking, he said, that America, a country which had not been at war with Turkey and did not sign the armistice, gave this imperative notification separately and without participation on the part of the Allied Powers. The French High Commissioner immediately cabled Paris and two days later, on August 25, Clemenceau raised the matter in the Council of the Heads of Delegations. He said that one Power could not dictate the terms of the Peace with Turkey, and entered a protest against the American action. As to saving the Armenians, he did not know what could be done. There were no British or American troops available and France was not permitted by Britain to send troops to Asia Minor or " to play any part in Asia Minor." The Turks were powerless, and he did not see where help could come from. Balfour asked him whether, but for British opposition, he would send troops to prevent massacres. Clemenceau replied that he was not making any commitments, though he would consider the matter. After some prodding by Balfour, he agreed to inquire of the French military authorities if troops could be sent. At the end of the discussion on the President's letter to the Sultan, it was agreed that no pressure should be brought on the Sultan by any Power acting alone.[59]

Polk, the American representative on the Council, told Washington that he had explained to the French that the President was stating the views of the American government alone and did not purport to be acting for all the Allied and Associated Powers. Two days after the discussion in the Council, Polk went on, Clemenceau

[58] Telegram 157 from Constantinople, August 25, 1919; 867.00/914.
[59] *Foreign Relations*, Paris Peace Conference, VIII, 839–40.

said that France would send 10,000 men to Armenia; this was rather an attempt to get a foothold in Asia Minor, Polk thought, than an effort to help the Armenians. He had asked Balfour later whether Britain would agree to the " palpable attempt " of France to gain control of the Caucasus. Balfour replied that since the British were withdrawing, and the United States could not send troops, they could not very well object.[60]

7.

Throughout the summer and autumn of 1919, the Nationalist movement under Mustafa Kemal gathered strength. The Congress of Erzurum continued its sessions until August 17; its most important accomplishment was the drafting of a declaration of the rights of Turkey and its people, which formed the basis for subsequent manifestoes adopted by the Sivas Congress and ultimately by the Ottoman Parliament. On September 4, the National Congress opened at Sivas with delegates from all over Turkey. Mustafa Kemal was again elected chairman. The decisions of the Erzurum Congress calling for national independence and the integrity of Turkey were adopted and made more specific; the loyalty of the people to the Sultan-Caliph was affirmed, but the government was denounced as a gang of traitors and criminals, its acts without force, and to whom no obedience was due from patriotic Turks. A resolution calling for an American mandate for all of Turkey was heavily defeated, though the Congress did send a telegram to the United States Senate, inviting it to send a delegation to Turkey to see for itself the conditions there and to form its own judgment as to the truth of the lies and rumors being circulated about massacres of Christians and also about the nature of the Nationalist movement itself.[61] In October the Nationalists had established themselves so firmly in the country that the government was forced to open negotiations with Kemal which ended in the practical recognition of the Nationalists by the government and its acceptance of the principles of the Nationalist program. New elections were called under pressure from Kemal, and in January, 1920, the new Parliament met with a

[60] *Ibid.*, 1919, II, 838–39.   [61] 763.72119/7533.

majority of Nationalists. The National Pact, embodying the national principles enunciated at the Erzurum and Sivas congresses was passed by the Parliament, and it appeared that the supine and ineffective cabinets of the preceding year had given way to a firm and patriotic government that could meet the Allies on an equal footing and not as mere tools of the occupying powers.

The information on these events relayed by the High Commission in Constantinople to Washington and Paris varied in value; Admiral Bristol was extremely suspicious of Allied policy in Turkey (the normal course of international politics seemed to have been something of a shock to him) and this suspicion colored his reports; he seemed not to be able to separate the wheat from the chaff among the many rumors he reported to Washington, and he took at face value many of the pro-American statements made to him by Turks in official positions. On August 14 the High Commission reported that Mustafa Kemal's party had held a preliminary congress at Erzurum which had demanded that Turkey not be dismembered. This did not mean that it opposed a mandate, said the report, but rather wanted a single mandatory for all of Turkey, though they would prefer none at all; Mustafa Kemal had stated in private letters to his supporters in Constantinople that he preferred an American mandate. In the meantime, he hoped by temporizing to gain control of Turkey and establish a strong government. The High Commission believed that the delay in settling the Turkish treaty was working in Mustafa's favor.[62]

Later cables had much to say of British policy with respect to the Nationalist movement. One said that there was good circumstantial evidence that the British were supporting Kemal, since his movement was the first sign of political strength in Turkey since the Armistice, while the Constantinople government was incompetent and of no significance. The British were disgusted with it and were seeking to establish relations with Kemal, who had 20,000 men under him as well as large numbers of irregulars.[63] A cable sent a day later said that the British authorities in Constantinople were apparently taking a firm stand against the Kem-

[62] Telegram 150 from Constantinople, August 14, 1919; Peace Conference files 867.00/363.
[63] Telegram 1357 from Constantinople to Peace Mission, August 21, 1919; Peace Conference files, 867.00/368.

alists, and this might lead to serious consequences. The rumors
of a British approach to Kemal were again mentioned, with the
addition of a further rumor that the British were merely making
a show of opposition to Kemal while secretly supporting him.[64]
Some days later another cable reported that rumors were " rife "
that Britain was contemplating active intervention in Turkey, that
the Nationalists deported to Malta in the Spring had been persuaded to swing the Nationalist movement to a British mandate
and were being released and sent back to Turkey to work on the
Kemalists, and that Britain and Turkey were about to sign a treaty
similar to that just negotiated with Persia; while these rumors
were not trustworthy, the cable added, they did indicate the trend
of thinking in Constantinople.[65]

On August 30 Senator Ahmad Riza, a representative of the
Council of National Defense, called at the High Commission.
He told Ravndal that he was hoping to leave for Switzerland or
Italy in the near future to work openly for an American mandate
for Turkey. He said that Britain was working very hard to obtain
support for a British mandate and that the Sultan was in league
with them; he believed that there was actually a secret agreement
between the British and the Sultan to this end. He called the
present ascendancy a new form of German imperialism and said
the Nationalist program was solely aimed at preserving Turkey
from a repetition of the years before and during the war. The
Commission cabled the Department a report on this interview
adding that in view of British ambitions in Turkey and the
inability of France to counteract them, the United States could
not remain indifferent to the situation.[66] The Department was
less worried about British ambitions and about their implications
for American policy, and sent instructions to take no action in
the matter and to refrain from taking sides or appearing friendly
with any Turkish party; the Commission was reminded that it
had already been instructed to " scrupulously avoid advising Turks
or expressing any opinion " on the question of the Turkish
mandate.[67]

When the Sivas Congress opened, Bristol was convinced that

[64] Telegram 165 from Constantinople, August 22, 1919; 763.72119/913.

[65] Telegram 160 from Constantinople, August 26, 1919; 867.00/915.

[66] Telegram 4 from Constantinople, August 30, 1919; 763.72119/6452.

[67] Telegram, unnumbered, to Constantinople, September 4, 1919; 763.72119/6452.

the majority of the Nationalists wanted an American mandate; he had been told so many times in Constantinople by the local Nationalists, and he had not yet discovered that this was standard political practice among the Turks, to set one power against the other. He reported that the British and French had apparently abandoned the whole idea of a mandate for Turkey because of the support in Turkey for an American mandate, and in order to thwart the pro-American feeling had been talking of independence under Allied auspices.[68] Later he cabled that the Sivas Congress "unanimously" wanted an American mandate, but the Allies were spreading the rumor that the Congress did not want any mandate at all, and had adopted the Erzurum resolutions only because the Nationalists had not received any American encouragement or any assurance that, if they asked for an American mandate, the United States would accept the offer. He said that if the United States would indicate that it would accept the mandate for Turkey, the Congress would issue a proclamation to the whole country stating that Turkey was not capable of proceeding without assistance and that the Congress had asked for American aid.[69]

The cables from Constantinople in September and October were full of the growing strength and influence of the Nationalist movement, together with conflicting rumors of the part played by Britain and the other Allies in its success; this was attributed either to actual support of the Nationalist movement or to the conflicting ambitions and jealousies of the Powers.[70] On October 2 the High Commission received a memorandum from the Sivas Congress stating the position of the Nationalist movement and its attitude toward the Constantinople government. The Cabinet was nothing more than a collection of traitors and rogues, said the memorandum, who were completely undeserving of the allegiance of patriotic Turks; the Congress would therefore sever all allegiance to it. It was thus also necessary that new elections be held to place in power a government representative of the people; in the meantime the Nationalist movement would maintain order. It was hoped that the Powers would approve of the actions of the Congress (but the tone of the memo-

[68] Telegram 18 from Constantinople, September 10, 1919; 763.72119/6696.
[69] Telegram 16 from Constantinople, September 12, 1919; 763.72119/6973.
[70] These are to be found in 763.72119/6700 ff., and 867.00/900 ff.

randum indicated that it would not affect the Nationalist program if they did not).[71]

On October 31, a little later than a week after representatives of the government and the Nationalists had met at Amasia and come to an understanding that virtually amounted to recognition of the Nationalists, the High Commission cabled that the Nationalists were still strengthening their hold on the country (it apparently did not know of the Amasia meeting since it did not report it) and that the elections, which would now certainly be held, would result in an overwhelming majority for the Nationalists and a Cabinet under either Tewfik or Izzet Pasha. Opposition to the Nationalists, under British encouragement, was growing stronger, said the report; the British were planning to create as much trouble as they could for the Nationalists before the election, thus opening the way for an enlarged area of occupation by British troops. The Sultan was completely committed to the British but the Nationalists, backed now by the Crown Prince, were certain of success in the elections and were in no mood to yield.[72] On the same day Bristol cabled a separate report; he said that attempts to prevent new elections by bribery and the plots to engineer a coup had failed, but, by intrigue, the Christian population and the anti-Nationalist element had been persuaded not to participate in the elections, thus they would not properly represent Turkish feeling. The anti-Nationalists, in any case, were belittling the significance of any election before the terms of the peace treaty were known.[73]

[71] Telegram 29 from Constantinople, undated, received October 3, 1919; 867.00/942.

[72] Telegram 49 from Constantinople, undated, received October 31, 1919; 867.00/980.

[73] Telegram from Constantinople, unnumbered and undated, received October 31, 1919; 867.00/981.

CHAPTER VII

THE BREAKDOWN OF WILSON'S CONFERENCE POLICY

1.

The two preceding chapters have described Wilson's attempts in the Council to establish and preserve the positions of the United States in the Eastern settlement, and the parallel attempts of the other parties to the settlement—the British, French, Greeks, and Turks with their already well-established claims—to improve their respective bargaining positions vis-à-vis one another and the United States by direct action in the field. It was difficult enough for the United States to control this movement before the signing of the Treaty of Versailles on June 28, 1919, when the possibility of the United States refusing to sign the Treaty put a limit on the extent to which the Allied Powers could pursue their ambitions and on the choice of methods used; the Treaty of Guarantee, which was not signed until June 28, was an additional check on France. But after the United States had, as the Allies thought, committed itself to the settlement with Germany by signing the Versailles treaty and the Treaty of Guarantee, these restraints on the Allies were removed. This new freedom soon appeared at the Council table and in the Allies' actions in the Middle East, and the United States found that control of the situation was slipping rapidly from its hands.

With the Treaty of Versailles signed, the major work of the Peace Conference was accomplished and the treaties with the lesser Central Powers could now be given the full attention of the Conference. The Turkish treaty was considered to be the least urgent of these treaties. As mentioned in the last chapter, Turkey was thought to be under the complete control of the Allies and, in any case, her problems were of less importance to Europe than those of European states; in addition, the question of mandates and their distribution had still to be settled. Turkish questions, except where they touched on the interests of the great powers, were discussed only when more important matters were not pressing. It was not until May 13 that the actual negotiation of a treaty was mentioned in the Council of Four, and then merely to decide whether the Turks would be invited to Paris to receive the terms of peace or whether they should be met somewhere else. Wilson suggested that, since some of the Allied and associated powers had not been at war with Turkey, a commission should be sent to meet the Turks away from Paris. His own position in the matter, he said, was that, as a member of the League of Nations, the United States would have to guarantee the arrangement. Lloyd George rejoined that he hoped it would be a good deal more than that, for he hoped that the United States would accept a mandate. It was decided that, in view of the pressure on the drafting committee, the Turkish treaty would " not be put in hand just yet." [1] Wilson's position, that the United States while a signatory of the Treaty would not participate in the negotiations with the Turks, was taken also in the various commissions of the Conference, set up to consider details of the several settlements, though American advisers were appointed. This did not mean that the United States would leave a clear field to the Allied Powers; there was every intention of maintaining vigorously the American position vis-à-vis the Allies.

With the approaching completion of their work on the German and Austrian treaties, the commissions began to turn their attention to Turkish matters, and the American members asked the Secretary of the Peace Commission what their part in these proceedings was to be. The question was referred to the President, who replied that they were to act as advisers but not as participants.[2] The same question arose a month later in connection with the appearance of the Turkish delegation before the Conference; liaison committees of Turkish and Allied representatives were set up to facilitate the negotiations and instructions were given

[1] *Foreign Relations*, Paris Peace Conference, V, 588.
[2] Wilson Papers, Series VII A, Box 47; Wilson to J. C. Grew, May 13, 1919. Peace Conference files, 185.5/14.

that there would be no American participation in these commit-tees " since the United States was not at war with Turkey." [3]

The Turks were permitted, as the Germans and Austrians were not, to present their case to the Conference. They had been invited to attend the Conference after the Council of Four had received a request from the Grand Vizier for permission to come to Paris to "enlighten the Conference" on the actual state of affairs in Turkey and on the facts of the Turkish participation in the war on the side of the Central Powers.[4] The matter was pre-sented to the Council by Clemenceau on May 30. Lloyd George supported the proposal, adding that it was not necessary to treat the Turks in the same manner as the Germans. Wilson com-mented that their first object would be to protest against the Smyrna landings, but both Clemenceau and Lloyd George saw no harm in that, and it was decided to grant the application of the Turks.[5] Instructions were accordingly sent to the several high commissioners in Constantinople to communicate the decision of the Conference to the Turkish government.[6] The French han-dling of their part in the transaction gave rise to considerable resentment among the British. Their High Commissioner cabled the Foreign Secretary on June 4 that the French High Commis-sioner, who had received his instructions on June 1, whereas, the British instructions were not sent until June 3, had immediately seen the Grand Vizier privately and had attempted to give the impression that the decision of the Conference to hear the Turks had been due to French pressure; he was carrying on a press cam-paign to this effect, and had "mobilized all the agents, and is employing all the means, at his disposal to start on these lines a campaign of propaganda which he is no longer at any pains to conceal." The American High Commission reported these occur-rences to Paris, saying that the French and British were making " desperate " efforts to control the selection of the Turkish dele-gation to the Conference and the French had tried to make it appear that the invitation was due solely to the good will of France toward Turkey. The British had protested vigorously to

[3] *Foreign Relations*, Paris Peace Conference, XI, 230.
[4] The Turks sent requests to each of the Allied leaders and to Wilson; telegram 619 from Constantinople, May 31, 1919; Peace Conference files, 867.00/228.
[5] *Foreign Relations*, Paris Peace Conference, VI, 116.
[6] *Ibid.*, p. 134.

the French High Commission; the latter had later called on the American High Commission to soothe the feelings of the Americans, though no action had been taken by them in the affair. When the delegates were chosen, the American High Commission reported that they represented a balance between the British and French interests, that is to say, between the members of the Turkish government who were actively pro-British and actively pro-French, respectively.[7]

The Turkish delegation duly arrived in Paris and appeared before the Council of Ten, which had been reconvened on June 17 for the purpose of hearing them. Damad Ferid, the leader of the delegation, spoke for Turkey. He denied that Turkey had any responsibility for the war and placed the blame for Turkey's participation on the machinations of the Germans, particularly referring to the attack on Odessa as solely the work of the German Admiral commanding the *Goeben*, and on the leaders of the Committee for Union and Progress. The Committee and its works had been repudiated by the Turkish nation as the first step in the rehabilitation of the Ottoman people, though they were attempting to regain control of Turkey, as the Bolsheviks were in Russia. He asked the Council not to revenge on the Turkish people the massacres of Christians. This was the work of a few men and should be offset against many centuries when such things had not been done in Turkey. Moreover, the massacres were not solely motivated by religious fanaticism, for many Muslims had also been massacred. He concluded by asking that the Ottoman Empire not be divided but maintained in the *status quo ante bellum* in conformity with the principles of President Wilson.[8]

This statement had no effect on the opinions of the members of the Council. They were in fact contemptuous of what they considered the transparent attempt of the Turks to avoid responsibility, and amazed at their colossal impudence in asking that the Ottoman Empire be maintained. The Council made its formal reply in a memorandum sent a few days later. It rejected the Turks' disclaimer and stated that a people must bear the responsibility for the acts of its government. The record of the Turks in ruling subject peoples made it impossible to accept the claim for

[7] Peace Conference files, 867.00/238 *et seq.*; telegram 666 from Constantinople to Peace Mission, June 4, 1919. See, also, *British Documents*, Series I, XIII, 12.
[8] *Foreign Relations*, Paris Peace Conference, IV, 508–12.

the integrity of the Ottoman Empire, and this position was not affected by any claims that the partition of the Empire would injure the Muslim religion.[9] On June 28, as the major work of the Conference ended with the signing of the Treaty of Versailles, the Turkish delegation was coolly told (in so many words) that it was wasting its time in Paris, since the Conference would not be taking up the treaty of peace with Turkey for some time and (the death blow to the hopes of the Ottoman delegation) it would in any case cover interests other than those of Turkey. It was suggested that the delegation therefore return home.[10]

2.

On June 25 the question of peace with Turkey was raised in the Council of Four by Lloyd George. He said it would be unreasonable to maintain a state of war with Turkey while President Wilson returned to the United States, and suggested that the Council agree to peace terms which would include the future frontiers of Turkey, with the final disposition of the former Turkish territories left until the United States could say whether it would take a mandate. Wilson agreed and proposed that Turkey be stripped of the territory it was to lose, with the Treaty of Peace stipulating that Turkey accept the disposition made of it by the Allied and associated powers. His present view, he said, was that a mandate over Turkey would be a mistake, but that some Power ought to have a " firm hand." Constantinople and the Straits should be left as a neutral strip; it was already in Allied occupation, and the Sultan would be moved out of Constantinople.[11] On the following day the question was discussed again, with the effect of Italian actions in Anatolia forming the chief topic together with the difficulties the Powers would face in forcing the Turks out of Constantinople should the Conference decide to deprive them of the city. No conclusions were reached, though Wilson stated that he could not go back to the United States and tell the Senate that the treaty he was presenting them

[9] *Foreign Relations*, Paris Peace Conference, VI, 688–91. Constantinople cabled on July 1 (telegram 110, 867.00/894) that the Turkish government was " dismayed " at the reply of the Peace Conference to the Turkish statement.

[10] *Ibid.*, p. 729.

[11] *Ibid.*, pp. 675–76.

with re-established peace if Italy were left a free hand. " It would on the contrary be a Treaty preparing war and could not be guaranteed by the Powers." [12]

Discussions continued in the Council, but it was found impossible to settle the problems of Constantinople and of Greek and Italian activities in Anatolia until the United States could state definitely that it would accept a mandate in Turkey, either of Armenia or Constantinople or both. In the first instance, the status of the city would depend on which country controlled it— if the United States, it would be for the purpose of intra-European politics a neutral city, but if one of the European powers were in control, the whole balance of power in the Middle East would be upset and would have to be re-established by a very careful limitation on the nature of the control to be exercised in the city and by a redistribution of control in the rest of the Middle East. In the second instance, until the question of mandates was settled, the question of occupation troops in Anatolia must be left in abeyance, for once a treaty was signed, occupation troops would have to be withdrawn and, unless there was some means of keeping Allied or American control in Armenia vis-à-vis the Turks, the whole country would be overrun. It was formally decided, therefore, that consideration of the Turkish treaty would be postponed until the United States could state whether it would accept a mandate.[13]

3.

Questions affecting Turkey continued to be considered by the Council of the Heads of Delegations, the successor to the Council of Four, after June 28, though the treaty of peace was left in abeyance. These questions were the Greek occupation of Smyrna and the hinterland, the activities of the Italians and Greeks in Anatolia, and the treaty of peace with Bulgaria. The last question touched on Turkish affairs in respect to the boundary of Bulgaria with Turkey, and thus concerned Greek claims to Turkish territory in western Thrace. The other two, insofar as they concerned the work of the Council, continued as they had started in the Council of Four, with the Greeks pushing inland from

[12] *Ibid.*, pp. 711–14.   [13] *Ibid.*, p. 729.

Smyrna, the Italians matching the Greeks in the south, and the Council attempting, half by threat and half by persuasion, to control the rush of events in Turkey. For most of July the American representatives on the Council did not participate actively in the consideration of these questions. Unlike the representatives of the other powers in the Council, neither Henry White nor Lansing had attended the meetings of the Council of Four and were thus not well informed on the background of the various disputes that occupied the attention of the new Council. They were mainly concerned, therefore, with holding the line and preventing the Council from making decisions until the United States could decide the nature of its role in the Eastern settlement, rather than attempting to arrive at solutions. Some things were accomplished. A resident Commissioner, an American, Colonel Haskell, was appointed for Armenia and the Caucasus after the British withdrawal from the Caucasus. The Commission of Inquiry for Smyrna was given an American member.[14] At Paris the American position was preserved, for the time being.

Secretary Lansing aroused the ire of Clemenceau shortly after he took his place as the chief American delegate. On July 3 the Italian delegate, Tittoni, raised the question of coal mines in the area occupied by Italian troops and said that while Italy did not desire to obtain sovereignty over the area of Anatolia it was occupying, it did desire to obtain concessions for certain coal mines at Heraklia and the oil wells at Van. Lansing said he was sympathetic to the Italian desire to secure the coal mines, but that Armenia was too poor to be deprived of her resources and the oil wells at Van should not be taken from her. Clemenceau pointed out that the French had concessions at Heraklia and the Italians were proposing to surround them. Lansing asked Tittoni whether Italy had any coal mines. Tittoni answered that it had none. Lansing then asked Clemenceau what coal mines France had; he replied testily that of course Mr. Lansing knew what coal resources France possessed. Lansing rejoined that under these circumstances Italy should also have coal mines. " Thereupon," the minutes of the meeting record, " M. Clemenceau became somewhat excited and stated very emphatically that he could not bar-

[14] *Ibid.*, VII, 28.

gain away the rights of his people." Later in this meeting the Italians agreed that the Treaty of London should be abandoned as a basis for negotiation on Adriatic questions.[15]

At the Council meeting on July 18 Henry White laid before the Council a telegram from President Wilson which stated that considerable delay might be expected before the United States could commit itself to accepting a mandate and asked " what attitude towards Turkey the Powers propose to take in the mean-time." Clemenceau said that the only attitude the Powers could adopt as far as he knew was one of expectancy. He himself was not, for certain reasons, ready to talk about Asia Minor, and he did not know what the President expected of the Council. White replied that he thought the President was referring to the mainte-nance of order; to which Clemenceau rejoined that the Council would take necessary measures in concert but that he himself could not make any pledges—if the Greeks, Italian, and Turks were fighting, that was not his fault. When White asked if it was Clemenceau's intention to wait until the United States could state whether it could accept a mandate, Clemenceau retorted that he would not wait indefinitely and that at the moment he could not make any statement; the Turkish treaty would be taken up as and when the other work of the Conference permitted, and all he could say to the President's message was that the Council had taken note of it. The President knew " full well " what the diffi-culties were, he added. Balfour hastened to smooth over this impertinence. He agreed that no definite answer could be given; the President was unfortunately prevented by the American Con-stitution from undertaking any responsibility in Turkey at the present time, but meanwhile the Council would try to maintain order.[16] The tone of Clemenceau's remarks on this occasion and on the one related above was symptomatic of his increasing con-fidence in his ability to force matters in the Conference now that the Treaty of Versailles and the Treaty of Guarantee had been signed, and the principal desiderata of the French gained from the United States. Clemenceau also apparently thought that, with

[15] *Ibid.*, pp. 17–18.

[16] *Ibid.*, p. 193. Telegram 2568 to Peace Commission, July 15, 1919; Peace Conference files, 867.01/43.

Wilson gone, his American colleagues on the Council would be more easily handled. But, on the whole, July passed without serious complications for the United States in the Peace Conference.[17]

4.

The month of comparative quiet that followed the conclusion of the major work of the Conference—the Versailles Treaty— was rudely shattered in the beginning of August. On July 29 White cabled the Department of State reporting a conversation with Clemenceau, who had told him that he suspected the Greeks and Italians had come to an agreement on the occupation of western Anatolia. White had then queried Tittoni about the agreement. Tittoni had said that no agreement had been reached, though he and Venizelos were having conversations on the matter and hoped to come to terms. Clemenceau also told White that he was glad that the Turkish treaty was delayed until the question of an American mandate was settled. He was highly suspicious of British designs in Syria, he said; Lloyd George had gone back on his word on Syria seven times, and he and Balfour would have to thrash the whole thing out before the Turkish treaty could be settled. White commented in his report to Washington on the conversation that, on the other hand, Balfour had told him he feared Syria must be given to France, and that there was no chance of any other solution under the circumstances. " Bliss and I think considerable danger in Asiatic situation will result from further delay in final settlement of Asia Minor questions . . ." he cabled, adding that Polk agreed with this prognosis.[18]

Frank L. Polk, Under Secretary of State, had been sent to Paris as the new chief American delegate; the original Peace Commission of Wilson, Lansing, White, House, and Bliss was breaking up as the major work of the Conference was completed, and at the beginning of August Polk took over the American representation in the Council. On August 1 he sent his first report to Washington. He said it was clear that the British arbiters in the dis-

[17] President Wilson cabled to White on July 25: " I greatly value and admire the way you have been handling the Italians in the matter of the Adriatic and Asia Minor . . ."; 763.72119/5874.

[18] Telegram from Peace Mission 3378, July 29, 1919; 736.72119/5866.

pute over Greek claims to western Thrace had engineered an agreement between the Italians and Greeks. Tittoni admitted that, in return for concessions from the Greeks in Anatolia, Italy had promised to support Greek claims to western Thrace. All the peace commissioners were agreed, said Polk, that a strong stand must be made on the Bulgarian treaty, even up to the point of threatening to withdraw if justice were not done. He himself was beginning to think that it might be desirable to tell the great powers that the United States was considering withdrawing from the Turkish and Bulgarian treaties. The negotiations were being carried on in " a spirit of barter," he said; " it is in the end a land-grabbing scheme." It would be difficult to get such a treaty accepted by the American people. He asked the Department's opinion on making an approach to Clemenceau and Balfour, putting the American fears to them and stating that the United States might withdraw from all future negotiations if the present course continued. He pointed out that the French, Italians, and Greeks might actually welcome such a move, as it would mean that they would get what they wanted without a fight, though on the other hand the British probably wanted American participation. But, he added, since this threat might be accepted, the Department might wish the American delegation to continue in the negotiations since the settlement would be guaranteed by the League of Nations.[19]

On receiving a copy of this telegram, Wilson wrote immediately to Secretary Lansing. He was " distressed by these developments," he said, and it was " little less than intolerable " that Tittoni and Venizelos " should be suffered " to prejudge the settlement in Asia Minor by a private agreement. " I am clear in my judgment that Greece should *not* be given Bulgarian Thrace," and the American delegation should take a firm stand on this position, he said; on the other hand, it would be a serious matter to give it back to Bulgaria. " We have a clear voice in these matters," he went on, as guarantors of the final settlement, and suggested a temporary arrangement under the League until an impartial commission could decide the matter. The United States must make it plain, he said, that it would not stand for such bartering about of territory, contrary to American principles. If American co-operation in the settlement was desired, the settle-

[19] Telegram 3441 from Peace Mission, August 1, 1919; 763. 72119/5920.

ment must square with American principles. The United States would simply be cutting the ground from under its own feet if it permitted the Greeks and Italians to settle the matter on their own terms. " I should assume Mr. Venizelos is clear headed enough to see that he can gain no advantage by alienating us and making us regret that we ever let him take possession of Smyrna." [20] The substance of this letter was cabled to Polk on the same day.[21]

Polk learned more of the agreement during the next few days. Tittoni told him that the Greeks had agreed to stop at the Meander River, and the Italians were to occupy the country from there to Adalia. He also said he believed the French were sympathetic to this arrangement, but was vague about the boundary between the Italian sphere and the French sphere in Syria. Polk relayed this information to Balfour, who was very disturbed; he did not think, or so he told Polk, that the Italians should get anything in Asia Minor, though, as Polk noted, he was very much in favor of giving western Thrace to the Greeks. He also learned that the British military authorities who had personal knowledge of the situation in Bulgaria were opposed to giving western Thrace to Greece, since it would inevitably lead to war. British and French military leaders, including Marshal Foch, held that Bulgaria had the only strong military force in the whole area, for the Greeks were completely engaged in Asia Minor and the Allies had no forces there, or would shortly have none. Analyzing this situation in a cable to Washington, Polk said that the military picture had dampened somewhat the enthusiasm of the British and French for giving western Thrace to Greece, but when he had pointed out the danger of a conflict they had told him that they were the victors in the war and could dictate any terms they chose. Polk suggested to the State Department that he tell the Conference the Thrace question should be left until the Turkish treaty was settled and it was known whether the United States

[20] Letter from President to Secretary of State, August 4, 1919; 763.72119/5920. See, also, below, p. 212, fn., for Wilson's threat to leave the Conference. In the telegram of August 9 to Polk on the French refusal to consider the " A " mandate, below, p. 211, Wilson said, " The United States will certainly not enter the League of Nations to guarantee any settlements of this nature or any such intolerable bargains as the Greeks and Italians appear to be attempting."

[21] Telegram 2411½ to Peace Mission, August 4, 1919; 763.72119/5920.

would take a mandate for Constantinople; it would be possible then to set the terms of the settlement of the western zone.[22]

On August 11 Polk cabled that " all sorts of deals are in the air " on the question of Thrace; he had, he thought, given the Italians and Greeks some pause in their exchange of favors in Anatolia and Thrace by telling the Italians that the United States would never consent to Italy's obtaining the coast of southern Anatolia. He asked the Department of State for authority to propose as a compromise that western Thrace be included in the territory of the international state to be established for Constantinople and the Straits.[23] Again on August 15 he asked the Department for authority to propose his compromise solution, and requested the Secretary of State to see the President about it, otherwise, he would not be able to prevent the adoption of the proposals already being discussed.[24]

Before any decision could be reached, however, Venizelos himself sent a message to the President on August 24 through the American delegation, proposing a compromise on the distribution of Thrace between Greece, Bulgaria, and the international state of Constantinople, reducing somewhat the original Greek claim.[25] The President's reply was cabled on August 28 and was handed to the Council on September 1. He found Venizelos' proposal unacceptable, not out of lack of friendship for Greece or because the United States did not appreciate the national aspirations of a brave people, he said, but because the only possible basis for a settlement was the avoidance of future wars and the permanency of the settlement based on its justice and equity. However, the President went on, moved by a strong desire to meet the wishes of the Greek nation he would agree to the cession of the western portions of west Thrace, while all of the rest of Thrace would be included in the international state; Bulgaria would receive a right of way across west Thrace to Dedeagatch and the Agean. " The Greek aspiration to secure sovereignty over the greater part of eastern Thrace is of course denied." He noted that unless the international state of Constantinople and the Straits had a " considerable territory " attached to it, the power or group of powers

[22] Telegram 3508 from Peace Mission, August 5, 1919; 763.72119/6040.
[23] Telegram 3625 from Peace Mission, August 11, 1919; 763.72119/6117.
[24] Telegram 3705 from Peace Mission, August 15, 1919; 763.72119/6190.
[25] Foreign Relations, Paris Peace Conference, VIII, 48–49.

charged with its government would be at a constant and very considerable expense.[26]

On receiving this message the Council requested the Territorial Commission to draw up specific proposals taking into consideration the President's wishes,[27] and on September 2 the Commission reported to the Council a scheme for the delimitation of the Bulgarian frontier in Thrace which followed, reasonably closely, the President's plans. Polk accepted this on behalf of the United States and it was adopted by the Council.[28] However, Greek claims in eastern Thrace were left undetermined by the scheme, and, on September 5, Clemenceau, Tittoni, and Balfour cabled a note to Wilson through the American delegation, pointing out that the President's proposal would place 700,000 Greeks in the international state; there would be continual racial strife between the Greeks and Turks in the area and, moreover, it would be unfair to Greece, an ally, in favor of Turkey and Bulgaria, who had been enemies. Polk commented to the Department that this was an exaggeration, since none of the territory was " incontestably " Greek, the Greeks being actually in a minority.[29] A similar message was sent by Venizelos, but by this time the President had left on his ill-fated tour of the country and no answer to either of these messages was sent.

Venizelos wrote again to the President on September 27, answering the argument against giving east Thrace to Greece on the grounds that there was no Greek majority in the area. Venizelos said while this might be true at the present time, it was not so before the war. During the war the Greeks had been deported from Thrace; when they returned to their homes they would probably constitute a majority, though many had perished due to Turkish ill-treatment. Those who had died should be added to the enumeration of the population to reach a just comparison of the relative strength of the two races. The Turks should not be rewarded for their mistreatment of the Greeks.[30] This letter was not considered for many months, and it was not until December 11 that any note was taken of it by the President. On that date the President's private secretary, Tumulty, wrote to the Secretary of State returning the letter and saying the Presi-

[26] *Ibid.*, pp. 50–51.   [27] *Ibid.*, pp. 35–37.   [28] *Ibid.*, p. 55.
[29] Telegram 4066 from Peace Mission, September 5, 1919; 763.72119/6543.
[30] Letter, Venizelos to the President, September 27, 1919; 763.72119/10927.

dent had asked him to inform the Secretary that he would take it up as soon as he could discuss it with him.[31] There is no record that this was ever done.

5.

While the Council had been considering questions concerning Turkey and Allied ambitions there, the Commission on Model Mandates was attempting to lay down a working method of controlling these ambitions and of implementing the system of international trusteeship established by Wilson's efforts at the very beginning of the Peace Conference. On June 27 it was decided in the Council of Four that a commission be set up to consider the form of the mandates,[32] but work on this subject was already well advanced at the time. During the period that Wilson had been deciding fundamental American policy in the Council of Four, almost out of contact with his colleagues, the latter had been active in the fields left open to them, one of which was the drafting of model mandates. The members of the British delegation who were also concerned with mandates had very much the same outlook on them as their American colleagues, and the British and American experts worked very closely during the whole Peace Conference.

Anglo-American co-operation in determining the nature of the mandates had in fact been close since the previous fall; even before this there had been general agreement on principles, but in the weeks before the Conference opened discussions on specific details of the form international trusteeships should take had been held, notably during an informal conference in November, 1918, between several British and American experts on international relations. Here the provisions that should be included in a trusteeship over backward peoples were agreed on—the prohibition of forced labor, the liquor traffic, the use of the natives as troops, and training for self-government were to be dealt with by the Covenant of the League, and the League itself was to exercise continuing supervision over the administration of each territory

[31] Letter from Tumulty to the Secretary of State, December 11, 1919; 763.72119/10927.
[32] *Foreign Relations*, Paris Peace Conference, VI, 728–29.

and also was to have the right to dismiss a mandatory in case of a violation of the terms of the mandate.

As the German treaty neared completion, the terms of its implementation (and of the implementation of the other treaties) had to be determined. The mandate system, with the Covenant, was to be a part of each treaty; the general terms of the mandates had been laid down in Article Twenty-two but now precise instruments had to be drawn to fill in the broad outlines. Milner had already drawn up brief drafts of the Class " B " and " C " mandates in connection with his attempt earlier in the year to come to an accommodation with the French, but on March 11 Lloyd George had told him to drop the matter until President Wilson returned to Paris, and he had heard no more about it.[33]

Westermann was the first to draw up a draft of the Class " A " mandates. On April 24 he completed the outline of the terms of a model mandate for the territories of the Ottoman Empire. The mandatory power was to exercise supervision for twenty-five years under League control and provision was to be made for preparing the people for self-government. The capitulations were to be abolished and religious freedom guaranteed. Each mandated territory was to take a pro rata share of the Ottoman debt. Fortifications were to be prohibited and troops were to be raised for the maintenance of public order only.[34] This plan was submitted to the peace commissioners on the twenty-sixth, together with the suggestion that the general clauses of the mandates be agreed to before specific clauses designed to meet the requirements of individual areas, since this would make the mandates more readily acceptable by the powers. An American commission might be set up to study the question and later perhaps expanded into an inter-Allied commission. The peace commissioners approved the memorandum and suggested that, since the whole idea was so important, the President should be notified of the memorandum and the plan of an American commission.[35] The draft

[33] Cf., House Papers, Diary, March 11, 1919; on March 4 Milner called on House to discuss mandatories and to see if an agreement could be reached on a formula for mandates. House suggested he draw up a memorandum on the subject and then a commission might be appointed to go over the draft; Diary, March 4.

[34] Peace Conference files, Memorandum on the General Clauses of a Mandate, April 24, 1919; 185.1111/1.

[35] Foreign Relations, Paris Peace Conference, XI, 165.

was sent to Wilson on April 28.[36] One weakness of Westermann's draft was the absence of a guarantee of the Open Door in mandated territories, but on May 1 William Yale submitted a further memorandum on mandates in which he pointed out the importance of including in the clauses of all mandates provisions protecting American trade, particularly, in those for the Ottoman Empire, in regard to oil. This was also forwarded to the President as an addition to the draft previously sent.

The British experts were also active in attempting to give reality to the mandates system and to get it down in concrete terms. Lord Robert Cecil, in particular, was anxious to put the mandates before the Conference. On May 3 the Belgians requested that the former German colonies be ceded directly to the states concerned rather than through the Principal Powers. Wilson pointed out that while the League would distribute the mandates if their allocation was postponed until the League was in operation, until that time the mandates would be assigned by the principal Allied and Associated Powers. Lloyd George then said that Cecil had begged him to get the question of mandatories and the form of mandates settled. Wilson asked why the mandates needed to be settled immediately after the question of the mandatories; the general outlines had been laid down in the Covenant. However, he added, he wanted to decide the question of mandatories and he was willing to decide the question of mandates. Balfour said in his opinion the mandates should be settled first, to which George replied that this was the opposite of his view and Wilson added that the only controversial part of the question was that concerning the mandatories. (The Italian landings in Anatolia were then occupying the attention of the Three.) Lloyd George agreed; the real difficulties would arise in the Turkish mandates. Wilson thought that this would be particularly true in regard to Palestine, owing to the Zionist question, to which the United States and Britain and, he thought to some extent, the French, were committed.[37]

The controversial nature of the form of the mandates was revealed to Wilson two days later, when Clemenceau asked in the Council for the insertion of a specific clause in Article Twenty-two

---

[36] Wilson Papers, Series VIII A, Box 42; Letter, Secretary of State to the President, April 28, 1919.

[37] *Foreign Relations*, Paris Peace Conference, V, 459–60.

of the Covenant giving the mandatories the right to raise troops in the mandates for the defense of the mother country. " It is very important to France," he said. Wilson referred him to the discussion of January 30 in the Council of Ten, where an agreement had been reached that the wording of the resolution then passed covered the French case.[38] Later in the day Wilson told House what had happened [39] and House sent a memorandum to the President pointing out that a good reason for not accepting Clemenceau's amendment would be that it might mean that, for example, if France and Britain were at war, Arab would be fighting Arab; such provisions might prevent the acceptance of the mandate system by the backward countries.[40] Clemenceau had not waited for his colleagues, however, but had ordered the printing of the treaty with the offending amendment to the Covenant included in the draft. Wilson discovered what was going on while the presses were running; he ordered them stopped, and the copy taken from them and reprinted without the amendment.

Cecil also sought help from House in getting the mandates down in black and white, and asked him to get the President's help in establishing the form of the mandates before they were distributed. If it were left until afterward, he said, there would be difficulties in forcing acceptance of liberal terms. House agreed to see what he could do and wrote to Wilson about Cecil's request. Wilson replied on May 19 saying that he agreed with Cecil; he would do what he could, but discussions on the distribution of mandates had reached a point which would make their formulation a delicate matter. (The Italian action in Asia Minor was still before the Council.) He suggested that Cecil draft model mandates for the three types projected so as to make them as uniform as possible. The individual provisions would then be " less invidious." [41]

Cecil did as Wilson suggested and sent his draft to House on May 24 to be given to the President. In the covering letter he emphasized the need for provisions, even against opposition, for giving the League " real opportunities " to insure that the man-

[38] *Ibid.*, p. 463.

[39] House Papers, Diary, May 5, 1919.

[40] Wilson Papers, Series VIII A, Box 45; letter, House to the President, May 6, 1919.

[41] *Ibid.*, Box 50; letter, President to House, May 19, 1919.

dates were not looked upon as disguised annexations. He mentioned parenthetically his difficulty in drawing up an acceptable draft of the Class " A " mandates because of the peculiar circumstances of each case. Wilson apparently did not receive this immediately.[42] On June 4 Cecil wrote again to House, pressing for the publication of the mandates as soon as possible because they represented a new international system second only to the Covenant and should be subjected to the same sort of criticism. Publication would ease tension in the East; Faisal would see that the mandates protected him and the Arabs fully. House sent this to Wilson, who replied that he was willing to co-operate with Cecil in the mandates and wanted to see what he had drawn up.[43]

6.

As the time for the signing of the German treaty drew near, Lloyd George was pressing, under the prodding of Cecil, for the determination in the Council of the forms of the mandates. On June 25 he " insisted " on the importance of the matter. Wilson agreed but said that he wanted time to " read the question up," [44] and the next day told the Prime Minister that he had read only Cecil's drafts. He was told that Milner's drafts would be circulated in the Council on the twenty-seventh.[45] In the meantime Wilson wrote to House telling him that Lloyd George was pressing for a decision and asking for House's advice, particularly on the differences between Cecil's and Milner's draft clauses. House advised him to do nothing for the moment. The United States disagreed sharply with Britain in some essentials, he said, and these differences would have to be ironed out; this might be done by an inter-Allied commission.[46] Later, on June 27, he sent the two British drafts with explanatory notes by the peace commissioners stating that neither draft was quite satisfactory. They

[42] *Ibid.*, Box 52; letter, Cecil to House for the President, enclosing drafts of the mandates; copies are also in the House Papers.
[43] *Ibid.*, Box 56; letter, House to the President, enclosing Cecil's letter to House. Letter, the President to House, June 5, 1919.
[44] *Foreign Relations*, Paris Peace Conference, VI, 678.
[45] *Ibid.*, p. 703.
[46] House Papers, Diary, June 27, 1919.

did not provide fully for the Open Door nor give adequate protection to the native populations. Provision for the free activities of missionaries was lacking also.[47] In the covering letter, House wrote that Cecil was very concerned lest the Conference break up without having acted on mandates. He himself agreed and thought that there should be " a clear and ringing statement of principle." [48]

In the 4 P. M. Council session of that day Lloyd George introduced Milner's drafts into the Council. (They included only model clauses for the Class " B " and " C " mandates since, Milner said, the number and nature of the territories covered by the Class " A " mandates were so varied that it was difficult to conceive of any single form of mandate which would be applicable to them all.) Wilson commented that he had some criticism to make of Milner's proposals. " In his view," he said, " they hardly provided adequate protection for the native population; they did not provide sufficiently for the Open Door; and the Class C mandates did not make provision for missionary activities." However, he thought that if the Council devoted itself to the question now, it would be drafting the mandates; the best plan would be to appoint a special committee for the purpose. Lloyd George took issue with the President's comment on the lack of provision for the Open Door; in his view the drafts went too far, but he agreed to refer the matter to a special committee and suggested that it might conveniently meet in London, since Milner would be there and Colonel House was planning to go also. Wilson suggested that the committee be set up at once and that it hold a preliminary meeting in Paris to arrange procedure. It would be a good plan, he added, to draw up the mandates and publish them in order to invite criticism before adopting them. He was prepared, however, to leave this to the committee.[49] The terms of reference of the committee were then set up. As redrawn the next day in the interests of clarity, the committee was to: (1) consider the drafting of model mandates; (2) hear the Belgian and Portuguese claims to German East Africa; (3) hear " Aboriginese Societies " in the same matter; and (4) make a report on the two powers' claims.

[47] Wilson Papers, Series VIII A, Box 67.
[48] Ibid.
[49] Foreign Relations, Paris Peace Conference, VI, 727–29.

Milner, who was appointed Chairman of the Commission on Colonial Mandates, as the committee had been titled, called a meeting for the following day, but since the German treaty was to be signed on the twenty-eighth, House decided not to bother attending and instead sent G. L. Beer as his deputy with instructions to tell the Commission that he would take up the work of deciding on colonial mandates in London. The next meeting of the Commission was set at ten days' time.[50]

Wilson had a final word of advice for House before the Commission began its substantive meetings. On July 1, during his journey home, he sent a cable to him from the S. S. *George Washington*. It read:

I neglected before leaving to speak to you about the Committee to formulate model mandates of which we asked Lord Milner to act as chairman, associated with yourself, Simon, Chinda and Crespi. Milner is inclined to go the full liberal length, I think, and will have to be supported as against his chief, who thinks that the outlines he drew go too far. I believe that by devoting your most watchful attention to this business you can probably get it into shape that we will all be willing to support. The British chief is too much inclined to think that this is a business for the great Powers and only in form for the League of Nations, and is apt to verify the impression that the Mandates are after all a means of distributing the spoils.[51]

7.

The second meeting of the Commission was held in London on July 6, and the sessions continued for the next two days. There was general agreement on almost all points of the provisions of the mandates and upon the basis on which they were to be distributed—that the principal Allied and Associated Powers confer the mandates on trust and that the League would then supervise their performance. House wrote to Wilson that he was agreeably surprised at the unanimity of purpose at the sessions. There was, however, one major point of difference. On July 5 Dutasta, Secretary-General of the Conference, had sent to Milner, the chairman of the Commission, the new French text

[50] House Papers, Diary, June 28, 1918.
[51] Wilson Papers, Series VIII A, Box 68.

of the Class " B " mandates, which included the words " and the defense of its territory whether colonial or metropolitan " added to the clause on the raising of troops in the mandated territory. The French delegate had positive instructions to insist in the Conference on this French text in the exact words as presented; this French position was based on the proceedings in the meeting of the Council of Ten on January 30. It was House's opinion that the procès-verbal, while it was not clear, partially supported the French claim, but that he would " stand firm " if Wilson approved. The British, Japanese, and Italians were sympathetic to the American position, House added, when he had objected to the French amendment in the sessions.[52] (The United States had later to admit the French claim to raise troops in Togoland, but not in any of the other mandated territories.) [53]

The Class " B " and " C " mandates were finished by the eleventh, except for the homeland defense clause, which House protested and the French reserved. The texts were cabled to Wilson with the added notation by House that the Class " A " mandates had been postponed until August because of the uncertainty regarding the distribution of mandates in Turkey. Wilson replied on July 18 that the Class " B " and " C " mandates were " quite satisfactory," but that he did not understand why it was not possible to continue work on the model Class " A " mandates; they should be all alike irrespective of the mandatory.[54]

8.

Though the meetings of the Commission were postponed, the American and British experts attached to it, chiefly Beer and Cecil, continued to work on the drafting of the model Class " A " mandate. When the Commission reconvened on August 5, a draft

[52] Wilson Papers, Series II, Box 159; letter, House to the President, July 14, 1919; this was a personal letter, not an official report.

[53] Telegram, House to the President, August 20, 1919 (via London 2650); 763.72119/6294. Telegram 3001 to Peace Mission, August 30, 1919; 763.72119/6294.

[54] Telegram, House to the President via Embassy, July 11, 1919; 763.72119/5619. Telegram, President to House, via Department of State, July 18; 763.72119/5683. Copies in the Wilson Papers, Series II, Box 159; House sent official drafts to Wilson on July 17; Box 159.

was ready and was laid before the members. But now the difficulties experienced by the United States in the Council began to appear in the Mandate Commission also. The French delegate was not present at the meeting. After inquiries were made he was finally reached by telephone, whereupon he informed the Commission that he was under instructions not to attend. There are two versions of what took place, one by Milner in a report to Dutasta and the other in House's report to Wilson. Milner's version is somewhat milder. He said that Simon had informed him that the French government objected to the consideration of Class " A " mandates at the present stage of development until a political settlement with regard to the Turkish Empire had been arrived at. He went on to say that Simon could not, for other reasons, be at the meeting, but that he was given to understand that the French delegate would not have taken part in the discussions of the Class " A " mandates if he had been present.[55]

House's version gives a different picture. He informed Wilson that his draft was on the agenda but the French delegate refused by telephone to come to the meeting and discuss this form of mandate, maintaining that it had not been decided whether there should be mandates for the Turkish Empire. House and Cecil insisted that Article Twenty-two of the Covenant established the " A " mandate when the question was taken up by that body, mandate principle, but the Commission decided to refer the question to the Supreme War Council. House suggested to Wilson that Polk be instructed to present to the Council the draft Class " A " mandate when the question was taken up by that body, otherwise, House warned, the Ottoman Empire would be divided and distributed without any previous agreement as to the administration of the territory and " the whole mandatory system will receive a severe blow which public opinion will hardly forgive." [56]

Wilson was furious when he learned of the French action. He wrote to Lansing telling him that a question had been raised by the French in the Mandate Commission about mandates in the Turkish Empire. He rejected outright the French contention that there was no certainty of applying the mandate system to Turkey, saying that when the mandates were being discussed in Paris the

[55] House Papers, Milner to Dutasta, August 6, 1919.
[56] Telegram, House to the President and Secretary of State, August 6, 1919; 763.72119/6024.

Turkish Empire was used as an illustration and that Syria and Arabia in particular were discussed with Lloyd George and Clemenceau in terms of the mandate system. " I will withdraw the French Treaty rather than consent to see the Turkish Empire divided as spoils." He wanted Lansing to send a message to Polk to transmit to the French with " a very strong statement of our inflexible determination to allow nothing that will alter the understandings hitherto reached in this vital matter." He went on to comment that he would not press the German treaty on the Senate if the other treaties followed this course, nor would the United States enter the League to guarantee such settlements as the Greeks and the Italians seemed to be attempting, he added parenthetically.[57] (House sent his draft to Wilson, describing it as a composite by Beer agreed to by Cecil, with the other commissioners reserving comment.[58] Wilson wrote that he was satisfied and hoped that the differences with the French could be overcome.) [59]

Lansing cabled to Polk the substance of the President's statement on August 9. The next day Polk saw Clemenceau and asked him if the report from London was true, that the French delegate on the Mandate Commission had been instructed not to take up the Class " A " mandates. Clemenceau admitted this was the case but that the action had been aimed at Lloyd George, not at the United States, to force a decision in Syria. (This was probably true, for it tied the whole Turkish settlement to the Syrian settlement. If the French could not get a speedy decision from Faisal and the British in Syria, the British would not get one in Mesopotamia and Palestine.) Polk answered that, nevertheless, it concerned the United States, for it touched also on the League

[57] Letter, President to Secretary of State, August 8, 1919; 763.72119/6294½. In one of Lansing's private memoranda (Lansing Papers) on " The President's Feelings as to the Present European Situation," August 20, 1919, he notes the President's comments: "When I see such conduct as this . . ." (referring to Allied intrigues in Central Europe) " When I learn of the Secret Treaty of Great Britain and Persia . . . I am disposed to throw up the whole business and get out." Lansing states that this was the third time Wilson had said he was ready to " get out." The other occasions were when the Greeks demanded all of western Thrace and when the French insisted on their Syrian claims.

[58] Telegram 2751, House to the President and Secretary of State, August 9, 1919; 763.72119/6103. Printed in Miller, *Diary*, XX, 383–89.

[59] Wilson Papers, Series 11, Box 161; letter, President to House, August 15, 1919.

of Nations and the German treaty. It would look very bad, he told the French leader, if France seemed to be delaying the mandates. He hinted that it might be necessary to withdraw the Treaty of Guarantee with France if these tactics continued. Clemenceau was conciliatory and promised to proceed with the Class " A " mandates, asking for a letter outlining the American position so that he could show it to his colleagues in the Ministry, some of whom were very hot-headed on the Syrian issue.[60] Polk complied and on the thirteenth he sent the letter, reporting the same day to House in London what was happening in Paris.[61]

The French Premier was not a man to abandon a position so tamely. Nothing was said on the subject for two weeks or so and the Commission remained inactive. Then on August 24 he returned to the attack. He wrote to Polk giving the French case for postponing the mandates. He had studied the case in detail, he said, and wished to report his findings. His basic argument centered around the wording of Article Twenty-two of the Covenant (from which the French had fortunately been able to delete the names of specific countries in the meeting of the League of Nations Commission on February 8). There had been no decision reached that any particular portion of the Ottoman Empire would be detached and given a separate political existence, and the mandates would vary with the area concerned. It could not be determined what areas were to be dealt with by the mandate system until a definite territorial settlement had been reached. This was waiting upon the Turkish treaty and this in turn was delayed because the United States had not yet decided whether she would take a mandate. Therefore, until the United States made up her mind it was impossible to go ahead with the Class " A " mandates. (The French, it would seem, wanted nothing more than to get on with the mandates, but in the face of American dilatori-

[60] Telegram 3624 from Peace Mission, August 11, 1919; 763.72119/6114.

[61] The Department cabled to Polk approving his action and stating that Clemenceau's agreement not to block the mandates was " highly appreciated." The President felt, the cable continued, that any deviation from the agreements arrived at during the discussions between himself and Clemenceau would be " highly inadvisable " and might lead to " serious complications." Telegram 2820 to Paris for Polk, August 4, 1919; 763.72119/6114. Polk's cable to House is in Peace Conference files, 185.1111/7A.

ness they could merely acknowledge political facts; it was not the French who were delaying the mandates at all, but the Americans.)

Polk answered that the main point was to lay down broad principles applicable to any state and any territory. The delay of the United States in accepting a mandate should not affect general consideration of model mandates. He urged that the Council act on the problem; it could take substantial steps toward a solution. This exchange was cabled to Washington with an inquiry if the President's threat to withdraw the French treaty should be used to force the French to act.[62] Lansing replied, rejecting Clemenceau's arguments. Article Twenty-two laid down that at least a portion of the Ottoman Empire would be placed under mandates, therefore it was perfectly proper to consider the general terms of Class "A" mandates at this time. He instructed Polk that since Clemenceau was merely delaying the mandates and not actually opposing them, the use of the President's threat would be left to his discretion.[63]

Negotiations continued but without success, and on September 5 Polk cabled House in London that Clemenceau was still opposing the formulation of the Class "A" mandates. He (Polk) was still hoping for a favorable outcome, he said, but it would take time.[64] No progress was made, however, and in the middle of September House and Milner decided to go to Paris themselves to see if they could expedite matters, but after tackling the Conference both men decided that there was nothing they could do for the present and that they would let the Class "A" mandates go until the Turkish treaty was taken up.[65] The French had made their point. House conceded this in a cable to Lansing on September 26. He had come to Paris, he told the Secretary, hoping to finish up the Class "A" mandates, but he had decided that it was impossible to do anything until the Turkish treaty was formulated. "The French maintain that there will be several

[62] Telegram 3897 from American Peace Mission, August 25, 1919; 763.72119/6371.

[63] Telegram 2996 to American Peace Mission, August 29, 1919; 763.72119/6371.

[64] Peace Conference files, 185.1111/14A.

[65] House Papers, Diary, September 15, 1919.

forms of Mandate according to the territory," he said, and thus they could not proceed.[66]

---

[66] Peace Conference files, 185.1111/14B. G. L. Beer, House's deputy on the Mandate Commission, wrote to House on October 24, 1919, giving a summary of what had happened since House sailed for the United States. Drummond, the Secretary-General of the League, wrote to him on October 4 stating that no progress had been made in inducing the French to withdraw their reservations on the mandates, but that Milner hoped to do this before he left for Egypt. In view of this, Drummond said, he thought it advisable that the League Council take up the entire matter under paragraphs eight and twenty-two of the Covenant. Beer commented that of course Drummond based this opinion on the assumption that the United States would soon ratify the Treaty. If the Senate turned it down, some other course would have to be adopted. Australia and New Zealand were clamoring for an early settlement and the matter could not be left suspended indefinitely. There had been informal discussions of a second type of " A " mandate, in addition to those for former Turkish territory; this type would be applied to countries such as Persia and Liberia, which would retain control of their own foreign relations but would receive advice and assistance from a great power. The United Kingdom and Persia intended to submit their treaty to the Council of the League as soon as it was operative. (House Papers.)

CHAPTER VIII

THE FRENCH OCCUPATION OF SYRIA

1.

Since the signing of the Treaty of Versailles and the departure of President Wilson from Paris, American policy on Syria had been conducted in the Mandate Commission. The King-Crane Commission had ended discussion of Syria in the Council of Four and in its successor, the Council of the Heads of Delegations, except for a brief outburst by Clemenceau on July 18 against General Allenby during a discussion on the question of putting all Allied troops in Anatolia under a single Allied commander in order to stop the confusion that followed the Greek landings at Smyrna. Clemenceau claimed that General Allenby or his subordinates were carrying on a deliberate campaign against France in Syria; this was strongly denied by Balfour. Outside the Council, however, Clemenceau had carried on a vigorous attempt to force the British to come to terms with him on Syria; he had blocked any settlement of the mandates in the Mandate Commission, tied the whole Arab question to the future of Syria, and during the entire summer had conducted a press attack in the leading French newspapers on the alleged anti-French activities of the British in Syria and the " farce " of the American Commission. The British protested to the French government these attacks, but were told there were dossiers full of evidence and that the British government seemed to be unaware of the intense feeling in France on Syria which would sweep away any government which did not protect French interests there.

On August 11 Balfour wrote a memorandum on the effect on Anglo-French relations of the Syrian question. It was causing him " considerable anxiety," he said, " an anxiety which is not dimin-

ished by the fact that little is openly said about it, much is hinted
. . . ." He noted that Britain, France, and the United States had
" got themselves into a position over the Syrian problem so inex-
tricably confused " that it was impossible to find a satisfactory
answer to it. The agreements entered into by the Allies during
the war had not taken into consideration the principles of the
mandate system, which presupposed that the Arab states were
ready for independence, with some guidance. The literal fulfillment of the various declarations made by the Allies to the Arabs
were not capable of being carried out, and Balfour proposed
therefore that the basic principles of the Sykes-Picot agreement,
though not necessarily its precise terms, should be followed in
the settlement of the Arab question; that is, the settlement be
based on the principle of a French sphere in Syria, a British sphere
in Mesopotamia, and a home for the Jews in the Jordan Valley.
Within this framework the British and French could come to an
agreement between themselves, and then could agree together
with the Arabs.[1]

Lloyd George accepted this analysis to the extent of being prepared to accede to the basic French demand to occupy Syria. This
would eliminate at least the chorus of French protests, official and
journalistic, that Britain was attempting to destroy the French
position in the Middle East. Accordingly, he prepared a memorandum for submission to the French and the Arabs, stating that
steps would be taken immediately for the evacuation of Syria and
Cilicia by the British Army and that responsibility for garrisoning
these areas would be handed over to French and Arab troops in
accordance with Britain's commitments; in Syria this would mean
that west of the Sykes-Picot line French troops would replace the
British, the area east of it, including the towns of Homs, Hama,
Aleppo, and Damascus, being occupied by Arab forces; British
troops would remain in Palestine " from Dan to Beersheba," and
in Mesopotamia, including Mosul. Britain also agreed to the
dispatch of French troops to Armenia, France having accepted
responsibility for the protection of the Armenian people.[2]

Lloyd George presented his memorandum to Clemenceau at a
private meeting on September 13 in Paris, but before doing so he

---

[1] *British Documents*, Series I, IV, 340–49.
[2] Text in *Foreign Relations*, Paris Peace Conference, VIII, 216–17; also in
British Documents, Series I, I, No. 57, Appendix B.

sounded out Polk to get the American reaction. On September 12 Polk dined with Lloyd George, Allenby, and several members of the Cabinet; Lloyd George discussed in detail the situation in the Arab lands and read the text of the memorandum. The Prime Minister told Polk that the British had 400,000 men in the Middle East and somehow they had to be reduced, hence the plan to withdraw from Syria. He said he thought he could live up to the commitments to the French and Arabs, but the French were insisting on providing the garrisons for Damascus, Homs, and Aleppo. Allenby commented that as soon as British troops were withdrawn, and the French took over, Faisal would attack them. Lloyd George said he had invited Faisal to come to London in order to explain to him the necessity of withdrawing British troops. Polk kept his counsel and did not comment on the plan.[3]

Clemenceau would not commit himself to the memorandum beyond accepting the withdrawal of British troops. Polk saw Lloyd George again after the September 13 meeting. He was told no conclusions had been reached. Clemenceau had proposed, in an answer to the memorandum, that only the Arab areas of the Ottoman Empire be detached from the Ottoman Empire; the rest should be left to the future Turkish state, and the Sultan maintained in Constantinople with a French Commissioner, on the pattern of Kitchener in Egypt. Lloyd George told Polk this was unacceptable. The only possible solution for the Straits and Constantinople, he said, was an American mandate. Polk told him it was impossible to comment on this; it was not certain whether the American people would accept a mandate for Armenia, where there was a real call for it, much less a mandate for Constantinople.[4]

Lloyd George formally introduced the memorandum into the Council on September 15. He had felt it necessary to notify the Conference, he said, otherwise it might be said in the newspapers that these arrangements were being made behind the backs of his colleagues. Clemenceau maintained the position he had taken in his private talk with Lloyd George two days before, and

[3] Telegram 4217 from Peace Mission, September 15, 1919; 763.72119/6760.
[4] Telegram 4217 from Peace Mission, above. House discussed Syria and Eastern questions generally with Allenby on September 15. They covered much the same ground as Polk had with Lloyd George. House also spoke with Clemenceau on the same matters. House Papers, Diary, September 15, 1919.

formally stated that if, by sending troops to Syria and Armenia, France accepted the whole agreement he could not undertake to send troops. He was assured by Lloyd George he would not be committed to anything other than replacing British forces by French. Clemenceau's point was that France could not accept the assignment of the four cities to the Arabs in the ultimate settlement, and wished to make perfectly clear that the replacement of British troops by Arabs in any part of Syria, and the participation of France in the proposals under which this was carried out, could not be interpreted as French agreement to the Arab claims in Syria. When the future of Turkey was considered in its entirety, Clemenceau added, it might be possible to grant what could not be granted when Syria was discussed in isolation; he would always be ready to go to London. In other words, he was prepared to bargain, but the Eastern settlement must be taken as a whole.[5] Polk at this point put forward the American position, which he had been careful not to do informally; he wanted it to be on the record and official. Any agreement, he made plain, between the French and British was not binding on the United States nor on the Conference. The discussion between his British and French colleagues was merely an exchange of views; it was understood that the question would be debated as a whole.[6]

2.

Faisal had been informed on September 10 in Damascus, of Lloyd George's decision to withdraw from Syria. On the same day the Consul at Beirut cabled that Damascus was in a state of excitement following news reports of an Anglo-French agreement on occupation troops and the Anglo-Persian treaty; it was believed that the price for French approval of the treaty had been British approval of a French mandate.[7] The Syrian Congress had passed a resolution calling the Syrian nation to arms to defend

[5] Clemenceau made his formal reply to the memorandum on October 9, 1919; *British Documents*, Series I, IV, 452–54. Clemenceau gave Polk a copy on October 10; Peace Conference files, 185.5137/140; sent to the Secretary of State on October 20, 1919; 763.72119/7657.

[6] *Foreign Relations*, Paris Peace Conference, VIII, 205–8.

[7] Telegram 1374 from Beyrouth (sic) via Paris, September 10, 1919; 763.72119/607.

its rights. On September 12 the Consul at Damascus reported Faisal had left " hurriedly " for Paris that morning via Port Said. It had been understood he was to sail on a French ship but his departure had been " delayed " by the French authorities. Faisal had talked with the Consul the day before he left for Europe and told him that British and French representatives had urged him on September 9 to accept a French mandate for all of Syria excluding Palestine; his answer had been, he said, that the Peace Conference must decide. The situation as he saw it, the Consul cabled Washington, was that Britain wanted the mandate for itself or the United States, as did most of the Syrians, and hoped to get the United States to repudiate the Sykes-Picot agreement in the Peace Conference by insisting on self-determination as in the Fiume case.[8] In a report to London of the discussions with Faisal on September 9, the British representative, Meinertzhagen, said Faisal had demanded unity of Syria " from Gaza to the Taurus Mountains " and accepted Zionism within this framework, but a French mandate meant slavery and he would answer the question of a French mandate when the British and French governments had accepted the Anglo-French declaration of the previous November.[9] In a later talk with Meinertzhagen alone, Faisal had freely discussed his true policy, which was the " absolute exclusion " of France and everything French. He was inclined to ignore the British refusal to accept the mandate for Syria, reported Meinertzhagen, and was attempting to force Britain's hands into taking the mandate; his ultimate aim was an Arab federation including Syria, Mesopotamia, and a Jewish Palestine, all under British mandate.[10]

Faisal sent instructions to the Hejaz delegation at the Peace Conference to protest the new proposals. On September 10 the delegation delivered a memorandum to the British delegation. After referring to Article Twenty-two of the Covenant and to the sending of the King-Crane Commission by the Peace Conference, the memorandum called the attention of the British delegation to attempts being made to oppose the Commission and make light of its findings. It rejected the Sykes-Picot agreement and any claims made on the basis of privileges such as concessions

[8] Telegram from Damascus, September 12, 1919; 763.72119/6740.
[9] *British Documents*, Series I, IV, 381.
[10] *Ibid.*, pp. 382–83.

for ports and railways or permission to establish schools or hospitals, granted to a nation by the Ottoman government; such claims were incompatible with the " *droit sacré de* self-determination," which the Covenant of the League had recognized. The memorandum warned the Conference of the results of so-called temporary arrangements which would result in a *fait accompli* with respect to the future of the Arab countries.[11]

After passing through France and receiving an extremely cool reception from the French government, Faisal arrived in London on September 18. He had asked for an interview with Clemenceau and received what Lloyd George later described as a " somewhat insulting " letter. On September 19 he met Lloyd George, Allenby, and others at 10 Downing Street where the new British proposals to withdraw from Syria were explained to him. He bitterly opposed the occupation of any part of Syria by French forces, and denied the right of anyone to partition any of the Arab lands; he said the Arabs had fulfilled their obligations during the war and he expected that Britain would do the same now. He asked the Prime Minister three questions. Did the three great powers, Britain, France, and the United States, stand by the declaration of November 9, 1918? Would the subsidy he had been receiving from the British be continued under the new arrangement? Would the British Commander-in-Chief in Syria continue to exercise command over all troops in Syria? Lloyd George answered that Britain would stand by all its engagements as the " Arab forces had redeemed the pledges they gave to Great Britain." Faisal commented that " he could not stand before the Moslem world and say that he had been asked to wage a war against the Caliph of the Moslems and now see the European powers divide the Arab country." [12]

Faisal made his formal reply to the proposals in a letter of September 21 to the Prime Minister, asking for the complete abrogation of the memorandum of September 13, which was a return to the old system of imperialism; the Arabs would fight for their independence, he said, and he disclaimed all responsibility for the consequences if the memorandum were imple-

[11] *Ibid.*, pp. 375–77.
[12] *Ibid.*, pp. 395–404; copies of the minutes of this meeting were obtained by the Embassy; in 867S.00/50.

mented.[13] No reply was received for several weeks. In the mean-time he had a series of conversations with Colonel Cornwallis of British Intelligence. He told Cornwallis that if Lloyd George rejected his answer to the September 13 proposals, he would submit three counterproposals: Allenby to remain in Supreme Command of all troops in Syria—if this were done, and French troops kept to a minimum, Faisal believed he could keep his people in order; an international commission to consider tem-porary arrangements in Syria pending the final decision of the Conference; the consideration without delay of the future of the Arab lands by the Conference—there was no reason why this should await the peace treaty with Turkey since it had already been decided to separate them from Turkey. He also said that he intended to take his case to the world press if he failed in his efforts in Europe. He was "very anxious to send a commission to America," reported Cornwallis, "but is at present debarred by his inability to find suitable representatives. He talks of going there himself." [14]

Faisal wrote again to the Prime Minister on October 9, appeal-ing to him to cancel the arrangement with the French, or if this were not possible, at least to postpone it. The replacement of British troops by French forces would be a "great catastrophe," he said, and asked that the whole question be submitted to the Peace Conference, or to a commission composed of British, French, and Arab members under the chairmanship of an American, which would report to the Conference.[15] As it happened, Lord Curzon had answered the previous letter to Lloyd George on this same day; he went over the commitments to the French and the Arabs emphasizing two main points: Britain had an obligation to King Hussain to establish an Arab kingdom which would include Damascus, Homs, Hama, and Aleppo; also, as Britain had made clear to King Hussain, France had special interests in the lands to the west of the four cities. It was imperative that Britain with-draw its troops because of the enormous cost of maintaining them, and Curzon asked Faisal to accept the temporary measure pro-posed; it was not a permanent arrangement and the ultimate

[13] *Ibid.*, pp. 406–9; Faisal gave a copy to the American Peace Mission; 763.72119/ 7337.

[14] *Ibid.*, pp. 421–22.

[15] *Ibid.*, pp. 443–44.

future of Syria would be decided by the Peace Conference as a whole. He reminded the Amir that the liberation of Syria from the Turks had been made possible by the great sacrifice made by France in Europe.[16] The reply to Faisal's second letter was made by the Prime Minister. He rejected Faisal's two suggestions and stated that he could not discuss the matter further, since the matter had already been thoroughly clarified in the letter sent by Lord Curzon, and it was not possible for Britain to maintain the cost of the occupation.[17]

3.

The American position on the redistribution of occupation forces in Syria was governed by two factors; first, the United States, as Polk had stated in the Council, would not recognize as having any implications for the settlement of eastern questions the occupation of a given area by troops of a particular nationality; second, until the United States had ratified the Treaty of Versailles and the Covenant and had accepted a mandate in the Ottoman Empire, it would take no part in discussions which affected the future of the area, except to prevent decisions being made which anticipated the final settlement. Consequently, no attempt was made by the American Delegation to intervene in negotiations between the British and Faisal on the one hand and the British and French on the other, since they concerned temporary arrangements which Polk had, on September 15, declined to recognize as binding on the United States. However, to keep the Delegation informed of developments, William Yale was sent to London, as an unofficial observer, to follow the negotiations there and maintain contact with the parties involved.

Before leaving Paris, Yale had conversations with a number of Frenchmen who were playing a prominent part in French Syrian policy. He saw first Robert de Caix, on September 13, and discussed with him French plans for the occupation of those parts of Syria allotted to French forces. They would occupy the Baqaa, the Syrian coast, and the railway north of Aleppo, but not the four cities of the interior, he was told. De Caix said that the French were afraid that the British would make trouble for the

[16] *Ibid.*, pp. 444–49.   [17] *Ibid.*, pp. 451–52.

French by encouraging the Arabs. In conversations between himself and Faisal in Syria, the latter had continually brought up the subject of Arab-Turkish relations in the future and was not happy about the establishment of a big Armenian state which would separate Arabs and Turks. Finally, De Caix had told Yale, if the British gave up Mesopotamia, France would give up Syria, but not otherwise. However, he went on, if the United States participated in the internationalization of the Ottoman Empire, France would prefer that solution to its partition. In a talk with Jean Gout on the same day, Yale was told France would like to get a reasonable agreement with Faisal, but if he continued to behave as he had in the past months, France would by-pass him and deal directly with the Syrians.[18] On September 19 Yale saw Bertholet who told him that while France would restrict her occupation of Syria to the areas laid down in the Lloyd George memorandum, enough troops would be sent to occupy the whole of Syria. Yale commented in his memorandum of the conversation that it was his opinion the French would do this at the first pretext.[19]

At the end of September Yale went to London. He saw the American Ambassador, Davis, on September 29, and it was agreed Yale would have no official connection with the Embassy and would carry out his mission as a private individual. Yale immediately began a series of interviews with British and Arab personalities. Rustem Haidar, the chief delegate from the Hejaz after Faisal, told him Faisal would not accept the British proposals. Yale replied that the United States could not be of any assistance in the problem until the three parties came together and agreed on basic principles. He outlined to Haidar a compromise plan of his own devising under which Mount Lebanon was to be established under its own government, and Syria, from the Taurus to the Red Sea, constituted an Arab state; both were to be under French mandate, though the Arab state would retain a greater degree of independence. Palestine from the Jordan to the sea would be under a British mandate, and the Zionist program, " with due restraint," would be allowed to proceed. Mesopotamia would also be divided into two zones, one, reaching from Baghdad

[18] Peace Conference files, 185.5137/131; Memoranda of conversations, September 13, 1919.
[19] Peace Conference files, 185.5137/137; Memorandum of conversation, September 19, 1919.

north and including Mosul, would be an Arab state under British mandate, and the southern zone, including Basra and Muhhammera, would have local self-government under British mandate. The United States would act as arbiter in any disputes that arose in the implementation of the scheme.

Three days later, on October 2, Yale lunched with Faisal and his advisers. Faisal was very bitter against Britain and rejected entirely the Lloyd George memorandum. He told Yale that if the British insisted on the memorandum, he would make a final appeal to the United States, and if this was unsuccessful, he would return to Syria and lead his people in armed resistance to any invasion of their freedom. Yale put forward his plan and asked Faisal for his opinion, emphasizing that it was his own idea and had no official standing; but if a compromise solution could be reached, he could then present the plan to the American government with a reasonable expectation that it would assist in implementing it. Faisal however was guarded and did not commit himself, confining his comments to saying that he would accept anything the United States approved. Later in the month, on October 13, Yale met Rustem Haider and Nuri Said, who had been the field commander of the Arab Northern Army under Faisal; they said that they would accept Yale's plan if it were modified to provide for the establishment of a single Arab state rather than the two in Syria and Mesopotamia, and Nuri felt that Faisal would accept it when the time came to make a decision.

Yale also saw many of the British leaders concerned with Middle East affairs, as well as the experts and military men handling the Syrian question. On October 5 he had an interview with a Colonel Gribbon of the War Office Intelligence Bureau. Gribbon said the French were being unreasonable but Britain would live up to her wartime promises, and all unofficial commitments made by British officers to the Arabs in the war would be disregarded. Yale's most important discussion was with Mr. Wickham Steed, editor of the *Times*. Steed said that his only interest was in maintaining good relations with the French and he saw no way out of the difficulties with the Arabs. When Yale described his own plan, Steed said that if he would write it in the form of a letter to the *Times*, he would publish it; he also urged him to draw up a memorandum and submit it to the British government. This Yale did, and, with Steed's help, it was brought to the attention of

Lloyd George. The Prime Minister agreed to consider it if the French accepted it also. The plan was thereupon cabled to Washington and permission requested to adopt it as an official American proposal for submission to the French government. The Department of State, however, declined to change the policy of non-intervention in Turkish affairs until the Covenant and the Armenian mandate were accepted by the Senate, and there Yale's plan lapsed.[20]

American consular posts in the Arab countries had also been instructed to keep Washington and the Peace Commission informed of the effects of the British withdrawal from Syria on local conditions. Beirut reported on September 23 that the trustworthy consensus in Syria was that the withdrawal would have the " most serious consequences." [21] Throughout September and October reports and rumors were cabled describing the increasing unrest in the country. The Consul at Beirut reported on October 2 that, hearing reports of a serious outbreak between the Christians and Druses in Lebanon, he had asked the local British political officer for information; he had been given the bare outlines of the situation, but, he added, whereas up to this time the political officer had discussed local affairs freely, he now was reserved and his attitude seemed to indicate that he had received instructions to support the proposed French mandate.[22] However, on October 19, the Consul reported the political officer had told him about a secret instruction that all British wives and children of British army personnel were to be evacuated from the French and Arab zones of occupation, in view of impending disorders in those regions. He had also told the Consul that if the disorders were organized by the Arabs there would be no danger to British and other European residents, but if they were spontaneous, as he believed they would be, then it would not be possible to guarantee anyone's safety. The Consul asked the Department to send an American warship to Beirut on November 1, the date of the British withdrawal. The only chance for a peaceful solution, he said, was an American mandate.[23]

[20] Yale's conversations in London are filed under Peace Conference file 185.5137/141.

[21] Telegram 14 from Beirut to Peace Mission, September 23, 1919; Peace Conference files, 867.4016/18.

[22] Telegram 1473 from Beirut via Paris, October 2, 1919; 867.00/946.

[23] Telegram 30 from Beirut, October 19, 1919; 867.00/968.

As the date for the British withdrawal drew near, the cables from the Middle East grew more and more anxious in tone, and in their stress on the probability of widespread outbreaks in Syria.[24] There were rumors that Mustafa Kemal, with the knowledge and approval of the local Arab authorities, was planning an attack on Aleppo. It was feared that the French would not be capable of maintaining order, and it was strongly urged that Britain postpone its withdrawal. The Consul at Beirut stated again that the only way to prevent open war and meet the conflicting interests of all elements in the dispute was an American mandate. The Department of State cabled him: "You are instructed scrupulously to avoid discussing with Syrians questions of or expressing any opinion in regard to mandates or encouraging any hope that America will take a mandate over Syria." [25] On October 30 the Department cabled London instructing the Embassy, in view of the reports from the Middle East on the scattered fighting that had broken out between French forces and local groups, to ascertain whether the British government had any fears of disturbances breaking out on the withdrawal before other measures could be taken to insure the maintenance of order. Inquiries were also made about the reported evacuation of British wives and children from the area.[26] An informal approach was made by the Embassy to the Foreign Office, where it was learned that there was no information on the evacuation of British families; the Embassy was informed that every effort would be made to synchronize the withdrawal with French troop movements into the zone. It was hinted that the reports sent by American posts in the area were somewhat exaggerated.[27]

4.

Notwithstanding Lloyd George's reply to Faisal's letter of October 9, a further interview was arranged to discuss the Amir's proposal of an international commission; it took place at Downing Street on October 13. The Prime Minister told Faisal that such a commission would be very difficult to set up, particularly with

---

[24] These cables are filed under 867.00.
[25] Telegram to Beirut, October 25, 1919; 763.72119/7445a.
[26] Telegram 6136 to London, October 30, 1919; 867.00/975.
[27] Telegram 3474 from London, December 1, 1919; 867.00/1031.

respect to the appointment of an American as the chairman of the group; the President was ill and the American representatives in Europe were without instructions. Faisal said that he was very concerned to have an American member on the commission and that it probably could be arranged, and Lloyd George agreed to ask the American delegation if this could be done. He also agreed, and this was the most important result of the discussion, to approach the French government on the subject of the commission.[28] Accordingly, he sent a telegram to Clemenceau asking that French representatives be sent to London to discuss occupation policy, adding that he was asking the United States to be represented in the talks. In addition he instructed the British Embassy at Paris to ask informally whether Clemenceau agreed to the presence of American representatives.[29] Lord Derby, the Ambassador at Paris, made repeated attempts during the next two days to obtain a reply from Clemenceau, but was not even successful in reaching him.[30] Finally, on the fourteenth, Clemenceau cabled a reply to London " in a temper of acid resentment, and full of insinuations against British good faith." At the same time he sent a letter to Derby giving his answer in more detail. The gist of his reply was that he could not accept the suggestion of the commission and, in so many words, that the British government had no business suggesting one, to say nothing of negotiating with Faisal, who should conduct his business with the French government. The solution of the Syrian problem, he went on, could not consist of sacrificing the rights of France as laid down in the Sykes-Picot agreement; what the British government should do was to tell Faisal to adhere to the letter and spirit of the existing accords. However, he was willing to talk to Faisal if he came to Paris.[31] On the eighteenth Lloyd George wrote to Clemenceau rejecting his charges of British bad faith. He went over the history of the Syrian problem from the exchange of letters between the Arabs and the British to the Anglo-French declaration of November, 1918. He assured Clemenceau that Britain acknowledged " France's rights and claims " in Syria and reminded him that Britain had formally stated to the Council of Four on March 20 that Britain would under no circumstances

[28] *British Documents*, Series I, IV, 458–62.
[29] *Ibid.*, p. 463.
[30] *Ibid.*, p. 467.
[31] *Ibid.*, pp. 468–69.

accept the mandate for Syria. But, he added, Britain was under a
" solemn obligation " to the Arabs as well as to the French.
Faisal had begun the Arab revolt at a time when allied fortunes
were far from promising, he had been loyal to the alliance to the
end, and he and the Arabs had played an indispensable part in
the victory over the Turks. He was entitled to the courtesy and
consideration due to an ally and should not be treated high-
handedly, but as the representative of a proud and historic race
" with whom it is essential that both the British and the French
should live in relations of cordial amity." [32]

The United States learned of these events by stages. On October 16 Curzon, the Foreign Secretary, called in Ambassador Davis
and gave him a brief account of what had been going on. He
said that an interview between Faisal and French representatives
had been arranged to discuss the British withdrawal. Faisal was
distrustful of the French and would meet any infringement of
Syrian sovereignty by force, said Curzon, and was unwilling to
make temporary arrangements until the final status of Syria had
been settled. Faisal had asked for an American representative to
be present at the discussions, and the American Peace Commission
in Paris would be asked if they agreed. Everything pointed to
the urgent necessity of deciding, not only the question of occupation forces, went on Curzon, but also the question of the ultimate status of ex-Turkish territory. Faisal was willing to postpone the latter question until the United States made its decision
on taking a mandate, but this was further delayed by the illness
of the President, which in addition made more unlikely an American mandate. He told the Ambassador that, the situation being
so, the British government, and the French also, asked if the
United States would be willing to proceed with final discussions
concerning the non-Turkish portions, at least, of the Ottoman
Empire. Davis reported this interview to Washington, but no
reply was received.[33]

On the following day, Faisal called on the Ambassador. He
told him that he had been summoned to London to be told by
the British that they had agreed with the French on the replacement of British troops with French in Syria; he now understood

---

[32] Ibid., pp. 479–89.
[33] Telegram 3254 from London, October 16, 1919; 763.72119/7285.

that Britain and France had come to a final agreement on the division of the Arab countries, with Mesopotamia and Palestine going to Britain and Syria to France. " Against this he protests bitterly, insisting that the Arabs were promised a united country," reported Davis to Washington. Faisal told him that any effort to divide his people or to put them under French rule "would be resisted by force of arms, preferring a hopeless struggle to shameful submission." Faisal said that he understood that Clemenceau had agreed to American representation at the proposed conference on occupation policy. His policy in Paris would be to insist first, that an American be present at the conference, and second, on Arab unity. If these were refused, he said, he would return to Syria and " put himself in the hands of his people." He thought a separate Palestine under British mandate useless and unwise, but that it was a minor matter to which he could probably agree. He stressed the unrest which British and French plans would create in the Middle East and added, apparently conscious of the implications of his remark, that the Turks who were the enemies of the Arabs yesterday might be their friends tomorrow. Davis commented in his cabled report; " He concluded by saying that he would do anything which met with the approval of President Wilson. I am impressed by his evident sincerity." [34]

On the following day, Polk, to whom a copy of the cable to Washington had been sent, cabled his own thoughts on the settlement of military questions in the Middle East and on the talk between Faisal and Davis. He did not think that the French were willing to discuss Syria and occupation policy in isolation; they hoped to get control of all of Turkey through the appointment of a French Commissioner in Constantinople, with the city and the rest of Turkey maintained as a political unit. This might satisfy them for not getting what they want in Syria, said Polk, " so you see the two are tied together." If the United States attempted to settle this issue, and the " dangerous " question of military occupation, Polk continued, there was a good chance of having the three nations—British, French, and Arabs—dissatisfied with the United States. It should be borne in mind, he added, that the present American Commission at the Peace Conference was not equipped to deal with the situation.[35]

[34] Telegram 3264 from London, October 18, 1919; 763.72119/7327.
[35] Telegram 4732 from Peace Mission, October 19, 1919; 867.00/965.

Faisal left London for Paris on October 20. On October 21 Polk reported to Washington that an agent of Faisal, Auni Abdul Hadi, had been sent from London to see him. Abdul Hadi had told him that Faisal wanted two things; first a conference with American participation, with General Bliss joining General Allenby, General Gouraud, and himself in discussing occupation policy; second, he wanted the United States to settle the entire Syrian question. Faisal believed that the Syrian people would accept any decision made by the United States, but they would fight a British or a French settlement. Polk told Abdul Hadi that he had no authority at that time to speak for the American government on the question, but he felt sure that the United States would not accept the position of arbiter, either in military or political matters, unless all the parties concerned joined in requesting American intervention. Polk concluded his cable by saying that General Bliss had always been of the opinion that occupation policy now in force, or imposed in the future, would decide the political future of the territories in question. It would " irrevocably fix the future political status of the component parts of Turkey in Asia," Bliss had told Polk; the Powers had evaded coming to a political decision and were now letting the military decide for them by default. American arbitration would be futile. The fundamental question was one of right or wrong, and therefore the decision of the American arbiter would be made in advance. There should be a conference to settle all Turkish questions, held away from Paris or London; if the Powers declined, the United States should withdraw from the whole affair.[36]

Faisal himself called on Polk two days later and told him of the progress of the proposals for a commission on Syria. He said the British had accepted the idea as far as military matters went, but refused to consider its having any authority in political matters; however, Clemenceau refused to accept the proposals even for military matters. This was an unacceptable situation, for divided control of Syria would make it impossible for his people to develop and the rivalry between the British and French would make it worse; some Arabs would be looking to France and others to Britain. He asked again for American arbitration of the problem, but Polk told him there was no chance of this. He then

[36] Telegram 4759 from Peace Mission, October 21, 1919; 867.00/967.

asked the United States to insist on French acceptance of his plan for a Commission. Polk told him again that it was not possible for the United States to intervene, but that he, Faisal, certainly could ask the Supreme Council (i.e., the Council of the Heads of Delegations) to consider the question. Faisal asked whether it would be wiser to ask for the Arab question to be settled alone, or to wait for the settlement of the whole Turkish question. Polk answered that it would be better to wait for the Turkish settlement, since it might be possible to satisfy France elsewhere. In his report of the conversation cabled on October 24, Polk said that Faisal would undoubtedly submit the question to the Council and that it would undoubtedly irritate the French. "Faisal is distinctly angry and while making no threats, it is evident that he feels ill used and some of those around him hint that a Jihad is possible and an alliance between Turks and Arabs more than likely." Polk added that he hoped the United States could withdraw from the "whole disgusting scramble." The Turkish treaty would be difficult to negotiate since it was the "last call" for spoils; it should not, in any event, be negotiated at Paris. It was essential that Britain and France do nothing to imperil the peace of the Middle East, but the plan they were trying to force on Faisal would bring trouble. The plea of the British that they could not support the occupation was nonsense since they had only 8,000 troops in Syria, and they could afford to maintain any number where oil was to be found. He said that there were only two courses that the Supreme Council could take— either to retain Allenby in supreme command in all of Syria or to appoint some other commander, British or French, to the supreme command.[37]

5.

The series of telegrams sent to Washington by Polk and Davis on the Syrian situation called for drastic action by the United States to prevent a complete collapse of the President's Middle East policy, but by the end of October policy-making in Washington had come to a standstill. For the past month the President had been completely incapacitated, and at the time of his

[37] Telegram 4807 from Peace Mission, October 24, 1919; 867.00/970.

breakdown in September he had not delegated any authority to determine policy in the Middle East, having kept control of Turkish affairs entirely in his own hands. Secretary Lansing made several attempts to get a decision from the President, but no answer had been received from the White House except a statement by Wilson's physician that the President could not be permitted to make any decisions. This was serious enough, but in November the Senate rejected the Versailles Treaty and the American position in Turkish matters was in effect destroyed through the rejection of the Covenant of the League. There remained nothing to do except make arrangements for the withdrawal of the United States from Middle Eastern affairs.

Lansing made a final effort to obtain some indication of the President's mind on Turkish matters under the new circumstances. On November 12 he wrote a short note to him:

MY DEAR MR. PRESIDENT,

I venture to lay before you the summary, as well as copies, of telegrams the Department has received from Mr. Polk and from the Ambassador in London regarding the political and military situation of Syria and the general question of the Turkish Empire, and of Mandates.

After a careful perusal of these telegrams, I venture to suggest the advisability, should it meet with your approval, of instructing Mr. Polk and Mr. Davis to inform respectively the Peace Conference and the British Government which had inquired as to our desires in the premises, that since the British feel that everything points to the urgent necessity of settling the question of military occupation as well as the ultimate political status of the component parts of the Turkish Empire, and since, on the other hand, our own present Mission is not prepared to take part in negotiations for such settlement, this Government would, therefore, have no objection to the other powers proceeding with these negotiations.

I should be very grateful for an expression of your views.[38]

The telegrams referred to were those from Davis and Polk, cited above, concerning occupation policy in Syria. The letter was never answered. The Department could send no other reply to the series of cables from Paris and London on the Syrian question and other Turkish affairs than a cable informing Polk that Lord Grey, who was the appointed Ambassador at Washington

[38] Letter, Secretary of State to the President, November 12, 1919; 763.72119/7802b.

(he had not yet been able to present his credentials), had inquired at the Department if any information at all could be given of American policy on the prospective negotiations of the Treaty of Peace with Turkey; he had been informed that the matter had been before the President for some time but he was not in a condition to render any decision.[39]

One of the very few instructions received from the White House at this time (the President was in a condition to issue formal instructions but could not decide between different courses of action) was to bring to an end the activities of the Peace Commission, in view of the rejection of the Treaty; in reply to inquiries by the Department of State, Mrs. Wilson replied on behalf of her husband that the Commission could sign the Bulgarian treaty if it were finished before they left Paris, but it was to make no special efforts in the matter.[40] In reply to Polk, who had asked for further instructions and guidance on the American position on the yet unnegotiated treaties with the Central Powers, Lansing cabled on November 14 that while he was unable to speak for the President, his own view was that since the only reason for American participation in the Bulgarian and Turkish treaties was the guarantee in the Covenant, which would make the United States a guarantor of the individual settlements, with the rejection of the Covenant by the Senate that reason had disappeared.[41]

6.

The defeat of the Treaty of Versailles in the Senate did not completely extinguish the hope that the United States would enter the League; the rejection of the Treaty had been due to the votes of those who supported the Treaty without reservations, as well as to the votes of those who were enemies of the League, and the version defeated had had added to it several reservations objected to by Wilson and by the League supporters. There might still be an opportunity for the United States to join the League if an acceptable version of the Covenant could be agreed on by all its supporters, who were in the majority both in the Senate and

[39] Telegram 3803 to Peace Mission, November 18, 1919; Peace Conference files, 867 n.00/182.
[40] *Foreign Relations*, Paris Peace Conference, XI, 672.
[41] *Ibid.*, p. 661.

among the people at large. The United States therefore, while withdrawing from an active part in the consideration of the Turkish treaty, maintained a watching brief in the negotiations. At first, Wilson had instructed the Department of State to close the American Peace Commission on December 1; Lloyd George and Clemenceau had begged the Americans to stay in Paris until the Germans ratified the Versailles Treaty, which they had shown signs of refusing to do, in order to present to the Germans a united front. Wilson had then agreed to extend the time of departure until December 9, but this was to be the limit of his concession.[42] However, Polk made repeated requests of the Department to have some American representation on the Supreme Council at least; he suggested that the Ambassador in France, Wallace, be appointed. Lansing wrote to the President endorsing Polk's arguments but recommending that Wallace sit on the Council as an observer not as a participant.[43] Wilson approved this,[44] and Wallace was informed by cable on December 8 of the President's decision. He was " to take no action and express no opinion on any subjects discussed by (the Council), but (to) report the proceedings to the Department and await instructions on any point on which an expression of the views of (the) Government is desired." [45] These instructions were reiterated on December 18, when the Council, apparently not yet accustomed to the new status of the United States in the Council, attempted to act as though it represented the principal Allied and Associated Powers.[46] When the Supreme Council adjourned after the Treaty of Versailles had been ratified and was in effect, and the Council of Ambassadors took over the handling of Peace Conference business, Wallace was authorized to continue to attend its sittings as an observer when it considered matters relating to Austria and Germany,[47] but when a preliminary meeting of Allied premiers was convened in London prior to the consideration of the Turkish treaty by the Supreme Council, Wilson refused permission for an American observer to attend.[48] However, when the Council met in San Remo in April for the Turkish treaty discussions, the Ambassador in Italy attended as an observer.

[42] *Ibid.*, pp. 677 ff., *passim.*
[43] *Ibid.*, pp. 694–96.
[44] *Ibid.*, p. 696.
[45] *Ibid.*, p. 697–98.
[46] *Ibid.*, 1919, I, 29.
[47] *Ibid.*, p. 32.
[48] *Ibid.*, 1920, I, 1.

CHAPTER IX

THE AMERICAN WITHDRAWAL: THE FORTUNES OF SELF-DETERMINATION

1.

For less than a year, American policy in the Middle East had been based on the active participation of the United States in Middle East affairs. During this brief interlude one lasting thing had been accomplished—the establishment of the mandate system—which, whatever its faults in its final form, profoundly affected the settlement of Eastern questions in two ways: first, the perfectly legal right of the victorious Allies to annex conquered territory outright was denied application to the settlement; and secondly, the right of the peoples of a territory, no matter what its relation to the conqueror, to have a voice in its future was admitted as a factor in the determination of the territorial aspects of the peace settlement. There was, of course, a vast difference between the mandate system as it appeared at the Peace Conference and as it was actually applied to the Turkish settlement. Lloyd George boasted that, in the mandate system, Wilson received " a bundle of assignats," whereas he had a pocketful of gold sovereigns in the form of the actual control of the countries involved. But he might have done better had he assayed the gold content of his coins, and he lived to see the day when Wilson's assignats were cashed at par.

The war ended with the European powers in firm control of the non-Turkish portions of the Ottoman Empire, and this control was maintained for twenty years or more. But the control they exercised was not in their own names but in the name of the League of Nations and the peoples of the territories. This may have been a matter of form, and the mandatories certainly considered it to be such, but it was not merely an empty form. In the first place, the people were left with a hope; their right to independence had been recognized, though it had been postponed for an indefinite term, and once the possibility of controlling their own affairs was admitted it would never be easy to persuade them that it would never come to pass. Second, the mandate system precluded the establishment of new Algerias in the Middle East; Syria could never be integrated into metropolitan France and could never be colonized by the French. Third, attempts to achieve independence could never be declared wholly illegal by the mandatories; specific actions to this end might be put down by the mandatory, but the principle could not be denied—for the mandate system itself declared that the territories were to be prepared for independence.

One of Wilson's major aims in the Turkish settlement was thus achieved: the terms of the settlement were such as would be acceptable to the American people and the mandate system gave to the United States a channel of influence in Middle East affairs, via the League, without direct involvement in the Middle East and without buying, as it were, a voice in these matters by direct involvement in the Middle East. The indirect interests of the United States in the former territories of the Ottoman Empire, based on their importance in world affairs generally, would appropriately be protected by indirect means. But all this was predicated on the assumption that world affairs were of sufficient importance to the welfare of the United States to warrant the country's active participation in world politics. The defeat of the Treaty of Versailles and the Covenant in the Senate was in effect a denial of this assumption and a return to a foreign policy based on the belief that the benefits, if there were any, to be derived from entangling alliances were simply not worth the price. The following chapters describe the development of a new Middle East policy to meet the requirements of this assessment of the national interest and the new conditions in the area itself.

2.

The rejection of the Treaty of Versailles had important effects on the policies of the Allies as well as on American Middle East policy. The withdrawal of the United States from the Turkish settlement was both a benefit and a problem for Britain and France. It left them with a clear field in the settlement, but it also deprived them of the services of the United States in the effective neutralization of disputed or unwanted territory such as the Straits and the Caucasus. But the most tragically affected of all the claimants to the remains of the Ottoman Empire were the Arabs and the Armenians. The effect of the withdrawal on the Armenians was direct; without the active participation of the United States in the settlement, their hopes for an independent state were ended. For the Arabs the effect was less immediate and it took many months for its implications to be completely realized, but it was as significant. The first impact of the American withdrawal on the Arab position was felt in Faisal's relations with the French at Paris. In the last chapter, Faisal's attempt to make the question of occupation troops a matter for the Supreme Council, rather than one between the French and the Arabs alone, was described. The United States was his sole hope for achieving this and when news of the probable Senate action on the Treaty reached Paris, Faisal abandoned his hopes of keeping occupation policy within the framework of the Peace Conference and entered into direct negotiations with the French.

During the course of these negotiations Clemenceau wrote to Faisal, on November 2, what amounted to an official statement of French policy with respect to the replacement of British troops by French. He noted Faisal's uneasiness about the September 15 agreement and his and his compatriots' fears that it would mean the partition of Syria. He assured them that his government was interested only in helping the Syrians and assuring them a regime of liberty, order, and progress. Neither the boundaries nor, indeed, the actual future of Syria were in question, he said. He gave to the Arabs and Faisal a full guarantee that the political future of Syria was reserved absolutely, local administration would be unchanged, and no decision would be taken on frontiers—all these points would be decided by the Peace Conference and not by the agreement to replace British troops with French units in any part of Syria. A new commission, said Clemenceau, would merely needlessly complicate the issue and would, in fact, be opposed to a decision of the Supreme Council.[1] (The September

[1] *British Documents*, Series I, IV, 511–13.

15 agreement was, in fact, not a Council decision; Polk had made that clear at the time.)

Faisal replied on the fifth. He said that the Arabs, who had fought for their freedom, could congratulate themselves on the new assurances given by M. Clemenceau in confirmation of the previous declarations and repeated promises of the Allies. However, he went on, even though the political future and frontiers of Syria were not to be called in question, a change in occupation policy would compromise greatly the public life and administration of Syria. More important, the implementation of the agreement would in effect put into execution the Sykes-Picot agreement, which the Arabs had not ceased to protest. A reading of the September 15 agreement sufficed to show that it was not a mere military arrangement but a delineation of spheres of influence.[2] On the following day Faisal submitted to the Supreme Council his interpretation of the present position in Syria and asked the Council to take the matter into its own hands. He asked for the appointment of a commission to consider occupation policy, a proposal which had been accepted by the British and rejected by the French. He made five points: (1) He found it " difficult to understand," he said, how the new arrangement could be described as a purely military one; it comprised political and economic factors that should be decided by the Council. (2) The division of Syria into three zones would be a " deadly blow " to the Arabs, and, moreover, that part left to the Arab government, while described as " independent," was actually divided again into British and French zones. (3) The withdrawal of British troops was based on an agreement that left out two of the parties involved—the Arabs and the United States. (4) When the Allied troops entered Syria, the Arabs had withdrawn from the coastal region of the country on the promise by the Allied Commander-in-Chief that Syria was being occupied in the name of all the Allies and that the regime thus established would remain in effect until the Peace Conference made its final decision on the Turkish treaty; no change could thus be made until the Peace Conference itself decreed it. (5) The unrest in the former provinces of the Ottoman Empire was no longer a secret; it was caused by unwise Allied actions, and if the status quo in Syria were disturbed there

[2] *Ibid.*, pp. 513–15.

would be serious trouble there.[3] On November 6 he also sent to
Lloyd George copies of his correspondence with Clemenceau and
his letter to the Council; he had been obliged to put the matter
in the hands of the Council, he said, and informed the Prime
Minister that the " Syrian Arab Nation " would do everything in
its power to defend its independence and unity. He asked him
for his help in presenting the Arab case to the Council.[4]

By this time, of course, the British withdrawal had already
begun. The French, in a note to the Council, on November 13,
rejected Faisal's request for a commission of inquiry,[5] and on the
same day Clemenceau wrote to Faisal informing him of this action.
Faisal replied on November 20 reiterating his demands for the
maintenance of the status quo, or at least retention of over-all
command in British hands, and for a commission of inquiry.[6]
The story at this point becomes obscure; neither French nor Arab
documentation is available, but a clue may be found in the
sequence of events as they are known. On November 16 the
commander of the U. S. S. *Biddle*, then at Beirut, radioed Admiral
Bristol at Constantinople that he had been informed, as a military
secret, by the French Administrator-in-Chief at Beirut, in an interview held at the latter's request, that the French intended to
occupy the Baqaa Valley (i. e., the valley between the Lebanon
and anti-Lebanon mountains; it had always been predominantly
Muslim and was not included in the Lebanon of the 1861 arrangement). This, the French authorities maintained, was in accordance with the 1916 agreement.[7] The Consulate at Beirut reported
on the sixteenth that the French had actually begun to occupy the
valley, and French and Arab forces there were facing each other
ready to fight.[8] There were skirmishes throughout the country
between Arabs and French. The Arab Chief-of-Staff, Yasin
Pasha, was arrested by the British and sent to Haifa for sending
troops to Baqaa to oppose the French and for refusing to take
orders from the British and French military authorities.[9] The
Consul in Beirut cabled that the Arab representative there had

[3] *Ibid.*, pp. 516–19.   [4] *Ibid.*, pp. 510–11.   [5] *Ibid.*, pp. 530–31.
[6] *Ibid.*, pp. 546–48; the text of Clemenceau's letter to Faisal is not available.
[7] Telegram 83 from Constantinople, November 17, 1919; 867.00/1012.
[8] Telegram from Beirut via Constantinople and Paris, November 16, 1919;
867.00/1004.
[9] Telegram 5498 from Paris for Beirut via Constantinople, November 26, 1919;
763.72119/8072.

asked him to intervene but he had refused. In a cable to Paris on November 24, Damascus reported being informed by the Arab authorities in the city of the certainty of trouble if the French occupied the Baqaa. Events were moving rapidly, the Consul said; the other Consuls were advising their nationals to go to the coast and were considering going there themselves. In the cable the Consul included a message from Faisal's brother and deputy in Damascus, the Amir Zaid, to Faisal for delivery via the American Embassy at Paris: " Do you authorize return of Sherif Ali to Hejaz? " The Consul commented that, as Zaid favored war on the French, he suspected it might be a code message, particularly as Zaid had asked for a reply as soon as possible.[10] The Embassy did not forward the message.

In the meantime, at Paris Faisal saw British Ambassador Lord Derby on November 21 and handed him a letter to Lloyd George stating that the French intended to occupy territory in the Arab zone promised to the independent Arab state. The army and all the Arabs would resist this move, he said, and he asked the British government, in the name of his father, for assistance. Faisal told Derby of the contents of the letter and also complained he was not being treated with proper respect by the French, nor would Clemenceau see him.[11] The British did not respond, and by November 25, under the threat of a general French advance into the interior of Syria, Faisal agreed to negotiate on the terms of a French mandate in return for a suspension of the French orders to occupy the Baqaa; the French also agreed to a commission of inquiry, but it was to meet in Beirut under the chairmanship of General Gouraud or his nominee.[12] The French intention to force the issue, by arms if necessary, had already been made clear to Faisal on November 6 by Gouraud, before the latter left for Syria, who had told him that while he sympathized with the Arabs he would carry out all orders he received and would not hesitate at bloodshed if his orders required it.[13] The Consul at Beirut cabled

[10] Telegram from Damascus via Paris, November 24, 1919; 867.00/1033.

[11] *British Documents*, Series I, IV, 543–46.

[12] *Ibid.*, pp. 554–58. The French Ambassador told the Foreign Office that the French withdrawal was part of an agreement by which Faisal accepted a French mandate; *ibid.*, pp. 559–60.

[13] Beirut cabled on December 10, 1919, that Gouraud had announced that the Baqaa would remain under Arab administration, but under certain conditions: (1) The French would occupy Rayak and guard the railway there. (2) A French

on the twenty-fifth a report that General Allenby would arrive
at Beirut in a few days and informed the Department, on " reliable authority," that the object of his visit was to arrange the
boundaries of Syria in consultation with Gouraud. The Consul
had also learned from the same source of the postponement of
the French occupation of the Baalbak and Rayak districts pending
the settlement of boundaries. The French, in any case, did not
have sufficient troops at the moment to meet determined Arab
opposition at these places, commented the Consul; they had asked
the British if they would come to their assistance if attacked by
the Arabs—the answer was no.[14]

The details of the agreement between Faisal and the French
were made known to Polk on December 1 by Faisal's representative, General Haddad, who gave him copies of the correspondence
between Faisal and Bertholet; a letter from Pichon to Gouraud
informing him of the agreement with Faisal; a similar letter from
Faisal to Zaid; and a letter from Bertholet to Faisal informing
him that the French would not occupy the Baqaa. In the course of
the conversation, Haddad asked several times if the United States
would send, unofficially, officers to help in administering Syria.
Polk told him he did not think France and Britain would approve
of the arrangement. He also told Haddad it was not at all certain
that Britain would take a mandate for all of Mesopotamia, due to
the Kurdish problem, and if they did not it would be easier for
Faisal to keep the French out of Syria—though he himself was
convinced they would occupy part, at least, of the coastal zone.
This was the second time Polk had seemed to hint more-or-less
broadly that Faisal should hold on in Syria since it was very possible the French could be compensated elsewhere when the final
settlement was reached.[15]

During the next month Faisal and the French came to an understanding on the broad terms of a mandate. On December 20
Derby reported to London that the French had made concrete

---

liaison officer would be stationed at Baalbek. (3) All " malefactors " would be
surrendered to the French authorities. (4) Arab troops would evacuate the Baqaa.
(5) There would be free commerce and communication between the French and
Arab zones. This would be a temporary arrangement and would not affect the
final settlement by the Peace Conference.

[14] Telegram from Beirut, November 25, 1919; 867.00/1025.
[15] Peace Conference files, 185.5137/-; Memorandum, December 1, 1919.

proposals to Faisal, and Faisal had submitted counter proposals.[16] On January 2, 1920, the Consul at Damascus cabled Washington that Nuri Said had told him he felt sure an agreement with the French would be reached shortly, uniting the east and west zones of Syria under Faisal but curtailing his independence. Nuri added that the British did not want Faisal to become too subservient to the French and might assist him to retain more freedom of action in the east zone.[17] Some days later the *Temps* of Paris reported Faisal had agreed to a French mandate before he left France (he had returned to Syria at the beginning of January). In an interview he had said there was no written agreement but something better—a " harmony of views " founded on a mutual feeling of confidence.[18] General Haddad gave a copy of the agreement to a member of the British Embassy at Paris on January 16, pointing out it was only a French draft and had not been signed by Faisal.[19] The Consul at Damascus discussed the agreement with Faisal on January 24 and was told there was no definite agreement yet with the French. The Consul commented to Washington that Faisal realized some foreign assistance was needed in Syria and that he had to accept the available power—France. He had reshuffled his Cabinet, which was much stronger now, with Amir Zaid as Military Governor and Ali Riza as Chief-of-Staff. During the past few days, added the Consul, Faisal had told several public meetings that he had had to change his policy because of the withdrawal of the United States from the Peace Conference.[20]

The version of the agreement given to the British by Haddad consisted of a preamble and six articles with an explanatory letter. The French government, with reference to the Anglo-French declaration of November 9, 1918, and to the principles of freedom enunciated by the Peace Conference, confirmed its recognition of the right of the Arab-speaking peoples of Syria, of all religions, to unite for the purpose of self-government as an independent nation. Faisal acknowledged on his part that, due to the disorganization resulting from Turkish misrule and the ravages of

[16] *British Documents*, Series I, IV, 592–95.

[17] Telegram 2 from Cairo for Damascus, January 2, 1920; 867.00/1069.

[18] *British Documents*, Series I, IV, 611–12; on Faisal's agreement with the French, see also *ibid.*, VII, 114–18, for discussions during the Conference of London on February 18, 1920.

[19] *Ibid.*, pp. 624–27.

[20] Telegram 93 from Beirut for Damascus, January 24, 1920; 867.00/1102.

war, the Syrian people required the advice and assistance of a great power to realize their unity and establish a state, under the auspices of the League of Nations. Faisal, in the name of the Syrian people, was to call on France for this assistance. The French government engaged to guarantee Syrian independence within boundaries to be established and would see to it that these boundaries were equitable. Faisal undertook to ask the French government, and only the French government, for the advisers, instructors and technicians necessary for the organization of the government; they would be put at the disposition of the Arab government. The French government and Faisal agreed to establish in Syria a constitutional regime which would assure all the rights of the Syrian people, with a government responsible to Parliament. A financial adviser would participate in drawing up the budget and would have control over that part of the Ottoman public debt allotted to Syria. A transport adviser would control all railways. France was to organize the *gendarmerie*, police, and army. Priority was to be given to French economic interests. Syria was to have diplomatic representation overseas, and France was to use its good offices to obtain the entry of Syria into the League of Nations; however, while Faisal was to have a diplomatic delegate at Paris, he was to confide to France the diplomatic representation allowed to him and France would represent Syrian interests in foreign countries. Faisal recognized the independence of Lebanon under French mandate. Arabic was to be the official language, though French was to have a special position. The most interesting article provided for the establishment of Damascus as the capital, while the residence of the French High Commissioner was to be at Aleppo, in the frontier zone, where the defense forces would normally be stationed. These forces would be sent into the interior only at the request of the Chief of State in agreement with the High Commissioner. The letter was an expansion of the provision relating to an independent Lebanon and the status of Beirut and Alexandretta. Faisal's proposed agreement followed the French proposals closely in almost all particulars, with two very significant differences: The complete political and administrative independence of Syria was to be recognized, and the present government of the country was to be the basis of the new Syrian state.

3.

While Faisal was negotiating at Paris and giving the appearance, at least, of agreeing to a French mandate, the Arab government at Damascus, under his brother Zaid, was laying plans for continuing resistance to the French and the British, not only in Syria but also in Mesopotamia. What part Faisal played in these plans is not certain; that he supported them to some extent on his return to Syria, is known. However, there are good indications that he was in secret communication with Zaid while he was in Paris, and the code apparently used was a type based on a prearranged course of action. He also had good reasons for maintaining his reputation as a moderate so as to give no excuse to the French for refusing to acknowledge him as the leader of the Syrians and to keep whatever support the United States might be in a position to afford him. There is no doubt that Faisal was informed of Zaid's activities, yet on his return to Syria in January he appointed him Military Governor with wide powers over the Arab forces. On the other hand, many of those around Faisal were hot-headed and irresponsible and had little patience with the subtleties of Faisal's negotiations with the French. In the latter part of 1919 the exploits of Mustafa Kemal in Turkey had encouraged the hot-heads to believe that a policy of action and resistance could achieve independence for Syria, and Faisal would have short shrift at their hands if he seemed to be bowing to French pressure. Lastly, a policy of continued resistance would make the final settlement of the Syrian question more difficult and would delay at least a French take-over before the Turkish treaty was signed. This was a principal aim of Faisal's policy, based partly on the belief the United States would step in at the last moment and save the Arabs. From the statements and actions of American leaders at the Peace Conference Faisal had some reason for believing this, and even though the defeat of the Covenant in the Senate had dampened Arab hopes, Polk had since then twice indicated to Arab representatives that if they held on they might yet keep out the French. It is possible Faisal read more into Polk's statements than were intended and believed they were hints the United States would intervene directly. Whatever the truth of the matter, the Arab authorities in Syria, with the active participation of Faisal, were from the end of 1919 to July, 1920, engaged in active military operations against Britain and France.

Before Faisal's return to Syria agents of Mustafa Kemal had approached the Arab authorities in Syria, and, particularly in the Aleppo region, had, by an extensive propaganda effort, succeeded in arousing a good deal of pro-Turkish feeling, notably among the ex-officers of the Turkish Army who had joined the Arab revolt. The most important of the Arab officials who entered into negotiations with the Turkish nationalists was Yassin Pasha, the Arab Chief-of-Staff, deported by the British to Haifa for his anti-Allied activities. Apart from an increase in local attacks on French military posts the first important effect of the growing understanding between Arabs and Turks was the attack on Dair ez-Zor, a small town on the Euphrates far in the interior of Syria; it was the most advanced British post manned from the Mesopotamian command and an important river crossing. The Consul at Baghdad cabled on December 16 that the Arab Governor of Rakka attacked Dair on December 11 with 2,000 men, taking the British authorities prisoner and burning the public buildings. It was believed in Baghdad, said the Consul, that the Turkish Consul-General and the frontier authorities were implicated, and that a large number of Turks had taken part.[21] A month later the Consul at Aleppo confirmed these rumors and added that the Amir Zaid was behind the Arab participation in the raid and had given the Arab leader 12,000 Turkish lira.[22]

On his return from Paris, Faisal found a great deal of antagonism to himself and to his negotiations with the French. He was accused of treachery to the Arab cause, of weakness, of selling Arab freedom to the French. This feeling had been carefully nurtured by the Turkish Nationalists and was particularly strong in the northern region of Syria around Aleppo. The Consul there reported Faisal had been threatened with assassination if he appeared in the city.[23] Consequently, when Faisal discovered that the Arab government had arranged for two emissaries to proceed to Constantinople to contact the leaders of the Turkish Nationalist movement, he was at first opposed to the plan. He was per-

[21] Telegram from Baghdad, December 16, 1919; 867.00/1048.
[22] Despatch 435 from Aleppo, January 5, 1920; 867.00/1121.
[23] Despatch 438 from Aleppo, January 15, 1920; 867.00/1160.

suaded to agree, however, apparently on the understanding that Turkish opposition to him as ruler of Syria would cease, and the two men left for Constantinople where they met with representatives of Mustafa Kemal. An agreement for joint military action against the foreigners was worked out and a provisional agreement on the relations between the Turkish nation and Arabs drafted. This provided for Arab and Turkish independence under a binational state on the pattern of Austria-Hungary, and a united front against the Allies " from the Black Sea to Ma'an " with Arab and Turkish forces under a unified command. When this agreement was brought back to Syria in April, however, Faisal refused to approve it; no doubt because it would have meant the complete subservience of Syria to the Turks.[24]

In the meantime the agreement on joint military action was in effect and Arab plans went forward accordingly. On February 28, 1920, the Consul at Aleppo reported that a meeting had been held in Damascus on that date to discuss a proposed boycott of all countries occupying Arab territories. The meeting had been called by Faisal and was attended by many prominent Syrians and most of the Arab government, including the higher military personnel such as Ali Jawdat Ayyubi and Jaafar Pasha. The Consul believed this indicated that the purpose of the meeting was to discuss military operations rather than commercial embargoes. He had information, he said, that an attack on the British in Mesopotamia was to begin in the middle of March. Faisal had made sure of all the tribes in the Syrian desert and the Kurds also would take part. The attack would take place in three columns. The first would follow the line Dair ez-Zor-Baghdad, the second Dair ez-Zor-Mosul and the third Aleppo-Ras al-'Ain-Mosul. Arab emissaries had talked with Mustafa Kemal at Sivas on joint operations, and the Turks had already begun to attack French posts in Cilicia. Dair ez-Zor was to be the headquarters of the invasion and Faisal's troops and Bedouins were assembling there and col-

[24] On the Syrian mission to the Turkish Nationalists, see Zeine, *Arab Independence*, pp. 147–48, fn. See also Ali Jawdat al-Ayyubi's account of his role in the Mesopotamian rebellion, *ibid.*, p. 146, fn. There are some vague references to Faisal's connection with the troubles in Mesopotamia in *British Documents*, Series I, XIII; the question of continuing the subsidy to Faisal in view of Arab attacks is raised on p. 286, and Faisal's relations with the Turks on pp. 289–90. Also, Harry St. J. Philby, *Arabian Days, an Autobiography* (London, 1948), p. 184.

lecting arms.[25] On March 3, Aleppo sent more information on these plans. The Arab government had issued a call for all Syrians between twenty and twenty-five to enroll in the Arab Army. Special secret orders had been issued to engage a number of competent officers, who were to be given three months' pay in advance, to go to Dair in Bedouin dress and there lead the tribesmen in the attack on the British.[26]

The next stage was the declaration of Syrian independence, including Lebanon and Palestine, on March 8 and the coronation of Faisal as King of Syria on March 20. But in the midst of these preparations the situation changed completely. The Senate decisively defeated the Treaty of Versailles and the Covenant in March, whereupon the British and French proceeded to divide the Ottoman Empire at the San Remo Conference, which was held to decide the terms to be offered the Turks in the Peace Treaty. France was allotted the mandate for Syria on April 24. In the meantime the Clemenceau government had fallen and was replaced by a group whose Middle East policy was diametrically opposed to its predecessor's, its main features being the protection of French financial interests in Turkey, which meant coming to terms with the rulers of Turkey—Mustafa Kemal and the Nationalists—and the reinstatement of traditional French policy in Syria based on a firm and direct control of the country.

Faisal felt the first impact of this when the French came to an understanding with the Turks whereby the French withdrew from the interior of Cilicia and the Turks recognized the French position in Syria.[27] This completely altered his plans for Mesopotamia, which had been based on Arab-Turk co-operation. He repeatedly attempted to persuade the Turks to keep their agreement, but without success. The great plan deteriorated into individual attacks on British posts and the part played by Syria in the revolt was confined to the individual participation of certain of Faisal's officers, except for the provision of money by Faisal to the rebels. In June Faisal made a last attempt to come to terms

[25] Despatch 464 from Aleppo, February 28, 1920; 890d.00/5.

[26] Despatch 467 from Aleppo, March 3, 1920; 890d.00/7.

[27] According to despatch 132 from Beirut, May 31, 1920, a delegation of Turkish Nationalists came to Beirut in the latter part of April and held secret conversations with De Caix; the French paid their hotel bill, and they returned on a French ship; 890d.00/31.

with the Turks without success. On June 17 the Consul at Aleppo reported that Faisal was in the city preparing for an expedition against Baghdad via Dair ez-Zor, but had failed to persuade the Turks to break their agreement with the French and had now decided to return to Damascus. The Consul said it was reliably reported that Faisal had paid the leader of the Iraqi rebels 30,000 Turkish lira and that members of his army were with the rebel forces attacking British installations near Mosul.[28]

The weakening of Faisal's military position came at the precise time when he needed all the strength he could muster. The allocation of the mandate to France meant two things—that France would not accept compensation for Syria elsewhere in the Middle East, and there would be no last chance for Faisal at the Peace Conference. The agreement between the French and the Turks meant that France would now turn all her attention to Syria and, since Syria was all France would get out of the spoils of the Ottoman Empire, it was certain that France would brook no opposition there from Faisal. French troops withdrawn from Cilicia were sent to Lebanon, and by the middle of July were in sufficient strength to insure a decisive superiority over the Arab forces at Faisal's disposal. A peremptory ultimatum was sent by the French Commander-in-Chief to Faisal. It was accepted in essence but, nevertheless, the French Army moved out of Lebanon into Arab-administered territory and marched on Damascus. Faisal, always a realist and realizing that resistance was futile, ordered his army not to resist, but a few thousand volunteers, together with some hundreds of the army who had ignored an order to disband, met the French outside Damascus at Khan Maisalum in a last attempt to hold the city. The Arabs were quickly dispersed by the superior French force, leaving many dead, including the Minister of War, who had gathered the Arab force for this final effort and had led them into battle. Faisal left the country shortly after and never returned. The revolt in Mesopotamia, once the spark had been ignited, no longer needed Faisal, and the Iraqis, with their own grievances against the British, were soon in full-scale rebellion.

[28] Despatch 520 from Aleppo, June 17, 1920; 890d.00/26. In a telegram from the Foreign Office to Curzon on June 21, 1920, there is a mention of Faisal's " reported visit to Aleppo to meet Mustapha Kemal's emissaries . . ." and a reference to a telegram from the British Consul-General in Beirut which apparently had something to do with this; it is not printed. See above, p. 247, fn.

4.

The United States played no direct part in these events. American Middle East policy was still in suspension, awaiting the final word of the Senate on the Covenant, and in the meantime the Department of State merely watched and gathered information, taking care not to become embroiled in the growing disruption of Syria and the Arab countries. American representatives generally maintained good relations with Arab, British, and French officials in the area; the Arabs in particular being anxious to keep on good terms with the United States as the only power in a position and, they hoped, of an inclination to help them. As a result, the United States had many channels of information and was acquiring a body of knowledge which would have been of great value in the event it had participated in the Eastern settlement. On the other hand, this information served to confirm the general American feeling following the rejection of the Covenant that, after all, the United States was well out of Middle Eastern affairs, the Fourteen Points notwithstanding.

The immediate American concern was the growing violence in the Arab countries in the spring of 1920 and its possible consequences to American missionary activities, to the missionaries themselves, and to the Christian inhabitants of the area. Reports from the Middle East were not encouraging. In reporting the arrival of Faisal at Beirut on January 14, 1920, the Consul there said Faisal had officially announced that a definite political agreement with France had not been reached but a united Syria was assured and it would be assisted by the French to reach its full development; he himself would help prepare the people for the French mandate, Faisal had said. However, the Consul added, it was felt in Beirut that the Arabs had been so much aroused against the French by Sherifian propaganda that if Faisal actually came to a definite agreement with the French he would be supplanted by another. Moreover, the tribes remained actively hostile and the brigandage prevalent in the country would continue until the French occupied Syria in force.[29] Aleppo sent a despatch two weeks later describing a visit of Faisal to the city to address a meeting of the notables; he had intended to tell the meeting the

[29] Telegram from Beirut, January 17, 1920; 867.00/1091.

full story of his relations with the French, but the hostile attitude in the city had made him confine his remarks to a statement that total independence had not yet been achieved but he had great hopes this would come about in the near future.[30] Faisal himself warned the Consul in Damascus that trouble was afoot. He told him on February 15 that the decisions reached in Paris on the Arab countries were illegal and opposed to the national aspirations of the Arab people; they would arouse much resistance, for the effects of which he would not be responsible. (There were already serious clashes between the local population and French officials, noted the Consul's report.) Faisal said that if the Peace Conference did not give independence to Syria the whole East would be incited to religious warfare against the Allies, and he himself would send his army against them.[31]

At this time the serious disorders in Cilicia had broken out and the entire region was torn by the conflict between the French and the Armenians on the one hand and the Turkish Nationalists on the other. This had its effect on north Syria both by reason of the overspill of the fighting into the Arab-speaking areas and, as mentioned above, as a result of the military understanding between the Turks and Arabs.

On February 6 the High Commission at Constantinople sent an instruction to Aleppo to make strong protests to the local government against attacks on Christians and foreigners by Muslims and to " demand " the protection of the " non-Muslim races " from these attacks. The necessity for all United States officials and citizens, especially relief workers, to remain neutral and to refrain from becoming involved in the quarrels between the French and the Arabs was impressed on the Consul. The Consul replied on March 2 saying that there was no cause for uneasiness on the latter count in the Aleppo district. He was taking no part in Franco-Arab disputes and his relations with the local Arab administration were cordial in the extreme; nor were any of the Americans in his jurisdiction affiliated in any way with the French, and no partisanship was being shown. As for protesting to the government about attacks on Christians, said the Consul, such

[30] Despatch 450 from Aleppo, February 2, 1920; 867.00/1139. The Consul accepted an invitation by the Arab authorities to meet Faisal at the railroad station and also attended the official reception.

[31] Telegram from Damascus, February 16, 1920; 867.00/1119.

protests must be made to the Arab authorities since there were no French in Aleppo; this he was doing continually, but had not had an opportunity to report individual cases to Constantinople since he was short of personnel and now had British interests in his charge. The problem of demanding protection for the non-Muslim races was even more difficult, he said, and he did not see how it could be demanded from the local government, composed as it was of " invaders " from the Hejaz and Mesopotamia whose interests were entirely foreign to those of the local people and were selfish and personal in the extreme.[32]

The situation was so confused that an official attached to the High Commission at Constantinople, C. van H. Engert, was sent on a special mission to Cilicia and Syria to tour the area and report firsthand on the problem. After spending two weeks in the French-occupied region of Cilicia and north Syria, he reported to the Department on February 28 that unless the French and Italians were prepared to send large forces to the Middle East, it would be better for them to withdraw completely rather than be thrown out. The Turks and Arabs were co-operating in anti-French activity in Syria and there were many ex-Turkish officers in the Arab Army. The French Army was sick of the whole affair, said Engert, and most French officers were more than ready to pull out of Syria, for their troops were Algerians and Senegalese and quite unreliable. In talks with Faisal and other Arab leaders he found a " child-like " belief that the United States would still come to their rescue.[33]

A few days later, the Consul at Aleppo also sent a report on conditions in the consular district. The chief causes of the unrest, he said, were British and French propaganda against each other; the use by the French of poor quality troops which, after the strong British administration, encouraged the Syrians; and the " imposition " on Syria of Faisal and his " coterie " of Hejazis and Mesopotamians, who were looked on as foreigners—the Syrians wanted to be rid of all outsiders, not just the French. The increase in brigandage, the Consul went on, was primarily due to encouragement by the Arab authorities, who wished to harass the

[32] Despatch 466 from Aleppo, March 2, 1920; 890d.00/6.
[33] Telegram from Damascus, February 28, 1920; 867.00/1135.

French by all means available. The French could end most of their problems by sending an adequate occupation force.[34]

When the independence of Syria was proclaimed, Faisal and his government made great efforts to secure American approval and to place their action before the United States in as favorable a light as possible. The Department of State, however, remained aloof. Independence was proclaimed on March 8, 1920. On March 9 the Consul at Beirut cabled his impressions of the significance of the action. He said Arab policy, in declaring Syrian independence and proclaiming Faisal as King (which they would do shortly), was to present the Peace Conference with a *fait accompli* by putting into effect what the Allies had proclaimed to be their policy and by actually implementing Article Twenty-two of the Covenant. This, they hoped, would so far embarrass the Peace Conference that it would not have the face to do anything about it. The Arabs, said the Consul, were willing to accept French advisers but nothing more. If the Peace Conference insisted on imposing the French on Syria, the Arabs would join with the Turkish Nationalists; and they were well enough equipped to make a European force of 100,000 men necessary to put them down.[35]

The United States took no official notice of Syrian independence and did not recognize Faisal as King. The Consul at Damascus cabled on March 11 for instructions if he were invited to attend the coronation.[36] The reply said that unless the British and French Consuls attended the ceremony he was to absent himself from Damascus for the period of the ceremonies, ostensibly going to Beirut to consult his colleagues there on " urgent business." [37] On the day of the coronation, the Prime Minister of the new government, Rikaby Pasha, sent two letters to " The Honorable Minister of Foreign Affairs, Washington "; one officially informing him of his appointment as Prime Minister and enclosing a certified copy of the proclamation of independence, and the second, of a more informal nature, in which the Prime Minister informed the Secretary of State that Faisal, at the first meeting of his Cabinet, gave a synopsis of the relations he had had with

---

[34] Despatch 467 from Aleppo, March 2, 1920; 890d.00/4.
[35] Telegram 163 from Constantinople for Beirut, March 9, 1920; 867.00/1148.
[36] Telegram from Beirut for Damascus, March 13, 1920; 890d.01/2.
[37] Telegram to Beirut for Damascus, March 16, 1920; 890d.01/2.

American statesmen and the political impressions he had brought back from Europe. His Majesty was convinced of the sympathy of the United States with Syria, said the Prime Minister, and of the fact that the American people were well disposed not only to recognize and support the independence of Syria in accord with their chivalrous traditions and the requirements of their real interests but also, insofar as was compatible with independence, to give to Syria aid and support. He was happy, he said, to have received this impression from His Majesty; it only strengthened the confidence the Syrians had always had in the great American nation and in the solemn declarations concerning Syria made by American statesmen.[38]

On March 28 Faisal cabled to President Wilson, informing him of the reasons for declaring his independence and asking for his support. After many years of Turkish misrule, said Faisal, and of the inability of the Arabs to gain their freedom because the balance of power did not permit them to obtain outside assistance, the Arabs seized the opportunity offered by the outbreak of war and sided with the Allies, ignoring the Caliph's call to Jihad which was thus rendered ineffective throughout the Muslim world. The Arabs had loyally helped in the defeat of the Central Powers with full confidence in the clear promises of the Allies of independence and in the President's own principles. But after the war the French and the British had begun to divide the country, and the only solution for the Arabs was the declaration of independence. The Arabs sought only their rights, said Faisal, and would fulfill all their obligations; he concluded by asking for Wilson's influence in obtaining the acceptance by the Allies of the independence of Syria. No answer was returned by the United States to any of these communications from Damascus.[39]

Faisal expanded his cable to the President in an interview he held at the end of March, at his own request, with Engert who was then in Damascus concluding his special mission. He had written to the President stating his reasons for the proclamation

[38] Telegram 29 from Cairo for Damascus, March 22, 1920; 890d. 01/14; this transmitted the texts of the messages. The originals were sent in despatch 5 from Damascus, March 24, 1920; 890d.00/10.

[39] Telegram 255 from Constantinople for Damascus via Beirut, April 2, 1920 (sent March 28 from Damascus); 890d.01/18.

of Syrian independence, he told Engert, but was very anxious to explain in greater detail his position and views, which he hoped might be communicated to the President in order that there should be no misunderstanding. He began by reviewing the reasons why his father had joined the Allies and revolted against the Turks; they were, Turkish misrule, and the promises made by the Allies of Arab independence. The Arabs had rendered important services to the Allies both militarily and in keeping the Muslim world quiet at a crucial time, and they had run great risks in case of an Allied failure to gain a decisive victory. On his first journey to Paris, said Faisal, he had been encouraged by the reception of the Arab cause by the Peace Conference; but since then the situation had radically changed, probably owing to the reluctance of the United States to participate in world affairs, for when he had visited Europe the second time he found Britain and France engrossed in purely imperialistic designs and he had difficulty in even getting a hearing. He was particularly disappointed in the British, on whom he had been relying for a united Syria; they had merely referred him to the French, whom he found laboring under the delusion that Syria was clamoring for a French mandate. They had offered to make a secret treaty with him, but the terms were completely unacceptable; he therefore had had to follow the advice of the more radical elements of his supporters, who were becoming more and more difficult to restrain, and proclaim the independence of Syria as a *fait accompli*, hoping that the world would support the legitimate aspirations of his people. He realized, he said, that Syria needed the help of a Great Power and was ready to accept advice and assistance, but he could never agree to the division of their country which would lead to a struggle for supremacy between the European powers to the detriment of the people. If the United States could not undertake the task, Britain was the only country the Arabs would accept; they found it difficult to understand, however, how Britain could take Palestine and give the rest of Syria to France. He concluded by stating that the Arabs would fight before submitting to the division of their country.

" The Emir spoke with great earnestness and undoubted sincerity," said Engert, in the report of the conversation he cabled to the Department, even if he overstressed the national consciousness of the Syrians which existed as a matter of fact only among very few educated Arabs; the educated Christians were by no means eager to support an Arab Kingdom, while the Jews were openly hostile. A year ago, said Engert, the great illiterate majority would have accepted any decision of the Peace Conference, provided they were given an efficient and impartial government and the Bedouin not interfered with too much, but since then they had been aroused by clever Turkish propaganda and encouraged by the successes of the Turks to believe that they could defy the Allies. They now believed also that the Syrian Christians were about to sell their country to the French and that Britain had already betrayed them by handing over Palestine to the Jews, and it was entirely possible at this stage that their bigoted leaders could lead them to armed resistance. Judging by the very frank and confidential statements made to him by Allenby and his Chief-of-Staff, added Engert, the British realized the dangers of the situation and were urging a conciliatory attitude to Syrian independence. France, however, was the stumbling block, and unless it could be persuaded to withdraw, in exchange perhaps for Constantinople, there would be no solution to the Syrian question without bloodshed. Britain had tried to carry out the Sykes-Picot agreement, but was being continually accused of intrigue by the French. Engert concluded by suggesting that if the French withdrew from Syria (and the French Army there was more than ready to do so, he added), the United States might recognize Syria provisionally; Mesopotamia should not be recognized, however.[40]

As events in Syria drew to their climax in the spring and summer of 1920, the United States continued to observe and continued aloof. With one exception no attempt was made to influence in any degree the actions of the powers, nor to intervene on behalf of the Arabs. No response was made to Faisal or his government, nor to the communications addressed to the United States through the Embassy at Paris by the delegation of the Hejaz, which still existed in Paris awaiting the conclusion of the Turkish treaty. The delegation sent a note to the Paris Embassy on May 19 protesting the decisions of the San Remo Conference on Mandates as contrary to all the Allied promises to the Arabs and to the Covenant; the delegation had not even been informed officially of the decision but had learned of it through the press. This was not answered.

[40] Telegram 27 from Cairo, March 28, 1920; 890d.01/10.

On July 19 the Consul at Aleppo reported that the expected clash between the Arabs and French was drawing nearer; the French had sent an ultimatum to Faisal and it was due to expire in twenty-four hours. He had been advised by a personal friend, who had the information from one high in Arab councils, that certain Arabs would make an attempt on his life. He had cabled at once to Damascus asking for all assistance necessary to protect the Consulate and all American citizens and British subjects who were now under his protection. The government had acted at once and had done everything possible to insure his safety. He was now making preparations, he said, for the protection of Americans and British if fighting broke out.[41] The French defeated the Arabs at Maisalun on July 24 and entered Damascus on the same day. On July 31 the Kingdom of Syria passed from the Department's view with the transmission of a cable from Beirut reporting that Faisal had abandoned Damascus and was then at Dera'a with some of his followers. The Consul said that official and other sources indicated Damascus and Alexandretta were calm, and Faisal's decision for peace or guerrilla war was awaited without anxiety.[42]

5.

It will be remembered that in August, 1919, Lloyd George and Clemenceau agreed in the Council that French troops would be permitted to go to Cilicia, ostensibly to protect the Armenians. In the middle of September a resolution was introduced in the Senate providing for the granting of authority to the President to send American troops to Armenia, to act either along or with the French Army. This had the full approval of the President. The Foreign Relations Committee was opposed to the idea, however, and it was dropped. As a substitute, it was proposed that regulations forbidding the recruiting of volunteers for foreign armies be suspended to permit Armenians in the United States to join the Armenian Army. It was pointed out by the Peace Commission that the United States would have to obtain control of the route from the sea to Armenia and hold it open to get the volunteers to Armenia, and nothing further was heard of this idea either.

[41] Despatch 534 from Aleppo, July 19, 1920; 890d.00/34.
[42] Telegram 434 from Constantinople for Beirut, July 31, 1920; 890d.00/27.

At about the same time as the agreement on occupation troops in Syria was being implemented, French troops were moved inland into Cilicia in the regions of Marash, Urfa, and Aintab. Most of the French troops were Armenians recruited by France in the Legion d'Orient. Soon the inevitable took place and incidents between the Armenian troops and local Turks occurred which led to wider outbreaks as the Nationalist forces came to the support of their compatriots. Resentment grew among the Turks as the French authorities moved out of the military sphere and began to interfere with local administration. At the beginning of 1920 Nationalist forces began to prepare for a full-scale attack on the French; reports came into American posts of attacks on Armenians and rumors of a new massacre began to circulate. The climax came with a full-scale attack on Marash by the Turks in which many Armenians were killed and two Americans shot. The French withdrew from the interior leaving the Armenians to the mercies of the Turks, and not long after negotiated the agreement with Mustafa Kemal which left Cilicia to Turkey.

In the middle of February the Consular posts in the region reported that thousands of Armenians were being massacred, but at the same time Admiral Bristol in Constantinople was cabling the Department of State that the reports of massacres were being grossly exaggerated for political purposes. Bristol had never been a supporter of an independent Armenia, considering it a part of Allied plans to carve up Turkey as spoils, and in January had sent to the Department his estimate of the politics behind the Armenian state. He said the idea of a large Armenia from Alexandretta to the Caucasus was a French scheme to offset the position of the British in the Arab countries; Britain had countered this by supporting an American mandate over a small Armenia.[43] On February 21 he cabled his estimate of the situation in Cilicia. A new condition had arisen in Turkey similar to the Smyrna episode, he said, caused by the French occupation of Cilicia and Syria. The use of Armenian soldiers and the arming of the Armenian population had led to the intervention of the Turkish Nationalists. Even in the parts of Syria where they were popular,

[43] Telegram 22 from Constantinople, January 10, 1920; 763.72119/8632. From the time he assumed his office as High Commissioner, Bristol had been sending similar warnings to Washington; cf. telegrams 1074 and 1085 from Constantinople to Peace Mission, July 23, 1919; Peace Conference files 867.01/46 and 47.

the French had antagonized the people by pulling down the local flag and substituting that of France, while taking over all government functions; this same behavior elsewhere had caused great anger. In Cilicia they had destroyed villages and misbehaved to the population, hence the outbreaks there, which, however, had been directed at the French troops not at Armenian civilians, who were not being persecuted, and all Americans in the area were safe. However, if the French advanced any further this situation might change, and the possibility of evacuating Americans was being considered. He had made representations to the Turkish government, said Bristol, and also to the French High Commission; would the Department of State consider approaching the French government with a request to withdraw all its troops of Armenian origin and replace them with French nationals?[44] A further cable from Constantinople on February 26 said that the Turkish government had sent instructions to the authorities in Cilicia to protect all American citizens; they were all in good health and it was believed that they were in no danger at present. The Armenians were not being massacred, reports to the contrary notwithstanding.[45] On March 4 Bristol sent a lengthy cable on the events in Cilicia during the advance of French forces on Marash and the subsequent retreat. He said while many Armenians had been killed, on the other hand French and Armenian troops had burnt Turkish villages and massacred the inhabitants. The entire situation was the result of French actions and France should bear the responsibility.[46]

While Bristol was sending his reports from Constantinople, sources closer to the events were giving a very different picture to the Department. Engert reported several times during February that Armenians were being massacred. On February 28 he cabled his impressions of the situation, derived from a two-week tour

[44] Telegram 150 from Constantinople, February 21, 1920; 867.00/1118. In a letter to the Secretary of State, March 9, 1920, Bristol sent a communication from the Turkish Foreign Office enclosing correspondence with the French High Commission at Constantinople regarding French activities in Cilicia and Syria. Beginning on November 25, 1919, the correspondence dealt with Armenians in the French army, incidents involving these troops, attacks on peaceful Turks and on villages, and French interference with the civilian administration of areas under French control.

[45] Telegram 161 from Constantinople, February 26, 1920; 867.00/1124.

[46] Telegrams 167 to 170 from Constantinople, March 4, 5, 6, and 6, 1920 respectively, and filed 867.00/1130, 1131, 1128, 1129 respectively.

of the area. He said that Mustafa Kemal and the Nationalists were determined to throw the Greeks out of Smyrna and the French out of Cilicia, and were making preparations for guerrilla warfare on a large scale. The same " insolent spirit " that prevailed during the war now ruled the Turks, he said, and they believed they could intimidate the European powers by threatening to massacre the Christians. It was a " crying injustice " to have induced the Armenians to return to their homes without providing any protection, and thousands of them had already lost their lives because of this. The decisions of the Peace Conference with respect to Smyrna and Armenian independence could only be implemented by large European forces, said Engert, and unless the French and Italians were willing to make more sacrifices to maintain law and order in the areas they claimed, it would be much better for them to leave now rather than be pushed out later.[47]

When the Department received these conflicting reports, it cabled to Bristol asking for a clarification of the statement in his cable of February 26 that the Armenians were not being massacred. Engert and others had reported that several thousand had been killed; did he mean that the massacres had stopped?[48] Before this cable reached Bristol, he sent a further report on the Armenians. He said recent stories in the European press on Turkish affairs and the Armenian massacres were misleading and merely propaganda for political purposes to support the selfish plans of the Allies. The recent killing of Armenians in Cilicia was due to the French advance, and there was no evidence that the extermination policy of 1915 was returning. The Turks were well aware of the effect of such behavior on the Peace Conference. The killings were neither as widespread nor systematic as the newspapers reported. Many rumors were being spread in Europe and America which were directly contradicted by local Armenians. Three Armenian bishops had recently asked him to do everything in his power to prevent a further advance by the French.[49]

On March 12 Bristol replied to the Department's cable of the fifth by reiterating what he had already said, and again urging

[47] Telegram from Aleppo via Beirut, February 28, 1920; 867.00/1127.
[48] Telegram 76 to Constantinople, March 5, 1920; 867.00/1124.
[49] Telegram 191 from Constantinople, March 9, 1920; 867.00/1154.

great caution in believing reports from Cilicia; Engert, he said, was reporting information obtained from Armenian sources.[50] Engert, however, sent another cable on March 15 saying that two Americans recently in the Marash area told him that all telegrams sent from Marash by Armenians after the French evacuation blaming the French for the fighting were sent under duress and should be read in that light.[51] Bristol sent several other telegrams repeating what he had said previously, but as they were received fresh information was coming in, not only from Beirut and Aleppo but also from Smyrna, describing the great peril of the Armenians, their desperate defense against the Turks, and their abandonment by the French. By the end of April they had been swept out of Cilicia and the scattered remnants were refugees once again. In the east of Turkey they suffered the same fate, crushed between the Bolsheviks, the Muslims of the Caucasus and the Turkish Nationalists. When, in accordance with his undertaking, President Wilson drew up the boundaries of Armenia and sent his decision to the Supreme Council, Armenia no longer existed; the miniscule enclave around Erivan was all that was left of free Armenia, and that too soon disappeared into the Soviet Union.

While the Armenians in Cilicia were being eliminated by the Turkish Nationalists, the Supreme Council had agreed to recognize the independence of Armenia. This decision was taken on January 19, 1920, and on January 24, the Ambassador in Paris, Wallace, who was acting as official observer on the Council, was informed by the Department of State that the American government " concurred " in the decision, and the attitude of the United States would be communicated to the Armenian representative in Washington. Two days later a further cable informed the Ambassador that, " through an inadvertance," the President had not been consulted in the matter and had not sanctioned the decision on the recognition of the independence of Armenia. Wallace had already communicated his original instruction to the Council, however, and he was obliged to recant to the extent of attempting, on instructions from Washington, to persuade the Council that what the United States government had meant was not to recognize

[50] Telegram 200 from Constantinople, March 12, 1920; 867.00/1156; telegram 201; 867.00/1157.
[51] Telegram from Beirut (number 14 from Engert), March 15, 1920; 867.00/1165.

Armenia but merely to indicate that it did not oppose it; to the actual recognition of the *de facto* Armenian government the United States was not in a position to pledge itself, explained Wallace.[52] American *de facto* recognition was eventually given to Armenia on April 23, 1920.[53] The Supreme Council sent, on April 27, a letter to President Wilson asking the United States to accept a mandate for Armenia. The letter noted that plans to include Cilicia had been " abandoned," but there remained the question of what portions of the eastern vilayets of Erzurum, Trebizond, Van and Bitlis—still in Turkish hands—should be added to the existing Armenian state of Erivan. The President was therefore also requested to undertake the responsibility of determining the boundary of Armenia with Turkey. The Allies were precluded from undertaking the protection of Armenia by their onerous obligations elsewhere in the former territories of the Ottoman Empire, said the letter, and thus were approaching the United States to undertake the burden, for without the support of a major power, Armenia could not maintain itself. Armenia needed loans and material, and the United States was in a much better position to supply these than the Allies, since she was rich and powerful and her resources had not suffered in the war as had those of the Allies.[54] The President's reply was to accept the request that he determine the Armenian boundaries. His decision was sent to the Supreme Council on November 24, 1920.[55]

6.

The United States was even less involved in the Palestine question than it was in Syria or Armenia. Such action as was taken was the direct result of representations made by American Zionists to the State Department and the President. In October, 1919, when the British and the French were arranging the limits of their new occupation zones in Syria, Felix Frankfurter wrote to the Department of State saying that the two countries were delimiting the boundary between Syria and Palestine in such a way as to defeat the economic viability of Palestine, since it would deprive

---

[52] *Foreign Relations*, 1920, III, 774–78.
[53] *Ibid.*, p. 778.

[54] *Ibid.*, pp. 779–83.
[55] *Ibid.*, pp. 789–804.

the latter of control of the water supply essential to its economic development; he asked if the Department would cable Polk at Paris to get assurances from Britain and France that no decision would be made that did not take into account the American and Zionist positions on Palestine. The Department declined to take any official action but agreed to send a personal cable from Frankfurter to Polk through Department channels if Frankfurter paid the charges.[56] This was done on October 18,[57] and on October 20 Polk replied that Britain and France had been informed that no decision on Palestine made between themselves would be binding on the United States; they had informed him that the only discussion on the matter so far had been whether to make an informal suggestion to the United States that the boundary question be left to American arbitration.[58]

When the consideration of Turkish matters was resumed in the Supreme Council in February, 1920, the American Zionists made even greater efforts to gain American support for an extension of the Palestine boundaries northward to include the valley of the Litany and the slopes of Mount Herman, as well as the Hauran and the Jordan Valley; increased pressure was now essential, for the United States had temporarily withdrawn from all activity at the Peace Conference. It was not now, as it had been in October, merely a question of the United States maintaining a well-established position, but of a new diplomatic departure. This could only be decided by the President, and so Justice Brandeis wrote to Wilson putting the case for the Zionists, saying that the French were insisting on the Sykes-Picot agreement as the basis for the Palestine boundaries and adding that it would be a betrayal of the promises of Christendom to the Jews embodied in the Balfour Declaration if Palestine were denied the opportunity of becoming a viable state. Wilson rose to the occasion, perhaps aroused by the mention of the secret treaties and the reference to Christendom's promise, and instructed the Secretary of State to instruct the Ambassador at Paris to impress on the French and British the points raised by Brandeis, with which he agreed. Accordingly, telegrams were sent to the ambassadors in Britain and France

[56] 763.72119/7398.

[57] Telegram 3480 to Peace Mission, October 18, 1919; 763.72119/7398.

[58] Telegram 4750 from Peace Mission, October 20, 1919; Peace Conference files 867 n.00/138.

giving the gist of Brandeis' letter to Wilson and the fact that the President agreed with it; the ambassadors were to impress these views on Britain and France and all the great powers committed to the Balfour Declaration, which was a solemn promise in no circumstances to be altered or broken. The transmission of the President's views was to be oral and informal, inasmuch as the United States government was not taking an active part in the discussions regarding the matter.[59] Apparently Britain and France were not impressed by this *démarche,* for when the boundaries were settled they followed the Sykes-Picot agreement.

Later in the spring, following an outbreak of rioting in Jerusalem and elsewhere in Palestine between Arabs and Jews, the Department cabled the Consul in Jerusalem that influential Jews in the United States were " greatly exercised " about " anti-Zionist demonstrations " in Palestine; he was to report fully on the origins, extent, and significance of the disturbance and the prospects of further outbreaks.[60] At the same time, a cable was sent to London containing the substance of the instruction to Jerusalem and also informing the Embassy that Jewish circles alleged the British authorities in Palestine had failed to prevent anti-Jewish excesses and had threatened to end all Zionist activities. The Embassy was to ascertain whether there was any conflict between British military policy in Palestine and that followed by the Foreign Office, or whether there was any definite indication that the British government had rescinded the Balfour Declaration.[61]

London replied on April 22 saying that there was no sign that the Balfour Declaration was being reconsidered, or of any discord on the subject between the military and the Foreign Office. As the embassy had reported before, Curzon " deprecated " the Declaration and had expressed " strong repugnance " to the Palestine mandate, but he had also said that Britain was committed in the matter.[62] Jerusalem replied on the twenty-fourth, giving the background of Muslim and Christian-Arab feeling on Zionism and an outline of the events which had led up to the riots. The consul said that responsibility for starting the riots could not at that time

[59] Telegram 295 to London, February 6, 1920; Peace Conference files, 867 n.00/195.
[60] Telegram to Jerusalem, April 17, 1920; 867 n.01/101A.
[61] Telegram 398 to London, April 17, 1920; 867 n.01/101B.
[62] Telegram 653 from London, April 22, 1920; 867 n.01/102.

be determined, but both Arabs and Jews had taken an active part in them. The British military had been impartial in controlling and putting down the rioting and several persons, both Arab and Jew, had been court-martialed and sentenced to imprisonment; a full investigation was underway and its findings would be sent to the Department as soon as possible.[63]

In June, 1922, a Joint Resolution of Sympathy for the National Home for the Jews was passed by each of the Houses of Congress; the final text was passed by both Houses in September. The wording followed very closely that of the Balfour Declaration. The Department of State did not support the Resolution. Secretary Hughes' position, as given to Senator Lodge, was that while he did not propose such a Resolution, he had no objection to its adoption. The officers of the Department were generally opposed to it on the grounds that American rights in the mandated territories were still in the process of negotiation and because the Resolution was an intervention in affairs from which the United States had deliberately withdrawn. The prevailing opinion in the Department on the value of the Resolution as a statement of American policy, as opposed to American statements of opinion (President Harding had made at least one favorable public comment on the Zionist program in recent months), was shown quite clearly in a discussion between a member of the Italian Embassy and William Castle of the Department in the latter part of July, 1922. The Italian called at the Department to ask Castle if the Congressional Resolution represented the views of the American government on the Palestine mandate. "When he asked this question, I only smiled, without answering, and Mr. Celesia then burst out laughing and said that he remembered very well that Congress had also passed a Resolution urging recognition of the Irish Republic and that did not represent the view of this Government. . . ."[64]

---

[63] Telegram from Jerusalem, April 24, 1920; 867 n.01/103.
[64] 867 n.01/175A, 199, 280, 311A.

PART III
THE SETTLEMENT

CHAPTER X

THE UNITED STATES AND THE TREATY OF SÈVRES

1.

In the period thus far covered in this study, American Middle East policy went through three district stages—neutrality and traditional non-involvement, war and strategic non-involvement, the Peace Conference and full involvement. Now, when the settlement with Turkey, postponed from the previous summer, was taken up by the Peace Conference in the spring of 1920, American policy had reverted to traditional non-involvement. But it was not possible merely to erase the past six years, and while the new goal of United States policy was to disentangle the country from the " disgusting scramble " in the Middle East into which it had ventured under President Wilson, as well as to come to terms with the new conditions prevailing in the area, this goal could not be accomplished by a purely negative policy of passivity and withdrawal. An active policy was necessary to liquidate the policies of Wilson with the least damage to American prestige and to insure in the postwar era the protection and advancement of such American interests as existed in the Middle East. During the war and the Peace Conference, American policy had, under the revolution in American relations with the rest of the world, been determined directly by the President; but in the return to non-involvement in the Middle East, policy was conducted on a single basic principle which allowed for no development, in vivid contrast to the preceding period when policy developed from day to day as the fortunes of war and the Peace Conference dictated. Under these circumstances Wilson kept the reins in his own hands since vital decisions might have to be made at any time, whereas, after 1919 American relations with the Middle East were diplomatic, not strategic. This section of the study will be concerned therefore to a far greater extent with the activities of the Department of State and American diplomatic representatives abroad than was the case with the two preceding sections, where attention was centered on the President.

The withdrawal of the United States from the Supreme Council's consideration of Turkish affairs did not indicate disinterest in events in the Middle East, but merely that the United States declined to integrate the protection of American interests there with Allied plans for the Eastern settlement. The close watch maintained by the United States on the Arab portions of the former Ottoman Empire has been described in the last chapter. Turkey proper was as closely observed, and after the withdrawal from the Conference the actions of the Allies in Turkey were subjected to the same careful scrutiny as the actions of the Turks; now that American interests had to be protected in the field, rather than at the conference table, the activities of the Allies provided a valuable source of information on their policies.

The chief source of information on Turkey was the American High Commissioner, Admiral Bristol. The Admiral had very definite ideas on Turkey and the settlement of Eastern problems. On January 29, 1920, as the Allies began to organize the negotiations on the Turkish treaty, he sent to the Department a lengthy telegram giving in detail his recommendations on the treaty and on the part the United States should play in it. " In order that there may be absolutely no misunderstanding of my attitude towards affairs in the Near East, I state emphatically that I have always, during my years of duty in Turkey, advocated the abolition of the old Turkish rule over all races and nationalities in the old Ottoman Empire," he said. His opinion was well understood in Turkey; he had continually advocated good government for Turkey without partition, either for the benefit of European nations or for particular racial groups, he said, for no European state had any just claims to any part of the Ottoman Empire. The subject races were not ready for self-rule and their leaders were all too often ambitious men who had set themselves at the head of the various national movements. They had demonstrated their complete inability to rule, a good example being the conduct of the Armenians in Russian Armenia. The Turks, too, were unable to rule themselves or others, and to reinstate Turkish rule anywhere would be a crime. If the United States were a party to such a move, it would be equally criminal with the other nations involved; and also if it remained silent while other nations restored the Turks, it would be guilty. The United States should raise its voice against the plans of the Allies and the American people should be told the facts, the Admiral concluded.[1]

All this may have been true but the conclusions as to American policy Bristol drew from the situation in Turkey were quite irrelevant. Essentially Bristol's position begged the question of American Middle East policy. The whole point at issue was whether the United States should participate in the Eastern settlement; this depended on whether American interests were involved in the Middle East to an extent that warranted direct American intervention. Wilson had determined that this question depended in turn on whether the United States participated in the general settlement of the war and in the League of Nations. This was still in suspension, and until the Senate acted there could be no question of American intervention except to safeguard the immediate interests of the United States. As for the ability of the Turks or the Armenians to govern themselves, or the right—or lack of it—of the European states to govern Turkey, or to obtain economic privileges, these were questions quite outside American interests, unless the United States was a member of the League.

The Department of State, however, was well aware of Bristol's proclivity for direct action and his somewhat pro-Turk and anti-Armenian feelings, and took them into consideration when assessing his cables. The factual information sent back to Washington by the Admiral varied in quality. His reports on the Nationalist attacks on the French and Armenians in Cilicia have already been related. While it was colored by his attitude to the Armenians, it did provide a corrective to the flood of anti-Turkish propaganda put out by Greek and Armenian interests in this country and in Europe. As the Nationalists' attacks in Cilicia grew in intensity, Bristol became increasingly concerned for the whole future of the Middle East. On March 6, 1920, he cabled the Department that the results of Allied policy in Turkey he had been predicting for so long seemed to be coming to pass. He wanted to point out " as strongly as possible," he said, that an extremely serious situa-

---

[1] Telegram 83 from Constantinople, January 29, 1920; 867.01/6.

tion existed in Turkey due to the long delay of peace, the Greek occupation of Smyrna and its accompanying atrocities, and the " shameful " acts of the French in Cilicia. If the European powers carried out their plans in the Middle East, the results would be catastrophic and make the solution of the Turkish question impossible. He urged that the United States declare its policy at once, and that policy should be that Turkey must not be partitioned among the Allies, that Turkish rule should not be restored, and that the whole of Turkey should be put under a single mandatory. It was very likely, he said, that the European powers would ask for American help in the Middle East soon, and the United States should be ready to announce its policy when this happened.[2]

At the end of March, Bristol sent a long cable urging again, with great emphasis, United States action in Turkey. The unrest in Cilicia and the anti-Western feeling aroused in almost all of Anatolia by the actions of the European powers and by the insistent propaganda of the Nationalists placed American missionaries and relief workers operating in the interior in considerable jeopardy, and, he said, these brave people were in great danger; this was not a new state of affairs, but conditions were now becoming intolerable. In large areas of Turkey there were no Allied troops, and it was there that the relief workers were, completely without protection. There were about five hundred altogether, taking care of 54,000 orphans and 500,000 destitute Christians. If the Muslims were aroused any further against the Western Powers, they might all be massacred. This situation was the direct result of Allied ambitions and greed in Turkey and the United States should throw all its weight against these Allied schemes before it was too late and the Muslims were driven to acts of desperation to save their country. While the Turks were all that people said they were, Bristol went on, they were still human and still had rights, and the other side of the coin was obscured by the flood of Greek and Armenian propaganda painting the Turks as completely inhuman and undeserving of any consideration, while suppressing all the facts in favor of the Turks and against the minorities such as had been brought out by the King-Crane Commission and the inquiry into the occupation of Smyrna by the Greeks. The Admiral asked the Department to appoint a com-

---

[2] Telegram 177 from Constantinople, March 6, 1920; 867.01/13.

mission of prominent Americans who knew the Middle East, such as Bliss, Crane, and Harbord, to which his cable could be submitted and its accuracy verified by an impartial jury. He reiterated his previous recommendations for Turkey—that there should be no partition, no restoration of Turkish rule and no establishment of independent states for minorities. He ended by stating that it was his duty to make the American government and the American people see the truth about Turkey.[3]

When this impassioned plea for American intervention in Turkey was sent, the Senate had already voted down the Treaty of Versailles, ending any possibility of American intervention, not only directly in the area itself but even through representations to the Allied governments. The Department of State could make only one response to Bristol's demands for American action in the Middle East. On April 6 a cable was sent to Constantinople stating that the Department was alive to the seriousness of the situation but, owing to the attitude of Congress, it was not in a position to make any demands of anyone—Turks or Allies. The Congress was unwilling to accept a mandate in the Middle East or even to authorize any funds for government action there.[4]

2.

During February the Supreme Council had, as has been mentioned, met in London to discuss the terms of the Turkish treaty. One of the major decisions reached was to keep the Sultan in Constantinople.[5] Though all meetings of the Council were held in secret and its decisions kept from the public, there were leaks to the Press from time to time, one of which concerned the decision on Constantinople. London cabled the background of the decision on February 25 "from a reliable source"; it was due to very strong pressure by the India Office on the Prime Minister because of the dangerous situation in India among the Muslims there,

[3] Telegram 241 from Constantinople, March 29, 1920; 867.00/1190. For the views of the British High Commissioner, Admiral de Robeck, on the Turkish settlement, see *British Documents*, Series I, XIII, 17–19.

[4] Telegram 25 to Constantinople, April 6, 1920; 867.00/1190.

[5] For Lloyd George's version of this phase of the history of the Treaty of Sèvres, see his *Memoirs*, II, 819–36. For the official record of the London conferences on the Turkish settlement, see *British Documents*, Series I, VII, 1–462, especially 99–112, the meeting of February 17, 1920.

who might rise if the position of Islam and the Caliph in Turkey suffered further at the hands of the Allies. The decision was taken in spite of the fact that it might, on the other hand, be detrimental to the British position in Europe. There had been much opposition in the Cabinet and Foreign Office, the Embassy said, but Lloyd George had overridden it and had personally insisted in the Supreme Council on keeping the Turks in Constantinople. After the news leaked out, there had been a great deal of opposition in Parliament and the Press.[6]

Leaks from the Supreme Council also brought the Russian Ambassador and the Greek and Bulgarian ministers to the State Department. The Russian Ambassador called on Under Secretary Breckenridge Long on February 24 to discuss the reported terms of the Turkish treaty. He asked the United States to take the position on the Straits that any arrangements made by the Council were temporary because there was no authority in Russia that could speak for Russian interests in the Straits. The Ambassador said that Russia would want the Straits closed to ships of war. Russia, he said, was now a defensive naval power and could not under the present circumstances become an offensive power, therefore there was no need to fear her in the Black Sea. Long told him it was a reasonable position which merited careful consideration, and he would write up the conversation and send it to the Secretary.[7] On the twenty-sixth the Greek Minister called on Long. He said he was very anxious to know the American attitude on the new settlement being made on Thrace and whether the new arrangements on Constantinople would have any effect on the position the United States had formerly held on Thrace. Long replied that it probably would. The Minister then asked what the President had to say on Smyrna, but was informed that the Department could not comment on that. Later in the day the Bulgarian Minister called to discuss the same subjects. He said if Greece got west Thrace, it would probably also get east Thrace. He intimated that in such an event Bulgaria should receive Adrianople, and gave the impression to the Under Secretary that his country would accept the Thrace decision if it got a railway to the Agean and the port of Dedeagatch internationalized.[8]

---

[6] Telegram 314 from London, February 25, 1920; 867.01/10.
[7] 763.72119/9502.
[8] Both conversations filed under 763.72119/9363.

3.

While the Allied premiers were debating Turkey's future, the Nationalists were rapidly gaining strength and self-confidence, and day by day appeared to be growing, not only in the disinclination to accept Allied dictates but also in their ability to frustrate them. The Parliament was under Nationalist control and had passed the National Pact, the government was riddled with Nationalists and their sympathizers who actually controlled the War Department and, to add insult to injury, Mustafa Kemal, who had been branded as a traitor and had a price on his head a few months before, had been appointed Governor of Erzurum. The French were thrown back in Cilicia and plans were going ahead to increase the size of the Nationalist forces in Anatolia from 30,000 men, plus irregular troops, to four army corps of 22,000 each, of which one was to be stationed north of Adana, two in the eastern vilayets, and the other in the Trebizond region. Arms were to be obtained from dumps of captured arms collected by the Allies, under the terms of the Armistice, and sealed.[9] Bristol cabled on February 23 that the British High Commissioner had informed the Turkish government that while it was the intention of the Allies at the present time to maintain Turkish sovereignty in Constantinople, if the government did not control the Nationalists in Anatolia and Cilicia, the final peace terms would be very severe. Bristol also reported in this cable that a big British fleet had arrived in Constantinople.[10]

In the latter part of February reports from the Allied high commissioners to the Supreme Council bore unmistakable evidence that events in Turkey were getting out of hand, and the Council determined to act. Orders were sent to the high commissioners to occupy Constantinople at their discretion. On March 6 Curzon called in the American Ambassador and informed him that in view of the massacres in Cilicia and the "growing disposition" of the Turks to flout the Allies, the Conference had instructed the high commissioners the day before to seize the capital and the government offices, including, most particularly, the War Office, to cut it off from any communication with the "insurgents." They

[9] Telegram 199 from Constantinople, March 11, 1920; 867.00/1103.
[10] Telegram 152 from Constantinople, February 23, 1920; 867.00/1123.

were also to demand the " instant dismissal " of Mustafa Kemal as Governor of Erzurum. Curzon exused the Council's not keeping the United States informed but, he told the Ambassador, it was a very complicated matter and the final decision had not been reached until the day before, when it was immediately leaked to the Press. The United States would have been informed before the actual occupation took place.[11] On the same day the Embassy received information from the Council of the background of the decision and the general policy it planned to follow: Constantinople must be occupied; the Turkish government required to dismiss Mustafa Kemal; the occupation to continue until the terms of peace were accepted by the Turks, and, in the event there were any further outrages, the terms of peace would be made far more severe. The high commissioners were to inform the Turkish government of this, and had been instructed to consult together on the steps necessary to control the situation, to secure the submission of the Turks, and to protect the Christian population. This information was being communicated to the United States, said the Council, in view of American interest in these affairs and it would welcome American co-operation in its policy, which was international " in the strictest sense." [12]

Allied troops landed in Constantinople on March 16 and immediately occupied all key points and began arresting as many of the Nationalist notables and deputies as could not escape in time across the Bosporus. Bristol reported on the eighteenth that among those arrested were Raouf bey and Karavasif bey, the chief representatives of Mustafa Kemal in the city, the famous Turkish feminist Halide Hanoum and her husband, and many other prominent men, as well as hundreds of lesser lights; they had apparently all been deported to Malta. Bristol said that the Turks believed that the arrests were made at the direct insistance of the Supreme Council and not merely by a decision of the high commissioners. The professed aim of the Allied action—to sup-

---

[11] Telegram 406 from London, March 6, 1920; 867.01/12. A copy of Curzon's memorandum of this conversation was sent to Washington in London's despatch 2375, March 8; 867.01/24. The record of the discussions of the occupation of Constantinople at the Conference is in *British Documents*, Series I, VII, 411–21, 494–98. Curzon sent a cable to the Washington Embassy on March 12 with an account of his discussions with Davis on Turkish matters and the occupation of Constantinople; *ibid.*, XIII, 22–24.

[12] Telegram 407 from London, March 6, 1920; 763.72119/9370.

press the Nationalists as a danger to peace and as perpetrators of massacres—was nonsense, the Turks were saying, as the occupation of Constantinople could not accomplish that; it was just another political move such as had been made in Smyrna and Cilicia to keep Turkey docile and obedient to the ambitions of the Allies.[13] On March 23 Bristol cabled that the situation in the interior, since the Allied landings, was obscure, for all communication had been cut. It was reported from London that the Greeks were about to launch a new offensive, but the local opinion was that it was merely a threat of doubtful effectiveness by the Peace Conference. A British officer on the staff of General Harding, the British Commander in the city, knew of no such plan, said Bristol, and the Greeks were in any case not strong enough to do it. He believed that they might try it anyway if they were offered a big enough reward, and said that " the hand of Venizelos " was visible throughout recent events. He also said if the Greek government were not allotted Smyrna by the Conference, it would set up an independent government there, as D'Annunzio had done in Fiume.[14]

4.

The first task of the new period in American Middle East policy that resulted from the final rejection of the Covenant by the Senate was to determine the new position of the United States in Middle Eastern affairs and from there to lay the groundwork on which could be constructed specific policies which reflected specific interests. The general nature of the Eastern settlement was no longer the major concern of American policy as it had been before the defeat of the Treaty of Versailles. In implementing American policy, the United States at this time was dealing exclusively with the Allied Powers. They were technically in control of Turkey, or at least of the legal government of the country, and the United States had no contact with the Nationalists. The immediate necessity was to put the American position categorically to the Allies before the Supreme Council acted on the Turkish treaty. This was done in March, 1920. The February meeting of the Supreme Council had decided that the Peace Conference

[13] Telegram 215 from Constantinople, March 18, 1920; 867.00/1174.
[14] Telegram 224 from Constantinople, March 23, 1920; 867.00/1181.

would reconvene in the near future to take up the treaty, and on March 9 the French Ambassador at Washington, Jusserand, informed the Secretary of State that work on the treaty had progressed far enough to warrant calling the Turkish delegates to receive the terms of the treaty at an early date. He said the French government would be happy to know as early as possible whether the United States intended to " desist " from any interest in Eastern affairs or whether it proposed " by taking part in [the Conference] to claim its share of influence, action and responsibility in the definitive and general reestablishment of peace."

The Secretary replied that he had no information on the nature of the settlement contemplated by the Allies, and before the United States government could respond intelligently to the request of the French government this information should be at its disposal. Jusserand cabled Paris for details of the Allies' plans and on March 12 wrote to the Secretary giving the major points of the terms to be presented to the Turks. The boundaries of Turkey in Europe were to be the Enos-Midia line or, more probably, the Chatalja line; in Asia the Black Sea, the Sea of Marmora, the Mediterranean, Armenia, Cilicia, Syria, and Mesopotamia. The Sultan and the government of Turkey were to be maintained at Constantinople, but no Turkish forces, except the Sultan's bodyguard, were to remain there, and the Allies reserved the right to garrison the zone of the Straits. The retention of Constantinople by Turkey was contingent on the execution of the terms of peace and the observation of the guarantees in favor of minorities. The freedom of the Straits was to be insured by placing them under the control of an international commission which would exercise complete authority, in the name of the Sultan, over all matters connected with the free and safe passage of the Straits in war and peace. The commission was to be composed of representatives of France, England, and Italy, and, under certain contingencies, the United States and Russia, each with two votes; Rumania, Greece, and ultimately Bulgaria, would have a representative with one vote. Greece was to have as much of Thrace as was not given to Turkey. Inserted at this point in the Ambassador's note, in the middle of the terms concerning territorial arrangements, was a reference to a " special arrangement " affecting the three great powers, which would set aside for each of them a particular region of Turkey where they would enjoy priority over the others in the matter of the furnishing of advice and instructors. The note then returned to territorial questions. The independence of Armenia was recognized; Turkey renounced all rights to Mesopotamia, Arabia, Palestine, Syria, and all the islands; Smyrna, except for Aidin, was to be administered by the Greeks under the suzerainty of the Sultan. Economic questions had presented many difficulties, and many of them had received only preliminary examination or had been postponed for further study by the Council; however, agreement had been reached on certain points: the liquidation of German property; maintenance of concessions in territories subject to a change in sovereignty, or at least payment of an indemnity in case of revision or cancellation; the creation of a financial commission having control of all revenues and expenditures; continuation of the Ottoman Debt Administration; and reimbursement of the cost of Allied occupation of the regions which were to remain Turkish.[15]

A few days after the receipt of the French note, a cable was received from London giving the background of the Supreme Council's decisions on the terms of the treaty. This information was obtained from the Foreign Office via " a reliable American source." The cable gave much the same information as the French note, but it added some interesting comments on the treaty terms. It said that the decision on Constantinople was a " triumph of the India Office." France was leaving Cilicia to the Turks because keeping it would be too difficult, but it would retain economic privileges there; Italy likewise would get out of Adalia for the same reason and on the same terms. The lack of direct control of Turkey would, said the Embassy, mean the continuation of misrule and the mistreatment of Christians. The French were being more conciliatory in Syria owing to the strong anti-French feeling there, but the proclamation of Faisal as King would increase the difficulties between the Arabs and the French. Armenia was to consist of the vilayets of Erzurum and Van, with a good deal of territory of the surrounding vilayets added and with an outlet at Batum consisting of a free zone under the League. If the Turks and other Muslim peoples presently inhabiting the area refused to leave, they would be evicted by the Greeks. Kurdistan was to be independent; its *raison d'être* to act as a buffer state

[15] *Foreign Relations*, 1920, III, 748–50.

between Turkey, Armenia, and Mesopotamia. The Nationalist Turks would certainly not agree to this. Britain wanted a weak Turkey to safeguard the British position in Persia and Mesopotamia. The Embassy's informant, commenting on the possible use of the Greek Army to enforce the terms of the treaty, said it would endanger the lives of the Greek and Armenian inhabitants of the region in question, but this would be used by the Allies as an excuse for even more extensive operations against the Nationalists. The official British theory, he said, was that the Turks would not accept the treaty without a severe lesson, and Venizelos was more than ready to apply this lesson.[16]

The French note was sent to the President, together with details of recent happenings in Turkey and the European capitals as reported by American representatives, the claims of the Russian and Bulgarian representatives in Washington, mentioned above, and the comments and suggestions of the Department of State. The Treaty of Versailles was before the Senate for the second time, and it was not until it had been defeated that the President answered the request of the Department of State for his comments on the note and the reply to be made to it. The Senate voted on March 19, and Wilson answered the Secretary on March 20. The Secretary's reply to the French note, sent on March 24, was based entirely on the President's remarks. The President did not " deem it advisable in the present circumstances that the United States be represented by a Plenipotentiary at the conference," said the Secretary, but felt, however, that as the government of the United States was vitally interested in the peace of the world, it should frankly express its views on the proposed solutions of the difficult questions connected with the treaty. It was also the duty of the American government to make known its views and urge a solution which would be both just and lasting, because while the United States had not been at war with Turkey, it had been at war with its principal allies and had contributed to the defeat of those allies and, therefore, to the defeat of the Turkish government.

After thus stating the American claim to be heard on the settlement, though declining to participate in it, the note went on to the specific points mentioned by Jusserand. While understanding

[16] Telegram 469 from London, March 17, 1920; 763.72119/9475.

the strength of the arguments for keeping the Turks in Constantinople, the United States government believed that the arguments against it were far stronger " and contained certain imperative elements which it would not seem possible to ignore." Nor would the reactions of the Muslim peoples to the expulsion of the Turks be such as to make necessary the complete reversal of Allied policy to end the " anomaly " of the presence of the Turks in Europe; the Muslim peoples had not only witnessed the defeat of the Turkish power without protest, but had even materially assisted in its defeat. The arrangements for the regime of the Straits were approved and, the Secretary said, the American government noted " with pleasure " that provision had been made for Russian representation on the International Council (sic), since it was convinced that no satisfactory arrangement on the Straits could be made without carefully providing for the " vital interests " of Russia. By the same token, the United States also noted with pleasure that questions of the passage of the Straits in time of war were still under advisement, since no decision concerning them could or should be made without the consent of Russia. On the boundaries of the new Turkey, the United States questioned the frontier with the Arab peoples, which, if it were based on ethnological consideration, would seem to need certain rectifications, and if it were not, the United States would appreciate being furnished with the reasons for the decision. The allotment of eastern Thrace to Greece was approved, with the exception of the northern part, which was predominantly Bulgarian; " justice and fair dealing " demanded that Bulgaria receive Adrianople and Kirk Kilisseh (sic) and the surrounding territory. As for allotting each of the three great powers a zone where it would have preference in supplying advisers and instructors, the United States felt that it was necessary to have more information on the plan before it could express an intelligent opinion. Armenia should be allotted the port of Trebizond in order to assure her of an adequate outlet to the sea. Turkey should place the Arab provinces and the islands in the hands of the great powers to be disposed of as these powers determine. The United States was not in a position, in regard to the arrangements for Smyrna, to express an opinion, since it did not have sufficient information as to what exactly was contemplated and the reasons for it. That economic questions should have caused difficulty, the United States could very well understand, but was confident that they would be dealt with " in a spirit of fairness and with scrupulous regard for the commercial interests of victor, vanquished and neutral." However, the note went on, the Council plan for concessions had " grave possibilities " and would " seem to require careful elucidation." The note concluded by expressing the understanding of the United States that whatever territorial changes or arrangements might be made in Turkey, they would in no way place citizens or corporations of the United States, or of any other country, in a less favorable situation than those of the powers who were parties to the treaty with Turkey.[17]

The note made three main points in addition to the comments on specific terms mentioned in the French note. The first point was that while the United States would not participate in the treaty of peace with Turkey, it had a well-established right to a voice in the settlement, not only as it affected American interests but also as it would establish in the Middle East a settlement that was both just and lasting. This right was based generally on the interest of the United States in the peace of the world, and specifically on the fact that while the United States had not been at war with Turkey it had contributed to the defeat of its principal allies and therefore to the defeat of Turkey. The second point was that the Open Door should be maintained. The third, that the treaty would not discriminate against the United States, or any other country, in favor of the signatories to the treaty. These three points together with a fourth—the maintenance of existing American rights—formed the basis of American Middle East policy throughout the period that ended with the final settlement in Turkey, through the administrations of three presidents. The insistence of the United States on maintaining its rights in the territories formerly comprising the Ottoman Empire went back to 1914 when it refused to accept the unilateral abrogation of the Capitulations by Turkey.

The reply to this note was made by the Supreme Council over a month later. The Council was then meeting in conference at San Remo to draw up the final terms of the Turkish settlement. The American Ambassador in Italy had been instructed to attend the conference as an observer, and on April 26 the Council handed

[17] *Foreign Relations*, 1920, III, 750–53.

him a note, signed by the President of the Council in the name of
the members, to be forwarded to the Secretary of State. The
Council noted that the United States, not having chosen to be
represented at the conference, apparently did not intend to become a signatory of the peace treaty with Turkey, though the
close interest of the United States in the settlement was welcomed.
The Allies had made no secret of their desire to have the United
States participate in the Eastern settlement, and had, in fact, delayed the negotiations with Turkey at the risk of gravely imperil-
ing the prospect of a satisfactory settlement without renewed
military action against Turkey solely in the hope and expectation
of American participation. But this delay meant that the difficulties of arriving at a satisfactory settlement had been increased,
and the Allies were bearing this burden alone. However, it was
hoped that the final solution would be satisfactory to the United
States. The American desire for a just and fair treaty was shared
by the Allies; but when it was urged that the settlement be made
"with a scrupulous regard for the interests of victor, vanquished
and neutral," it should be remembered that it would be unjust
to treat the Turks—who had joined the Central Powers in their
war of aggression—on the same level as their victims.

The Allied note then turned to the specific points raised by the
American note. After weighing the problem most carefully, the
Council was convinced that, supposing the exclusion of the Sultan
from Constantinople were desirable, the Allies were not in a position to incur the responsibilities, dangers, and sacrifices which
such a policy would entail. The southern frontier of Turkey had
been drawn, taking into consideration not only ethnic but also
geographic and economic factors, as had been the case in other
treaties with the enemy powers (the United States would readily
recognize that it was not possible to isolate these factors). With
respect to the Straits and Constantinople, the American concern
that Russia be fully represented on the Straits Commission was
welcomed, but it should be pointed out that the Commission
would have no control over Constantinople. The regime of the
Straits proposed by the Allies would, it was hoped, meet with
American approval; it had obviously been impossible to defer
the drafting of this part of the treaty pending consultation with
Russia. The statistics, on which the American note based its contention regarding the Bulgarian population of northern Thrace,

were out of date. The Tri-Partite agreement on zones of priority was, in effect, a self-denying ordinance to eliminate the old Turkish practice of playing one power off against another; it bound only its signatories and contained nothing which would impede the commercial activity of other powers. The precision with which the future status of the Arab lands and the islands could be formulated had been governed by the necessity of expediting the treaty, which had already been delayed " to the limits of expediency." In Smyrna the Allied solution of an autonomous region within Turkey had been based on two considerations. Turkish mistreatment of the Greek population required that it be put under Greek administration, but, on the other hand, extensive areas of the region were predominantly Turkish and these areas were economically dependent on Smyrna and, moreover, the Allies had been advised that the immediate cession of Smyrna, so closely linked with the economy of all of western Anatolia and for so long an integral part of the Turkish state, would have aroused national feeling to such a pitch as to make the implementation of the whole treaty difficult if not impossible. The economic provisions of the treaty were similar to those of the other peace treaties. With regard to concessions, these were obtained frequently by dubious means and the right to cancel them applied only to former Turkish territory under Allied tutelage, it being thought unfair to burden these new states with onerous concessions since they had no voice in incurring them. In general, the economic clauses of the treaty were designed to protect Turkey from exploitation and to establish a sound system of finance. Finally, the United States was assured that the Allied governments had in no way sought to place American citizens or corporations in an inferior position compared to their own nationals.[18]

5.

The application of the new American Middle East policy to particular events and situations that arose out of the Eastern settlement and the relations of the United States with the new Turkey will be taken up in later chapters.[19] But before turning

[18] *Ibid.*, pp. 753–56.
[19] On May 11, 1920, Sir Arthur Geddes, British Ambassador at Washington,

to the several topics that will be covered, it might be appropriate to follow the misfortunes of the treaty of peace with Turkey, the terms of which were set at the San Remo Conference in April, 1920,[20] and which was signed at Sèvres on August 10, 1920. The United States had an interest not only in the terms of the treaty but also in the likelihood, or the contrary, of these terms being enforced. (The San Remo Conference also distributed mandates for the Arab areas of the former Ottoman Empire and produced an agreement between Britain and France on Mesopotamian oil; these subjects will be a major concern of the rest of this study.)

The terms of peace were submitted secretly to the Turkish government on April 24, but on May 13 Venizelos had, for domestic political purposes, disclosed the terms. They were of such a nature that no Turkish government could accept them once they were known to the nation. The Turkish delegation was instructed to refuse to sign any treaty which deprived Turkey of Smyrna, Adrianople, or eastern Thrace. The government was supported in its stand by the knowledge that Mustafa Kemal had regrouped his military and political forces after the occupation of Constantinople and was again well entrenched in the interior, waiting for the Sultan's government to make just such a mistake as accepting the Allied terms. Bristol cabled on June 14 that the Nationalists had a well-organized government at Angora with a regularly functioning parliament composed of those deputies who had escaped deportation to Malta in March. This government was determined to stop the treaty and, with supplies sufficient for two years, was ready for a long struggle. Bristol said there was a decided change in sentiment in Angora to the United States;

---

cabled the Foreign Office, "on what appears to be reliable authority," that the President and Secretary of State "were extremely desirous of forcing United States to undertake mandate for [Armenia] and to participate, but this is less sure, in control of Dardanelles and Bosporous." On May 18 he reported that the Secretary of State had questioned him about the arrangements for the Straits and Constantinople in the Turkish Treaty and asked if the Supreme Council would reopen the question if the United States assumed responsibility for Constantinople. Geddes understood that the President was exploring ways to carry out his plan "over the heads and in the teeth of opposition of both Senate and House of Representatives." *British Documents*, Series I, XIII, 70–71, 76–77; I have been unable to find any trace of this in the files of the Department of State, though it is possible there may be other evidence which I have overlooked in the Wilson Papers.

[20] On the San Remo Conference see *British Documents*, Series I, VIII, 1–252.

it was thought there that the Americans had joined the Allies in their attempt to destroy the Turkish nation, and there was a growing sentiment to have all Americans leave the country. Bristol also reported that French and Italian delegations had visited Angora and a Turkish delegation had been sent to Moscow.[21] Two weeks later he reported that both the Constantinople government and the Nationalists under Mustafa Kemal were adamant against the treaty and the population was " solidly " behind the Nationalists. The Cabinet was, with few exceptions, pro-Nationalist and the Sultan was incapable of controlling it. The French and the Italians were opposed to the treaty; Britain was not in sympathy with it; and only the Greeks approved, they were " jubilant," and delighted at the opportunity to advance in Asia Minor. Bristol believed that, while the Turks might give up the fight due to war weariness, the Greek advance might also be the final pressure that would solidify the Turks. He now advised the United States to keep out of all Near East questions and to guard against Greek and Armenian propaganda.[22]

The Greek advance referred to by Bristol had been authorized by the Allies as a means of bringing pressure on the Turks to sign the treaty. In June, Mustafa Kemal advanced on the Straits, more as a gesture than as a serious attempt to force the Allied lines. Some shots were fired on the British positions at Ismid, but the attacking troops were driven off without difficulty. It has been noted that in March reports were received in the Department that Britain believed the Turks would have to have a sharp lesson before they would sign a treaty on the terms agreed to by the Allies and that they were considering using the Greek Army in Anatolia to administer this lesson. The recalcitrance of the Turkish government and the Nationalists, culminating in the attack on British troops, appears to have been the occasion the British government was waiting for. The British and French premiers were meeting at Hythe (they later moved to Boulogne) to consider means of bringing pressure on Turkey to sign the treaty. Present at the meetings was Venizelos. Neither the French nor the British had forces in Turkey sufficient to carry out a decisive military operation against the Nationalists, but in the area of

[21] Telegram 355 from Constantinople, June 14, 1920; 867.01/49.
[22] Telegram 388 from Constantinople, June 30, 1920; 763.72119/10089A.

Greek occupation around Smyrna there were almost 100,000 well trained and experienced Greek troops. Venizelos offered to the Supreme Council the use of these troops to clear the Nationalists from the zone of the Straits, and this offer was gratefully accepted by the premiers.[23]

On June 22 orders were received by the Greek Army, from Venizelos, to drive the Turks from the Straits and from the area west of the Smyrna-Panderma railway, and to occupy east Thrace and Adrianople. Venizelos had promised the premiers that the first part of this task would be accomplished in fifteen days; ten days later he announced that "western Anatolia was clear of Turkish forces," and on July 27 Adrianople was captured.[24] On July 19 Mustafa Kemal issued a proclamation calling for a Jihad against the Allies who, he said, with Britain at their head, were determined to exterminate the Turkish nation. In transmitting a copy of this to Washington, Admiral Bristol commented that it was "a rather fair statement" of the situation.[25] But on July 23 the Sultan's Crown Council, circumventing the pro-Nationalist Cabinet, designated three new delegates to the Peace Conference with instructions to sign the treaty. Constantinople reported that this had been done at the urging of Ambassador Rashid at Paris to avert even more disastrous terms.[26] The High Commission cabled again on the twenty-sixth that the government realized that in order to save Constantinople it would not only have to sign the treaty but also actively assist in enforcing its terms; however, its ability to do so was questionable.[27] The three new delegates proceeded to Paris and at Sèvres on August 10, 1920, signed the treaty of peace.

The immediate aims of the Supreme Council and the Greeks had been accomplished. But the very success of the Greek operation contained within it the seeds of future disaster. As soon as

[23] The discussions were transferred to Boulogne after a few days, and Venizelos' instructions to the Greek Army were actually sent from that town. Paris reported, in telegram 1314, June 30, 1920, that the suggestion to use the Greek Army had come from General Henry Wilson and Marshal Foch; 763.72119/10089. On the Hythe-Boulogne Conference, see British Documents, Series I, VIII, 307–79.

[24] Telegram 99 from Athens, June 23, 1920; 767.68/26. Reports from Athens and Constantinople dealing with the Greek advance are filed under 767.68/26 ff.

[25] Copy of the Proclamation, in translation with Bristol's comments, was sent from Constantinople on September 2, 1920; 767.68/64.

[26] Telegram 421 from Constantinople, July 23, 1920; 763.72119/10176.

[27] Telegram 36 from Constantinople, July 26, 1920; 763.72119/10580.

it was obvious that the Turks would sign the treaty, Greek military operations had been halted by the Council, leaving the Greeks in an exposed position, though, in spite of the Council's attitude, they continued limited operations to improve their front while pleading with the Allies for an opportunity to finish the Nationalists once and for all. This permission was not granted. The chief opponents in the Council to Greek expansion were France and Italy. They could not look with favor on the domination of Anatolia by the Greeks, who were, in their eyes, little more than puppets of the British. As a result, Greek morale suffered and the army had difficulty in maintaining its position, partly because of low morale but also because of the vulnerable position which the Council had wished on it. This in turn was a major factor in the morale of the Greek forces. The High Commission cabled on August 31 that there was good evidence that Greek morale was being badly undermined by the indecision as to further offensives against the Nationalists and by "misunderstandings" between the Greek and British high commands about Greek "deficiencies." Now that the first flush of success had passed, the Greeks seemed to realize, the cable went on, that they had fought chiefly for British interests. The British were admitting this openly and were telling the Greeks that they would not retain any of the territory they had occupied.[28] A week later Bristol reported that effective French and Italian opposition to decisive operations by the Greeks in Anatolia was daily more evident. The truth was, said the Admiral, that neither France nor Italy, for political and economic reasons, wanted the complete destruction of the Kemalist movement; he had heard that for the second time a plan to land Greek troops on the Black Sea coast of Turkey for an attack on Angora from the rear had been thwarted by the French and Italians, and Britain had assented. The British, in the absence of any decisive action and with the Greek lines of communication lengthening, were growing more and more apathetic in the support of the Greeks and were fast losing confidence in them, said Bristol; they were now playing their usual waiting game, to avoid blame if the Greeks were unsuccessful in maintaining their position in Anatolia.[29]

[28] Telegram 470 from Constantinople, August 31, 1920; 767.68/55.
[29] Telegram 477 from Constantinople, September 8, 1920; 767.68/56.

There was irony too in that at the moment when Allied plans for Turkey seemed to have reached their goal with the signing of the Treaty of Sèvres and the apparent defeat of Mustafa Kemal and the Nationalists at the hand of the Greeks, the Bolsheviks invaded Armenia and on September 29 Kiazem Karabekir occupied Kars and Ardahan. There was now a direct connection between the two outlaw regimes, and across this land-bridge arms, munitions and supplies could flow to the Nationalists. The Bolshevik regime in Russia lost no time in strengthening the enemy of its enemies. Assured thus of the means of making war and of feeding his people, Mustafa Kemal rested secure in the Anatolian plateau, knowing that only a full-scale military invasion could destroy him and knowing too that only the Greeks were likely to attempt such an invasion.

The strength and confidence of Mustafa Kemal were soon felt by the Allies. The treaty of peace had been signed and the Sultan's government pledged to assist in its enforcement. But there was little it could do outside Constantinople, and in October the Cabinet was dismissed at the instance of the Allies. Constantinople reported on October 21 that the government had been strengthened by the resignation of the Grand Vizier, and its ability to enforce the terms of the treaty had been enhanced, though the Allies themselves were at odds over enforcement of the treaty and had done little to help the Turkish government fulfill its pledge, while insisting that it do so. The one hope of reconciling the " rebels," said Bristol, was the presence of Izzet Pasha in the Cabinet, with whom Mustafa Kemal was prepared to hold *pourparlers*, but the British had apparently, or at least outwardly, changed their policy and now insisted on Mustafa Kemal being hunted down and executed. This might be in the nature of a preface to an apologia for British support of Greek military action of the summer, or camouflage to hide a move for reconciliation with the Nationalists, said Bristol.[30] After a new Cabinet was formed, Bristol cabled, on November 2, that it had done little to settle the question of the Nationalists. As for the Allies, the French, contemplating the Nationalist program of the return to Turkey of Smyrna, Thrace, and the eastern vilayets—which would necessitate the modification of the Treaty of Sèvres—were in a

[30] Telegram 536 from Constantinople, October 21, 1920; 867.00/1351.

dilemma in their policy toward the Nationalists, since the modification of Sèvres could be a precedent for the modification of Versailles. The British were standing pat at the moment; the Italians were deferring to their Allies, but the Nationalists and the Sultan's government were both making overtures to them as they had less at stake.[31]

The final blow to the Treaty of Sèvres was the overthrow of Venizelos. On October 2, 1920, the young King Alexander of Greece, who had taken the throne on the abdication of his father Constantine in 1917, was bitten by a pet monkey. Three weeks later he died. Venizelos then asked Constantine's third son, Paul, to take the throne. The Prince was living with his deposed father, and he replied that he would do so only if a plebiscite were held and the Greek people given an opportunity to choose between his father, his elder brother, and himself. Venizelos, in full confidence of his own popularity (he had been responsible for the deposition of Constantine and the adoption of a pro-Allied policy during the war) agreed to these terms, and allowed the general election (which would constitutionally follow the death of the King) to take place. He had two shocks. The election turned out his party and put the pro-Constantine royalists in power. The subsequent plebiscite confirmed the results of the election, and Constantine was overwhelmingly chosen as the King. This completely changed the relations of the Allies and the Greeks—and thus the relations of the Allies and the Turks—for the Greek Army was the only means at the disposal of the Allies for coercing Turkey. Constantine had been pro-German during the war and was considered to be the enemy of the Allies. It was not possible for them to continue the close relations that had existed under the Venizelos regime, even if the new King had chosen to do so. Nor was it now necessary for the Allies to be concerned about Greek interests in Turkey and the treaty, since the Greek people had apparently rejected the Allies and chosen a pro-German King. The big stumbling blocks to a settlement with the Nationalists were the allotment of Smyrna and Thrace to Greece. The question of the eastern vilayets had been settled by Mustafa Kemal and the Bolsheviks without reference to the Allies, and Armenia was no longer a factor in the settlement. Perhaps it was all for

[31] Telegram 545 from Constantinople, November 2, 1920; 763.72119/10608.

the best, except for Lloyd George, who had been the main supporter of the Greeks; but even he could not swallow, at least publicly, a Greek government headed by the man who had been, in substance if not in form, one of the allies of the Kaiser. From now on the Greeks were on their own.

CHAPTER XI

THE UNITED STATES AND THE MANDATES:
OIL AND AMERICAN RIGHTS

1.

The specific interests of the United States in the treaty of peace with Turkey and the general settlement of Eastern questions were the establishment of the principle of the Open Door and the maintenance of existing American rights and privileges in the territories which had comprised the Ottoman Empire—whether these territories remained under Turkish control, achieved independence, or came under the control of another state. The negotiation of definitive agreements on these points with the various powers concerned was of necessity delayed until definitive settlements had been arrived at between the Allied Powers and Turkey. An agreement governing American interests in the new Turkish state would have to take into account the form, effectiveness, and degree of independence of the new state, as well as extent of the privileges acquired in Turkey by the Allied Powers under the treaty. All these questions depended on the treaty of peace as it was finally ratified, and until that time the United States could do no more on the diplomatic level than to state the general American position, as had been done in the note of March 24, 1920, to the French Ambassador, since the treaty would not actually exist until it was ratified. The same was true of the mandated territories; until the League of Nations had approved the terms of the mandates and defined the nature of the regime to be established, it was not possible to negotiate agreements defining American relations with them. But while the United States could do nothing at this time of a formal nature, there was a great deal that could be done and had to be done to protect existing American interests; to prevent decisions being made and actions being taken by other powers that would weaken the American position in future negotiations; and to ensure that American decisions and actions were such as to strengthen the American position. For more than five years, from 1919 to 1925, the Department engaged in a highly technical, and tedious, diplomatic exchange with the Allied Powers. The success of these efforts reflects credit both on the professional competence and on the endurance of the officers of the Department.

Correspondence between the United States and France and Britain on oil and the maintenance of the Capitulations firmly established the principles of the new Middle East policy of the United States—the Open Door, the maintenance of existing private rights, the maintenance of the rights of the United States, and the refusal to acknowledge the termination of the Capitulations without the formal agreement of the United States—in the territory detached from Turkey and placed under mandate. In following this policy the Department of State was not trying to return to the days of 1914 or refusing to admit that the Middle East of the 1920's was totally different from what it had been ten years before. The whole purpose of American policy was to meet the new conditions, but to meet them on ground of American choosing, and so come to terms with the new political situation arising from the final partition of the old Ottoman Empire and the formal domination of the Middle East by European powers, which had completely changed the nature of American relations with the Middle East. The problem was how to accomplish this when the United States had no way of applying pressure directly in the Middle East and could only in the most general way apply pressure on the European powers concerned. The Department's solution was: first, to give nothing away without a *quid pro quo*; second, to proceed with great caution; third, to operate as far as possible within a legal framework so that a denial of American claims could be resisted as a breach of international law; and fourth, to make all the use possible of the rights that had accrued to the United States from its contribution to the defeat of the Central Powers, including Turkey. The first three of these procedures insured that in exchange for relinquishing American rights, which did not correspond to the current situation, other rights might be acquired by the United States and guaranteed by treaty; the fourth procedure was designed to give the United States a voice in the construction of the new Middle East and an opportunity to control, to some extent at least, decisions inimical to American interests while they were in the making.

2.

American interest in Middle East oil was a direct outgrowth of the increasing concern felt in the United States after the war at the apparent rapid depletion of the nation's oil resources. The great expansion in oil consumption during the war had directed the attention of the government to the state of the reserves available for future exploitation. Investigations undertaken seemed to show that little more than twenty years' supply at current rates of consumption was left in the continental United States. The result was an increased concern with the future supply of oil from overseas sources, and on May 31, 1919, an instruction was sent to all American consular posts in regions where oil might be found to report on the prospects for development, on the present control of oil resources, and on the prospects for American participation in the production of oil, in their districts.[1] In the Senate's consideration of legislation concerning oil leases on public lands, during August and the months following in 1919, there was much debate on the so-called " Aliens Clause " which prohibited aliens from holding oil leases in view of the anticipated scarcity of oil. During the debate there was much pointed comment on the alleged policy of Britain to control the oil of the world, and particular reference was made to British oil policy in the Middle East. This brought forth a sharp rejoinder by Ambassador Grey who, in a letter to the Secretary of State, denied any intention by his government to pre-empt the world's oil and referred to the vast resources of oil under the control of the American government.[2] The Secretary declined to accept responsibility for anything that was said in the Senate, and added that American production, while vast, was not keeping pace with consumption, and in view of the restrictive practices relating to the exploration

[1] *Foreign Relations*, 1919, I, 163–65.
[2] *Ibid.*, pp. 168–70.

and production of oil in territories controlled by other powers, the anxiety felt in the United States over the availability of oil for the future was not misplaced.[3] Over the next two or three years there was a great deal of public comment in the United States on British attempts to exclude American interests from participating in the development of foreign oil deposits, and corresponding protests by the British Embassy at the charges leveled against its government. This merely served to emphasize the efforts of the Department of State to achieve full American participation in the development of Middle East oil.

The rights of the United States in the oil resources of the former Ottoman Empire derived from two quite different sources; first, from existing rights claimed by American oil companies and, second, from rights claimed by the United States government under the Open Door principle. In both instances the policy followed by the United States was governed by—and to a great extent influenced in its turn—American policy on the mandates, the oil lands in question being located in mandated territory. The oil question arose while the United States was still an active partner with the Allies in determining the future of the Middle East and a year before the new policy of non-involvement was set forth in the note of March 24, 1920. But there was actually no break in policy, and the course followed by the United States was from the beginning continuous, notwithstanding the withdrawal from the peace settlement nor the change in administration.

In 1919, the Standard Oil Company of New York, which held concessions in Palestine and was interested in Mesopotamian oil, and a group of independent oil companies also interested in Mesopotamia, complained to the Department of State that their interests were being threatened by the actions of the British authorities in the Middle East. Standard Oil stated that officials of the British Administration in Palestine had entered its offices in Jerusalem and taken away documents relating to the concession; later in the year it wrote to the Department that its agents had been refused permission to investigate oil conditions in Mesopotamia, though a British geologist employed by the Shell interests had been working there for four months.[4]

[3] *Ibid.*, p. 171.
[4] *Ibid.*, II, 250–56; see also *British Documents*, Series I, IV, 501–3. On April 8, 1919, British and French representatives initialed an agreement, known as the

Ambassador Davis in London discussed these matters informally at the Foreign Office on October 6 and was told that, pending a decision on the Mandates, the British government felt bound to prohibit the activities of all concessionaires in the former territory of the Ottoman Empire and also the fulfillment of any concessions granted before the war by the Turkish government, since without such restrictions the country would be flooded with claimants and prospectors. As for complaints that British interests were being permitted to operate in Mesopotamia, certain oil wells had been operated by the British military authorities solely for military purposes because of a shortage of oil. There might have been laxity in permitting the Shell representative to make surveys, but he had been asked to leave the country once this was discovered by higher authority.[5]

The Department was dissatisfied with this reply, and Davis was told to make a formal presentation to the Foreign Secretary of the American position that a future decision on the control of the mandated territories could not affect existing rights of American nationals; that the prosecution of such rights was in full accord with the principles stated by President Wilson and agreed to by Mr. Lloyd George and with the principles of the mandates; and that the United States expected equal privileges to be extended to American nationals as were granted to the nationals of Britain or any other nation in Palestine as well as in Mesopotamia.[6] Curzon's reply repeated the points made by the Foreign Office in the discussions with Davis in October and added that the restrictions applied equally to new undertakings.[7] In the meantime, the Department had been studying the legal aspects of the Standard Oil Company's position and came to the conclusion that though the company had vested rights under Turkish law,

---

Long-Berenger agreement, regulating their mutual interests in oil around the world, including arrangements for dividing the holdings of the prewar Turkish Petroleum Company. The United States made inquiries on May 13 at Paris and was told that talks had taken place on oil, but there was nothing agreed on that excluded American interests. The agreement in fact covered much the same ground as the San Remo agreement signed a year later (see below, pp. 297–99). Lloyd George withdrew from the agreement, and negotiations were not finally concluded until the San Remo agreement; *ibid*., pp. 1089–96.

[5] *Foreign Relations*, 1919, II, 257.

[6] *Ibid*., pp. 258–59.

[7] *Ibid*., pp. 260–61. *British Documents*, Series I, IV, 541–42.

the Department had no legal grounds for pressing the British for permission to prospect in the Middle East. However, the Embassy at London was told to " maintain pressure " on the British government in order to impress on it the " vital concern " of the United States and to make sure it understood that it would be expected to protect the rights of American nationals during the negotiation of the Turkish treaty. While British good faith could not be questioned, said the Department, if any feeling arose in the United States that it was being discriminated against, the good relations of the two countries might suffer.[8]

3.

The signing of the Anglo-French oil agreement at San Remo on April 27, 1920, put an entirely different complexion on American policy on Middle East oil. It was now concerned with the national interest, not merely the individual interests of its nationals. The agreement covered the oil interests of the two countries in Rumania, Galicia, former Russian territory, and certain French and British colonies, as well as Mesopotamia; but while the extent of the agreement indicated to the Department of State the seriousness with which it was taken by France and Britain, American concern was confined to the agreement on Mesopotamia. Basically the agreement provided that in return for French acquiescence in the control of Mesopotamian oil by Britain, France was to receive a quarter of the oil produced or, if the oil were exploited by a private concern, French interests would receive a quarter of the shares. It was understood that if the oil were produced privately the company was to be under permanent British control. It was no longer merely a question of protecting American rights in the Middle East, but of preventing the pre-emption of practically the entire output of Middle East oil by Britain and France, in flat contradiction to the understandings previously arrived at on the mandates, and the exclusion of the United States from participation in what promised to be a great untapped source of oil.

The main points of the San Remo agreement were cabled to

[8] *Foreign Relations*, 1919, II, 650–51.

the Department of State from Paris on May 3, and the full text was sent on May 7. The Embassy had been given a copy by Mr. A. C. Bedford of Standard Oil of New Jersey, who had obtained it secretly from a member of the French delegation at San Remo.[9] The Department responded immediately. It was precluded from taking issue with Britain and France on the oil agreement itself, since officially the United States had no knowledge of it, and the American position was presented in terms of the general principles underlying the mandate system. On May 10 a note was cabled to London and on May 12 it was given to the Foreign Secretary. After restating the position already taken in the correspondence with Britain on Middle East oil, the note then gave a categorical statement of " the principles which the United States government would be pleased to see applied in the occupied or mandated regions": First, the mandatory power should " strictly adhere and conform to the principles expressed and agreed to during the peace negotiations at Paris and to the principles embodied in Mandate ' A ' prepared in London. . . ." Second, all nations should be guaranteed treatment equal in law and fact with respect to personal rights and in all economic and commercial activity. Third, no exclusive concessions should be granted which covered all the territory of a mandate nor any monopolies on the products of such concessions. Fourth, full publicity should be given to all applications for concessions and to government regulations dealing with the economic resources of the mandated territory, and regulations and legislation concerning concessions for the exploitation or exploration of natural resources should not have the effect of placing American or other nationals at a disadvantage with the nationals of the mandatory power. The United States recognized that concessions granted by the Ottoman government must be given practical consideration but claimed the right to participate in any discussions relating to the actual status of such concessions. This right was based on existing vested rights of American nationals and on the necessity of equitable treatment of such concessions to the initiation and application of the general principles in which the United States government was interested.

[9] 800.6363/108 and 800.6363/113, respectively; Ambassador Davis at London sent a similar account of the agreement; 800.6363/128. The text of the San Remo agreement is in *Foreign Relations*, 1920, II, 655–58.

Having stated the general American position, a carefully worded and extremely oblique approach was made in the note to the questions raised by the Anglo-French agreement, without mentioning the agreement itself. While recognizing that national emergencies might call for control of oil production (a consideration which the United States did not wish to discuss in the present communication), and the financial burdens placed on the mandatory power by the cost of administering the territory, the United States believed, the note stated, that any attempt to reimburse the mandatory by adopting a policy of monopolization, or exclusive concessions, or special privileges to its own nationals would not only be a repudiation of principles already agreed on but also economically and politically unwise. The note ended by requesting an early expression of the views of the British government " especially in order to reassure public opinion in the United States." [10]

The Foreign Office made no reply for several months. In July, however, the Anglo-French agreement was made public. It was now possible for the United States to acknowledge its existence and to make known to the French and British governments the American position on it. On July 28 a note was presented to the Foreign Office by the Embassy, asking for an early reply to the note of May 12. The United States government realized it was necessary for the British government to proceed " with due deliberation " in the inauguration of the new administrations in the mandates, the note continued, but the United States was primarily interested in " the effective application " to these territories of general principles " already clearly recognized and adhered to during the peace negotiations at Paris that such territories should be held and governed in such a way as to assure equal treatment in law and fact to the commerce of all nations." The treatment of the economic resources of the mandates was not merely a question of commercial competition or strategic control of raw materials, but involved principles far transcending such matters. The United States had made certain suggestions in its previous note

[10] *Ibid.*, pp. 651–55; the note here printed is an amended version of the original note submitted to the Foreign Office, which, with British approval, was withdrawn and the printed version substituted, omitting a reference to the discussions in the Council of Four, still secret at this time, in view of the proposed publication of the correspondence. See 800.6363/130 and 800. 6363/133.

about the measures which should be applied in order to guarantee the application of such principles, but, unfortunately, " occurrences subsequent to the submission of this note have not served to clarify the situation or to diminish the concern felt by the Government and people of the United States." The note then referred to the publication of the agreement and went on, " It is not clear to the Government of the United States how such an agreement can be consistent with the principles of equality of treatment understood and accepted during the peace negotiations at Paris." In the view of the United States government it would " as a practical matter result in a grave infringement of the mandate principle." [11] The substance of this note in summary was left at the French Foreign Office as an aide-memoire of an oral presentation of the American position on the agreement made by the Chargé in France to the Secretary-General of the Foreign Office.[12]

On August 9 Foreign Secretary Curzon replied answering in detail the points raised by the American notes of May 12 and July 28. The first topic he discussed was that of the alleged advantages given by the British authorities in Mesopotamia to British oil interests. Curzon said the hope had been entertained that the doubts of the American government in the matter had been satisfactorily dispelled. No development work on the oil fields had been undertaken except under military necessity, and the suggestion that Britain had, during the period of military occupation, been preparing for the exclusive control of Mesopotamian oil was " devoid of foundation." He then made a " passing reference " to the " very mistaken impressions " of British oil policy then current in the United States. He compared oil production under British control, which amounted to four and a half per cent of world production, with American oil production, which amounted to eighty per cent; American predominance was assured for many years and there was no justification for supposing that Britain could seriously threaten American supremacy. Yet the United States had laws which reserved American oil resources for American interests, and had used its influence in countries " amenable " to its control to exclude British oil interests. " The nervousness of American opinion, concerning the alleged grasping activities of British oil interests, appears singularly unfortunate

---

[11] *Foreign Relations*, 1920, II, 658–59.   [12] *Ibid*., pp. 659, 667–68.

in view of these facts," said Curzon. The attitude of the British government had been very different; it had fulfilled its obligations as the administrator of the territory, and had taken steps to protect the natural resources of Mesopotamia from indiscriminate exploitation, as well as the absolute freedom of action of the future authority which would eventually administer the country.

Curzon then turned to the specific " suggestions " made in the note of May 12. The first was that the regimes established in former Turkish territory should reflect the principles accepted at Paris and in the draft " A " mandates. He pointed out that the draft mandates agreed on at Paris had been abandoned, and the drafts prepared in their place, which would secure equality of treatment and opportunity of all states members of the League, would, when approved by the Allied Powers concerned, be submitted to the Council of the League of Nations. In this case, while appreciating the desire of the American government to discuss the terms of the mandates, the British government was of the opinion that these terms could only properly be discussed at the Council of the League by the members of the League. The next issue was that of concessions. The British government agreed with the American government that all legally acquired rights must be given due consideration, and provision for this had been made in the Turkish treaty. Certain rights had been acquired by American interests while British interests, such as the Turkish Petroleum Company, also claimed rights, and these rights would have to be given practical consideration and equitable treatment consistent with the interests of the mandated territory. Under the Turkish treaty the oil deposits of Mesopotamia would be secured to the future Arab state, but there was no intention to secure a monopoly for the mandatory power. The arrangement with the French government for participation in Mesopotamian oil production derived from the long-standing interests of France in the Mosul region, and the share allotted to France was in consideration of an agreement to permit oil to be transshipped from the oil fields across Syria by pipeline. The arrangement did not exclude other interests, while the Mesopotamian state was free to develop the oil fields in any way it judged advisable.[13]

The State Department was not satisfied with this reply. Yet

[13] *Ibid.*, pp. 663–68.

another note was therefore addressed to the Foreign Secretary, this time by Secretary of State Colby, himself. It was not delivered until December 6, having been delayed by questions concerning the proposed publication of the correspondence on oil and the propriety of the Secretary of State communicating directly with the Foreign Minister of another power, which Secretary Colby wished to do. The Secretary accepted " with a full sense of the good faith of the British Government " the statement that it had refrained from exploiting the oil resources of Mesopotamia and that its operations there were for purely military purposes. The United States government welcomed the pledges of the British government that no monopolies were contemplated and the resources of Mesopotamia were being reserved for the future Arab state and its people. Referring to the mandate for Mesopotamia, the Secretary called the attention of the British government to the fact that while the form of Mandate " A " adopted at Paris had been discarded, the British government had expressed agreement with the draft. The United States believed that territories acquired from the Central Powers should, in the interests of future world peace, be administered in such a way as to insure equality of treatment to the citizens and commerce of all nations, and indeed it was in reliance on an understanding to this effect that the United States was persuaded to agree to the acquisition of conquered territory under mandate by the victorious powers. Accordingly, it was assumed that Lord Curzon's statement in the note of August 9, that draft mandates for Mesopotamia and Palestine had been prepared with a view to securing equality of treatment to the states members of the League of Nations, did not indicate a supposition that the United States could be excluded from the benefits of equality of treatment. Nor could the United States concur in the view that discussion of the draft mandates could only take place in the Council of the League; such powers as the Allied and Associated Powers enjoyed in the disposition of the territories in question accrued to them as a result of the war against the Central Powers, and the United States, as a participant in that war, could not consider any of the associated powers debarred from the discussion of any of its consequences. In like manner, the United States was entitled to be consulted for its opinion on the drafts, before the draft mandates were submitted by the Allied Powers to the Council for approval.

The Secretary then brought up the main point at issue. He referred to the importance of economic equality in the mandates, a principle which was an " outstanding illustration of the type of question which the Mandate System was designed to meet, to obviate those international differences " that grow out of a desire for the exclusive control of the resources and markets of annexed territories. The United States government found difficulty in reconciling the agreement, by which France was to receive a quarter of the oil production of Mesopotamia, with the statement by Lord Curzon that the oil resources of the country were to be secured to the future Arab state, or with the statement that claims on these resources were to remain in their prewar condition. The American government had noted a statement by a British Minister that the San Remo agreement was based on the principle that concessions granted by the Ottoman government must be honored; it would be " reluctant to assume that His Majesty's Government has already undertaken to pass judgment upon the validity of concessionary claims in the regions concerned." Such information as the American government possessed indicated that the Turkish Petroleum Company did not own any rights in Mesopotamia to petroleum concessions or the exploitation of oil, and the Secretary said he was " at some loss to understand how to construe the provision of the San Remo Agreement that any private petroleum company which may develop the Mesopotamian oil fields ' shall be under permanent British control,' " in view of Lord Curzon's assurances that it was not the intention of the British government to establish on its own behalf any kind of a monopoly. As for Curzon's comments on the dominant American position in oil production, the Secretary stated that he would " regret any assumption " by the British government that the American position on mandates was " dictated to any degree " by considerations of domestic needs or production of petroleum or any other commodity. He also noted that American oil resources were only one-twelfth of the world resources and were being used up rapidly; the demand for petroleum products exceeded the supply and only by the unhampered development of the world's resources could the demand be met. He mentioned these matters, said the Secretary, only to correct certain confusing inferences in Lord

Curzon's note which might arise from certain departures in it from the underlying principles of a mandate.[14]

This note was as unsatisfactory to the British as its note of August 9 was to the United States, though the dissatisfaction was apparently not with the substance of the note but the fact that the United States insisted on maintaining its position. Lord Curzon replied to it on February 28 and, shifting tactics, now based his arguments on the proposition that the Allied arrangements on the Mesopotamian oil fields were based on a valid concession obtained before the war. ". . . I desire to make it plain," he said, " that the whole of the oil fields to which those provisions refer are the subject of a concession to the Turkish Petroleum Company. The position of such concessions in territories detached from Turkey is expressly safeguarded by articles 311 and 312 of the Treaty of Sèvres." He then went into the history of the concession, concluding, ". . . the oil rights in the vilayets of Baghdad and Mosul cannot be treated as a matter of abstract principle . . ." and adding that the rights of the Standard Oil Company, which the United States presumably expected the British government to honor, were based on a prospecting license and were no stronger than those of the Turkish Petroleum Company. The rest of the note was a restatement of what had already been submitted by the British government. (Lord Curzon addressed his communication to the American Ambassador, not the Secretary of State.) [15]

The American reply to the claim that a valid concession to Mesopotamian oil existed was not made for several months. The Harding Administration took office in March and the new officials of the Department had to learn their way. A partial answer was given to the Foreign Office on August 24, 1921, in a memorandum on the principles which the United States considered to be involved in the determination of precise terms for the mandates.[16] *Inter alia*, the memorandum made reference to the British note of February 28 which mentioned the concession said to have been made to the Turkish Petroleum Company before the war. " This Government has already pointed out in its note of November 20, 1920, that such information as it then had indicated that prior to the war the Turkish Petroleum Company possessed in Meso-

[14] *Ibid.*, pp. 668–73. [15] *Ibid.*, 1921, II, 80–84. [16] See below, pp. 315–16.

potamia no rights to petroleum concessions or to the exploitation of oil. The information possessed at present by this Government confirms this view." The United 'States government, continued the memorandum, would shortly take up this subject with the British government; if the claims put forward by the British government continued to be asserted, it was desired that provisions be made for the arbitration of the claim.[17]

A full statement of the American position on the claims of the Turkish Petroleum Company was presented to the British government on November 17, 1921. The Department of State had received an account of the company's negotiations with the Turkish government immediately prior to the outbreak of war, from the Consul-General at Berlin, who had obtained his information from F. J. Gunther, a German, the chief negotiator for the company in the company's negotiations in 1914.[18] The British claim was based on a letter written by the Grand Vizier, Said Halim, to the company on June 28, 1914, stating that the Turkish government " consents to lease [the petroleum resources in Mosul and Baghdad vilayets] to the Turkish Petroleum Company," with the conditions of the contract to be determined later. The United States held that this letter,

even in connection with the communications to which it is understood to have been a reply, cannot well be considered a definite and binding agreement to lease. . . . The relations between the Turkish officials concerned and the Turkish Petroleum Company would appear, therefore, to have been those of negotiators of an agreement in contemplation rather than those of parties to a contract.

The United States did not believe that any presumption should rest in favor of contracts covering mandated territories which were in the negotiation stage and not consummated, and again put forward the proposal that the claim of the company, if it were continued to be asserted, be determined by arbitration. As for American claims in Palestine, which the British government had referred to, these were of an entirely different category than the British claims since they were based on concessions regularly granted by the Turkish government, and were, in contrast to the British claims, far from monopolistic.[19]

[17] *Ibid.*, pp. 106–10.   [18] *Ibid.*, pp. 85–86.   [19] *Ibid.*, pp. 89–93.

4.

No answer was made to this note, but, significantly perhaps, at about the time the note was sent, Sir John Cadman, an important figure in the British oil industry and shortly to become the head of the Anglo-Persian Oil Company, was in the United States and opened discussions with American oil interests looking to American participation in the development of Mesopotamian oil. Seven companies had indicated to the Department of State their interest in investigating this oil and their readiness to begin work in the country as soon as conditions permitted. They had been told that current British policy was not to permit exploration during military occupation, and also that there were certain claims still to be determined, but, the Department said, the companies would be informed as soon as the country was open for prospecting. These were the companies approached by Cadman. Negotiations between American and British interests continued through 1922 and into 1923. The Department maintained the position it had followed in the negotiations with the British government—while favoring private negotiations between the oil interests of the two countries, it would not approve any private arrangement which did not meet its requirements for the Open Door. On June 22, 1922, A. C. Bedford, who had given the Paris Embassy the copy of the San Remo agreement, called at the Department on behalf of the seven oil companies to ascertain the Department's attitude toward the negotiations between British and American interests looking to American participation in the Turkish Petroleum Company. He was told that the Department had no objections to such negotiation provided that any reputable American company willing and ready to participate would not be excluded by arrangements arrived at through the negotiations and provided that the legal validity of the Turkish Petroleum Company's claims would not be recognized until after an impartial arbitration of them. It was suggested that it would be possible at the proper time to obtain a new or confirmatory grant of a concession to the Turkish Petroleum Company, if that company were to be the basis of the proposed agreement.[20] In December, 1922, certain British companies with an interest in the Turkish Petro-

[20] *Ibid.*, 1922, II, 337–38.

leum Company attempted to make American participation dependent on an undertaking by the Department not to question the title of the company to the concession it claimed. On being informed of this by the representative of the American companies, the Department replied by citing its correspondence with the British government, and nothing more was heard of the plan.[21]

During the Lausanne Conference on the treaty between the Allied Powers and the Nationalist government of Turkey, the validity of the Turkish Petroleum Company's claims was again asserted by the British in discussions on the Mosul vilayet, which the Nationalists claimed as part of Turkey and the British as part of Mesopotamia, or, as it now was, the kingdom of Iraq. The mission at Lausanne was instructed to bring to the attention of Lord Curzon the American note of November, 1921. This was the last of the correspondence. In February, 1923, the British interests in the Turkish Petroleum Company agreed to accept the Department's position on the validity of the company's claims, and in April an " Open Door Formula " was drawn up to meet the American government's position. It provided for the negotiation of a new concession with the government of Iraq, and for open bids for oil rights not reserved for the company, which would be confined to twenty-four areas of eight square miles each.[22] On a draft concession being submitted to the Department in October, 1923, approval was given to the arrangement; the desiderata of the United States were considered to have been attained.[23] Final approval was given when the concession was finally granted by the government of Iraq in 1925. The American oil companies, now organized as the Near East Development Corporation, continued detailed negotiations with the British and other interests and on July 31, 1928, the so-called Red Line agreement was signed which made a final settlement of the terms under which the various interests participated, including their respective shares of the company (which had now changed its name to the Iraq Petroleum Company), and the renunciation of the right of any participant to engage independently in oil activities in the Middle East within the boundaries of an area corresponding roughly to the old Ottoman territories. This boundary was marked in red on a map, hence the name of the agreement.

[21] *Ibid.*, pp. 347–52.   [22] *Ibid.*, pp. 243–45.   [23] *Ibid.*, pp. 246–64.

This agreement nullified the claims of the Standard Oil Company of New York in Palestine.[24]

5.

Paralleling the efforts of the Department of State to maintain existing private American commercial and economic rights in the former territories of the Ottoman Empire and in Turkey, as well as rights acquired by the United States as a result of American participation in the war against the Central Powers, were the Department's efforts to protect rights stemming from treaties and usage. These rights were embodied in the Capitulations and in customary practice, and concerned the legal status of Americans in Turkish and former Turkish territory, their rights to be exempt in certain cases from Ottoman jurisdiction and police power, economic and commercial rights, rights to establish schools and missions, and rights with respect to taxation. The Turkish government had attempted to abolish the Capitulations shortly after the outbreak of war and the United States had denied the right of the Turks to end rights established by treaty, except by treaty. The American position did not change with the end of the war and the defeat of the Turks. It has been mentioned that attempts by the Turkish government and the Allied high commissioners in Turkey to increase taxes had been resisted by the Department of State on the ground that taxes were set by the Capitulations. The most significant diplomatic actions with respect to the Capitulations, however, took place not in Turkey, where the Sultan's government was not in a position to challenge the United States, but in the mandated territories, now ruled by the Allied Powers who had just conquered these lands and were not in a frame of mind to give up anything of what had been so onerously won. This was particularly true of the economic wealth of the former Turkish territories, as we have just seen, but it was

[24] For general accounts of the Middle East oil questions, see De Novo, *American Interests*, chap. VI, particularly for material on the domestic American aspects; B. Shwadran, *The Middle East, Oil, and the Great Powers* (New York, 1955), pp. 204–13; and, from the British point of view, S. H. Longrigg, *Oil in the Middle East* (London, 1954), pp. 45–47, 67–70. The Red Line agreement is in Hurewitz, *Diplomacy*, p. 161.

also true of the mandatory powers' rights to govern them as they saw fit.

The question arose in the former Turkish territories after the Treaty of Sèvres had been signed and the position of the occupying powers apparently confirmed. The mandates had been assigned at San Remo, and the treaty had formally transferred the territories to the Allied and associated powers for disposal. Shortly afterwards, the British authorities in Palestine attempted to exercise jurisdiction over American nationals there. When the Embassy at London protested, Curzon replied " that with the coming into force of the Turkish Treaty and the severance thereby from Turkey (of Palestine) the capitulations in Palestine will definitely be at an end." The particular case that called forth this exchange never came to trial, and the United States did not raise the basic issue with the British government beyond refusing to accept British jurisdiction in the case. However, the British continued to attempt to bring Americans before the local courts instead of turning them over to the American Consulate for trial. The Consul protested, and the Foreign Office asked the United States, in view of the fact that the majority of the judges in the Palestine courts in which Americans would be tried were British, to reconsider its position. The United States declined to do so.[25]

By this time it was obvious that the Treaty of Sèvres would never be ratified in its original form. In March, 1921, the Foreign Office accepted the American position that the consular court retained its jurisdiction, but it did so " in deference to the United States Government's representations and as a mark of [His Majesty's Government's] friendly sentiments . . ." while " regretting the legal reasons and somewhat technical considerations " for the American action and reiterating the position taken in the note of December 29 on the status of extraterritorial rights.[26] The Department's reply, sent in April, restated the American position and ignored the Foreign Office's comments on the reasons for the Department's actions and the spirit of complaint in its remark that overriding the Palestine court would risk " adversely affecting the authority and prestige of the responsible British authorities in Palestine and render more difficult the heavy

[25] The correspondence is in *Foreign Relations*, 1920, II, 675–78; and 1921, II, 119–20.
[26] *Ibid.*, pp. 120–21.

tasks which they have accepted, with, as they hoped, the cordial good-will of the United States Government. . . ." The reply merely referred to previous statements reserving the question of the Capitulations, and indicated " that the Government of the United States is not at present disposed to concur in the view of His Majesty's Government that the regime of the Capituations in Palestine will be terminated as a matter of course when the Treaty [of Sèvres] and the Mandate become effective." [27] In a case that arose later in the year, an American citizen was arrested for carrying a revolver, contrary to local law, and was tried and sentenced by the District Governor to thirty days in jail. When the Consul at Jerusalem heard of the case, a week after the trial, and demanded that the American be turned over to the Consulate for trial, the local authorities declined on the grounds that the prisoner had been apprehended in a military reservation and had not claimed American citizenship or protection at the time of his trial. The Department took the position that the rights of separate jurisdiction could not yield to rights asserted by military authority to apprehend persons in a military zone nor, since these rights were accorded to the government of the United States, could they be relinquished at the will of an individual citizen. [28]

After the Department's April note, over two years passed before the American position was challenged again. During 1922, and the first half of 1923, peace with Turkey was in abeyance and it was not until August, 1923, that the Treaty of Lausanne settled the relations between the Allies and Turkey. During this period no question was raised as to the validity of American claims, and, in fact, the local administration and the Consulate at Jerusalem, with the approval of their respective governments, negotiated in February, 1922, a provisional agreement on procedure in civil and criminal cases, purely for the convenience of both parties, which recognized implicitly American rights. [29] On July 20, 1923, however, the Vice-Consul at Jerusalem cabled the Department that the Attorney General of Palestine had informed him he would no longer apply the provisions of the provisional agreement, [30] and on August 11 he cabled that the Supreme Court of Palestine had handed down a decision asserting that American

[27] Ibid., pp. 121–22.
[28] Ibid., pp. 122–23.
[29] Ibid., 1923, II, 218–21.
[30] Ibid., pp. 221–22.

capitulatory rights were not in accordance with British law governing the jurisdiction of courts in Palestine, and therefore the courts should ignore the provisional agreement. He was insisting on the maintenance of American rights, said the Vice-Consul, but the law would have to be changed if the local courts were to recognize the jurisdiction of the Consulate. The Department instructed him to tell the British authorities that until the treaty with Turkey was ratified and an agreement between the United States and British recognizing the British mandate was negotiated, it was hoped that the provisional agreement would be followed. The Embassy at London was instructed to inform the Foreign Office that the United States trusted appropriate instructions would be sent to Palestine to have any cases pending in the Palestine courts involving American citizens treated in conformity with the provisional agreement, as the capitulary rights of Americans in Palestine " remain intact in the absence of an agreement concerning the formal recognition by the United States of the British mandate. . . ." [31]

Lord Curzon's reply was a complete surrender. The American claim to the maintenance of the Capitulations was admitted; the British government was prepared to have the law of jurisdiction changed, though, said Curzon, this would entail fresh legislation and its " effect on the local situation would be particularly unfortunate at the present time, when the justification of His Majesty's Government in singling out United States nationals for special treatment would not be properly understood either in Palestine or by the League of Nations," in view of the fact that the United States had already agreed, in its treaty with Turkey of August 6, to surrender its capitulatory rights. " In these circumstances His Majesty's Government earnestly hopes that the United States Government will agree that the best method of regularizing the present situation is by taking immediate steps to negotiate the convention . . ." (i.e., the convention between the two countries providing for American recognition of the mandate).[32] This was a far cry from the note of December 29, 1920, and the peremptory tone used in it.

[31] *Ibid.*, pp. 222–24.
[32] *Ibid.*, pp. 225–28.

6.

The principles of American policy being established and American rights admitted by the Powers, it remained to settle the precise terms to implement this policy and define these rights, and to bind the other Powers. The mandate system would create *ab initio* new states, and the terms of the mandates would in effect be the constitutions of the several mandated territories, defining their political, economic, and legal regimes. American rights would be affected in all these spheres. When the terms of the mandates were discussed in the Council of the League, in early 1921, it was the policy of the Wilson Administration to deal directly with the Council in order to insure that the terms of the mandates contained nothing injurious to American interests. The mandates had been assigned by those of the principal Allied and Associated Powers convened at the Conference of San Remo; this decision had been ratified by the Treaty of Sèvres. But, under the Covenant, the terms of the mandates had to be approved by the League of Nations, and in the latter part of 1920 those powers which had received mandates had submitted drafts for the consideration of the League. Copies of the drafts of the mandates for Syria and Palestine were obtained by the Embassy at Paris through an American official of the League and sent to the Department in January, 1921,[33] and draft mandates for certain former German colonies were sent officially by the Secretary-General of the League to " President Warren Gamaliel Harding " on February 17, 1921.[34]

On the same day, Ambassador Wallace in France cabled the Department that the " A " and " B " mandates would be taken up by the League Council at its next meeting, beginning on February 21. " According to information received," said the Ambassador:

the Council is under pressure from interested parties, but is anxious to bring mandates into accord with the Covenant. American views may be

---

[33] Despatch 2017 from Paris, January 7, 1921, 890D.01/30. On December 10, 1920, Beirut cabled the Department that the Consulate had been informed the French government had a complete draft of the mandate for Syria; on December 14 Paris was instructed to obtain a copy (telegram 1698), 890D.01/27.

[34] *Foreign Relations*, 1921, I, 118–20.

reasonably expected to receive consideration of Council. Your oil note to the British Government [i.e., the note of November 20, 1920, from Secretary Colby to Curzon, mentioned above] is, of course, known to the Council, but I am informed that as the note has not been presented to them officially they cannot act on it.[35]

Wallace was instructed to notify the President and Council of the League that the United States had been informed that the mandates would come before the Council at its next meeting and wished to submit to the Council an explanation of its views, which had already been communicated in part to the principal Allied powers. There were also other observations which the United States government wished to present, and it " respectfully requested " that no final decision on the mandates be taken until after the receipt of the American position, which would be communicated to the Council at an early date.[36] At the same time a cable was sent to the Embassy in Brazil with instructions to " ascertain discreetly " whether the Brazilian government would be disposed to instruct its delegate to the League to cause a postponement of any immediate action on the mandates.[37] On February 21 the text of a note from the Secretary of State to the President and members of the Council of the League of Nations was sent to the Ambassador in France; he was instructed to deliver it exactly as transmitted, since he had no official contact with the League and it was " desired that the communication should be presented and delivered as coming directly from this Government. . . ." The Ambassador was to enclose with the note a copy of the oil note of November 20.

The note referred to the statements in the note of November 20 of the wish of the United States government to have submitted to it the draft mandates before they were submitted to the Council, so that the Council might " have before it an expression of the opinion of the Government of the United States on the form of such mandates, and a clear indication of the basis upon which the approval of this Government, which is essential to the validity of any determinations which may be reached, might be anticipated and received." (The note also pointed out that the mandate for

[35] *Ibid.*, pp. 87–88.
[36] *Ibid.*, p. 88.
[37] Telegram to Rio de Janeiro, February 16, 1921; 763.72119/10980A.

the German islands in the Pacific north of the Equator was mis-worded; it stated that the award of the mandate to Japan had been made on the agreement of the principal Allied and Associated Powers, but the United States, which was "distinctly included in [that] very definite and constantly used descriptive phrase," had never agreed to the terms or provisions of this mandate; it had in fact been opposed to the inclusion of the island of Yap in any mandate to Japan, President Wilson having made a specific reservation of this point in Paris.[38]

The President of the Council replied on March 1. The claims of the United States were freely admitted—"The rights which it acquired [in the war] are not likely to be challenged in any quarter . . ."— but the situation had been complicated by the failure, so far, of the United States to ratify the peace treaty. However, no conclusions would be reached on the "A" mandates until the United States had an opportunity to express its views, and the United States was invited to take part in the discussions of both the "A" and "B" mandates at a forthcoming meeting. The Japanese mandate in the Pacific had been allocated by the Supreme Council and the League was concerned only with its administration, thus the misunderstanding would seem to be with the principal Allied Powers rather than the League.[39]

7.

The procedures adopted under President Wilson to safeguard American rights in the mandates were completely abandoned when President Harding took office. In his first message to Congress, of April 12, 1921, he stated, "In the existing League of Nations, world-governing with its superpowers, this Republic will have no part."[40] The new Administration refused to acknowledge the League's existence, and the correspondence with the Council on Mandates was allowed to lapse. Instead, a policy of separate negotiations with the powers concerned was followed. Several requests from the League for the statement of the American position on the mandates, pending the receipt of which the

[38] *Foreign Relations*, 1921, I, 89–92.
[39] *Ibid.*, pp. 93–95.
[40] *Ibid.*, pp. xvii–xviii.

Council of the League had agreed to postpone consideration of the mandates, were ignored in Washington. In July, 1921, the French Embassy asked the Department of State for an expression of its views on the mandates for Togoland and the Cameroons, and on August 1 Curzon sent an informal note to the Ambassador in Britain, recalling to him that he had twice mentioned the subject of " Asiatic mandates " in seeking to obtain a statement of the criticisms or objections which he understood the American government wished to raise. The matter was urgent, said Curzon, since the League Council was pressing the British government; on the other hand, it might be assumed that the United States had already given its objections, since it had communicated a protest to the League in March.[41]

In carrying out the new approach to the mandates, it was the American attitude that the United States should not go from country to country seeking the protection of its rights, but that the powers, if they wanted American approval of their plans, should approach the United States to obtain it. The Allies having raised the question, therefore, Secretary of State Hughes responded. The text of a note was immediately cabled to London and it was given on August 21 to the Foreign Secretary.[42] It reiterated the stand already taken on the mandates in the correspondence on oil and in the note to the League Council under the previous Administration—that though the United States had not declared war on Turkey, victory over it had been made possible by the victory over Germany; therefore, and also by reason of the recognition by the powers of the principles of the mandates agreed to at Paris, the United States assumed " there would be no disposition in relation to any of the [former Turkish] territories to discriminate against the United States or to refuse to safeguard equality of opportunity." Several specific points relating to the " A " mandate drafts were presented. Consular tribunals should continue until the new legal organs created to replace the Ottoman legal system were actually functioning, and provision should be made for the revival of the Capitulations on the termination of the mandate; the prohibition of discrimination against members of the League should be broadened to include

[41] Ibid., II, 106.
[42] An almost identical note was sent to the French Ambassador in reply to the query mentioned above; ibid., I, 922–25.

the United States, particularly with respect to concessions. Provisions for the protection of missionaries in the mandate for Syria and Lebanon should not be confined to " the domain of religion " but should include educational and charitable activities. The consent of the United States to any change or modification of the mandate " shall be necessary." [43]

The French and British governments replied on the same day, December 22, 1921, and, allowing for the differences between the two languages, in substance almost word-for-word in the same terms. The position in the mandate question claimed by the United States by virtue of its participation in the war was fully accepted. With respect to the mandates for Middle East territories, the position of such territories being still legally undefined, the respective governments stated they would make them the subject of later notes. As for the general considerations put forward by the United States, both countries declared their intention of meeting the American proposals, and suggested that the placing of the United States on the same footing as the members of the League, and the acknowledgment of the right of the United States to be consulted before any changes were made in the mandate, could best be secured by the exchange of notes, rather than by the addition of clauses to this effect in the text of the mandates.[44]

The British reply was expanded a week later in a letter from Sir Eyre Crowe, and by Lord Balfour in talks with Secretary Hughes during the Disarmament Conference at Washington in January, 1922. Crowe's letter emphasized British acceptance of the American position as a whole but raised some new points. The mandate, in the special case of Palestine, expressly provided that the Administration might arrange with the Jewish agency to develop the resources of the country, in view of the conditions in Palestine and the undertaking to establish a Jewish National Home. Judicial tribunals were already established under British administration, since the Turkish courts had ceased to exist in 1918, and, therefore, the American requirement that consular courts be continued did not apply. In Mesopotamia, the position of the British government there was " peculiar "; the situation was quite different from Palestine " as the course of events since the grant of the mandate and in particular the coronation of King

[43] *Ibid.*, II, 106–10.　　　　　　[44] *Ibid.*, pp. 110–15.

Faisal and the appointment of an Arab cabinet for that country make it necessary for His Majesty's Government carefully to consider the manner in which they can best fulfill the obligations undertaken by them in the draft mandate. . . ." It was hoped to give the United States the " fullest assurances " at an early date.[45]

Hughes, in his talks with Balfour and also in a formal reply sent on April 3, 1922,[46] maintained the position set out in the note of August 24, 1921, since the views then advanced were " confined to the purpose of safeguarding the interests of the United States " and these interests had not changed. The guarantees of American rights required by the United States could not be secured by an exchange of notes; American rights derived from treaties with the Ottoman Empire could only be modified or abrogated by treaty. The United States would agree to the exercise of jurisdiction over American nationals by local courts, in view of the British assurances that the majority of judges would be British, but only after a treaty had been signed, and with the proviso that the treaty provided for " the immediate and complete revival of American capitulary rights on the termination of the Mandate." It would not be sufficient to provide in the treaty merely for consultation with the United States should Britain desire to modify the terms of the mandate in the future; the consent of the United States would be necessary. If the British government was willing to meet the wishes of the United States on these matters, negotiation of the treaty could begin immediately. (The mandate for Iraq was dealt with later.)

The British reply, given to the Embassy a few days later, accepted all the American terms: " The proposals now made by the Government of the United States are acceptable to His Majesty's Government who will be prepared to enter without delay into negotiations for the conclusion of a treaty on the lines proposed." However, since the terms of the mandate were to be recited in the preamble of the treaty, it would be necessary to settle those terms before the treaty could be signed, and this would have to wait on the determination, by the League of

[45] *Ibid.*, pp. 115–18.
[46] For the Hughes-Balfour discussions, see *ibid.*, 1922, II, 268–71; the American note of April 24 is in *ibid.*, pp. 271–75.

Nations, of the final terms of the mandate.[47] A draft of the treaty was sent to the Department of State by the British Embassy on July 5, 1922. The preamble mentioned Article Twenty-two of the Covenant of the League, the Treaty of Sèvres whereby Britain was entrusted with the mandate for Palestine, the Balfour Declaration, the terms of the mandate, the participation of the United States in the war against Germany and its contribution to the defeat of Germany and its Allies, and the non-ratification of the Treaty of Versailles by the United States. The Convention itself consisted of six articles providing respectively for the " concurrence " of the United States in the mandate; the enjoyment by the United States of all the engagements of Britain defined in the mandate, including equality of commercial opportunity, notwithstanding the United States was not a member of the League; maintenance of American property rights; the submission of a duplicate of the mandatory's annual report to the League; and the assent of the United States to any modification and to the effective date of the Convention.[48]

An American counterdraft was sent to the British Embassy on July 12. It contained several important changes from the British draft. The reference to the Balfour Declaration was omitted from the preamble, since it did not " appear to be explanatory of the reasons underlying the negotiations of the proposed convention and therefore seems to be unessential," and the preamble of the mandate was also omitted from the preamble of the Convention. In the Convention, the United States " consented " to the mandate instead of concurring in it; the United States was to have the rights and benefits secured to members of the League; an additional article was inserted providing for the free establishment and maintenance by American nationals, subject to local law for the maintenance of public order and morals, of educational, philanthropic and religious institutions, and for them to receive voluntary applicants and to teach in the English language. The United States also suggested a change in the mandate itself to remove ambiguity from the article dealing with the suspension of capitulatory rights.[49]

[47] *Ibid.*, pp. 275–76.
[48] *Ibid.*, pp. 281–84.
[49] *Ibid.*, pp. 287–91. The final terms of the mandate as submitted by Britain to

The British reply, sent on October 2, " substantially (accepted) the operative clauses of the convention now proposed by the State Department " subject to certain modifications. The British government was " anxious " to have the policy of establishing a national home for the Jewish people mentioned if possible in the Convention, partly because of American interest in it (there was a reference here to the Joint Resolutions of the Congress in support of the Jewish National Home) and because one of the articles of the mandate referred to it. This could be done by including the preamble to the mandate in the preamble to the Convention. However, if the United States still found difficulty in accepting the insertion of the mandate preamble the British government would " reluctantly be prepared in the last resort, to accept the draft convention as put forward by the United States " provided mention was made of the policy of the Jewish National Home in the Convention preamble. The substitution of " consent " for " concurs " was accepted; in view of the fact that the mandate provided for freedom of educational activities and undertakings, and with the assurance which the British government was prepared to make regarding American requirements for missionary and educational institutions, it was felt that the United States would agree that an article providing for these points was unnecessary.[50]

8.

At this point in the negotiations there was a hiatus of almost eighteen months. Negotiations for the Allied-Turkish treaty of peace were about to start at Lausanne and the Department wished to postpone the mandate convention until a definitive settlement was reached on Turkish matters. In the meantime, negotiations with the French on the mandate for Syria had made some progress. In the French note of December 22, 1921, the French government had said, as had the British, that a fuller exposition of the French position would be made in a " later Note." The British had sent theirs on December 29, but nothing had been heard from Paris.

---

the League of Nations were sent to the Department by the British Embassy on July 15, 1922; *ibid.*, pp. 292–300.

[50] *Ibid.*, pp. 304–10.

In May, 1922, the French government stated in the League of Nations that they had not proceeded with the Syrian mandate because they had not been able to arrive at any agreement with the United States on the matter.[51] The truth of the matter was that France had been allowing the British to carry the weight of the negotiations with the United States and, furthermore, was not unhappy to have the definition of the mandates postponed until its position in Syria was firmly established.

The reference to the United States made by the French in the League and a report that the French government would oppose the Palestine mandate until agreement had been reached in the Syrian mandate, led the Department to instruct the Ambassador at Paris to remind the French Foreign Office that the " further Note " was still awaited in Washington.[52] At the end of May the Ambassador was told that proposals would be sent to the American government shortly,[53] and a month later a draft Convention was delivered to the Embassy. It repeated, *mutatis mutandem*, the terms of the draft Convention submitted by the British government on Palestine.[54] The Department replied on July 12, submitting a counterdraft which followed closely the proposals sent to the British government on the Palestine mandate, and this in substance was accepted by the French government.[55]

The conclusion of the Convention on Syria was postponed, as in the case of the Palestine Convention, until after the Lausanne Conference. The League of Nations confirmed the French mandate in September, 1923, and on October 23 the Department instructed the Embassy at Paris to notify the French government it was ready to resume negotiations for a Convention, reserving in the meantime all capitulatory rights of American citizens in Syria.[56] The French agreed and on November 2, 1923, sent a note in reply to the American note of July 12, 1922, accepting in substance the American position.[57] After further correspondence

---

[51] Letter, Minister Grew at Berne to Assistant Secretary Harrison, May 25, 1922; 890D.01/70.
[52] *Foreign Relations*, 1922, II, 117.
[53] *Ibid.*, p. 118.
[54] *Ibid.*, pp. 118–27.
[55] *Ibid.*, pp. 127–33.
[56] *Ibid.*, 1923, II, 2–3.
[57] *Ibid.*, pp. 4–6.

clearing up details concerned with the consular regime, American educational and missionary activity, and extradition, the Convention was signed on April 4, 1924, at Paris.[58]

Negotiations on the Palestine Convention were not resumed until April, 1924, when, shortly after the Syrian Convention was signed, the Department instructed London to bring the recently concluded Convention to the attention of the Foreign Office and to suggest it be taken as the basis of renewed negotiations.[59] The British government agreed and with minor changes accepted the Syrian Convention.[60] The United States agreed to the recitation of the preamble to the mandate, including the reference to the Jewish National Home. The clarification of these minor points continued for some months, but the Convention was finally signed on December 3, 1924.[61] The exchange of ratifications was delayed by differences between the two governments on the disposition of cases of American citizens before Palestine courts. The United States held firmly to the maintenance of its rights up to the actual exchange of ratifications. In December, 1925, the ratifications were exchanged and the Convention went into effect.

The Convention dealing with the mandate for Iraq was the last to be negotiated. The final form of the mandate was not determined until some time after the other " A " mandates had been settled, due to the particular circumstances obtaining in Iraq, where Faisal had been installed as King with an administration considerably more independent than those set up in Syria and Palestine. Faisal had objected to Britain's obligations as mandatory being established by the fiat, as it were, of the League, as in Syria and Palestine. Instead a treaty between Iraq and Britain was signed which provided for the exercise of certain rights by Britain in the execution of the requirements of Article Twenty-two of the Covenant; this treaty was approved by a resolution of the League Council in September, 1924.

When news of the League action reached Washington, the Embassy at London was instructed on October 21, 1924, to ask the Foreign Office for information on the arrangements for Iraq

[58] *Ibid.*, 1924, I, 741–46. Ratified by the United States, June 5, 1924; by France, July 13, 1924; proclaimed by the President, August 13, 1924.
[59] *Ibid.*, II, 203–7.
[60] *Ibid.*, pp. 207–9.
[61] *Ibid.*, pp. 211–22.

and to bring to the attention of the British government the fact that the United States had been neither consulted on nor informed of the action.[62] The Embassy cabled on November 3 that the Foreign Office had said that the League resolution and the Anglo-Iraqi treaty constituted the mandate for Iraq; the form of mandate used in Syria and Palestine had been dropped because of Iraqi objections.[63] The Department did not take further action until the following April when an instruction was sent to London giving a résumé of the American position on mandates and the text of a note to be handed to the Foreign Office. The note referred to the previous correspondence on the mandates and the position of the United States as developed therein. " [The United States government] is firmly of the opinion that no arrangements to which it is not a party could modify the rights to which it is entitled in Iraq by virtue of the Capitulations of the Ottoman Empire. . . ." The United States did not ask for the abrogation of the present arrangements, the note stated, but wished to know whether Britain was prepared to negotiate a convention similar to that recently concluded with respect to the Palestine mandate.[64]

The British government indicated that it was willing to proceed with negotiations, and in July, 1926, a draft convention was submitted by the United States following closely the Palestine Convention.[65] British counterproposals based on the American draft were sent to Washington in January, 1927,[66] and these were accepted by the United States.[67] After further correspondence dealing with certain minor changes, and a delay caused by the demand of Iraq that it be a party to the convention (which was agreed to by the United States), the final instrument was signed by the three states in January, 1930.[68] It was ratified by the United States in April and ratifications were exchanged in February, 1931.

[62] *Ibid.*, 1925, II, 230–31.
[63] *Ibid.*, p. 231.
[64] *Ibid.*, pp. 231–38.
[65] *Ibid.*, 1927, II, 781–87.
[66] *Ibid.*, pp. 799–802.
[67] *Ibid.*, pp. 802–4.
[68] *Ibid.*, 1930, III, 291–308.

Chapter XII

AMERICAN RELATIONS WITH TURKEY

1.

So far, American Middle East policy in the postwar period has been described in terms of American relations with the Allies as the conquerors of the Ottoman Empire. These relations were undoubtedly the most significant in the formation and evolution of American policy, particularly toward the former Ottoman territories that came under direct European control but also toward the Turkish state itself. Initially, American relations with Turkey, or rather, so much of Turkey as was left to the Turks by the Allies, were conducted through the Allied high commissioners at Constantinople in practice, though formal relations were carried on through the Swedish Embassy which had charge of American interests while diplomatic relations were still broken. However, as the Turkish state under Mustafa Kemal began to regain its identity, after the establishment of the Angora government in 1920, and to act as an independent force in international affairs, so did American interests in Turkey require closer relations between the United States and the Nationalist regime.

The policy followed in Turkey was that followed in the mandated territories and outlined above—the establishment of the Open Door and the protection of existing private and public rights—together with an interest in the Christian populations of Asia Minor strong enough to call forth diplomatic action, but nothing further, by the Department of State, and a continuing concern for American missionary and educational activity in Turkey. During the period between the final abandonment of the Treaty of Sèvres and the negotiation of the definitive settlement at Lausanne, the United States was concerned to maintain its position against the encroachments of the Allies and, at the same time, as the prospects of the Nationalist government grew brighter, to begin to prepare the way for the day when the relations between the United States and the new Turkey would be regularized.

2.

From the beginning of his installation as American High Commissioner in Turkey, Admiral Bristol had carried on a running fight with the Allied high commissioners and the Sultan's government to maintain American rights, under the Capitulations and under treaty, against constant attempts to ignore or override them. Under the prewar system, customs duties had been levied by the Turkish government on all imports at a rate of eleven per cent ad valorem, with all receipts over eight per cent set aside to service the Ottoman debt. After the war the Allied high commissioners attempted to increase the revenue of Turkey by imposing a consumption tax over and above the eleven per cent duty; their reason for doing this was that, since under the law all import taxes over eight per cent went to the debt service and since more money was needed for the expenses of the government, the only way this additional revenue could be raised was by imposing taxes other than import duties. Bristol's response was to point out, first, that if the Allies could do one illegal thing—impose consumption taxes on imports—they could do another, and increase the ad valorem duties without assigning the excess to the debt service. Second, since the United States was the principal exporter of foodstuffs to Turkey, consumption taxes would fall most heavily on American trade, whereas an increase in customs duties would fall on all alike.[1] In his despatch of May 18, 1921, reporting these developments, Bristol commented: " The whole history of my negotiations with the Allied Representatives on the subject of the tariff indicates a desire on the part of the Allies to keep me completely in the dark, and to foster the trade of their nationals at any cost. . . ."[2]

In June of the same year the Allied high commissioners in-

[1] *Foreign Relations*, 1921, II, 890–92; the whole correspondence is in *ibid.*, pp. 890–916.
[2] *Ibid.*, pp. 893–95.

formed Allied nationals trading into Turkey that they could ignore any taxes imposed on imports by the Turkish government which increased the aggregate import tax to an amount greater than eleven per cent ad valorem. This, said Bristol in his cable of June 7 informing the Department of the Allied action,

exposes the hypocrisy of the Allies in urging the United States Government to tolerate the consumption taxes for the purpose " of increasing the receipts [of] the Turkish Government." . . . I have become convinced that Allied representatives work on the principle of what is best for their interests commercially without regard to legality or justice. This seems to be the principle that actuates the Allies in the whole procedure in . . . the obtaining of peace in the Near East.

Bristol flatly refused to agree to any imposition of taxes not authorized by treaty.[3] The Allies then attempted to persuade the United States to accept the new tax regime by direct representations to the Department of State while maintaining pressure on Bristol at Constantinople.[4] These efforts were also unsuccessful. The Department instructed Bristol on September 14, 1921, to " insist on the integral application of the pre-war regime. . . ," [5] though in response to urgent requests from the Turkish government it agreed to permit the collection of certain municipal taxes, without prejudice to American rights.[6] Attempts were also made by the Greek authorities at Smyrna to collect port dues and other taxes from American traders, and these too were rejected by the United States.

The stubborn attitude of Bristol infuriated the Allied high commissioners, particularly the British, who sent back to his home government numerous complaints of his American colleague's unco-operative attitude. The situation came to a head in April, 1922. On the twenty-eighth of that month the First Secretary of the British Embassy, Craigie, called on Allen Dulles, Chief of the Near East Division of the Department, to discuss with him the differences between the American and British high commissioners at Constantinople, as reported by the British High Commissioner, Sir Horace Rumboldt. Rumboldt had complained to London several times, said Craigie, that though the Allied high commissioners had made several concessions to Bristol in an attempt to meet his

[3] *Ibid.*, pp. 895–97.
[4] *Ibid.*, pp. 906–7.
[5] *Ibid.*, p. 908.
[6] *Ibid.*, p. 916.

demands, nothing had so far improved relations; the British government was at a loss as to what it could do to improve the unfortunate situation, and Ambassador Geddes had suggested to Craigie that, as he had known Dulles from previous posts, he discuss the matter informally with him and get his views of it, in the hope that this might make matters clear that were not understood in London or Constantinople. Dulles told him that the crux of the affair was that while Bristol recognized that the Allied military occupation and the enforcement of the Armistice of 1918 gave the Allied high commissioners certain rights, which Bristol was the first to respect, he did not admit that this gave the Allied civil and military authorities any right to modify the Capitulations or to institute general trade regulations without the approval of the United States, nor did it give the Allied political representatives a position of superiority over the political representatives of the United States.[7]

Dulles drew up a memorandum of the conversation for the Secretary, and told him that unless there were objections he planned to discuss the matter further with Craigie. The Secretary approved [8] and on May 2 Craigie again came to the Department. He brought with him a report from Rumboldt to Curzon which had been sent to the Embassy, and read it to Dulles. Rumboldt stated that while the Allies had actual responsibility for the safety of Constantinople, and the Allied forces of occupation there, through which responsibility a large share of the burden of civil administration devolved on the Allies, Admiral Bristol, who was unable to share this responsibility, had been inclined to block Allied measures, especially taxes necessary to provide the funds for the functioning of the government. Rumboldt said further that Bristol seemed to have the opinion that the Allies were using their position to promote their own commercial interests to the detriment of the United States, and the Admiral had not been at any pains to conceal this opinion from prominent Americans visiting Constantinople. The report indicated that Bristol apparently did not appreciate the difficulties of the Allied position or that American trade benefited by the fact that the United States was not at war with Turkey and could thus trade throughout Anatolia

---

[7] Memorandum of conversation, April 28, 1922; 867.01/138.
[8] *Ibid.*

while the Allies were prohibited from so doing. (No mention was made by Rumboldt or by Craigie of the agreements made by two of the Allies with the Nationalists in 1921, both of which contained provisions for trade in Anatolia.)

Dulles told Craigie it was his opinion that the difficulties between Bristol and the Allied authorities were due to the fact that the Allied representatives had not consulted Bristol on the measures proposed; he cited cases where, while there was no actual discrimination, American interests had been hard hit—in none of these had Bristol been informed of the action taken nor his opinion asked for. When the Allied high commissioners met to decide on policy, they met secretly and Bristol never knew what went on at these meetings. The Allied high commissioners also claimed precedence over Bristol though he had held office at Constantinople longer by two years than any Allied High Commissioner. Keeping Bristol in the dark about Allied decisions accentuated the problems that existed, for Bristol was forced to send a succession of protests, inquiries, and notes, none of which would be necessary if personal contact were maintained. If Bristol were invited to attend the high commissioners' meetings many difficulties would disappear. Dulles mentioned, as an example of the problems created by the secrecy in which decisions were made, the " unfortunate incident " when the Allied high commissioners had protested to the Turkish government the erection of Standard Oil Company oil tanks without even informing Bristol. Craigie said he would report their conversation to the Ambassador, who would probably call on the Secretary shortly to see what could be done about the situation.[9]

Ambassador Geddes called on the Secretary on May 4. Dulles was present at the interview and, at the Secretary's request, gave a summary of the problem and a brief statement of the American position similar to the one he had given to Craigie two days before. Geddes referred to the Rumboldt report to Curzon containing the British case against Bristol, and asked if there was any basis for the charge of discrimination against American trade. Dulles replied that in certain cases there was good cause for complaint, for example, the retention of consumption taxes at the insistence of the Allied high commissioners, over Bristol's

[9] Memorandum of conversation, May 2, 1922; 867.01/139.

complaints, was especially hard on American goods; the illegal granting of permission for Allied companies to build storage tanks on the Bosporus while refusing permission to American interests; and the imposition of the Miri tax on American schools. At Geddes' request he gave details of these. Geddes then recited some specific complaints made by Rumboldt and referred to the tax on alcohol, which had been imposed to reduce consumption; Bristol had made this very difficult to impose. Bristol had also demanded precedence over the other Allied high commissioners. The Secretary pointed out that Bristol had seniority of tenure in Constantinople, and it was not clear on what ground precedence over him was claimed by the Allied high commissioners. Geddes did not reply to this. Dulles informed the Ambassador that the main source of trouble was the fact that Bristol was not adequately informed of the actions of the other high commissioners, and repeated the substance of what he had told Craigie on this point. Geddes then turned to Bristol's alleged anti-British feeling. He said that after Mr. Ochs, the publisher of the *New York Times*, had visited Bristol at Constantinople, his paper had printed several stories about British trade discrimination against the United States, the source of which was apparently the Admiral. He also referred, "in strictest confidence," to reports by Rumboldt's predecessor, Admiral Roebeck, that Bristol was anti-British and unnecessarily and deliberately blocked measures proposed by the British High Commissioner. Dulles replied that Bristol was not at all anti-British, and in fact some of his best friends at Constantinople were British and he was on particularly good terms with the British Commander-in-Chief, General Harrington. The Secretary summed up by referring to Bristol's difficulties in protecting American interests when he was not fully informed by the other high commissioners and was often placed in a position where all he could do was to send letters of protest. After the conclusion of the formal interview, Geddes told Secretary Hughes he was going to write to Curzon saying that Bristol and Rumboldt ought to come together and settle their differences between themselves. The Secretary told Dulles to draft a cable to Bristol on the same lines.[10] The problem was ultimately settled by the Nationalists, as were many other problems of the occupation

[10] Memorandum of conversation, May 4, 1922; 867.01/140.

period in Turkey, when they ended the regime of the high commissioners by their victory in Anatolia.

3.

Except for the cities of Smyrna and Constantinople with their hinterlands (including Thrace) and the fringes of Turkish territory held by the French and Italians, the character of the rule of Turkey exercised by the high commissioners grew more and more an academic question. The greater part of Turkey was under the control of the Nationalist government at Angora, and with the failure, in the summer of 1921, of the Greek drive to unseat the Nationalists this control would probably continue to be exercised by them. The United States made no effort to establish relations with Angora until the fall of 1921, however, and even then was content to have these relations conducted in an entirely informal and unofficial manner. It was the Angora government that made the first move, apparently as part of its policy of dividing the Allies by coming to terms with each Power individually; in the spring of 1921 it negotiated agreements with France and Italy, as well as with the Bolsheviks and Afghanistan.

At the beginning of January, 1921, a representative of the Angora government secretly approached the commander of one of the American destroyers stationed temporarily at Samsun and suggested that American and Turkish representatives meet at Adalia to discuss relations between the two countries.[11] A month later more serious efforts were made to establish contact with the American government. A local official at Samsun again approached the destroyer commander, stating he had " very secret instructions " from the Foreign Minister at Angora to convey to the American High Commissioner his government's wish to resume " the friendly political and economic relations with the United States which existed before the severance of relations. . . ." The naval officer stated that he could do nothing officially but agreed to forward the Foreign Minister's message unofficially to Constantinople. The Foreign Minister then sent to Admiral Bristol, through this channel, a four-point proposal for the consideration of the United States: (1) The chief aim of the Grand

[11] Despatch 17 from Constantinople, January 18, 1921; 711.67/11.

National Assembly was to secure the political and economic independence of the people of Anatolia. (2) The Turkish people had no enemies within or without Turkey except those who would obstruct this aim. (3) The Angora government wished to resume friendly relations with the United States, the basic condition being the abolition of the Capitulations. Once this was done, other problems, such as those concerning the status and welfare of schools and orphanages, would easily and automatically be solved, and with both countries working together the greatest economic benefits to both countries would be assured. (4) If, therefore, the United States recognized the political and economic independence of Turkey within the boundaries laid down before the Armistice of Mudros by the Ottoman Parliament, there would remain no obstacle to the resumption of prewar relations.

Bristol noted in his despatch of February 9, enclosing this proposal, that there were many evidences of the Turks' desire for American good will. American newspaper reporters had been welcomed, schools had been assisted, and in an interview with the United Telegraph Agency, Mustafa Kemal had said that Turkey recognized the United States as the protectress of the rights of liberty. All this should not be taken entirely at its face value, Bristol said. Certainly the demands of the Turks presented to the United States were not the final Turkish terms but a bargaining position. He suggested that no action be taken for the time being, but if the existing situation in Turkey continued after the forthcoming London Conference, with two Turkish governments claiming to represent the country, then a delegate of the High Commission should be sent to Angora to follow the activities of the government there.[12]

Bristol's advice was followed and for the present no action was taken to establish relations. In June, R. McDowell, an official of the Near East Relief Organization, visited Angora and he was asked to tell the High Commissioner of the desire of the Angora government for a response by the United States to the previous request for recognition. On his return to his station at Samsun, McDowell sent a memorandum to Bristol informing him of the action of the Angora government. He said the Acting Foreign Minister, with whom he had spoken, laid great stress on the note

[12] Despatch 45 from Constantinople, February 9, 1921; 711.67/15.

sent to Bristol in February and on his government's desire to know the response of the United States. McDowell also said that Angora was very anxious to interest American capital in the development of Anatolia, and he had been told so by many government officials. This memorandum was sent to the Department by Bristol on June 20,[13] and on the same day he also cabled that there was no immediate prospect of reconciliation between Angora and Constantinople, and the protection of American commercial and philanthropic interests throughout Turkey required the assignment of a delegate of the High Commission to Angora. He would have the same status as the delegates at Beirut, Aleppo, etc., and would be sent without any implication of the recognition of the regime. Both the British and French had recently sent informal missions to Angora, and the Italians had maintained close relations with the Nationalists through Adalia, said Bristol, and unless the United States wanted to be excluded from Anatolia action should be taken at once.[14] The Department replied two days later that the usefulness of a delegate at Angora was thoroughly appreciated, but his position would be very different from those at Aleppo and Beirut, where they could have official dealings with the authorities, whereas this would not be possible at Angora. Could the High Commission therefore suggest someone who could go in an unofficial capacity? [15]

The question of sending a delegate was postponed during the unsettled period of the Greek offensive in the summer of 1921 when the existence of the Angora government was in the balance. In the meantime, the Nationalists, not having been successful in their attempts to establish contact through Bristol, made approaches through an American Embassy in Europe. It was intimated to them that the re-establishment of relations between Turkey and the United States was in the hands of the Turks since they had severed relations with the United States, not vice versa. On October 28 Bristol cabled that France had just concluded a treaty with Angora, and the Italians and British were reported to be sending missions to the Nationalists. The United States could not keep open the door of economic opportunity, he said, by maintaining an attitude of aloofness based on the fear of con-

---

[13] Despatch 311 from Constantinople, June 20, 1921; 711.67/18.
[14] Telegram 201 from Constantinople, June 20, 1921; 711.67/17.
[15] Telegram 54 to Constantinople, June 22, 1921; 711.67/17.

structively recognizing the Nationalist government, which was after all in real control of the country, had the support of the majority of the people, and was, in effect, recognized by all the Allied Powers. Nor could the United States attempt to protect its interests by protesting the grant of economic privileges to other powers since the Turks badly needed economic assistance. He suggested that Julian Gillespie, the Assistant Trade Commissioner at Constantinople, be sent to Angora as his delegate. He was an official of the Department of Commerce, and his assignment would be less formal and official than if a State Department representative were sent. Unless he received instructions to the contrary he planned to send Gillespie to the Nationalist capital.[16] The Department replied that it had no objection to Gillespie's going to Angora and understood that the Department of Commerce approved also. It must be understood, Bristol was informed, that Gillespie's position would be purely personal and unofficial. (The telegram as drafted in the Near East Division ended with the words, ". . . and that he shall have no dealings with the Government of Angora." These were deleted on the official telegram form by the Assistant Secretary approving the instruction.)[17]

Bristol made discreet inquiries of the Nationalist representative in Constantinople if an American delegate would still be welcomed in Angora and was informed he would indeed be most welcome. The Nationalists read more into the American approach than was justified. They immediately began to make plans to send a mission to the United States and to establish official, but informal, representation in Washington as they had in the European capitals. This was the last thing the Department wanted. Questions of diplomacy aside, it would have called down on the Administration's head the wrath of the people and Congress, who had been roused to a fever of anti-Turk feeling by the reports of mistreatment, and worse, of Christians by the Nationalists. Bristol was urgently instructed to discourage any idea of a Nationalist mission.[18] He replied in a lengthy despatch sent a month later on December 17. He said that as Gillespie was

[16] Telegram 259, from Constantinople, October 28, 1921; 711.67/20. See also despatch 491, October 10; 711.67/21.
[17] Telegram 88 to Constantinople, November 3, 1921; 711.67/20.
[18] Telegram 96 to Constantinople, November 15, 1921; 711.67/24.

leaving for Angora in the near future, he would instruct him to "intimate discreetly" to the authorities the position of the American government if the matter were brought up. It would be a great help, said Bristol, if the Department could inform him of the reasons for its decision, as he believed the question of receiving a Nationalist delegation in the United States merited very careful consideration. There was no reason to fear that it would involve recognition of the Angora government; Britain, France and Italy had received delegations and none of them had officially recognized the regime. The Nationalist government had maintained itself for two years and controlled most of Turkey; the Constantinople government was a mere shadow, and the shadow of the Angora government at that. The Nationalist movement must be taken seriously and be allowed to present its case to the world. It had been given the opportunity to do so in most of the capitals of Europe, and only the United States was closed to it. Politically, the American position could be maintained through the contacts of the High Commission in Constantinople, through the consulates at Beirut, Aleppo and elsewhere, and through relief activities. But American commercial interests were another matter, for here the United States had no contacts at all, Bristol warned. The Nationalists believed that the United States was not interested in trade and commerce in Turkey and therefore disregarded the United States in determining their economic policy.

The despatch then went into a detailed critique of American Middle East policy. The United States was too rigid and unimaginative in its handling of Middle Eastern questions, said Bristol, and too legalistic. Since 1919 there had in fact been no American policy, with two exceptions, both unfortunate—the participation in the Smyrna landings and the delimitation of the boundaries of Armenia, through both of which the United States had a share in the present situation in the Middle East. But leaving the past aside, Bristol continued, the final settlement of Middle Eastern questions was of the greatest importance to the United States as well as the Middle East, and active American participation in that settlement was essential if it was to be based on justice, fair play, and the Open Door.[19]

[19] Despatch 606 from Constantinople, December 17, 1921; 711.67/24.

Looked at strictly from the point of view of Constantinople, there was a good deal to be said for Bristol's attitude. But the Department had also to look at the problem from the point of view of Washington, of the people of the United States and their elected representatives, and of the other states concerned with Middle East affairs. Bristol's suggestions, advice, and pleas for a more active American policy, while they were not ignored in the Department and were in fact of great value as a source of information on Turkey, could not be followed as a guide to American policy without dilution and without considerable caution, and then only as one factor among the many that went into the making of American policy.

Gillespie set out for Angora at the end of December, 1921. He went by American destroyer to Ineboli and then overland by carriage to Angora, a journey of eleven days. He met all the leaders of the government, including Mustafa Kemal, Adnan bey, Yussuf Kemal bey, the leader of the pro-American group in Angora, and Raouf bey, making a point of explaining he had no connection with the Department of State but was a representative of the Department of Commerce. He was given a very friendly reception. After a series of interviews, Gillespie decided to deal as much as possible with Raouf bey as he spoke excellent English and struck Gillespie as an honest and sincere man. Raouf told him that his government wanted two things, to finish the war successfully and to be able to say to the European powers at the Peace Conference that all concessions in Turkey had been already allotted to others, for example, to Americans. He was also told that Turkey would maintain its claim to Mosul. The oil in that region and around Lake Van was very important, said Raouf, and proposals from any American oil group would receive preferential treatment. Gillespie was quite impressed by Mustafa Kemal, who received him very courteously and seemed to want to intimate that the American visitor was most welcome in Angora. In order to save time and an interminable round of the several ministries, with their numerous officials, and also to get specific answers in writing, Gillespie drew up a list of forty questions relating to general economic prospects in Turkey and to particular conditions that might affect American trade and business. This list was submitted to the government departments concerned and written answers obtained. While the list is too detailed and circumstantial to reproduce here, three of the questions may be cited as of immediate interest. The first asked for a clarification of the attitude of the Turkish government toward United States business. The answer was that the National government was very favorable to its participation in the economy of Turkey, not only in trade but also in the development of the country, and sincerely wished to see American capital in Turkey. The second question referred to the Chester concession (see below) and the attitude of the government toward it. The Turkish reply stated that the government was ready to study any proposals for a concession which did not impinge on Turkish sovereignty, but it could not comment on a specific undertaking until concrete proposals were submitted. The third question was a request for the Turkish policy on monopolies. The answer was that the Government was prepared to approve monopolies, but only with the participation of Turkish capital and under Turkish control.

Gillespie returned to Constantinople in the middle of February and drew up a report on his findings for Bristol, as much political as economic. He also sent a report to the Department of Commerce on the purely commercial aspects of his visit to the Nationalist capital. (He had managed to send a brief report to Bristol at the end of January by way of an American newsman who was in Angora at the time and about to return to Constantinople.) [20] He said that the Turks sincerely desired closer economic and commercial relations with the United States, for three reasons. First, Turkey needed financial assistance and hoped to get loans from American financial interests in connection with the granting of concessions. Second, these American financial interests, unlike their European counterparts, were commercial not political institutions, and the American government would not intervene on their behalf in the internal affairs of Turkey. Third, the Turks believed that American firms would be protected from foreign pressure by the American government. Moreover, these American interests would not be amenable to foreign pressure to relinquish concessions because their government was in a position to protect them from any foreign power.

The immediate prospects for American trade, said Gillespie, were not good due to the war, but when the situation was more

[20] Despatch 66 from Constantinople, February 7, 1922; 867.00/1488.

settled they could very well be promising. Thus in Cilicia there would be many opportunities in such fields as irrigation works, where the Turks were very anxious to get American experts and equipment. Agricultural machinery was another field which would be open to American exporters in the future.[21] In the report to the Department of Commerce Gillespie said the Turks were particularly anxious to give American firms options on certain construction works and on the development of natural resources in order to prevent monopolization by the European powers through the treaty of peace. There was also a disposition to revive the Chester project and a definite willingness to discuss American participation in the exploitation of the oil deposits of "Kurdistan" (i. e., of the Mosul region), claimed by Britain on behalf of the new state of Iraq. The Department's attitude on Turkish offers to American companies of concessions in this disputed area is given below in the account of the Chester concession.[22]

Shortly after Gillespie's visit to Angora, Yussef Kemal bey, the leader of the pro-American group in Angora and now Mustafa Kemal's Foreign Minister, passed through Constantinople on his way to the London Conference of March, 1922. While in the city he called on the Allied high commissioners and on Admiral Bristol. (Bristol remarked incidentally, in his despatch reporting Yussef Kemal's visit to the American High Commission, that he was given a warm reception by the French High Commissioner, "marked coolness" from the British High Commission, and a reception that was neither warm nor cold from the Italians.) In his conversation with Bristol, Yussef referred to Turkey's need for American assistance and said that the United States, of all countries, should appreciate Turkey's struggle for freedom. Bristol replied that if Turkey wanted help it should first help itself, and start by restoring order and preventing massacres such as the one at Marsovan. Yussef returned that the Greeks were responsible for all the present disorders in Turkey and the best way to stop them was to get the Greeks out of the country; only those Greeks helping the Greek Army were being forcibly deported. Bristol suggested that the proper way to handle the situation was to do as the Turks were already doing in Cilicia; moreover, such actions made an excellent impression abroad. Yussef said that

[21] Despatch 120 from Constantinople, March 6, 1922; 867.01/103.
[22] Telegram 20 from Constantinople, February 23, 1922; 867.01/81.

the Nationalist government was doing all it could to establish an adequate administration in the country and would in time succeed when conditions were more settled.

Some days later Yussef's call was returned, not by Admiral Bristol, by design, but by the Assistant to the High Commissioner Allen Dulles. At this meeting the conversation turned to specifics. Yussef said that Turkey must be freed from the burden of the Capitulations and Turkey on its part would establish a modern system of laws. This would make for better relations between Turkey and the other powers and would remove a constant source of irritation to the Turkish people. Dulles asked whether American businessmen would actually be able to rely on the Turkish courts if they engaged in commercial or other activities in Turkey, as it was understood was the wish of the Angora government. Yussef assured him that, under the system to be established, foreigners would be on exactly the same basis as natives in the courts, just as they would be in any European country. He then raised the question of the restoration of diplomatic relations, and asked whether it would be accomplished by the United States joining in a general treaty or whether a separate treaty would be signed between the United States and Turkey. Dulles answered that it was most unlikely the United States would participate in a general treaty, and Yussef rejoined that in that case he hoped the two countries would negotiate their own treaty before a general treaty of peace was taken up. Dulles told him that the initiative lay with Turkey since it was Turkey that broke relations with the United States. Yussef said the Grand National Assembly was ready at any time to pass a law annulling " with emphasis " the decree of 1917 severing relations, and this would be done whenever the United States informally indicated such an action would be acceptable.[23] (When the despatch reporting these interviews reached the Department, the Near East Division noted on the margin: " This was suggested to them last summer.")

The progress of American relations with the Nationalist regime was again interrupted by events of more immediate importance to Turkey—the London Conference, negotiations with the Allied Powers, and the renewal of the war with the Greeks and the final victory of the Nationalists in September, 1922. After Gillespie's

[23] Despatch 93 from Constantinople, February 22, 1922; 867.00/1497.

return from Angora it was decided to send a delegate there on a more or less permanent basis and in June, 1922, Robert W. Imbrie, a Foreign Service Officer of the Department of State was appointed to the post. His relations with the authorities were cordial, but little of significance developed in Angora in the first four months of his tour. In October he returned to Constantinople briefly. Shortly after his arrival there he was instructed by the Department to return at once to Angora in view of the seriousness of the situation, but before he left he sent a despatch to the Department describing briefly his impressions of the interior and his opinions on trade possibilities. This was his first report, communications between Angora and Constantinople being so bad and the chances of his mail being tampered with so great that it was not considered worthwhile to send routine reports.

During his four months in Anatolia, he said, he had traveled through seven vilayets seeing a great deal of the country under Nationalist control. He had had no official escort and so there was no chance of the Turks prearranging what he saw of conditions there. Most of Anatolia was quiet, except for the Kurds and some bandits, but he had never been molested. There seemed to be no lack of food. He had seen no cases of oppression of the Christians; this was not to say there had not been any, but on the other hand Turkish oppression of the Christians could be matched by Christian oppression of Turks. The Christians in areas controlled by the Turks were quite as bad as the Turks in their religious prejudice, Imbrie said, and did not co-operate with the government nor make any attempt to contribute to the general welfare; thus they did not receive all they might from the government. American commercial interests, except for tobacco, were negligible, though a representative of the Chester interests was in Angora and there seemed to be good prospects that a concession would be negotiated. He emphasized that the Capitulations were absolutely necessary to American commercial enterprises in Turkey. The courts were venal, bribes were essential, and interference by minor officials looking for bribes was endemic. The government was trying to remedy this situation but at present he did not see that the Department could recommend American companies to invest in Turkey except under very strict conditions.[24]

[24] Personal despatch from Imbrie, October 14, 1922; 867.00/1560.

4.

One of the principal concerns of the United States in Turkey during this period was the condition of the Christian people still under Turkish rule. On one occasion the High Commission made direct but informal representations to the Angora government on behalf of Greeks of Samsun. Bristol cabled on July 18, 1921, at the height of the Greek offensive, that the Nationalist government had ordered the deportation of all Greeks from Samsun following reports that the Greek government was about to land troops and occupy the region. There were about 15,000 Greek women, children, and old men left in the city, all the young men of military age having already been deported to the interior— large numbers of them had been killed on the journey.[25] He had sent a " vigorous " protest to Angora, said Bristol, asking Mustafa Kemal in the name of humanity to stop the deportations, ending his telegram with the words, " I would be pleased to receive from you an early and favorable answer which I would convey to my Government." He recommended that the Department bring pressure on the Allies, Greece, and the Nationalists to end the frightful slaughter of civilians. The general situation of the Nationalists was critical he said, driving them to acts of barbarism, and the safety of Americans in the interior might be in jeopardy.[26]

This cable was sent to the Secretary of State by the Near East Division when it reached the Department the next day, with a note attached stating that conditions in Samsun and generally in Anatolia were terrible, but the Division was not at all sure that Bristol's action in protesting directly to Mustafa Kemal was correct. The United States had never admitted his existence officially, and he might think the protest came from the State Department and even construe this as a form of recognition. However, under the circumstances, the Division was not either approving or disapproving Bristol's action; the chance of saving 10,000 or 15,000 lives would seem to be worth taking. The writer of the note added, " I have considered all along that Bristol was mildly under the influence of the Turks and was pro-Turk and anti-Greek. This statement of his makes me believe therefore that

[25] On the deportations, see telegram 181 from Constantinople, June 2, 1921; 767.68/98; also despatch 366, July 25; 767.68/138.
[26] Telegram 220 from Constantinople, July 18, 1922; 767.68/123.

the situation is as bad as possible." [27] Yussef Kemal, the Angora
Foreign Minister, replied to Bristol some days later saying that
no orders for the deportation of women and children had been
given, and went on to protest Greek atrocities against Muslims
and asked that effective steps be taken to end them. Bristol reported on August 2 the results of his protest. He said the denial
of the deportations meant that his telegram had had effect, and
he had reports from Samsun that this was in fact true, and the
deportations stopped. No comment was sent from the Department on Bristol's action in communicating directly with Mustafa
Kemal.[28]

Samsun was, a year later, again the scene of events which called
forth a second protest to the Angora government, but this time
the protest came from the Department. On June 7, 1922, Greek
warships bombarded Samsun. There was a great deal of damage
and some deaths, but there were no American casualties. A building belonging to an American company was hit twice, but otherwise American interests were not affected. However, during the
bombardment American residents were not allowed to leave the
city, even at the request of the commander of the American
destroyer stationed there. On receiving Bristol's report of this
incident,[29] the Department cabled at once instructing him to state
orally to the Nationalist representative at Constantinople that
the action of his government in refusing to permit American citizens to leave Samsun had created a " most unfortunate impression " at Washington, that the Department of State trusted such
an action would not be repeated, and that the Angora authorities
would be held responsible for any injuries suffered thereby by
American citizens. The cable added a confidential comment for
Bristol, that the Department felt the bombardment of Samsun
by the Greeks at the present time, when an investigation of the
condition of Christians in Turkey was contemplated, was most
unfortunate in that it might tend to aggravate the situation in
Anatolia.[30]

Bristol communicated this to the Angora representative, Hamid

[27] Memorandum, July 19, 1921; 767.68/129.
[28] Despatch 385 from Constantinople, August 2, 1921; 767.68/138.
[29] Telegram 90 from Constantinople, June 9, 1922; 767.68/208.
[30] Telegram 69 to Constantinople, June 10, 1922; 767.68/208. On the Allied
investigation, see below.

bey, and was told that the reason for the order was that the local authorities in Samsun feared serious disturbances would break out if one group was allowed to leave the city. Shortly after this interview, the destroyer commander returned from Samsun to Constantinople, bringing with him a written statement by the Turkish authorities in the city that as soon as enemy forces appeared, martial law would be proclaimed and no one allowed to leave, but foreigners would be allowed to take refuge in the district hospital under the Red Crescent flag. The commander considered this to be unsafe as the hospital was close to a munitions dump. In view of this development Bristol decided to have a further discussion with Hamid bey, and repeated to him with emphasis the American position, stressing the extremely bad impression the Nationalists' action was making in Washington.[31] Meanwhile, the Department had been studying the legal aspects of the bombardment, and the Solicitor determined that there was no principle of international law under which the United States could insist that its nationals be permitted to leave the city.[32] An officer of the Near East Division commented, " In my opinion the Turks are getting much too uppish in their treatment of Americans, in expelling them from the country, restricting their movements very closely and now forcing them to remain in towns that are being bombarded. If we let this sort of thing go on, our prestige in Turkey will be seriously affected." [33] However, the Nationalists backed down. On August 24 Bristol cabled that Hamid bey had told him that in case of future bombardments of Samsun Americans would be evacuated.[34]

The affair that touched American policy most deeply was that of the commission of inquiry proposed by the British in the spring of 1922. The commission was not important in itself; it never actually conducted an inquiry and by the time it had been organized Anatolia was in the process of being reconquered by the Nationalists, from whom it would be necessary to request permission to conduct a field survey—an unlikely occurrence under the circumstances. On May 15, 1922, British Ambassador Geddes wrote to Secretary Hughes, referring to the reported massacres and deporta-

[31] Telegram 108 from Constantinople, June 22, 1922; 767.68/215.

[32] Memorandum, June 27, 1922; 767.68/215.

[33] Memorandum, June 30, 1922; 767.68/215.

[34] Telegram 159 from Constantinople, August 24, 1922; 767.68/259.

tions of Christians by the Angora authorities in Anatolia. The British government had assumed a "serious responsibility" toward the Christians of Turkey by its proposals regarding them in the terms of a peace treaty with Turkey put forward in March, said Geddes, and the British government therefore proposed that Britain, France, Italy, and the United States each appoint an officer to a commission which would investigate the reports of massacres and other atrocities.[35] On the heels of this note came a cable from Bristol, who had been informed by his British colleague of the approach to the United States, recommending that the United States decline to participate in the inquiry and giving six reasons for his opinion. They were: first, that the events which prompted the inquiry had taken place a year before and were the result of French actions in Cilicia; second, the behavior of the Greek Army at the time of the occupation of Smyrna in 1919, and the Greek atrocities in the summer campaign of 1921; third, there were many indications that the British were using the recently published report on these events—which was the immediate occasion of the inquiry proposal—as anti-Turkish propaganda to strengthen their position in the Near East; fourth, the plight of the minorities had been well known for a long time, and it was significant that the present outcry coincided with British attempts to induce the French to take a strong line with the Nationalists; fifth, the publicity which the British were giving the inquiry proposals indicated that its purpose was political propaganda; and sixth, within the last few days reports had been received at the High Commission that at Harput at least, where massacres were purported to have taken place, all was quiet.[36]

Secretary Hughes put the question to President Harding[37] and on May 20 Harding replied:

. . . Frankly, I very much hesitate to hold aloof from a participation which makes such a strong appeal to a very large portion of our American citizenship. At the same time I cannot escape the feeling that we will be utterly helpless to do anything effective in case an investigation proves the statements concerning atrocities are substantiated. I am very sure that there will be no American support for a proposal to send an armed force there to correct any abuses which are proven.[38]

---

[35] *Foreign Relations*, 1922, II, 919–20.
[36] *Ibid.*, pp. 920–21.
[37] *Ibid.*, pp. 921–22.
[38] *Ibid.*, p. 922.

The President had not answered Hughes's request for a decision, and Hughes would not take the responsibility at this time for what would be a radical departure from American policy as it had developed since the withdrawal from Versailles. The President's letter had put the difficulty very well, but had not resolved it. The Secretary therefore wrote again, presenting both sides of the question and outlining the probable consequences of each course open to the United States. If the United States declined to participate in the commission of inquiry, said Hughes, a large body of Americans would be offended, and the Turks might be encouraged to refuse permission for the commission to operate in areas controlled by them. The ability of the United States to protect its interests in the Middle East might be adversely affected, and it would be more difficult for the United States to exert a " helpful influence " in creating stability in the Middle East. On the other hand, if the United States consented to participate in the inquiry, it would be unlikely that the question of sending an armed force to Turkey would arise if the inquiry proved the charges against the Nationalists, since it was also unlikely that the British or the other Allies would be in a position to use force against them; there was a strong possibility that the mere fact of American participation would have a restraining influence and prevent future massacres, and might create a situation in which it would be easier to make peace. He concluded by stating that American participation would be helpful and a refusal " would entail a grave responsibility and expose us to severe criticism." [39]

The President decided to accept the British invitation and the British Embassy was so informed on June 3.[40] On July 19, however, the British Chargé informed the Secretary that, in deference to French opinion, it had been decided, in view of the fact that the Allies were still at war with Turkey, to place the inquiry in the hands of the International Red Cross.[41] Events in Anatolia caught up with this new proposal and the Red Cross did not carry out the investigation. During the Turkish advance to Smyrna, church groups in the United States advocated publicly the use of American armed force to end the reported massacres of Christians by the Turks. On one of these resolutions, passed by the General Conference of the Methodist Episcopal Church and sent to the

[39] *Ibid.*, pp. 922–26.   [40] *Ibid.*, pp. 927–28.   [41] *Ibid.*, pp. 929–30.

Secretary of State, Harding commented to the Secretary, " Frankly, it is difficult for me to be consistently patient with our good friends of the Church who are properly and earnestly zealous in promoting peace until it comes to making warfare on someone of a contending religion. . . ." [42] After the Smyrna disaster, the Episcopal Church sent to the President a resolution pledging support for any diplomatic, naval, or military effort the government might make " toward the establishment of justice, mercy and peace in the stricken lands of the Near East." [43] While the United States was not prepared to participate in joint action to protect Christians in Anatolia, it kept up a constant diplomatic pressure on Angora to follow a course of moderation in the treatment of minorities. The response of the United States to British requests for support of Allied action in the fall of 1922 will be taken up in the next chapter.

5.

A second illustration of American policy applied to a concrete situation is the Chester concession. In 1920 Rear Admiral Colby Chester called at the Department of State with the information that a group of which he was a member had acquired the interests of the Ottoman American Development Company which before the war had been negotiating for a concession in Turkey to build railroads and explore mineral resources. The disturbances in Turkey had prevented his company from pursuing its interest so far, he told Department officials, but it was intended to go ahead as soon as possible.[44] In February, 1921, he called again at the Department to get an opinion of the feasibility of proceeding, and was told that conditions there were not suitable and there was no possibility of the present Turkish government being in a position to take definite action.[45] Later in the year Chester called on the Secretary of State and requested the Department's support for his project. (He had earlier asked to be appointed Naval Attaché at Constantinople and had been refused.) He was told

[42] *Ibid.*, pp. 931–32.
[43] *Ibid.*, p. 938.
[44] *Ibid.*, 1921, II, 917–18. On the activities of the Chester group before the war see DeNovo, *American Interests*, chap. III, and in the postwar period, chap. VII.
[45] *Foreign Relations*, 1921, II, 918.

that the Department was deeply interested in the project. It appeared in this conversation for the first time that the Chester interests did not in fact hold a concession, the original application not having been approved by the Turkish Parliament. Chester asked for the support of the Secretary and the Department of State, and was told by the Secretary that he would give the matter further thought. The Near East Division commented on the interview that in view of the objections being made by the Department to British oil claims in Mesopotamia, it would be impractical for the Department to make a definite statement of support for Chester.[46] When Chester appeared again in May he was told that the United States was opposing the claims of the Turkish Petroleum Company because they were based on an unperfected concession, and, as Chester's claims were no more substantial, the Department could not contradict itself and support them.[47] In February, 1922, Chester wrote again asking for an interview with the Secretary but was informed that, as the Secretary had given his opinion at the interview of the previous May, there was no point in discussing it again.[48]

During 1922, after several reorganizations, the Ottoman American Development Corporation, the successor to the Ottoman American Development Company, sent a representative to Angora, and negotiations with the Nationalist government were begun. The High Commission was instructed by the Department to give the American company support, but not to take part in any negotiations nor to indicate either to the company or the Turkish authorities any preference for the Chester group over any other reputable American interest.[49] The negotiations of the Chester group with the Angora authorities were successful and in April, 1923, a concession was granted for the construction of railroads across Anatolia and for the exploitation of mineral resources along the right-of-way in lieu of a mileage guarantee. Before the concession was confirmed, General Goethals, who had acquired an interest in the Chester group, called at the Department and spoke with Allen Dulles, the Chief of the Near East Division; he said he expected the Department would give " vigorous support " to the concession and, referring particularly to

[46] *Ibid.*, pp. 920–21.
[47] *Ibid.*, pp. 921–22.
[48] *Ibid.*, 1922, II, 966–67.
[49] *Ibid.*, 1923, II, 1198–99.

Mosul, asked whether the Department would support his company's claims as defined in the draft concession against the British there. Dulles referred the General to the Department's previous position already communicated to the company, that the Department would not interfere in territorial settlements in the Near East. The dispute over rights in Mosul might depend on the settlement of the boundary between Turkey and Iraq, and this, according to the Lausanne negotiations then being resumed (see below), was to be settled by Turkey and Britain. Goethals mentioned that the French Ambassador had questioned him about the concesssion, whether it was a new grant or a confirmation of an old one. Goethals said he did not know, though he thought it was a confirmation, but, he told the Ambassador, he wanted to interest British and French capital in the project. He told Dulles that he wanted to make friends not enemies.[50]

The day after Goethals called at the Department, on April 13, 1923, the Department received a cable from Bristol reporting the French had lodged with the Turkish authorities a protest against the Chester concession as infringing on French rights acquired before the war.[51] An instruction was sent to Paris, London, and Rome (with information copies to Constantinople and Berne) informing the embassies of the French action and giving the Department's position on the French protest which was that the concession was a private affair in which the American government had taken no part; that the information available to the Department indicated that the concession was not monopolistic and the mineral rights granted in it followed the railroad, to which there was no objection per se; and that any dispute regarding the validity of claims should be settled by arbitration or a friendly understanding based on the relative merits of the claim involved.[52] On April 16, in the course of a conversation with the Secretary of State, the French Ambassador, Jusserand, went over the basis of the French protest. He did not want to make a formal protest, he said, but to draw the Department's attention to the French claims; he hoped that the two governments could work together in the matter. Hughes replied that the first thing to do was to get all the facts. He would like to know just what the French concession was and to what extent there was a conflict, then the two claims

[50] *Ibid.*, pp. 1200–1.   [51] *Ibid.*, p. 1201.   [52] *Ibid.*, pp. 1201–2.

could be considered. He did not have complete information on the Chester project and could not thus comment on it, but he assured the Ambassador that if the French supplied the Department with a statement of the French case, it would receive the most careful study. The Ambassador said he would like to be able to inform his government that the United States was disposed to co-operate in the matter. Hughes replied that private interests, not the United States, were the grantees of the concession. He did not know the attitude of these interests; he supposed it probable that they would be glad to have a basis for a friendly settlement, but he could not commit them beyond that point.[53]

The Department cabled Bristol on April 20 stating that the Department was " in entire accord " with his view that " the greatest reticence and circumspection " should be shown with respect to all matters connected with the Chester concession and no action should be taken until all the facts were known; the Department had followed this policy consistently. The cable then went on to say, " The granting of the Chester concession may be understood to mark the triumph in Turkey of the Open Door policy, as against such policies as inspired the tripartite agreement and the Bagdad railroad concession." [54]

The concession was actually ratified on April 29, 1923. In the following months, the Ottoman American Development Corporation tried to raise the capital to begin operations, but was unsuccessful. In the meantime, the French continued their representations to the United States on the matter during the negotiations at Lausanne. When the American delegation to the Conference requested instructions as to the position they should take, the Department repeated what it had already stated to be the American attitude in the conversation with Jusserand on April 16.[55] The British Ambassador, Geddes, addressed a note to Secretary Hughes on April 30 referring to the reported concession and suggesting that in order to avoid misunderstanding and ill-feeling which might " ruffle the surface of Anglo-American relations," the Department " convey to Admiral Chester and his associates an understanding of the elementary fact that the Turkish Government at Angora cannot grant rights in Mesopotamia which is not within its jurisdiction." Hughes replied that while a final text of the

[53] *Ibid.*, pp. 1204–5.   [54] *Ibid.*, pp. 1206–7.   [55] *Ibid.*, pp. 1212–14.

concession had not been received, " careful consideration will be given to the observations which you have presented when more definite information as to the exact nature of the grant is available." [56]

[56] *Ibid.*, pp. 1208–9.

CHAPTER XIII

THE RISE OF THE NEW TURKEY

1.

The increase in the political strength of Mustafa Kemal and the Nationalists—which resulted from the publication of the terms of the Treaty of Sèvres, the establishment of a working government at Angora, and the expansion of the area of Greek occupation, together with their slowly increasing military strength resulting from the flow of supplies from France and Italy and across the common frontier between Turkey and Bolshevik Russia—made the enforcement of the terms of the Treaty of Sèvres daily more difficult, if not improbable. The return of King Constantine to Athens made enforcement of the territorial terms of the Treaty less worthwhile to the Allies. The immediate result was the decision to make the treaty of peace more palatable to the Turks by such modification of the terms as could be made at Greek expense. In February and March, 1921, a conference called by Lloyd George and attended by representatives of Greece, the Constantinople and Angora governments, France, and Italy, proposed that the Smyrna zone remain under Turkish sovereignty with local autonomy under a Christian governor; Constantinople be evacuated under guarantees for the safety of the Christian populations of Turkey; Turkey be granted the permanent chairmanship of the Straits Commission; and the military terms of the treaty be altered in favor of Turkey. These proposals were rejected by both the Greeks and the Nationalists. The Greeks could not accept the return of Smyrna to the Turks, even under special conditions, and the Nationalists would accept neither the retention of Thrace by the Greeks, the independent state of Armenia, nor the financial and economic terms of Sèvres. Instead, the Greeks opened a new offensive in Asia Minor and the Nationalists signed a treaty with the Bolsheviks. At the same time both France and Italy opened talks with the National government, France looking to a settlement in Cilicia and Italy seeking commercial advantages in return for moral and material support.

The United States was concerned solely with the effect of the negotiations on American rights and did not enter into the Conference at all. The American position on the Turkish treaty had been put to the Allies a year before, and there was no reason to change it, but if the treaty were changed American rights might be affected and further representations to the Allies become necessary. The Department of State cabled London to send the results of the Conference to Washington immediately they were known,[1] and on March 19 the Embassy was instructed to state to the Foreign Office that the American government was following the progress of the Conference with great interest, as it might affect American rights and interests in the former Ottoman Empire; would the Foreign Office make confidentially available to the Department all information on changes in the Treaty of Sèvres agreed on by the Allies.[2] The Foreign Office told the Embassy that the press reports of the Conference were quite accurate and allowed the Embassy to see the official reports, which confirmed the British statement. The Embassy cabled this to the Department and also reported that no further action by the Conference was expected unless and until further developments warranted. The British had informed the Ambassador that the Smyrna clause was a big stumbling block to both Turks and Greeks, as was Armenia to the Angora Turks, who maintained that the Wilson boundary was not feasible. The British did not expect any immediate Turkish action but confessed that further armed conflict between the Turks and Greeks would clear the air.[3]

The Department had no intention of disclosing its hand until there was a reasonable assurance that the Conference would actually produce results; no action was taken in the meantime. A close watch was kept on developments in Turkey, therefore, to

[1] Telegram 152 to London, March 16, 1922; 763.72119/11045. For source material on the events in Turkey in the period covered by this chapter, see footnote 37, chap. VI.

[2] Telegram 161 to London, March 19, 1921; 763.72119/11045.

[3] Telegram 249 from London, March 25, 1921; 763.72119/11061.

insure that American policy was in step with the current situation and that representations of the American position would be timely. The rejection of the Allied terms by the Greeks and Turks meant that there would be no immediate prospect of a renegotiation of Sèvres. The next event of significance was the reopening of hostilities by the Greeks, which, if successful, might force the Allies to reconsider their sacrifice of Greek aims and force the Turks to accept Sèvres. The progress of the Greek Army was thus of great interest to the Department. When the Greek offensive seemed to be failing at the beginning of April, 1921, and press reports indicated that the Allies had decided to intervene in the fighting, instructions were sent to London to " investigate and report immediately" all information available.[4] The Embassy replied that no such proposals had been made to the British government nor did it contemplate making any, according to the Foreign Office, and the best that was hoped for was a stalemate; the Greeks were in serious difficulties, both militarily and financially.[5] Shortly after this the Allies announced their neutrality in the struggle and declared the zone of the Straits neutral territory. Athens cabled on April 21 that the Greek withdrawal from Afiun, announced some days before as a matter of slight importance, now proved to be a major defeat. King Constantine and his government felt that the new campaign was a mistake, and, Athens commented, there was little chance that it would be pressed from now on. The Greek failure, continued the cable, was due to the transfer of troops to Thrace to check Serbia, the lack of big guns, incorrect information and intelligence, and especially to the removal of hundreds of Venizelist officers on the eve of the offensive, carrying the " insane hatred " of Venizelist supporters to extremes.[6]

2.

The renewal of the war in Anatolia touched directly on American interests through the attempt of the Greeks to make the most of their superiority at sea. Admiral Bristol cabled on April 21 that the hostilities had given rise to a complicated situation

---

[4] Telegram 211 to London, April 12, 1921; 767.68/75A.
[5] Telegram 309 from London, April 14, 1921; 767.68/76.
[6] Telegram 57 from Athens, April 21, 1921; 767.68/84.

with regard to neutral states and Greek rights as *de facto* belligerents. The Greeks had declared a blockade of the Turkish coast and were stopping ships bound for Nationalist territory, while, under cover of the Allied control of Constantinople and the Straits zone, they were bringing supplies by sea to Broussa with British connivance. It was possible, said Bristol, that the Greeks might attempt to interfere with American ships on the high seas, as they had already done in Smyrna harbor. Local Greek officials were justifying their actions by claiming that a state of war existed between Greece and Turkey, but there had been no official confirmation of this. Bristol then added some sidelights on the complications of Allied activity in Turkey. The Allies were still technically at war with Turkey but had officially declared their neutrality between Turkey and Greece. Meanwhile, the Italians, and to a lesser extent the French, secretly were supporting the Turkish Nationalists, while the British favored the Greeks, and the Greeks were posing as the mandatory of all the Allies in their actions in Anatolia. The Italians took great pleasure in obliging the Nationalists when they took Bekir Sami bey from southern Turkey (where he had been negotiating with the French) to Samsun via Constantinople on an Italian destroyer so that he could evade the Greeks and get back to Angora. The whole situation was "tragic and ludicrous," commented Bristol, and peace in the Near East seemed no nearer.[7]

The Greeks, as their fortunes in Anatolia declined, pressed harder at sea. On May 6 Bristol cabled that they had declared a blockade of the southern shore of the Sea of Marmora and threatened the seizure and confiscation of any merchant ship found in the area trading with the Turks. The Greeks were not strong enough at sea to maintain an effective blockade, said Bristol, even if it were justified, and he recommended that the United States not recognize it nor allow it to be enforced against American shipping. Pending instructions he would not recognize it and would protest any interference with American interests.[8] Instructions were at once cabled to him and to the Legation in Greece not to recognize the blockade. Bristol was to make clear to the Greek General in command that the government of the United

[7] Telegram 138 from Constantinople, April 21, 1921; 767.68/80.
[8] Telegram 151 from Constantinople, May 6, 1921; 767.68112/–.

States could not admit of any interference with American trade, and the Legation was instructed to advise the Greek Foreign Office, " orally and informally," of Bristol's instructions.[9] Bristol reported on May 12 that the blockade had been lifted. The Greeks seemed to go as far as they dared in exercising authority, he said, but retreated if sufficient protests were made.[10] Athens also cabled on the same day that the Greeks had backed down. The Foreign Minister had taken pains to inform the Embassy that the whole thing was a mistake and no such action as was complained of had been intended—his government had merely sent instructions to take great care in checking passports and individuals and they had been misunderstood by the authorities in Turkey.[11]

The relation of the Powers with the three factions in Turkey— the Greeks, Constantinople, and Angora—was also of interest to the Department of State, for the outside support available to each could not only affect the military situation but could directly influence the final settlement and the treaty of peace. The relations between the Nationalists and the Bolsheviks, and between the Greeks and the British, were well known in Washington. Less was known of the relations between the Nationalists and the Italians and French, respectively, and reports on these relations received close attention in the Department. In April, 1921, the private secretary of the Ambassador in Italy was told by the Secretary of the Nationalist mission at Rome that the Angora government had cabled to the mission to buy two hundred carloads of arms and munitions from Germany, to be shipped via Italy, for use against the Greeks. The Embassy also learned that the Nationalists were negotiating with the Italian government, so far unsuccessfully, for the sale of arms.[12] On April 30 Rome sent an " absolutely secret " cable reporting that, according to the Secretary of the Nationalist mission, the Italian Foreign Minister, Count Sforza, and Djamy bey, the Nationalist representative, were negotiating a secret informal agreement whereby Italy was to send munitions to the value of fifty million Italian lira from

[9] Telegram 40 to Athens, telegram 34 to Constantinople, May 7, 1921; 767.68112/-.
[10] Telegram 156 from Constantinople, May 12, 1921; 767.68112/2.
[11] Telegram 70 from Athens, May 12, 1921; 767.68112/3.
[12] Telegram 94 from Rome, April 21, 1921; 767.68/83.

Taranto to Adalia in exchange for ratification of the Italian-Nationalist commercial treaty. The agreement had almost been completed when Sforza held up shipment of the arms—according to Sforza because the British and Greeks had heard of the agreement, but the Nationalists maintained it was because of a rumor that Mustafa Kemal had rejected the treaty. The Embassy's informant had said that lack of these munitions would seriously affect the Nationalist war plans. An attempt was being made to get information about the commercial treaty, said the Embassy, and the British Ambassador was discreetly queried; he had demanded and received a copy from the Italians. The Secretary-General of the Foreign Office had promised the Ambassador to ask Sforza for a copy for the Department of State.[13]

The French also had been in close contact with Angora. Since the middle of 1920 they had been attempting to come to terms with the Nationalists in Cilicia, and had not neglected the opportunities offered to increase their influence at Angora and to establish themselves as the main channel of communication between the Allies and the Turks. Bristol reported on May 25, 1921, that the most significant event at the moment in the Near East was the negotiations between Mustafa Kemal and the French General Gouraud, Commander of French forces in the Levant, for the acceptance by Angora of the London proposals of the previous March. This was the reason for the comparative quiet in Turkey. The French were making great efforts to end the fighting, and Franco-British hostility in the West was reflected in their relations in the East, for the British felt that the continuation of the " little war " in Turkey was in the interest of Britain. However, Bristol said, a Greek victory would in fact embarrass the British by justifying the extreme demands of the Greeks, and if the Turks won their army might be loosed either on Constantinople or on the British possessions in the East under the influence of the Bolsheviks.[14] On June 2 Bristol cabled that a crisis in Near Eastern affairs was approaching, with the Allies on the point of open disagreement and even perhaps a break. The British were not even united among themselves, said the Admiral, and the British High Commission and the military command were split on both military and political policy. The High Commission was domi-

[13] Telegram 105 from Rome, April 30, 1921; 767.68/89.
[14] Telegram 175 from Constantinople, May 25, 1921; 867.00/1411.

nated by commercial elements, and it had paramount influence at the Foreign Office and thus dominated British Near East policy. The British commander, General Harington, had gone to London to press for either sufficient reinforcements to enforce peace or complete evacuation. The Greeks and Turks were making every preparation for a renewal of the fighting and it was expected that Ismid would be evacuated by Greece. There were persistent reports that fighting in Cilicia between French and Turks had broken out.[15]

In the middle of June a meeting was held between the British and French foreign ministers, Curzon and Briand, in an attempt to arrive at a common Allied policy in Turkey. The principal result was a decision to make one more attempt to end the fighting in Turkey, and a note was sent by France, Britain, and Italy to Greece stating that a settlement of the conflict could not be made by force and asking if the Greek government would accept the Allies as mediators. If the Greeks accepted, an approach would be made to Angora; if Athens refused, the Greeks would be left to themselves. Briand and Curzon agreed on three proposals which went even further than those of the previous March—Smyrna was to be autonomous under international control, parts of east Thrace were to be internationalized, and a special regime set up for Adrianople. The Embassy at Paris commented that as all the concessions were to be made by Greece, it was unlikely it would accept the proposals, but the feeling was in Paris that the military situation would force King Constantine's hand. The French were openly pro-Turk, said the Embassy, but they admitted that Angora would not accept the proposals either.[16]

The Allied program was delivered to the Greek government on June 21. On the twenty-fifth Athens cabled that the Greeks had declined the Allied offer of mediation, asserting that only a military victory could bring peace to the Near East. Everyone was surprised that they had not even asked for the conditions of the Allied offer.[17] Izzet Pasha, the Foreign Minister of the Constantinople government, told Bristol that as far as the Angora government was concerned, the chief obstacle to peace was the insistence

[15] Telegram 184 from Constantinople, June 2, 1921; 867.00/1413.
[16] Telegram 398 from Paris, June 21, 1921; 767.68/109.
[17] Telegram 97 from Athens, June 25, 1921; 767.68/112.

of the Allies on economic privileges in Turkey. Angora was holding firm to its policy of not bargaining away the resources of the country, and it was this attitude which led to the failure to ratify the agreements Bekir Sami had made with the French and Italians. On the other hand, Izzet said, the economic interests of the United States and Turkey coincided and he believed that the Open Door policy in Turkey would clear the air.[18]

The reasons for the Greek firmness were not long in making their appearance. At the beginning of July the Greek Army, newly supplied with arms and munitions, opened a determined attack on the Turkish lines in an all-out effort to smash the Nationalists and capture their capital. By the end of July they had reached their first objective. On July 27 Athens reported a government announcement of a great victory over an army of fourteen Turkish divisions and the capture of Eskishehir.[19] The Embassy doubted the report, but on the same day the Consulate at Smyrna cabled that the Military Attaché of the High Commission had just returned from Eskishehir and confirmed the Greek triumph and the victory over a superior Turkish force. He said the population of the city was calm and seemed well treated, and the Greek Army was behaving well. The Turks were finished, he thought, and the Greeks could march on Angora if they chose.[20]

The Greeks halted their advance for three weeks to regroup their forces. On August 8 the Supreme Council met at Paris to discuss the plebiscite in Upper Silesia, and during the meetings the question of the Greco-Turkish war came up. Ambassador Harvey was present as an observer. Lloyd George brought up the question of Turkey, asking that the powers agree to permit the Greeks to purchase arms privately in Allied countries. He said that while the Turks got munitions from the Bolsheviks, the Greeks were forbidden to buy arms in many countries because they were neutral in the war. The Greeks should be assured of fair treatment and though the governments of the Allied countries might remain neutral, they should permit private interests to sell arms to the Greeks. The French, Italians, and Japanese agreed in principle. After the meeting Lloyd George took Harvey

[18] Telegram 204 from Constantinople, June 22, 1921; 867.00/1424.
[19] Telegram 113 from Athens, July 27, 1921; 767.68/130.
[20] Telegram from Smyrna, July 27, 1921; 767.68/133.

aside for a private conversation. He asked what the attitude of
the United States toward his proposal was. Harvey replied that
it was an academic rather than a practical question, but, as far
as he knew, President Harding had not departed from traditional
American neutrality. Harvey was asked several times but declined
to give an opinion on the proceedings and on the attitudes taken
by the other powers at the meetings.[21]

The Greeks renewed their advance on Angora on August 14,
and at first made good progress. At the end of the month they
were at the Sakaria River where a fierce resistance was encoun-
tered from the Turkish Army, fighting desperately to save the
capital. By the middle of September the Greek effort was exhausted and the Turks still held their line intact. On September
16 the Greek government announced that the assault on Angora
had been abandoned and the army was retiring to new positions.[22]
Athens cabled on September 29 that the details of the Greek
retreat and the losses of the army were being kept from the people. The King had just returned to Athens and the Council of
Ministers was to meet that day to discuss the immediate annexation of occupied territory in Asia Minor to the line Afiun, Kutaya,
and Eskishehir, and the expropriation of its revenue. The situation of the government was " desperate," the Embassy said.[23]
Though defeated, the Greeks maintained for the time being the
new positions to which they had fallen back.

3.

The Greek defeat had cleared the air, as the British had hoped
in the spring. Admiral Bristol reported on October 5, 1921, that
since the Turkish success there had been a revival of diplomatic
activity in Angora. It was difficult to obtain reliable reports, he
said, but was sending along such information as he had. Franklin-
Bouillon, the French Deputy and journalist, had returned to
Angora with a draft treaty. There were no details available,
but it was rumored that the French would evacuate large areas
of Cilicia and leave in place supplies of munitions at the disposal

[21] Telegram 489 from Paris, August 10, 1921; 763.72119/11411.
[22] Telegram 133 from Athens, September 17, 1921; 767.68/147.
[23] Telegram 136 from Athens, September 29, 1921; 767.68/148.

of the Nationalists in return for economic privileges and the restoration of Franco-Turkish relations along the Syrian border. He recalled that Franklin-Bouillon had gone to Angora earlier in the year with similar proposals, but without success; now the Nationalists were militarily secure, they might be more disposed to listen to reason. A Persian delegation had recently arrived in Angora also, hoping to negotiate a treaty similar to the Turco-Afghan treaty signed on May 21 last. The Turks were sending a military mission to Afghanistan to assist in training the army. There were rumors that an Indian delegation was actually in Angora to co-ordinate Muslim action in India with the Turks. The Greek failure was having a significant effect on British thinking, Bristol commented. Their military authorities in Constantinople had always been critical of their government's policy and now perhaps London would listen to them, he said. But British commercial interests favored the Greeks in the belief that, in co-operation, the commercial interests of the two countries could control the trade of the Middle East, with the Greeks acting as agents of the British in areas where the British did not wish to act themselves, such as Anatolia. There was also a third party in British policy, the India Office, said Bristol, which favored a pro-Turk policy in view of the large number of Muslims in India. The British government was hesitating, partly because of the three different policies being thrust at it but also because it had no intention of supporting the Greeks if they were unsuccessful—and it was obvious that the Greeks could not beat the Turks.[24]

Bristol's reports on French diplomatic activities in Angora were well founded. A treaty was signed on October 20, 1921, ending the state of war between the two countries, providing for the evacuation of Cilicia; for the rectification, in Turkey's favor, of the border with Syria; and, in an annexed note, for French support of Turkey in questions relating to the latter's sovereignty and independence—in return for concessions for iron, silver, and chrome, and other economic advantages.[25] Lord Curzon was outraged and protested violently, but there was little he could do. When he received a conciliatory letter from the French he accepted, with as good grace as he could muster, the French assurances.

[24] Despatch 483 from Constantinople, October 5, 1921; 867.00/1451.
[25] Text in Hurewitz, *Diplomacy*, p. 97.

For the Greeks, however, the situation was desperate, and the French action marked their realization that they were alone in Europe except insofar as they could persuade Britain not to abandon them. Curzon, no philhellene, agreed only to see what he could do to persuade the Allies to deal kindly with the Greeks. He called a conference, to be held in January, 1922, but the French Cabinet fell before it could open and Poincaré, no friend of the Greeks or of Curzon, took office as Prime Minister and Foreign Minister. He preferred the controlled method of diplomatic exchanges by note, to the conference system, at least as far as British difficulties in the Near East were concerned. Then the Italian Cabinet fell also, the beginning of the crises that brought Benito Mussolini to the premiership. Curzon's conference was postponed. The plight of the Greeks would not wait, however. On February 15, 1922, the Greek Prime Minister sent an appeal to Curzon, stating that if the present situation continued the Greeks would have to evacuate Asia Minor. The Nationalists were receiving aid not only from Russia but also from France and Italy, and if Britain could not support Greece to the same extent then there was nothing left but to withdraw while conditions permitted. No encouragement was received from the Foreign Office, and the Prime Minister sent word to the High Command to prepare for evacuation. Curzon did, however, repeat his promise of diplomatic assistance, and again he sent invitations to the parties concerned. The Greek evacuation was postponed, and in the middle of March talks began in London.

4.

The fortunes of the proposed conference on Near East affairs were followed closely by the Department. From Constantinople, Admiral Bristol once more began to urge active American participation in Turkish affairs. On January 18, 1922, he reported that Allied experts on Turkey were gathering in Paris to prepare for a conference of foreign ministers to settle Turkish questions, and re-emphasized the importance of American participation in the Turkish settlement as the only way to protect American interests. The Constantinople government was afraid to favor American business, he said, because it was under the thumb of the British, though the Nationalists had an entirely opposite atti-tude—they could not forgive British support of the Greeks and had no intention of giving away their resources.[26] In the middle of February press reports received in Washington indicated that plans for a Near East conference were being revived. The Near East Division of the Department circulated, in the Department, a memorandum stating that it was obvious the Treaty of Sèvres and its appendix, the Tripartite Agreement, must be greatly modi-fied and probably entirely redrafted; the reported conference at Paris had probably been called to do this, but the Department had not received any communication from the Allies on its pur-pose. The memorandum recommended that the embassies be instructed to keep the Department fully informed and a decision be made whether the United States should participate in the con-ference, send official observers, or depend on informal represen-tations through regular diplomatic channels.[27] The last course was chosen for the time being. On February 21 instructions were cabled to London, Paris, and Rome referring to press despatches indicating that Curzon had asked Poincaré and the Italian Ambas-sador to meet him to discuss the Near East situation and instruct-ing the ambassadors to ascertain " discreetly " the purpose of the conference and the plans of the respective Foreign Offices, to keep in close touch with the government, and to report to the Department at once any information they received. " For your information and guidance," the cables stated, it was important to the Department " to be in a position to take effective action before any commitments are made that might affect American interests disadvantageously." [28]

Due to the uncertainties attending the calling of the confer-ence—arising from Poincaré's indifference, problems between the British Foreign Office and the India Office, and the illness of Curzon—no response to this instruction was received for several weeks, except a cable on March 4 from Rome where the new Foreign Minister had told the Ambassador that no date had actu-ally been set for the conference despite the announcement it would open on March 14. The Ambassador mentioned the attitude of

[26] Despatch 33 from Constantinople, January 18, 1922; 867.00/1483.
[27] 867.01/83.
[28] Telegram 49 to Paris, February 21, 1922; repeated to London and Rome; 867.01/83A.

the former ministry to the American position and its support of the Open Door, and requested that the previous assurances be repeated when the question had been studied.[29] A further telegram from Rome on the fourteenth informed the Department that the Foreign Minister had assured the Embassy that the Italian position had not changed.[30]

On March 17 London replied to the Department's cable of February 21. Ambassador Harvey reported that the conference was now due to open in a few days, but might be postponed again due to the attitude of the India Office and Curzon's illness. The general purpose of the conference was to reconstruct "the entirely inoperative" Treaty of Sèvres, and if the Department planned to submit memoranda to the Allied governments the Ambassador suggested it recall the past American positions on the Eastern settlement to the memory of Ambassador Herrick at Paris, or send him fresh instructions if he had not received the instruction of August 5, 1921, with the "vital" paragraph 4.[31] (This was Hughes's cable giving his first statement of the Harding Administration's position on the mandates; see above, p. 315.) Harvey cabled again on March 21 with further details of his actions. He had seen Curzon and, "to guard against the possibility of the Foreign Ministers' manifesting surprise should [the Department] direct their attention" to the position of the United States on American interests in the Near East, he reminded the Foreign Secretary of the memorandum he had given him on August 24, 1921, based on the Department's instruction of August 5, and, "to make assurance doubly sure," gave him also excerpts from the memorandum—clauses one, four and five. Curzon thanked Harvey for the reminder, saying he did not think that matters affecting American interests would arise at the conference, as the purpose of the meetings was to stop the Greeks and Turks from fighting and it was his intention to keep the discussions from being diverted to other topics, although provision would have to be made at the conference for a complete reconsideration of the Sèvres treaty. He would in any case take a copy of the American note with him to Paris. He told the Ambassador that to force a settlement on the Greeks and Turks he intended

[29] Telegram 33 from Rome, March 4, 1922; 867.01/89.
[30] Telegram 35 from Rome, March 14, 1922; 867.01/93.
[31] Telegram 114 from London, March 17, 1922; 867.01/94.

to take advantage of the financial needs of both parties; they were exhausted financially and only Britain was in a position to make loans. Harvey commented, in his report to the Department, that Curzon should use this lever "to the limit," as it was the only hope of success for the conference. Curzon complained that Admiral Bristol was "unwarrantably suspicious" of everything the British did in Turkey, but, Harvey commented, his "well-informed" military attaché disagreed, saying that the British were simply annoyed by Bristol's "unceasing proper vigilance." [32]

The Department replied stating that the memorandum of August 25, 1921, referred only to the mandates and it was felt that American rights and commercial interests would necessarily be affected by any revision of the Sèvres treaty made at the forthcoming conference. Harvey was instructed to continue his "informal and discreet" conversations with the British.[33] The Conference opened at Paris on March 22, 1922, and on the same day agreement was reached on the terms of an armistice in Turkey; they were immediately cabled to Athens and Angora.[34] Bristol cabled Washington on the twenty-fifth that it was locally reported the Nationalists would not sign an armistice on the Allied terms because the proposed armistice line was unsatisfactory; the time given to the Greeks to evacuate Asia Minor was too long; and, in any event, they did not trust the Allies to enforce the terms against the Greeks. They insisted on a Greek withdrawal to the line Broussa-Ushak—the line held by the Greeks before the advance in the summer of 1921—before even discussing armistice terms.[35] The Conference ended on March 26 and proposals for the modification of the Treaty of Sèvres were sent to Athens and Angora on the following day. Ambassador Herrick reported from Paris that the conference had almost broken up over the boundaries of Thrace but a compromise put forward by General Harington and seconded by Marshal Foch had been accepted. The Allies felt confident they could persuade the Greeks to accept their terms, but the Nationalists were another matter. Izzet Pasha was not optimistic that Angora would accept, because Curzon had proposed the terms and he was considered to be pro-Greek; the

[32] Telegram 118 from London, March 21, 1922; 867.01/97.
[33] Telegram 84 to London, March 24, 1922; 867.01/97.
[34] Telegram 133 from Paris, March 23, 1922; 867.01/98.
[35] Telegram from Constantinople via Paris, March 25, 1922; 767.68/167.

French expected the Nationalists to continue their intransigence. The only suggestion he had heard for applying pressure on the Turks, said Herrick, was a threat to evacuate Constantinople and leave it to the Greeks. Herrick particularly drew the attention of the Department to two proposed commissions—one for the revision of the Capitulations as they touched on financial matters, and a second on judicial reform.[36]

On the day after the Allied proposals reached Athens, the Greek Foreign Minister begged the American Chargé to make an appeal to the Department of State for American intervention in the Near East settlement, alleging that the Greeks and the Christians of Asia Minor were being sacrificed by the European powers to save their influence in the Muslim world. The Chargé told him that it was his opinion that American intervention was impractical. The Foreign Minister then asked him to cable the Department " asking for sympathetic American interest in the fate of the Christian populations of Asia Minor," as the Chargé's report to the Department put it.[37] The Chargé was informed by the Department that it did not desire to make any expression of opinion on the situation in the Near East. His explanation of the American position to the Foreign Minister was approved, but he was instructed to avoid any discussion on the subject of American intervention.[38]

The reports of the Conference sent by the embassies in Europe contained little comment on the terms of the Allied proposals. Not so the reports from Constantinople. Bristol sent a cable on April 1 containing an extensive analysis of the Allied plans. He said that despite the confidence with which the Allied governments had published their peace proposals in Constantinople, there were many reasons for the opinion that they were in accordance with " the most authentic traditions of the worst kind of temporizing and ambiguous diplomacy." For example, he said, Adrianople and Gallipoli were to remain Greek, which would be a fertile source of future trouble. Second, Turkish sovereignty was recognized from the Mediterranean to the Black Sea and from Transcaucasia and Persia to the Aegean—the Department should note that these boundaries included parts of Azerbaijan and Geor-

[36] Telegram 137 from Paris, March 27, 1922; 867.01/104.
[37] Telegram 33 from Athens, March 28, 1922; 867.01/105.
[38] Telegram 24 to Athens, April 6, 1922; 867.01/105.

gia now under Bolshevik rule, not to mention the fact that Turkish sovereignty might be impaired by the attempts of the League of Nations to find a national home for the Armenians. Third, the financial clauses, or as they were referred to in the peace proposals, economic interests, were full of problems. As for the Capitulations, an Allied Commission was to have full powers to decide on their revision. These terms were significant for two reasons, said Bristol: they showed that the Allies, and particularly the British, were unwilling to face reality in the Middle East; and they showed that the Allies would not pay the least attention to the desire of the United States for the fair and equal treatment of American interests unless they were made to do so. In this connection, he said, he recommended that the United States abandon its role of simple observer in the Middle East in favor of a policy of the formulation of and insistence on concrete demands. He also urged the Department to give the public the full background of the situation in the Middle East and to place the responsibility where it belonged. He thought it might do some good to publish the report on the Smyrna occupation he had helped to draw up in 1919.[39]

The Department instructed Bristol to send copies of this cable to London, Paris, and Rome, omitting the last two paragraphs.[40] The embassies were instructed to send their comments on Bristol's report and to use their " utmost endeavors " to obtain, discreetly, full information on the Conference and Allied aims; the Department was " very desirous " of being kept fully informed.[41] Rome replied on April 7, reporting that the Conference had been discussed informally with the Foreign Minister but he had been " too timid " to make a clear declaration of Italian aims and expectations, but from other sources it was understood that the Foreign Minister believed Mustafa Kemal would not accept an armistice and would insist on obtaining all of Thrace. He had, however, categorically informed the Ambassador that no action was taken at the Conference infringing on American rights, and repeated that if such an attempt were made he would have supported the United States in the Conference, referring to his " well-known " position in the matter. He promised a memorandum of the pro-

[39] Telegram 40 from Constantinople, April 1, 1922; 867.01/108.
[40] Telegram 29 to Constantinople, April 5, 1922; 867.01/108.
[41] Telegram 105 to Paris, April 5, 1922; 867.01/108.

ceedings at Paris. The Ambassador, commenting on Bristol's report, said he agreed with Bristol that the United States should put forward concrete demands, but this should not be done at the present time.[42]

Paris answered on the tenth. While he did not agree with Bristol's conclusions on the Conference, said Herrick, he did agree with his suggestion that the United States take an active part in the settlement. The only way the United States could protect its interest in the Near East, he said, was by having a representative at the conference which had been proposed to be held in Constantinople in the near future, where questions in which the United States had an interest would be discussed.[43] The Embassy at London also supported Bristol's suggestion of active American participation in the settlement.[44]

The Department of State had understood that three weeks after the close of the Conference, on March 27, invitations were to be sent to the Greeks and Turks to meet with the Allied foreign ministers to discuss a final settlement, provided the two belligerents accepted the Allied proposals in principle. When the three weeks had passed and no word had been received in Washington of the meeting, instructions were sent, on April 15, to London, Rome, Paris, Athens, and Constantinople to cable promptly whether any action was being taken on summoning the meeting, the probable place of assembly, and the agenda in case any subjects not mentioned in the Allied note to the Greeks and Turks were to be taken up.[45] The Department was aware that the Turks had not accepted the Allied proposals—neither in substance nor principle—but had submitted in their turn counterproposals. The chief of these was that there should be *pourparlers* on a Greek withdrawal before any armistice talks, the Nationalist position being that the Greeks must return to the lines held by them before the advance of July, 1921.

The replies from the embassies were all to the effect that no conference was expected in the near future since the Turks had rejected the Allied terms. Rome reported that a new note had been sent to Angora and, pending a favorable reply, no action

[42] Telegram 54 from Rome, April 7, 1922; 867.01/109.
[43] Telegram 156 from Paris, April 10, 1922; 867.01/111.
[44] Telegram 167 from London, April 21, 1922; 767.68/181.
[45] Circular telegram, April 15, 1922; 767.68/174A.

would be taken to call a conference; the Italian government also had information that the Nationalists were preparing for a new offensive. Constantinople said that the latest Allied tactic was to threaten again that the Allies would put Constantinople under Greek occupation if the Nationalists were intransigent.[46] Three more weeks passed, and again the Department cabled the embassies for information on the conference; again the replies stated that proposals and counterproposals were being passed between the Allies and Angora without any sign of the Nationalists giving way. Athens reported that there was considerable agitation in Smyrna against an evacuation of Asia Minor by the Greek Army, but the government was ignoring it since it was a Venizelist movement.[47] From Paris came information that the French were still waiting for a reply to their note to the British declining to assume responsibility for asking Angora for a definite " yes or no " to the Allied proposals and urging the acceptance of the Nationalist proposal to hold preliminary *pourparlers.* They believed that as long as negotiations were going on—no matter of what kind—neither the Greeks nor the Turks would resume hostilities, and therefore they were insisting that nothing be done to disrupt the negotiations.[48] The Italian Foreign Office had received a note from Britain insisting that no preliminary evacuation take place in Anatolia, as the Nationalists might then refuse to accept the Allied terms with the Allied position weakened by a Greek withdrawal. The British position was that there must be no evacuation until after an armistice, unconditional acceptance of the Paris proposals of March, and a joint meeting to draw up final terms of peace. Both the French and the Italians had accepted the last point.[49]

By the middle of June no progress had been made. Negotiations had been held up by the British proposal of a commission of inquiry on the condition of the Christians in Asia Minor. Constantinople cabled on June 14 that during Poincaré's forthcoming visit to London all phases of the Turkish settlement would be discussed, and it was quite possible that an important agreement would be concluded settling the differences between the Allies;

[46] 767.68/175-180.
[47] Telegram 57 from Athens, May 5, 1922; 767.68/185.
[48] Telegram 191 from Paris, May 9, 1922; 867.68/188.
[49] Telegram 74 from Rome, May 11, 1922; 767.68/199.

there were rumors that in exchange for a free hand in Tangier the French were ready to give Britain a free hand in Constantinople.[50] The Department sent this cable to London for comment and information;[51] the Embassy replied that the Foreign Office had stated that the Tangier-Constantinople agreement report was false, for the Straits of Gibraltar were too important to Britain, and French interests in Turkey, too great for bargaining.[52] No agreement came out of Poincaré's visit to London, and during the rest of June the situation remained unchanged. The British still insisted on an unconditional acceptance of the Allied terms by the Nationalists, though Italy and France were willing to meet the Nationalists for preliminary talks.[53]

5.

For Greece this delay did not mean a respite. The condition of its forces had been deteriorating since the failure of the previous summer, the situation on the Anatolia front worsened day by day as the Nationalists grew stronger, and money was running out. At the beginning of June the Greek fleet had bombarded Samsun, but this had no effect on the Nationalists and had merely resulted in the Pontic Greeks being even more severely treated by the Turks. On June 28 the Legation at Athens reported that the Greek high commissioners at Smyrna and Constantinople and the Commander-in-Chief in Asia Minor had been called home for consultation with the Cabinet in the hope that a definite decision could be made. The situation was critical, said the Legation, as a result of " the prolongation of affairs " in Asia Minor. The British were anxious for the Greeks to maintain their present position on the Anatolia front, but the Greeks could not hold out much longer—they needed money badly and the troops wanted to end the fighting and return home. The Cabinet meeting was held on June 29 under the presidency of King Constantine. According to information reaching the Legation, one Minister had

[50] Telegram from Constantinople to London, June 14; reported in telegram 243 from London, June 15, 1922; 867.01/122.
[51] Telegram 171 to London, June 16, 1922; 867. 01/122.
[52] Telegram 259 from London, June 23, 1922; 867.01/126.
[53] See 867.01/122, 124; 767.68/213,216,226.

suggested forcing the issue by some desperate move such as a march on Constantinople but the King had opposed it and no definite action was taken, except that the army in Thrace was put under the command of the Commander-in-Chief in Asia Minor.[54]

The Legation was instructed to keep the Department informed on the situation.[55] Athens answered on July 5 that consultations were still going on in the Cabinet. More conservative influences now prevailed and the Greeks, on British advice, were again waiting and hoping for some definitive Allied decision in July. The King was still personally popular, said the Legation, but the Cabinet was hated; however, the regime was not yet in danger.[56] As July passed, the Greeks heard nothing from the British or the Allies. By the end of the month Greece took matters into her own hands and decided to occupy Constantinople. It was first announced that the Greek Army would withdraw from Smyrna and turn the country over to a civilian administration. Athens reported on July 27 that the Greek Foreign Minister had handed identical notes to the Allied representatives, stating that the situation had become " intolerable " and the Greek government was forced to take measures to end it. The Legation believed a march on Constantinople possible.[57] A substantial part of the Greek Army in Anatolia was transferred to Thrace. Then on July 29 a second note was handed to the Allied representatives, expressing the hope that the Allied Powers would not oppose a Greek advance on Constantinople. The Greek Foreign Minister told the Legation that if the reply were negative the Greeks would not march [58]—but the army was already moving and soon was at the Chatalja lines. On July 31 the Allied governments informed the Greek government that they would not permit a Greek occupation of Constantinople.[59] On August 3 the Greek Foreign Minister replied to the Allies that, as they had denied to the Greeks the means of ending the war, the entire responsibility for

[54] Telegram 81 from Athens, June 29, 1922; 767.68.
[55] Telegram 49 to Athens, June 30, 1922; 767.68/220.
[56] Telegram 86 from Athens, July 5, 1922; 767.68/222.
[57] Telegram 90 from Athens, July 27, 1922; 767.68/231.
[58] Telegram 91 from Athens, July 29, 1922; 767.68/233.
[59] Telegram 93 from Athens, July 31, 1922; 767.68/237.

continued massacres of Christians in Asia Minor fell on their shoulders.[60]

Italy now took on the role of mediator. Admiral Bristol learned that the Italians had sent a note to Angora on August 10, through Jalal ad-Din Sherif, Nationalist representative at Rome, with six questions addressed to the Angora government: (1) What were the minimum Turkish conditions for peace? (2) Was Turkey willing to grant concessions to the minorities and was Turkey willing to give adequate guarantees to the Powers? (3) What compensation would Turkey be willing to give for the abolition of the Capitulations? (4) Would the Turks modify the zones of influence if the Capitulations were abolished? (5) What would be the relationship between the Sultan and the Angora government when peace was achieved? (6) (A secret clause) What oil concessions would Italy get in Turkey in a peace settlement? Bristol cabled Washington that the Turks had replied they were ready to accept any terms which did not impair the nation's sovereignty and independence. Bristol commented that the phrase had been repeated so often by Angora that the Allies were sick of it, and were treating the Turkish reply accordingly. In the meantime they were trying again to arrange a conference to be held at Venice. He added that his latest information was that the British had withdrawn their objections to the holding of a conference before an armistice was agreed on.[61]

The Department instructed Bristol on August 26 to repeat his cable to London, Paris, and Rome and to keep the Department fully informed on the Venice conference;[62] similar instructions were sent directly to the embassies concerned.[63] Before the cable was sent, however, Paris reported on August 23 having learned from the Foreign Office that the Turks had resumed hostilities. The full extent of the Nationalist offensive was not apparent for several days. On August 28 Bristol cabled that all communication with the interior had been cut off as the Turks opened an offensive along the entire front; Athens reported that the attack had caused considerable depression in Greece, and the government was being blamed for sending too many troops from Asia Minor

[60] Telegram 98 from Athens, August 3, 1922; 767.68/240.
[61] Telegram 155 from Constantinople, August 19, 1922; 767.68/251.
[62] Telegram 110 to Constantinople, August 26, 1922; 767.68/251.
[63] Telegram 269 to Paris, August 26, 1922; 767.68/251.

on the "foolish Constantinople escapade." [64] For the next few days reports came into Washington from Athens, Smyrna, and Constantinople of the headlong flight of the Greek Army to Smyrna.[65] Smyrna cabled on September 2 that the military situation was "extremely grave" owing to the exhaustion and low morale of the Greek troops; it was in fact so serious that it could not be saved; the local Christians were in a panic and trying to leave the city. When the Greek Army reached the city, said the Consul, serious trouble was possible and he had heard threats that it would burn Smyrna. He advised that a cruiser be sent to protect American lives.[66] The Department asked for and received permission from the President to send an American ship to the port.[67] On the fourth, Smyrna cabled to the Department a copy of a telegram sent that day to Admiral Bristol, describing the terrible conditions in the city with thousands of refugees pouring in from the country. "I beg you in the name of humanity to intercede with the Angora government," said the Consul, to grant an amnesty to permit the Greek Army to evacuate Smyrna. It might prevent the destruction of the city, for the Greeks were planning to blow up all munitions dumps and the destruction caused by the acts of individual soldiers bent on revenge would be avoided. He had been authorized verbally by the Greek High Commissioner to make the appeal, he said, and the British Consul-General had told him he was making the same appeal to his High Commissioner.[68]

This cable was also sent to the President by the Department, for a decision, but the covering letter advised against American mediation. The President agreed, and no action was taken.[69] A further cable from Smyrna came in on the following day asking that marines be landed to protect lives, but instructions had already been sent by the Navy to the local commander to use his own judgment on the use of American forces ashore to protect Americans.[70] On September 6 Paris reported that the Foreign Office had information that the situation in Asia Minor was "lamenta-

---

[64] Telegram 163 from Constantinople, August 28, 1922; 767.68/262.
[65] See 767.68/263, 264, 265, 273.
[66] Telegram from Smyrna, September 2, 1922; 767.68/274.
[67] 767.68/274.
[68] Telegram from Smyrna, September 4, 1922; 767.68/276.
[69] 767.68/276.
[70] *Ibid.*

ble "; the Greek Army had been completely routed and was burn-ing and massacring in its retreat. The Turks were expected in Smyrna within two days, the French reports said, and it was doubtful that the Greek Army could be evacuated. The Foreign Office was very pessimistic and feared more slaughter, and ex-pected the Turks to be completely intransigent.[71] Information reached Admiral Bristol on the seventh that the Greeks had asked for an armistice and that a meeting would take place soon at Ismid, with British, French, and Italian generals present. He said the Greeks wanted the armistice to permit them to evacuate Asia Minor, but the Nationalists would not accept any terms which did not include the evacuation of Thrace also.[72] When the cable reporting this was sent to the Under Secretary, the Near East Division attached a note saying that it indicated Mustafa Kemal was seizing the opportunity to settle affairs his own way, which was directly opposed to the plans which the powers spon-soring the Venice conference had in mind.[73]

On September 8 the Consul at Smyrna cabled for instructions on his relations with the Nationalists, who were expected to arrive in the city in a day or so.[74] The Department instructed him to bear in mind that the United States did not recognize either the regime in Greece or that in Angora and that diplomatic rela-tions had not been resumed with Constantinople; nevertheless, for practical reasons it would be advantageous for him to remain at his post unofficially as American Consul without exequatur and as delegate of the High Commissioner.[75] On the ninth Bristol cabled that the situation was "most alarming" with the Greek Army in panic and troops pouring into Smyrna; Aidin and Nazil were already burned and Smyrna might be fired by the Greeks next. He said the British, French, and Italian consuls had tele-graphed the Greek Minister of War asking for assurances that Smyrna would not be burned, but the reply was that it was not pos-sible to give any assurance.[76] The Turks entered Smyrna on Sep-

---

[71] Telegram 351 from Paris, September 6, 1922; 767.68/291.

[72] Telegram 169 from Constantinople, September 7, 1922; 767.68/293. Bristol's informant was Hamid bey.

[73] 767.68/293.

[74] Telegram from Smyrna, September 8, 1922; 767.68/296.

[75] Telegram to Smyrna, September 9, 1922; 767.68/296.

[76] Telegram 171 from Constantinople, September 9, 1922; 767.68/297.

tember 9, " in perfect order " according to the Consul.[77] Bristol informed the Department that the Nationalist Army was " practically intact " at the close of operations against the Greeks— well-organized disciplined, and in good condition. The Greek defeat was accepted in Allied circles as a great blow to British prestige, he said, and now the French were worried about the magnitude of the Turkish victory and its implications for French interests in the country. They were particularly concerned about the possibility of the abrogation of the Capitulations and the repudiation of the Ottoman debt. There was also considerable general apprehension about the Turks' next move and the possibility of their marching on the Straits and Constantinople. General Harington had issued a proclamation warning the Nationalists against any infraction of the neutral zone.[78] The end came at Smyrna with the burning of the city, the flight of hundreds of thousands of Greeks and the slaughter of thousands of others.

While the Turks had been flooding back across Anatolia to victory, the Venice conference was still being discussed in the three Allied capitals. The Foreign Office told the Embassy at London, on August 31, it believed formal invitations to the conference would be sent to the Greeks, the Constantinople government, and the Nationalists in a few days. It was hoped it would begin sometime in September, and it was the official view that the present fighting would not affect the conference in any way.[79] But on September 2 the Italian Foreign Office told the Rome Embassy that nothing but the place of the conference was decided; no invitations had been sent, nor in fact any prepared.[80] On the same day the British Foreign Office told the Embassy a note had been sent to the French stating that Britain no longer insisted on an armistice as a prerequisite to the conference.[81] This was the last obstacle, from the Allied side, to the conference, and on September 5 an invitation was sent from the Italian Foreign Minister to the Greek government to attend a conference to be held at Venice, on a date to be set after September 15 and agreed on by the Greek government and the Turkish Nationalists.[82]

[77] Telegram from Smyrna, September 9, 1922; 767.68/304.
[78] Telegram 180 from Constantinople, September 13, 1922; 767.68/314.
[79] Telegram 31 from London, August 31, 1922; 767.68/267.
[80] Telegram 154 from Rome, September 2, 1922; 767.68/271.
[81] Telegram 384 from London, September 2, 1922; 767.68/272.
[82] Telegram 157 from Rome, September 6, 1922; 767.68/289.

But by this time it was patent that the Turks would sweep the Greeks out of the country, and the British government had second thoughts. Athens reported on the sixth that the invitation had not actually been handed to the Greeks by the Italian representatives. The British Chargé had received instructions to request it be held up for the time being because of the present general attitude of the Turks. The cable added that the Greek government still hoped for British intervention.[83]

The Turks were now in effective control of all of Asiatic Turkey except the zone of the Straits. Only an Allied invasion of Anatolia in force could change that situation. Accordingly, a month after the Smyrna disaster, an armistice was signed between the Nationalists and the Greeks, and shortly thereafter a new conference was organized, which met at Lausanne in November, to make the final and definitive settlement of the Eastern questions. This was accepted by the British only after they had made one last effort to coerce the Nationalists. This was the movement to protect the Christians of Asia Minor in which the support of the Allies and the United States was canvassed to apply, first, diplomatic pressure and when, as was anticipated, this failed, then armed force was to be used to prevent the deportation of the Christians. When the British Ambassador approached the Secretary of State on November 10, 1922, to request American cooperation in the British plan, it called forth a statement which summed up, with a bluntness not often found in the relations of friendly states, American reaction to Allied policy in the Middle East. For four years the United States had watched the Allies scrabbling over the richest prize of the war, and the Secretary's statement is a masterly presentation of the American attitude which had developed since 1918.

6.

The official public American position on the desperate situation in Turkey after the Smyrna disaster had been given by Secretary Hughes in a speech at Boston on October 30. " While nothing can excuse in the slightest degree or palliate the barbaric cruelty

---

[83] Telegram from Athens, September 6, 1922; 767.68/290.

of the Turks, no just appraisement can be made of the situation which fails to take account of the incursion of the Greek army into Anatolia, of the war there waged, and of the terrible incidents of the retreat of that army, in the burning of towns, and general devastation and cruelties," said the Secretary. There were those, he said, who proposed that the United States should have actively intervened in Turkey. The situation in Turkey was the result of a war to which the United States was not a party, and if the Allies, who were close to the scene, did not choose to intervene, the American people would not shoulder the burden. It would also be futile to talk of going to war in Turkey at the present time, when all the other powers were preparing for a peace conference. The United States had properly confined its efforts to the protection of American interests in Turkey. It had no connection with the political ambitions of the Allies there and did not propose to become involved with them.[84]

The Secretary's statement to the British Ambassador was a good deal blunter. The Ambassador asked if the United States would support an ultimatum to the Nationalists that they would be held accountable if they persisted in their mass deportation of the Christian population of Asia Minor. The ultimatum would have to make clear that forcible measures would be used if necessary, he said, since the Turks would pay no attention to purely diplomatic moves. The Secretary said the United States was prepared to use diplomatic pressure " to the utmost extent " but was not ready to threaten war unless it was ready to go to war. The Administration had no legal right to go to war in Turkey unless the Congress authorized it. The Ambassador then referred to the part the United States had played in Turkish affairs at the Peace Conference at Paris and the delays in the settlement in deference to American wishes, which delays were largely responsible for the present difficulties. Britain had not desired mandates, said the Ambassador; the whole idea of mandates was President Wilson's and the British government had deferred to him in the hope of getting American co-operation in the Middle East. " The Secretary asked, if they did not wish the mandates, whether they desired the territories or whether the Ambassador meant to imply that they did not wish any territories at all as a result of the war,"

[84] *Foreign Relations*, 1922, II, 947–49.

reads the memorandum of the conversation; "The Ambassador did not directly meet this question." He referred to the burden of the mandates and he said Britain had taken up the burden in the expectation that the United States would share it, and now it was felt Britain was being left alone. The Department's own records would bear him out.

Hughes replied that he had no desire to engage in a controversy over what took place at the Peace Conference. It was quite obvious that British and American ideas on the mandates were quite different. While he preferred not to enter into a discussion of the general subject,

he would say that he could not for a moment assent to the view that this Government was in any way responsible for the existing conditions. . . . The United States had not sought to parcel out spheres of influence in Anatolia; [it] had not engaged in intrigues at Constantinople; [it] was not responsible for the catastrophe of the Greek armies during the last year and a half . . . diplomacy in Europe for the last year and a half was responsible for the late disaster. The Secretary said that that was the American point of view and that he was quite ready, if the Ambassador desired, to elaborate and substantiate it at any time.

(This was fair warning that the United States was ready to defend itself against any public attempt by the Allies to place the blame for the Turkish debacle on American shoulders.) The Secretary continued, "What troubled the dreams of the British statesmen was their maintenance of their imperial power, the question of India, the question of Egypt, of the Suez Canal, and their relations to the Near East in connection with their vast imperial domain." He did not wish to criticize this attitude and was quite ready to admit that the British Empire was a supporter of civilization, but he must point out that whatever these imperial ambitions and difficulties were, the American government was not associated with them. The Ambassador replied that he did not care to discuss the matter further at the present time, but if the Secretary examined the Department's records he would see that his statements were well founded. The Secretary closed the interview by mentioning that a lecture at West Point by a well-known British historian had been canceled by the Secretary of War because of statements reflecting on American honor which had appeared in his writings.[85]

[85] *Ibid.*, pp. 952–55.

CHAPTER XIV

LAUSANNE

1.

The elimination of the Greek forces in Anatolia and the establishment of the authority of the Nationalist government over the whole of Asiatic Turkey, except the zone of the Straits, established two political facts: first, that the Allied countries were not prepared to reinstate by force their authority in Turkey, and second, that the already discredited and inoperative Treaty of Sèvres would not be replaced by a treaty negotiated on the basis of the results of the war between the Allies and the Central Powers. In September, 1922, the military victory of the Nationalists was manifest; the diplomatic struggle had yet to be fought. The Allies had declined a military contest, but they had powerful political and economic weapons. Turkey had much to gain from a negotiated settlement and the restoration of normal relations with Europe and much to lose if it stood on its military victory and defied Europe. On the other hand, Turkey had much to offer, from economic privileges to influence in a strategically important area of the world. The Allies could deny to Turkey the benefits of a restoration of relations, economic aid, and such additional stability as would be afforded by a recognition of the Nationalist regime. However, the effectiveness of these weapons depended on the degree of unity among the Allies, for many of the Turkish desiderata could be provided by a single European state. The diplomatic settlement would depend on the nerve and tenacity possessed by the Turks on the one hand and on the reality of the common purpose of the Allies on the other. The Turks had their purpose clearly defined in the National Pact—to be masters in the lands occupied by the Turkish nation—and had already demonstrated their nerve by defying the military strength of the Allies. The purpose, and nerve, of the Allies was an unknown quantity. They had been shielded from the ultimate consequences of their actions in the Near East by the Greek Army in Anatolia. Now this shield was removed. The achievement of Allied purposes in Turkey would be at the expense of the Allies themselves, and it remained to be seen what price the Allies were willing to pay for these purposes, which of them would be jettisoned along the way, and which were worth the maintenance of unity.

For the United States this situation contained elements of advantage and loss. Those privileges and benefits which the Allies had attempted to extract from Turkey as spoils of war, to the exclusion of the United States, would undoubtedly be whittled down with a corresponding increase in the opportunities afforded to American economic and commercial enterprise. But on the other hand, those other privileges in Turkey which had been shared by all the powers, including the United States, would also be jeopardized. The United States had thus a direct interest in the outcome of the negotiations not only from the point of view of the relations of Turkey with Europe but also with respect to American relations with the new regime. The reactions of the Allied Powers and Turkey to the new era in the Near East which began with the Turkish victory over the Greeks and, insofar as the Greeks were the agents of the Allies, over the Allies, were closely followed by the United States, for these reactions would indicate policies and on these policies would depend American interests in Turkey.

The diplomatic situation was obscure, partly because it was new and partly because it was complicated by domestic crises in Britain, Italy, and Greece. The Greek failure completely discredited Constantine, and he was ejected by a coup at the end of September. The coalition government of Lloyd George that had ruled Britain since 1916 was also a victim of the Smyrna disaster. It lasted three weeks longer than Constantine, but in the middle of October the Conservative party withdrew its support and the government fell. A general election in November placed the Conservatives in control of the Commons. Italy was in the throes of the constitutional crisis that led to the triumph of the Fascio and Benito Mussolini. The Department of State's principal source of information on diplomatic developments at this time was the

London Embassy, to which Sir Edward Grigg, private secretary to Lloyd George, passed remarkably complete information of the discussions in the Cabinet of the Near Eastern crisis. On the day before the Turks took Smyrna, London cabled the substance of a recent Cabinet meeting on the Near East situation. The chief topic was the freedom of the Straits. This was the main achievement of the war, Lloyd George said, and must be maintained, and as the Greeks had been barred from Constantinople, so must the Turks. The Prime Minister was greatly incensed at Constantine for his "empty gesture" at the city which had drawn two key divisions from the Asia Minor front and so helped the debacle. The Cabinet decided that if the French would not assist in maintaining the Allied position at the Straits, Britain would do so alone, as the position was based on the Armistice of Mudros and the Treaty of Sèvres and was thus not affected by the defeat of the Greeks. The Embassy was also told that the Greeks were still demanding western Thrace, but not even the French could help there, since both Rumania and Serbia were opposed to it. The British government did not expect the Turks to grant an armistice to the Greeks readily, but once an armistice was reached a conference would be called of all the signatories of Sèvres.[1]

A week later, when the Nationalists, having smashed the Greek Army, were approaching the zone of the Straits and Constantinople, a special meeting of the Cabinet was called which was also reported fully by Grigg to the Embassy. A French note of September 14, supporting the British position on the Straits, was received "with much satisfaction," by the Cabinet, particularly since the French government had instructed the French Commander, Pelle, in the Straits, to co-operate with the British military, and agreed that more troops should be sent to the area. The French had also agreed that Angora be told the Allies expected the neutral zone to be respected and that instructions be sent to the Allied admirals to prevent the Nationalists from crossing the Straits. The Cabinet also discussed Bulgarian and Serbian fears of the re-establishment of the Turks in Thrace and decided that an early conference of the Allies, Greece, Turkey, Serbia, and Bulgaria would be desirable, though no conclusions were

[1] Telegram 394 from London, September 9, 1922; 767.68/303. See footnote 37, chap. VI, for source material on events in Turkey.

reached on the sending of invitations to Serbia, Bulgaria, or the United States. In view of French support it was decided to meet any threat from the Nationalists with full military force, and the dominions, the Allies and the Balkan states were asked to join the British government in resisting the danger to the freedom of the Straits from the Nationalist advance.[2]

The Embassy at Rome, however, had been earlier informed by the Italian Foreign Office that it was hoped, though a British reply to the last Italian proposals for moderation in handling the Nationalists had not been received, that Britain would not maintain its intransigent position in view of the military situation. (The British reply was received on September 12; it rejected the Italian proposals and the British Ambassador made clear to the Foreign Office his government's intention to defend Constantinople.) [3] The Greek Chargé at Rome told the American Ambassador that he had been told by the Foreign Office that the French government had indicated to the Italian Ambassador at Paris that while it was not enthusiastic about a conference, if Italy insisted, France would agree. The Chargé added that he thought the Italian government was inspired by a fear of continued conflict in the Near East threatening general peace and of French ascendency menacing British and Italian interests there. The representatives of the Little Entente countries had told him that though they were without instructions they believed their governments would hold serious objections to an extension of Turkish rule in Thrace and a common Turco-Bulgarian frontier.[4]

The information gathered by the Department was summarized by William Philips, the Acting Secretary, and sent on September 18 to the President and to the Secretary of State, who was cruising on the U. S. S. *Maryland*. (Almost no news had been sent by the Paris Embassy, and an instruction was sent to "telegraph promptly" all information on the French attitude on the Near East situation, as the Department was not being kept adequately informed.) [5] The letter to the President gave the gist of the cable from London of September 16 reporting the Cabinet meeting of the fifteenth and enclosing also copies of other cables on the Near

[2] Telegram 410 from London, September 16, 1922; 767.68/326.
[3] Telegram 162 from Rome, September 12, 1922; 767.68/309.
[4] Telegram 160 from Rome, September 12, 1922; 767.68/308.
[5] Telegram 287 to Paris, September 20, 1922; 767.68/339A.

East situation. After giving the Department's assessment, Philips continued:

I assume that the position of this country is really in line with the position of the Allies [on the Straits]; that is, in favor of a neutral zone and the internationalization of the Straits, and the moment may not be far off when it would be desirable for us to state our position. I am keeping the Secretary fully advised by wireless and shall not fail to advise you if I receive any comments from him.[6]

Harding replied on the nineteenth: " It may be possible that the United States will be invited to confer relating to the situation [in the Middle East], but I should be very slow to commit this nation to any sort of participation except as we express concern for American Nationals whose lives and property are endangered by the activities of the Turkish-Nationalist Armies." [7]

The cable to Secretary Hughes went into greater detail, giving a full summary of recent events. The situation in the Near East was " extremely critical " it said, with a possibility that Britain and the Allies might come to war with Turkey. The Department's actions had been limited to the protection of American lives and property and helping the relief activities of the Red Cross, Near East Relief, and other agencies. It had been made clear to the Allies, and via Admiral Bristol to Allied authorities in Turkey, that while responsibility was theirs, the United States was willing to give any assistance to refugees. The cable then came to the nub of the matter, the interest of the United States in events in the Near East. The United States would seem to have an interest in Allied efforts to prevent a forcible occupation of Constantinople by the Turks, said the Acting Secretary, for it would mean a repetition of the Smyrna disaster. Moreover, any further failure by the Allies to restrain the Turks would mean the end of the Capitulations and would endanger all American interests in Turkey and the Near East. Also, the United States had a direct interest in the internationalization of the Straits. Reports of Turkish atrocities had deeply stirred the country, he added, and pressure would undoubtedly be brought to bear on the government to take action in Turkey; at the same time, it was

[6] 767.68/326.
[7] 767.68/635

difficult to see what action could be taken which would not risk embroiling the United States in serious complications.[8]

2.

As the above cable indicates, American policy was still in the stage of raising the issues involved. The political situation in Europe and Turkey was still far too obscure for the United States to come to any definite decision on the part the United States should play in this particular stage of Near East politics, to say nothing of evaluating the significance of the policies of the individual powers at any given time. More than a month passed before the United States felt that the time had come to make any commitment on the position it proposed to take vis-à-vis the Powers and Turkey. (This was the time it took for the Allies to come to terms among themselves on their attitude towards Turkey and a peace conference.) In point of fact, of course, the United States had been waiting for an appropriate opportunity to put its position before the Powers since the Conference at Paris in the previous March. Since then, one major fact had been clarified—that Turkey could not be treated as a conquered state. September and October were taken up with clarifying a second question—whether the three major Allied Powers would decide, respectively, that, notwithstanding their very different interests in Turkey, they could gain more by united action than by acting alone.

The apparent agreement between Britain and France reported by the Embassy at London in the cable of September 15 did not last long. Britain had made plain to its Allies that it intended to maintain control of the Straits, by force if necessary. But on September 17, while Curzon was out of London, Winston Churchill and Lloyd George decided to commit the British government so deeply to an active policy in Turkey that, despite the growing public opposition in Britain to strong measures and the disinclination of France and Italy to offer more than diplomatic resistance to the Nationalists, it would be impossible for Britain to draw back from its announced policy in Turkey. This was

[8] Telegram 50 to Secretary of State on U. S. S. *Maryland*, September 18, 1922; 767.68/333A.

accomplished by the issuance of a strongly worded communiqué, made public on the seventeenth, stating the inflexible opposition of the British government to handing over the Straits and Constantinople to the Nationalists, and its determination to resist any Turkish attempt on the Straits by all necessary force. This communiqué had the effect of a bombshell in Paris. It ended any possibility of Britain being persuaded to a moderate course; worse, it served notice on the French and the rest of the world that Britain had no intention of being persuaded. It gave back to Britain the initiative in Turkey; it might even be successful in stopping the Nationalists without a fight, and this for the French was the worst possibility, for it would restore British prestige at French expense. Both France and Italy ordered their troops on the Asiatic shore of the Straits to withdraw to the European side.

Through Grigg the Embassy at London learned that on September 18 a French note on the communiqué had been received in London and considered at a meeting of the Cabinet. The note expressed great surprise at the tone of the British statement and regret at its untimeliness, and said that France would not cooperate with British forces if they attempted to prevent Nationalist troops from crossing the Straits. It stated the conditions for a settlement acceptable to France: these were, Turkish sovereignty over Constantinople, Adrianople, and Gallipoli; the boundary in Thrace to be the Maritsa River; and the freedom of the Straits under the guarantee of Turkey. Grigg said the Cabinet was firm in its decision to adhere to the Paris proposals on Thrace of the previous March and the retention of effective European control over the Straits. British unwillingness to restore Constantinople to the Turks had already been asserted as inconsistent with the Mudros Armistice and the Treaty of Sèvres. As for the threat of the Nationalists to invade the neutral zone, this would be a breach of the Mudros Armistice and would automatically renew hostilities between the Allies and Turkey. Grigg told the Embassy that Curzon was to go to Paris at once, as it was felt another exchange of notes would be unsatisfactory.[9]

The Department received reports on the Paris conversations from the British, French, and Italian points of view. Grigg told the Embassy on September 21 that the news from Paris was fairly

[9] Telegrom 414 from London, September 19, 1922; 767.68/332.

good and the situation easier. The French were making every
effort to keep Mustafa Kemal from aggressive action, but they
were having difficulty in view of Russian support of the Turks.
Britain was insisting on keeping Chanak in its hands as no decision on the evacuation of the Straits and Constantinople could
be taken until after a peace conference. The Embassy gained the
impression that British intransigence on Thrace was easing and
that Lloyd George's view now was that its ultimate disposal was
of secondary importance. On the Straits it was understood he
now favored placing them under an international commission and
though he was adamant on Turkish control he was indifferent to
Turkish sovereignty over them. " It was quite intelligibly hinted,"
said the Embassy in its report to Washington, " that American
participation in the conference would be welcomed, though no
illusions are held on that score." [10]

Paiis reported that the Foreign Office had told the Embassy
there was complete agreement at the inter-Allied meeting of September 20 on the necessity of preserving the freedom of the Straits
and preventing the Nationalists crossing the Straits until after a
conference, but at this point difficulties arose. Curzon insisted
that the Nationalists be prevented from entering the zone of the
Straits, by force if necessary, whereas the French and Italians
thought this might lead to war, which they wanted to avoid at all
costs—they refused to risk everything merely to save some territory for the Greeks, who had proved they could not hold it. Poincaré believed that if the Nationalists were assured the conference
would give them satisfaction, they would not make trouble. The
Foreign Office told the Embassy that its point of view was so reasonable the British would have to fall in line with it eventually;
the difficulty lay in British psychology, which looked at the situation from the point of view of 1918, instead of four years later,
and after a Turkish victory.[11] The Italian Foreign Office told the
Rome Embassy that according to the telegrams from Count Sforza
the situation was more hopeful and the British more amenable
to French and Italian pressure. The attitude of the Italian government, the Foreign Office said, was that while it believed the
freedom of the Straits was vital, the lengths Italy would go to

[10] Telegram 420 from London, September 21, 1922; 767.68/342.
[11] Telegrams 367 from Paris, September 21, 1922; 767.68/348.

preserve it depended on how Turkey was treated in the immediate future. If a conference were unjustly delayed and Turkish demands brushed aside, Italy would refuse to participate in any warlike action. Italy's position was that east Thrace should be returned to Turkey, west Thrace given to Bulgaria to provide access to the Mediterranean, and the freedom of the Straits maintained.[12]

On the twenty-second, the Paris discussions almost ended in a burst of anger. In London, Grigg told the Embassy the meeting had begun by Poincaré going over the military dispositions of the Nationalists, which he said were so ominous that the sole chance for peace was to make overtures at once to Mustafa Kemal granting the " indispensable condition " of the immediate cession of the Maritsa frontier. Curzon disputed this reading of the situation and said if General Harington had not been abandoned by his Allies there would be no question of being forced to evacuate the Straits. There was a violent outburst by Poincaré at this supposed slur on the French troops; he attacked Harington bitterly for his alleged insults to the French on their withdrawal from the zone of the Straits. Curzon tried to persuade Poincaré that these reports were not true, but the French Premier refused to listen and continued " shouting at me," cabled Curzon to the Cabinet, " like an angry schoolmaster at a guilty schoolboy." Curzon left the conference room, but half an hour later Poincaré came out and apologized and the discussions resumed. Curzon maintained the British position, that it was " absolutely impossible " to abandon the freedom of the Straits under European guarantees, but he asked London for approval of a definite statement to Poincaré of what the British government was prepared to offer Mustafa Kemal. The Cabinet replied that it would consent to the return of east Thrace to Turkey and had already consented to the return of Constantinople, but that in view of the massacres at Smyrna the passage of the Nationalist Army into Europe could not be permitted and the Straits must be held by the Allies until after the peace conference.[13]

On September 23, the Allies agreed on a public statement of the proposals to be made to the Nationalists for an armistice

[12] Telegram 170 from Rome, September 22, 1922; 767.68/357.
[13] Telegram 427 from London, September 23, 1922; 767.68/360.

and the eventual settlement of Eastern questions. Couched in suitably general terms, the statement was a compromise between the British, French, and Italian views in that while it mentioned the effective insurance of the freedom of the Straits, the question of the methods to be employed to insure this freedom was not raised. This called forth an official American comment on the Eastern situation in the form of an answer by Secretary Hughes to a question on the American attitude on the Allied proposals made during a news conference on September 26. The Secretary declined to comment on the territorial aspects of the proposals, but stated " unequivocally " the approval of the American government of the proposals for the freedom of the Straits and the protection of minorities.[14]

3.

The agreement of September 23 among the Allies was, as that of a week before, short-lived. On the day the Allied statement was issued, Bristol cabled from Constantinople that war was imminent due to the firmness of the British stand, with which he was in agreement; however, the French and Italians having withdrawn their troops, the British forces were not sufficient to stop the Nationalists should they decide to attack. He raised once more the question of a more active American role in the crisis " to prevent a war of such destructive possibilities." [15] A second cable of the same day reported that all British troops in Constantinople, except for 600 men, had been sent to Chanak, and General Harington, the British Commander, had asked Bristol if American sailors from the destroyers at Constantinople would help to maintain order in case of trouble in the city, for it was reliably reported that the Turks in the city were being secretly armed. Bristol told him there were only 400 men available and they would be needed to protect American lives and property; in any case the United States was neutral and could not join in any joint defense of the city.[16]

The crisis came with the fall of Constantine's government in

---

[14] *Foreign Relations,* 1923, II, 880.
[15] Telegram 212 from Constantinople, September 23, 1922; 767.68/361.
[16] Telegram 213 from Constantinople, September 23, 1923; 767.68/363.

Greece. Encouraged by this seeming indication of the weakness of the Allies, Mustafa Kemal advanced his forces to the barbed wire surrounding the main British position at Chanak.[17] The cables from London, Paris, and Rome showed the frailty of the unity of the Allies. It was painfully apparent that France and Italy were quite willing for the Turks to occupy the Straits and Constantinople by force, and their interest in the freedom of the Straits was limited to the degree of freedom that could be obtained by matching diplomacy against armed force.

The British Commander, General Harington, called Mustafa Kemal's bluff and maintained his position against the far larger force of Turks facing him at Chanak. The Nationalist move against the Straits and the prospect of a Turkish eruption out of Asia into Constantinople and Thrace was stopped without bloodshed. On October 11 an Allied delegation headed by Harington met Ismet Pasha, the victor of Inonu, at Mudania to arrange an armistice between the Greeks and Turks. The Turks demanded that they be allowed to cross the Straits and occupy Thrace. The French representative, with the support of his government, was willing to agree to the Turkish demands, but Harington refused. The Turks thereupon issued an ultimatum that they would attack in force if they were not permitted to advance peacefully. Harington again stood firm. Much pressure was brought to bear on the French government by Curzon to end its support of the Nationalist demands, and with a few hours still remaining before the ultimatum expired a compromise was reached whereby the Greeks evacuated Thrace to the Maritsa but were to be replaced not by Turkish troops but by Allied contingents who were to occupy

[17] The Department cabled to Bristol on October 10 saying that the Secretary of the Navy had just informed them that a request had been received from Bristol for the "immediate despatch" of the U. S. S. *Utah* to Constantinople. Bristol was instructed to cable immediately his reasons for this request—" You will appreciate that the use of our naval forces in the Near East under present circumstances has a political as well as naval bearing which makes it important that the Department be kept informed fully by you of any request for changes in these forces and the reasons therefor. It is felt here that the augmentation of our naval forces by sending a battleship to Constantinople at this time might be misinterpreted." Telegram 185 to Constantinople, October 10, 1922; 767.68/435A. Bristol replied that in view of the critical situation and the inadequate forces at his disposal for the protection of Americans in Turkey, he had asked the squadron commander in the Mediterranean, who was due to visit Constantinople anyway, to make his visit in the *Utah*. Telegram 263 from Constantinople, October 12, 1922; 767.68/441.

the territory until after the Peace Conference; the Straits and Constantinople also were to remain under Allied control.[18] On these terms an armistice was signed on October 11 and preparations for the Peace Conference then began.[19]

During these diplomatic and military maneuverings, the Powers, each in its own way, attempted to influence the attitude of the United States, none of them going so far as to suggest direct American involvement in the crisis but seeking, rather, insurance in case the growing feeling in the United States against the Turks might not after all force the American government to take some action. Britain had taken care to insure that its position was known and understood by the United States government. On October 4 Venizelos called on Ambassador Harvey in London to present, he said, an urgent request to the American government on behalf of the government of Greece. Before he submitted it Harvey suggested he state in what capacity he spoke. Venizelos replied that the new government of Greece had asked him to act as its representative in defining its position to all the Powers in the present emergency, but he was not yet speaking with authority because he had based his acceptance on certain conditions—i.e., that he should be empowered to concede the ultimate control of east Thrace to Turkey and to pledge the immediate withdrawal of Greek troops on condition that the Allied Powers occupy the territory and assume direct responsibility for its safety pending the evacuation of its Greek, Armenian, and other Christian inhabitants.[20] He was so convinced of the necessity of a Greek withdrawal from east Thrace, he said, he felt fully warranted in asking the American government to urge with the utmost insistence on

[18] See files 767.68/350 *et seq.* and 767.68119/1 *et seq.*

[19] See telegrams 254, October 10, and 259, October 11, 1922, from Constantinople; 767.68119/14 and 767.68119/15.

[20] The Department cabled to London on October 23 requesting the Embassy to cable any information which would indicate the nature of Venizelos' position in relation to the authorities now functioning in Greece " and in what capacity he is received by the Foreign Office." Telegram 321 to London, October 23, 1922; 767.68/409. London replied that Venizelos had told the Foreign Office that he had been entrusted by the present Greek government with the foreign affairs of Greece; although he was without credentials, the Foreign Office dealt with him as a kind of special ambassador sent to London to deal with broad questions of policy. The accredited Greek Minister at London was no longer given full diplomatic recognition, and he confined himself to running the Legation. Telegram 488 from London, October 25, 1922; 767.68/484.

all the Powers, in the name of humanity, to insure the safety of the lives and movable property of the Christians of Thrace and to prevent the slaughter which would otherwise ensue. His sole request was for adequate time to evacuate the province. Harvey promised to place his request before his government,[21] and asked him at the time if he had put it to Curzon. Venizelos said he had, but the response was not wholly satisfactory. Curzon had assured him that adequate guarantees would be exacted from the Turks, to which Venizelos had "vehemently" replied that Turkish guarantees were worthless and had been so proved over many centuries.

Surprisingly, Harvey said in his report to the Department, Venizelos made no criticism of the British for withdrawing their support after encouraging the Greeks. His resentment was at the United States for refusing to make good the promises given at the Peace Conference and declining to see them through their troubles "to the end of time," as Harvey put it. "The impressiveness of this rebuke was impaired by its lack of novelty," he commented.

Later in the day Harvey had a long talk with Curzon, who mentioned that Venizelos had called on him and had made approaches similar to those made to Harvey. He had turned "truculent," said Curzon, after a remark by the Secretary of War, Worthington Evans, expressing doubt at the efficiency of the Greek Army. Curzon told Harvey that he agreed in substance with Venizelos, but the danger of fresh fighting was a factor which required consideration also. Venizelos, said Curzon, was entitled to great respect as an extraordinary man of undoubted patriotism and sincerity, stirred to the depths by the real or fancied dangers of his countrymen, and his proposals also warranted attention because of the encouragement he had "unfortunately" received from "certain quarters in this vicinity." However, as to Thrace, the matter could be settled by an Allied occupation, and the Turks seemed amenable according to word

---

[21] The Department cabled London on October 12 in reply to London's telegram 443, that the terms of the Armistice of Mudania apparently made provision for Allied supervision of the Greek evacuation of Thrace and would obviate the necessity of replying to Venizelos' request. "If an appropriate occasion appears, you may tell Venizelos of the active steps being taken by American relief organizations to assist refugees from Asia Minor and Thrace."

received in London. Curzon, at the end of the conversation, expressed great satisfaction at the Secretary's statement of September 26 and said it had helped his government's insistence on the freedom of the Straits.[22]

On October 6 a member of the London Embassy staff had a conversation with Rechad bey, the diplomatic agent of the Angora government at London. The discussion consisted almost entirely of an exposition by Rechad of his government's position. The Nationalist government wanted the immediate occupation of Thrace, he said, to prevent the Greek Army from reorganizing there. If this were not accepted, then the Allies must order the Greeks to withdraw and then administer the province temporarily. On the Straits, the Turkish position was that they should be completely demilitarized within a zone thirty miles wide along both shores, under the surveillance of an international commission of all interested countries, including Russia. Control by the League was unacceptable as it was considered to be dominated by Britain and not truly international. Since demilitarization would leave Constantinople defenseless, the Powers must bind themselves to guarantee possession of the city to Turkey. The Capitulations must be abolished, particularly insofar as they conferred economic privileges—the economic rehabilitation of Turkey would be impossible under the present restraints, especially on customs duties. There would be no objection to continuing the consular courts until Turkish justice was properly organized and reformed. Rechad appeared very conciliatory, the Embassy reported, and had said Mustafa Kemal realized that, in a war with Britain, Turkey would be defeated eventually and was therefore anxious for a peace settlement. He would never agree to a permanent British occupation of the Straits, however, said Rechad, and cautiously hinted that Russia would give Turkey full support on this.[23]

On the same day, Chambrun, French Chargé in Washington, called on Secretary Hughes to inform him that the Turks had asked the Allied Powers to assist in protecting the lives and property of the Turkish inhabitants of Thrace; his government had therefore instructed him to ask the American government if it was prepared to make representations at Athens similar to

[22] Telegram 443 from London, October 4, 1922; 767.68/409.
[23] Telegram 446 from London, October 6, 1922; 767.68/415.

those made by the Allies. Chambrun did not explain why his government had asked him to make this gratuitous approach on behalf of a third power. The Secretary told him that the position of the United States was to protect the lives and property of all, but he was not prepared to say that the American government would make representations of any kind in the present case until more information was available to it. Admiral Bristol had not been approached by the Turks and the Department of State had no information of any imminent trouble which would make it advisable to approach the Greek government.[24]

4.

As the prospects for a definite settlement increased, so did the necessity of defining the American position. This problem had two aspects: first, would the United States take part in the forthcoming conference and, if so, in what capacity; and second, and most important, what were the specific interests of the United States likely to be affected by the conference and what action should be taken to insure that these interests were not adversely affected by decisions taken at the Conference.[25] This was quite

[24] Memorandum of conversation, October 6, 1922; 767.68/435.

[25] The Near East Division sent, on September 29, a long memorandum to the Secretary of State on the policy the United States should take towards the Nationalist regime in Turkey. The Division suggested that a strong line be taken with Mustafa Kemal. The United States could influence events in the Near East without recourse to armed intervention. American good will counted tremendously with the Turks because of the financial and commercial position of the United States; they wanted to re-establish diplomatic and trade relations and might in the future apply for a loan. Yet they were now placing themselves in a position where public sentiment against Turkey would make this out of the question. The peace not only of the Middle East but of Europe, too, was at stake if Turkey could defy the Powers with impunity, and abolish the Capitulations and re-establish itself in Constantinople. "We should immediately address a communication to Mustafa Kemal indicating our interests in the freedom of the Straits, the protection of minorities, the peaceful settlement of the present crisis and reconstruction in Asia and Europe." The communication should add that intransigence on the part of Mustafa Kemal would be interpreted in the United States as a desire to retard the reconstruction of the world and would brand him as a troublemaker; it would also affect an early restoration of relations. If the Allies knew of this démarche, they would be strengthened in their dealings with the Turks. The Secretary replied on the same day that the memorandum was " a forcible representation of the matter but there are other considerations which cannot be ignored. I

separate, of course, from the question of the direct relations between the United States and the new regime in Turkey and any
agreement that might be reached between them. The question of
American representation at the Conference had been raised by
Admiral Bristol and others at the time of the Paris Conference of
the previous March. The example of the Treaty of Sèvres and
the great difficulty experienced by the United States in protecting
its interests in the face of a *fait accompli* was always before the
Department, but on the other hand, so too were the dangers of
becoming involved in the aftermath of ten years of war in the
Near East. On September 23 Acting Secretary Philips wrote to
Secretary Hughes, shortly before the latter returned to Washington, giving him a summary of events in the Near East and
the Department's action with respect to them. He referred in
particular to the telegram sent from London on September 21.
" You will note that Mr. Harvey," he said,

. . . intimates that the British would be glad to have us take part in
the prospective Near Eastern conference to be held perhaps at Venice.
Furthermore, Mr. Craigie of the British Embassy, during the last two or
three days, has twice called at the Near Eastern Division and intimated
that his Government was very much interested to know whether an
invitation to participate would be favorably received here. . . . It seems
to me that it might be better for us not to receive an invitation to participate because in all probability we should have to turn it down. We
do not want to take part in discussions, I assume, relating to territorial
settlements, etc., which will come up at the Conference. Nevertheless I
feel that we ought not to convey the impression to the Powers that American interests can be ignored. We seem to have as much interest in the
settlement of the Near Eastern situation as we had in the Genoa Conference. Do you see any reason, therefore, why Mr. Child could not be
instructed to attend the Venice meeting, if the Conference takes place
there, in the same capacity as he attended the Genoa meeting? In this
way he could refrain from taking part in territorial discussions but would
be ready to make known this Government's views in the settlement of
important problems affecting American interests.

Here Mr. Philips mentioned the letter of the President, of September 19, deprecating American participation in discussions relating to the current situation in Turkey. " I have not taken up

---

am giving the subject close attention and shall talk with you soon." 711.67/44.
The United States did not follow this advice.

with the President," continued Philips, " the question of our informal representation, preferring to await your return, but I have called to the President's attention Mr. Harvey's telegram of September 21. . . ." [26]

This question was not decided by the President until October 25. In the meantime, the British government continued to urge American participation in the settlement, particularly with regard to the Straits. Curzon, on October 12, took particular pains in a long interview with Ambassador Harvey to make the point that American interests would be well served by active participation in any negotiations in the forthcoming Conference that touched on the Straits. He said he earnestly hoped that the United States government would take as active a part as possible in the Conference under the traditional American policy of detachment from purely European affairs. He understood perfectly that the United States was under no obligation to assist in replacing the Treaty of Sèvres nor would he think of pressing this, but he thought that the United States could justly claim the right, and might properly wish, to take part in drawing up a plan for securing the free passage of the Straits. From what he had heard from Washington he believed the government did in fact feel disposed to participate. The co-operation of the United States would actually make the securing of the freedom of the Straits easier. He was prepared, he said, if the United States indicated a wish to participate, to request the other Powers to issue an invitation. Harvey asked if he should understand that Curzon wished to be informed whether the United States would be inclined to take part in the Conference only insofar as it touched on the Straits, on the clear understanding that the American representatives would not join in discussing other topics. Curzon replied that Harvey had taken his meaning precisely.

Harvey cabled his report on the conversation to the Department at once. [27] The reply came on October 20. He was informed that the subject of American participation was " receiving careful consideration " and that instructions would be sent as soon as possible. In the meantime he was to hold the question " entirely in abeyance " and to give no encouragement to the idea of American

[26] 767.68/375A.
[27] Telegram 460 from London, October 12, 1922; 767.68119/20.

participation.[28] Harvey mentioned in a cable of October 21, dealing with other matters, that Curzon had been asking him, without pressing and entirely informally, whether he had received an answer from the Department to the inquiry about American participation.

During this period, the Near East Division had been preparing studies of American interests as they were likely to be affected by a Near East settlement, and on October 11 a memorandum drawn up by Allen Dulles was sent to the Secretary suggesting that the time might be appropriate to negotiate a new treaty with Turkey since the Allies would probably be doing so in the near future. This raised the question of American participation in the forthcoming Conference, said the memorandum, though the position of the United States in the settlement was very different from that of the Allies. American interests in Turkey fell under seven categories, according to the memorandum: capitulations, commerce, education and missionary activity, claims, the Straits, minorities, and international financial control of Turkey.[29]

The Division was instructed to expand this memorandum and a second version was sent to the Secretary on the sixteenth which went more fully into the implications of the points raised.[30] This was approved by the Secretary who then had the Division draft a letter to the President embodying the substance of the memoranda. On October 24 Secretary Hughes, using the draft, wrote a long letter to the President setting forth in detail the position of the United States as interpreted by the Department of State and its recommendations for action to protect American interests, and requesting the President's approval of the Department's interpretation of the United States position and its recommendations. This letter was the culmination of two years' bitter experience in Middle East affairs and shows a considerable advance in sophistication over previous analyses. It formed the basis of all subsequent American policy, at the Conference between the Allies and Turkey and during the negotiations for the Turkish-American treaty.

The Allies were about to hold a Conference with the Turkish Nationalists to negotiate a treaty of peace, said the Secretary. The

[28] Telegram 316 to London, October 20, 1922; 767.68119/20.
[29] Memorandum, October 11, 1922; 767.68119/197.
[30] 767.68119/197.

United States was not at war with Turkey, and thus would not be a party to the negotiations, but the Conference would take up many questions affecting American interests. He was sending, therefore, a brief statement of the considerations involved. American treaty rights were, in the main, defined in the treaty of 1830. There were two other agreements in force, the extradition treaty of 1874 and the real estate agreement of the same year. In order for relations to be established with the new regime in Turkey, it must either recognize these treaties or enter into negotiations for a new treaty. The 1830 treaty had long been inadequate, and the only way adequately to protect American interests would be a new treaty. At the same time, negotiations for a new treaty would be greatly influenced, if not practically controlled in considerable measure, by the results of the negotiations between the Allies and Turkey.

The Secretary's letter then turned to the specific American interests involved. First were American rights under the Capitulations. In view of conditions in Turkey, said the Secretary, it would be desirable to hold intact our rights, but the Turkish Nationalists were strongly opposed to the Capitulations as derogating from Turkish sovereignty, and were disposed to insist on their abrogation, or at least their limitation; to the extent that the Allies surrendered their capitulatory rights it would be difficult for the United States to maintain its own rights. The United States could of course demand that they be left intact and refuse to recognize the Turkish government if this were denied, but if that government were recognized by other Powers, the United States "would be left in an unpleasant situation of indefinite continuance." There was also a danger that individual Powers would bargain away specific rights for special privileges, which would leave American interests at their mercy. Under the best of conditions it would be difficult to maintain all American capitulary rights; under the present circumstances the United States should endeavor to insist on retaining the most essential rights: (1) The right to come and go in Turkey, to navigate Turkish waters, and to trade in all legal goods. (2) Freedom of religion for Americans and the right to follow their own customs and habits. (3) The right of foreigners to be judged by their own ambassadors or consuls in civil and criminal suits among themselves. (4) The right to have present in Turkish courts a consular dragoman in suits between Turks and foreigners. (5) The inviolability of domicile. (6) The right to bequeath by will. (7) The right to hold property. Other rights under the Capitulations were economic or related to taxation, customs, etc., which the United States could relinquish in return for most-favored-nation treatment.

Second was the protection of American educational and philanthropic institutions. This, said the Secretary, would depend to a great extent on the degree to which the Capitulations were retained, but it would also require special undertakings by the Turkish government allowing these institutions to operate effectively and recognizing them individually. Third was the protection of American commercial rights. The Allies had entered into several agreements for the protection of their own trade, for example, the Tripartite agreement for the partition of Turkey into zones of economic interest; these agreements could have a detrimental effect on American trade, and the United States should aim at the abandonment of spheres of influence and the establishment of a definite policy of the Open Door. There should also be no discriminatory taxation. Fourth, claims for damages against Turkey should include indemnities for all losses suffered due to illegal action by the Turkish authorities since 1914. Fifth, the protection of minorities would be demanded of the American government by national sentiment. However, due to deportations only a scattered remnant of the Christian population of Turkey remained and it would be difficult to formulate a program to protect them. The best solution might be an exchange of populations. As for Armenia, when conditions in Russia were more settled it might be possible to establish a national home in the Russian Caucasus.

Sixth was the very important question of the freedom of the Straits. There were two aspects to this, conditions in time of war and in time of peace. There should be little difficulty in arrangements for the passage of merchant ships in time of peace, said the Secretary. The best guarantee for maintenance of this freedom if Turkey controlled Constantinople and east Thrace would be the right of warships to free passage of the Straits, so that American ships could be sent to Constantinople to protect American interests and also pass into the Black Sea, which should not be under the exclusive control of Turkey and Russia. In time of war, the regime of the Straits would present an entirely different situation, and, the Secretary said, he did not suggest that the United States become involved in any arrangement for the maintenance of the freedom of the Straits in time of war if the great powers were involved.[31] Last was the question of the international control of Turkey's finances. United States financial interests might be asked by the Turks for loans, and proper consideration should be given whether such loans should be included in the consolidated loans so that the United States might claim a place on the Financial Commission and thus have more influence on Turkish finances.

The Secretary summed up by saying that, generally speaking, the United States was not a party to the Near East settlement, but the Allies and Turkey could not conduct their treaty negotiations without touching on American interests, and it would be taking a serious risk to permit the Allies and Turkey to negotiate without the American position being presented and assurances obtained. This would require continuous and expert observation at the Conference, and the United States should, before it took place, formulate, in identical notes or memoranda to the several powers, the American position outlined in the letter. As for American relations with Turkey itself, the United States and Turkey were not at war, but diplomatic relations were broken and therefore a treaty would be needed, which the government should be ready to negotiate whenever it seemed necessary or advisable.[32]

On the day after this letter was sent, the President saw Hughes, and after some discussion Harding approved the proposals sub-

[31] The General Board of the Navy sent, on November 10, 1922, to the Secretary of the Navy, at the latter's request, its recommendations on the policy which should be followed by the United States on the freedom of navigation of the Straits in the light of the present and future situation in the Near East and present and future American interests there. The Board recommended: (a) that the United States be represented on an international control commission if one were established; (b) that the Straits be open to the free navigation of the merchant vessels of all nations; (c) that the United States enjoy all the privileges granted to any other nation; (d) that the Straits be open to the free navigation of ships of war of all flags; (e) that no belligerent rights be exercised or hostile acts committed within the Straits; (f) that all fortifications be razed and no new ones erected. Basic American policy had of course been established by the time the Board submitted its recommendations, but they reinforced the Department of State's position. *Foreign Relations*, 1923, II, 893–97.

[32] 767.68119/62A.

mitted and agreed that they be used as the basis of memoranda giving a statement of the nature and scope of American interests to be communicated to the powers concerned. He also approved of the proposal that the United States be represented at the Conference by observers and that the United States negotiate a treaty with Turkey at the first appropriate opportunity.[33] Instructions were sent to London, Paris, and Rome, by cable on October 27, to hand to the respective foreign ministers an *aide-memoire*, the text of which was given in the cable, embodying in outline the points raised in Hughes's letter, except for that referring to international financial control, and adding that the United States was prepared to send observers to the Peace Conference to present the position of the United States government. The *aides-memoire* also referred to

the attitude of the United States Government in respect to secret treaties and agreements. It is not felt that arrangements previously made with respect to Turkish territory which provide for the establishment of zones of special commercial and economic influence, such, for example, as the Tripartite Agreement of 1920, are consonant with the principle of the equality of economic opportunity. It is assumed that the Allied Powers will not now desire, and do not now intend, to carry into effect previous arrangements of this nature.[34]

Simultaneously, cables were sent to the embassies giving in some detail, and following identically in form, the substance of the letter to the President and the decisions reached in the discussion of October 25 as to the actions to be taken by the United States. Added to the seven points in the letter was an eighth, also mentioned in the *aide-memoire*, referring to the adequate provision for opportunities to carry out archeological research. The embassies were instructed that they might orally make " guarded use," in submitting the *aide-memoire*, of the references in this cable to American interests in the Conference, the presence of American observers, the purpose of the *aide-memoire*, and Points 1, 2, 3, 4, 5 and 8; " most careful use " of the section of Point 6 referring to American interest in the peacetime passage of the Straits; and not to discuss at all Point 7 referring to the financial control of Turkey, nor the general observations of the Secretary.[35]

[33] 767.68119/56A.
[34] *Foreign Relations*, 1923, II, 884–85.
[35] *Ibid*., pp. 886–88.

London was also instructed, in taking up the *aide-memoire* with Curzon, to express the Secretary's " appreciation of the friendly, courteous and informal manner in which he has discussed [the Near East settlement] with you." [36]

When the President had decided on American representation at the Conference, on October 25, a carefully guarded and completely informal intimation had been made to the British Embassy of this fact. On October 27 the British, French, and Italian Embassies addressed identical notes to the Department stating that they would "welcome the presence of a United States representative at Lausanne in a similar capacity [to] or a more active capacity" than that of the American representative at the San Remo Conference of 1920.[37] The response in London to the *aide-memoire* was very favorable, in Paris moderately so, and in Rome no response at all was made. Harvey in London reported that at the interview on October 30 at which it had been handed to the Foreign Secretary, Curzon had "chatted freely" about the contents of the *aide-memoire*, agreeing fully with the points made in it. He made particular reference to the Straits and the Capitulations; repeated what he had said on October 12 about the American interests in the freedom of the Straits, and said he still hoped the American government would see its way to participate fully in working out a new regime. According to Harvey's report, Curzon's views on the capitulations were identical with those of the United States, and he had added that he had been " gravely concerned" by the French attitude on the Capitulations.[38]

When the *aide-memoire* was handed to Poincaré, he commented only on the Capitulations and the Tripartite agreement, refraining, said Herrick's report, " intentionally and with his habitual reserve from unnecessary discussion or comment." The formal French reply, made on November 2 (the *aide-memoire* had been presented on October 30), stated that the French government would take every precaution during the conference for the protecton of American interests inasmuch as the interests of the Allied Powers, particularly France, were similar to those of the United States. But, it went on to say, this undertaking would not be easy since Angora showed every evidence of refusing to grant

[36] Telegram 333 to London, October 28, 1922; 767.68119/20.
[37] *Foreign Relations*, 1923, II, 889.
[38] *Ibid.*, pp. 890–91.

former privileges. The French government also declared that it had not had at any time a wish to conclude secret pacts detrimental to American interests.[39] The Embassy at Rome cabled that " under existing political conditions " it was impossible to make contact with responsible Italian officials to amplify the *aide-memoire*, which had been duly delivered. There is no record that any reply was made by the Italian government. This was, of course, the time of the march on Rome.[40] When the oral replies from the two governments were sent to the President on November 1 he remarked, referring particularly to Curzon's statement, that American policy was given a better reception abroad than among the extremists at home.[41]

5.

The history of the American role in the negotiation of the Treaty of Lausanne is uncomplicated and straightforward, and as it has been related more than adequately elsewhere,[42] it will be but briefly covered here. During the first phase of the negotiations from the opening of the conference on November 20, 1922, until the breakdown in February, 1923, the function of the American delegation—headed by the Ambassador in Italy, Child, with the Minister in Switzerland, Grew, as the second delegate—was to present to the Conference the American position as outlined in their instructions based on the Secretary's letter to the President, to be ready to submit objections to decisions injurious to American interests, but not to take part in actual negotiations or to vote in the sessions of the Conference. The weight of the American delegation was thrown behind the Allies on the question of the Straits and the maintenance of the Capitulations, but when it came to

[39] *Ibid.*, pp. 891–92.
[40] *Ibid.*, pp. 889–90.
[41] 767.68119/94.
[42] See, J. C. Grew, *Turbulent Era* (Boston, 1952), I, 475–585. For the official correspondence, see *Foreign Relations*, 1923, II, 879–1039. For the record of the Allied negotiations with the Turks, see *Documents Diplomatiques, Conference de Lausanne sur les affaires du Proche-Orient (1922–1923), Recueil des actes de la Conference* (Paris, 1923); Cmd. 1814, Turkey No. 1 (1923). See also Earl of Ronaldshay, *The Life of Lord Curzon* (London, 1928), III, 259 ff.; and Harold Nicholson, *Curzon, the Last Phase, 1919–1925* (New York, 1939), pp. 246–350.

the Open Door, the position taken by the United States greatly strengthened the hand of Ismet Pasha, the head of the Turkish delegation, in opposing the attempts of the Allies to retain what they could of the economic privileges of the Treaty of Sèvres.

The Conference broke down on February 5, 1923, over the juridical and economic clauses of the draft treaty submitted by the Allies which the Turks refused to accept. Certain of the economic clauses were also objectionable to the United States, and on February 4 Ambassador Child addressed an informal note to Lord Curzon, the head of the British delegation, stating that these provisions were " ambiguous and might be interpreted in such a way as to work injustice to various national and private interests." The United States had not been given an adequate opportunity to state its attitude on the provisions, said Child, and the delegation was therefore somewhat anxious about them. He felt, however, that the difficulty could be met by inserting an additional clause with a blanket provision that all conflicting claims arising under these provisions be settled by arbitration.[43] Curzon left Lausanne before the letter was answered and the British Embassy in Washington took the matter further on March 17 by suggesting to the Department that the offending clauses mentioned in Child's letter to Lord Curzon be specified. The Department replied on March 31 that

without undertaking an exhaustive survey of the economic and financial sections of the Lausanne draft treaty, it may be stated that the provisions which Ambassador Child had chiefly in mind in his letter of February 4 were such as appeared to have possible bearing upon rights or concessions granted or alleged to have been granted before the war or more recently by the Turkish authorities at Constantinople or Angora.

The specific articles containing these provisions were articles Ninety-four, Ninety-six, and Ninety-seven. Article Ninety-four confirmed concessions if they had been put into operation or had formed the object of agreements between the Ottoman government and an Allied government " notwithstanding the non-fulfillment by Turkey of all the conditions requisite for their final confirmation." Article Ninety-six applied the same provisions to concessions granted in territories since detached from Turkey. Article Ninety-seven stated that the Allies would not be bound

[43] *Foreign Relations*, 1923, II, 968.

by the validity of any grant or transfer of any concession, in territory detached from Turkey, made by the Ottoman government or local Turkish authority since October 29, 1914. " This Government considers," said the American note, " that it would be unfortunate for the Allied Powers to insist upon the insertion in the treaty of any provision designed to confer upon Allied nationals . . . rights which were more extensive than those which were acquired under or by virtue of the conventions, contracts, agreements, or decisions in question." With respect to Article Ninety-seven, the note stated that the impairment by the operation of this Article of any rights acquired by American nationals in good faith could not be admitted.[44]

The Allied response was to attempt to exclude the United States from participation in the Conference when it was reopened in April. When the Allies, in the latter part of March, convened to consider their reply to the Turkish counterproposals, the Department instructed the embassies to request the respective governments for information on the discussions. These requests were met with a complete silence and the results of the discussions were not known in Washington until they were published in the press on April 2.[45] The United States, however, took the position that the Conference had merely been postponed in February, and when the renewal of negotiations at Lausanne was announced Minister Grew was instructed to attend as observer on the same basis as and in the same capacity he and Ambassador Child had enjoyed in the earlier discussions.[46] The French Foreign Office had second thoughts and made a little political capital by telling the Paris Embassy informally that Curzon had intimated to France and Italy that the United States need not be invited to the renewed Conference. France and Italy wished to do so, said the Foreign Office, and asked if the United States desired to be formally notified of the opening date of the conference.[47] The Department cabled

---

[44] *Ibid.*, pp. 972–74.
[45] See *ibid.*, pp. 974–80, for a memorandum by Dulles to the Secretary of State giving a summary of events from February 4 to the date of the memorandum, April 4, 1923.
[46] *Ibid.*, pp. 981–86.
[47] Telegram 195 from Paris, April 12, 1923; 767.68119/536.

the Embassy that it could ask the Foreign Office for information on the " resumption " of the Conference.[48]

Though the necessity of insisting on the American right to attend was thus avoided, the British delegation—or rather its head, Rumboldt—proceeded to put every obstacle in the way of effective American participation in the discussions and attempted to exclude the American delegation from meetings of subcommittees and other working groups while denying it full information on the progress of the discussions. Grew, however, found out all he needed to know from the other delegates, except on economic matters in which all the delegations had an interest. The Conference had been in session for several weeks when, on June 5, Grew was informed by Ismet Pasha that he was under pressure from the Allies to accept the treaty provisions confirming unperfected concessions. Grew went to the British, French, and Italian delegations and was told that they were indeed pressing for such provisions.[49] The Department instructed Grew to present to the Conference the American position as set down in the memorandum to the British Embassy on March 31; [50] at the same time instructions were sent to London and Paris to make similar representations to the respective foreign offices. The Allies made certain minor changes in the wording of the Articles concerned, but these were not satisfactory to the United States and Grew continued to press for the complete elimination of the provisions while urging Ismet to stand firm against the Allied demands.[51] Eventually, by the combined efforts of the Turkish and American delegations, the United States' point of view prevailed and the Treaty of Lausanne contained no provision for special economic privileges.

The final terms agreed upon by the Allies and Turkey and incorporated in the Treaty of Lausanne, signed on July 24, 1923, represented a partial achievement of American goals as set down in the Secretary's letter of October 24. The chief failure was the Capitulations; they were completely abrogated—though Allied nationals were to be given the right, for a period of seven years

[48] Circular telegram to Paris, London, Rome, Berne, and Constantinople, April 13, 1923; 767.68119/536.
[49] *Foreign Relations*, 1923, II, 1016–18.
[50] *Ibid.*, pp. 1019–20.
[51] *Ibid.*, pp. 1021 ff.

from the ratification of the treaty, to submit cases involving their own personal status or domestic relations to courts in their own countries for settlement; and the Turks agreed to appoint European legal advisers to assist in the reform of the legal system, to observe and report on the operation of the Turkish courts on behalf of the Ministry of Justice, and to receive complaints of the operation of the legal system. American policy on the Open Door was a complete success; the Allies agreed to the principle of equality of opportunity, no mention was made of spheres of influence, and the status of concessions was not mentioned. The provisions relating to the Straits fulfilled the most important American requirement in accepting the principle of freedom of transit by sea and air in peace and in war. The Straits were to be demilitarized, though in place of a system of guarantee by treaties with the individual powers—as the United States wished and in which the United States could take part—an International Straits Commission was entrusted with the carrying out of the Straits Convention under the auspices of the League of Nations, thus effectively barring American membership in the Commission should the United States have decided to participate. Philanthropic, educational, and religious institutions were recognized by Turkey and were to be put on an equal footing with Turkish institutions. Turkey agreed to guarantee full religious freedom for all minorities, protection of life and property, and civil and legal equality with Muslims; these guarantees were placed under the guarantee of the League of Nations.[52]

6.

From the point of view of the United States, the Treaty of Lausanne was merely a prelude to a Turkish-American treaty. Though it was true that the results of the negotiations between the Allies and the Turks would, to a large extent, determine the content of the Turkish-American treaty, yet it was this treaty that made the negotiations at Lausanne of more than academic interest to the United States. It will be recalled that the Nationalists had made several approaches to the United States for the renewal of

[52] Texts of the Treaty and the supplementary agreements are in Cmd. 1929, and League of Nations, *Treaty Series*, XXVIII.

relations and had been told that, as Turkey had broken relations, the onus of restoring them was on Turkey. The rapid fluctuations in the status of the Angora government had, from the American point of view, precluded any definite advance in relations until after the victory over the Greeks, the establishment of the authority of the Angora government over all Asiatic Turkey, and the acknowledgment by the Allied Powers of this authority. The final seal on the right of the Angora government to act as the sole voice of Turkey was the flight of the Sultan from Constantinople on a British destroyer in November, 1922. There was now no bar to the United States treating the Nationalists as the legal government of Turkey.[53]

The first cable sent by the American delegation at Lausanne on November 19, 1922, included a request for instructions on the discretion left to the delegation to " engage in preliminary and informal discussions with Turkish delegates tending toward basis for treaty after recognition of Angora." [54] The Department replied that there was no objection to holding informal conversations, but it should be kept in mind that no authority existed to make any commitments.[55] The first approach was made by the Turks some days after the opening of the Conference. Jalal ad-Din, the second Turkish delegate, had, even before the Conference opened, called on Child at Rome on his way to Lausanne and outlined the Turkish position. On November 22 he called on the American delegation at Lausanne and discussed again his government's aims. In both of these conversations Jalal had emphasized the desire of Turkey for American participation in its economic development, particularly in oil, and had assured his listeners that American interests would be fully respected by Turkey.[56] The question of a treaty was first raised by Ismet Pasha in a conversation with Child on November 29. He showed " haste and eagerness " to enter into preliminary negotiations, said the cabled report, and it was evident that the Turkish delegation desired some assurance that whether peace were signed or the negotiations broke down, the United States would be willing

[53] See, Grew, *Turbulent Era*, I, 586–605; the official correspondence is in *Foreign Relations*, 1923, II, 1040–1190.

[54] *Ibid.*, p. 1041.

[55] *Ibid.*, pp. 1041–42.

[56] *Ibid.*, pp. 1040–41.

to start negotiations with them. Child told Ismet that any prospect of negotiations with the United States must not be allowed to interfere with the current negotiations. The American delegation had no hesitation in stating its various positions, said Child, but would make no commitments; conversely it would be glad to hear what the Turkish delegation had in mind as the ground work for future negotiations. The American position, in this matter of American-Turkish negotiations, was very delicate in relation to the Allies, added Child, and he would not hesitate to make the American attitude known to them, which in fact had already been done.[57]

The Turks were anxious to persuade the United States to begin negotiations at once and conclude a treaty before the treaty with the Allies was completed, apparently because they believed it would be much less difficult to obtain terms acceptable to Turkey from a nation acting alone; the agreement thus obtained could then be used in the negotiations with the Allies. Toward the end of December a member of the Turkish delegation, in a confidential interview with the American mission, intimated that the American position in Turkey would perhaps suffer if a treaty with the Allies were signed first. When he was told that the present intention of the United States was not to sign first, he replied that the Open Door would be reserved for the United States in any case, but made it very clear that early applicants for economic privileges would take precedence over later ones.[58] In Constantinople, Adnan bey, the Nationalist Governor and well-known as a pro-American (his wife was Halide Hanum, a graduate of the American-sponsored Women's College), told the Acting High Commissioner that he saw no reason why a treaty of peace should not be negotiated at once between the United States and Turkey. It was desirable from the Turkish point of view, he said, that negotiations be commenced immediately through the delegation at Lausanne; there was only one difficulty, the Capitulations, since on this the Turkish government could make no concessions as its position in the country and with the Grand National Assembly was based on the repudiation of the Capitulations.[59] The Department cabled that it presumed Adnan was aware the United

[57] Telegram 37 from Lausanne, November 29, 1922; 711.67/30.

[58] *Foreign Relations*, 1923, II, 1042–43.

[59] Telegram 399 from Constantinople, December 28, 1922; 711.672/5.

States and Turkey had never been at war and therefore no treaty of peace was necessary.[60]

In January, 1923, when it appeared that the completion of a draft Allied-Turkish treaty was approaching, the Department cabled the mission requesting specific recommendations on whether it would be desirable to enter on direct negotiations with the Turks as soon as they received the Allied draft treaty. A treaty of amity and commerce, continued the cable, should provide for the resumption of diplomatic and consular representation and for most-favored-nation treatment, as well as for matters of particular interest to both countries. Following the pattern of the treaties recently concluded with the Central Powers, the treaty with Turkey could refer specifically to certain provisions of the Allied-Turkish treaty and contain a provision that the United States and its citizens should enjoy all rights conceded to the Allies.[61] The mission replied that it thought the time was opportune to begin negotiations and asked for a summary of the treaty terms considered desirable by the Department.[62] The Department informed the mission that precise instructions would be sent and in the meantime the mission was authorized to approach the Turks informally.[63] On January 15, therefore, in the course of a conversation with Ismet, a member of the mission " mentioned to him indirectly and cautiously the question of initiating discussions looking toward a Turkish-American treaty of amity and commerce." Ismet said positively that he was ready to begin the discussions at any time, preferably at once, but the mission told him it did not consider it desirable to begin negotiations until there was a definite prospect that a treaty would be signed between the Allies and Turkey.[64]

With the breakdown in the negotiations between the Allies and Turkey and the withdrawal of the various delegations from Lausanne, talks between the Turks and Americans also lapsed and were not resumed until the reconvening of the conference in the following April. Shortly after Ismet arrived in Lausanne, on April 22, he met Grew, who was now the head of the American delegation, and the two discussed, among other things, the re-opening of negotiations for a Turkish-American treaty. " Ismet

[60] Telegram 301 to Constantinople, December 30, 1922; 711.672/5.
[61] Foreign Relations, 1923, II, 1043. [63] Ibid., p. 1044.
[62] Ibid., pp. 1043–44. [64] Ibid., pp. 1044–45.

exhibits a strong desire to enter at once upon negotiations looking toward a treaty with the United States," cabled Grew to the Department.

He argues that an early settlement with the Allies would be promoted by a prior agreement with us. He regards the Chester concession as the initiation of economic relations with the United States which he hopes will become more intimate. His idea is to restore diplomatic and consular relations under a treaty of friendship and commerce, which would be supplemented by declaratory pledges from the Turkish Government offering protection of American missions and schools in accordance with Turkish law and guaranteeing fair treatment of Americans in trade and the courts.[65]

Grew had a second interview with Ismet on the twenty-seventh at which the latter inquired "urgently" whether positive instructions had been received from the Department of State regarding the treaty. Grew replied that the government of the United States was awaiting "with expectancy" an opportune moment for making a treaty, but he could not suggest a time for beginning negotiations as that was contingent on a number of other matters. He said that the Capitulations would present a very difficult problem in discussing the terms of the treaty. The United States government had never recognized the unilateral abrogation of the capitulatory regime, and, though it recognized the necessity of revising the old treaties, "some appropriate arrangement, however temporary, as a substitute for the capitulatory regime" would be necessary.[66] Grew cabled the Department on April 29 suggesting that he offer to proceed to negotiate with the Turks on the understanding that the treaty would not be signed until after the treaty with the Allies.[67] The Department approved,[68] and on May 1 Grew informed Ismet and each of the Allied heads of delegation that the United States was now prepared to negotiate a treaty with the Turks; that such a treaty would be signed only after the Turks had reached a settlement with the Allies, and after the conventions referring to the rights of foreigners and foreign institutions and a declaration on the rights of minorities, to be annexed to the Allied-Turkish treaty, had been drawn up to the satisfaction of the United States; and that the United

[65] *Ibid.*, p. 987.
[66] *Ibid.*, pp. 989–91.
[67] *Ibid.*, pp. 993–94.
[68] *Ibid.*, pp. 994.

States was prepared to assist in framing these instruments and would be disposed to conclude similar ones with Turkey.[69]

On May 5 Ismet addressed a formal note to the American mission suggesting that negotiations begin. (The United States still maintained its position that the Turks should initiate any move for the resumption of relations.) [70] Grew was instructed to reply to the note in terms which would not commit the United States to negotiations until after informal talks had indicated there existed a satisfactory basis for agreement.[71] When this was presented to Ismet he seemed to be disappointed, Grew reported, but agreed to consult his experts on the details of the terms.[72] On May 16 the American and Turkish experts met for the first time, on the understanding that the discussion was unofficial and not binding on either side. The American position, which had been sent to the delegation on January 18 when it seemed possible that the Allied-Turkish treaty would be shortly concluded, was based on the general outlines of the standard treaties recently concluded with Japan and Siam with seven additional points covering matters not touched on in these treaties: protection of philanthropic and religious enterprises; special arrangements providing for customs dues, taxation, personal immunities, and judicial reform as a substitute for the capitulations; free navigation of the Straits; compensation for losses and requisitions; facilities for archeological investigations; protection of minorities; and the regulation of naturalization.[73]

The Turkish position was put to the Americans in a lengthy exposition by Mustafa Sherif, one of the Turkish experts in the delegation. "It was apparent that on every matter discussed the attitude of the Turkish expert was one of great reserve," reported the mission. "His remarks did not have that tone of generous and even cordial sympathy often shown by Turkish officials at Constantinople and Angora, as well as by the Turkish delegates here when considering affairs of interest to America." (It was one thing to be generous and cordial when it was a question of obtaining American support for the Turkish stand against the Allies, and another when there was face-to-face bargaining to be done.) The basis of the Turkish viewpoint was that " an

[69] *Ibid.*, pp. 997–99.
[70] *Ibid.*, pp. 1055–57.
[71] *Ibid.*, pp. 1057–59.
[72] *Ibid.*, p. 1059.
[73] *Ibid.*, pp. 1045–46.

express recognition of the abolition of the capitulations " was " a fundamental condition of negotiation." The treaty of 1830 was regarded as cancelled, since the prewar treaties, which were all capitulary, were voided on the abolition of the Capitulations. Turkey did not admit that there were any valid claims against it for wartime injury to American property; claims for requisitions would be considered when receipts were presented. There was considerable reluctance to agree to any reference to the Open Door in the treaty or the principle of equality of commercial opportunity, and in place of most-favored-nation treatment the Turks offered the same privileges as the Allies were granted. It was the intention of the Turks to make separate customs conventions with individual powers for favors received, contrary to previous practice. Though they were willing to admit American consuls to trials of American citizens, they would not agree to make any express promise of this in the treaty, even on the basis of reciprocity, and refused also to admit the right of Americans to be tried in courts located in the principal cities.[74] The Department of State, on receiving the mission's report of this exchange, cabled, " The Department realizes that the Turks will not be disposed to make concessions without resistance and it has no illusions as to the difficulties of negotiating with them." The mission might find it desirable, the cable said, to obtain assurances directly from Ismet on two points which the Department considered to be " fundamental and without which it would be most difficult to successfully continue negotiations." These points were that Turkey should be ready to grant to the United States the same privileges granted to the Allies, and that Turkey accept, in principle, most-favored-nation treatment. The Department also noted its concern at the Turkish proposals for separate customs conventions and suggested that the mission discuss the matter with the Allied delegations, calling to their attention the dangers inherent in such a system and proposing that the United States and the Allies insist on most-favored-nation treatment to keep the Turks from making special bargains.[75]

Formal negotiations began on June 1 and continued for two months. On August 6, 1923, the treaty was signed; a copy of the declaration concerning the administration of justice which had

[74] *Ibid.*, pp. 1061–62.　　　　　　　[75] *Ibid.*, pp. 1065–66.

been made to the Allies was handed to Grew by Ismet on August 4, and on the same day an undertaking covering American educational, philanthropic and religious institutions was made by Ismet on behalf of his government. Both governments agreed in the abrogation of the Capitulations; the personal status of Americans was to be subject to American courts situated outside Turkey exclusively, and American citizens were to benefit by the execution of the declaration regarding the administration of justice. American merchant and war vessels and aircraft were to enjoy complete freedom of navigation and passage of the Straits on a most-favored-nation basis under the rules established by the Straits Convention, though the United States assumed no obligations of any kind toward the implementation of the Convention. Most-favored-nation treatment was mutually assumed in navigation and commerce, import and export duties, consumption and export taxes, transit dues and the protection of trademarks and patents. Consular officers were to be received by both parties under the rules of international law and according to provisions, where applicable, similar to those prevailing in treaties between the United States and other countries. In each country taxes on the individuals and corporations of one country in the other were to be, respectively, the same as those assessed against the natives. Citizens of one country in the territory of the other were to be exempt from military service, contributions, and forced loans. The domiciles and other buildings of the citizens of the two countries could be entered and searched in accordance with the law applicable to natives. The citizens of the two countries could enter or leave each other's territories, subject to their respective laws, with complete liberty, and while in the territory were to have full freedom of their persons and property; liberty of conscience and worship; access to the courts; the right to possess and dispose of movable property; similar rights with respect to immovable property, insofar as foreigners were allowed them by local law; the right to engage in business and the professions, also subject to local law. American philanthropic, educational, and religious institutions in Turkey recognized by the Turkish authorities before October 30, 1914, were to be recognized by the Turkish authorities. Those established since then and not recognized would have their position examined with a view to regularizing their position. All recognized institutions were to receive the same treatment as Turkish institutions, but they were also to be subject, equally with Turkish institutions, to Turkish laws and regulations.[76]

The measure of success of American policy in the negotiations with the Turks is best summed up by Grew, the principal American negotiator. " The Treaty of amity and commerce which we have signed today with the Turkish delegation," said Grew in a letter to the Secretary of State of August 6, 1923,

is far from what I should have wished to have it. It represents a considerably greater number of concessions on our part to meet the Turkish point of view than concessions on their part to meet ours. Among other concessions we have given up the articles on naturalization and claims, we have failed to obtain the desired modifications in the Judicial Declaration and we have failed to obtain any provision whatever with regard to minorities. On the other hand, it was we who laid the original draft treaty before the Turks. Had they first submitted their own draft, the principal concessions would doubtless have been on the other side of the column. Our obtaining most-favored-nation treatment in the established articles was perhaps the most important principle gained. . . .[77]

(The question of claims [78] and naturalization were not eliminated entirely from the scope of the American-Turkish settlement but were left to later negotiation rather than included in the treaty.)

The Treaty of Lausanne was defeated by the Senate. The elements that had urged the Department of State and the United States government to intervene on behalf of the Greeks in 1922 brought great pressure on the Senate not to give its consent to a treaty with Turkey that did not provide for the restoration of the Capitulations, generous privileges for Christians, and an independent Armenia. But the treaty had been based on the realities of the situation, and these realities remained. The negotiations at Lausanne had clarified them and translated them into formal diplomatic terms acceptable to both parties to the negotiations, and though this formal interpretation of the realities of the relations between Turkey and the United States was never implemented, the defeat of the treaty by the Senate had relatively little effect on these relations themselves. The treaty in effect merely

---

[76] *Ibid.*, pp. 1153–66. An Extradition Treaty was signed on the same day; pp. 1167–71.

[77] *Ibid.*, pp. 1148–50.

[78] *Ibid.*, pp. 1172–97.

laid down the rules for dealing with specific cases in the light of present circumstances, and it was here that the absence of a treaty was most severely felt, both on the public and private levels. However, this situation was gradually repaired over the next several years. Diplomatic relations were restored by the exchange of notes, and commercial relations and the status of persons were regularized by executive agreements, which did not require the consent of the Senate. Once again, after ten years, the United States could look with equanimity on events in the Middle East— or so the official policy of the United States interpreted the state of the world.

7.

To assess American Middle East policy is not easy. One can say that Wilson's wartime policy was a success, but it was after all a negative policy. As for the Peace Conference and the American attempt to influence events in the Middle East, Wilson's policies were never brought to a conclusion. Much of the postwar settlement in the Middle East was negotiated with European powers, and the political relationships that determined the settlements were, with the exception of that with the new Turkey, based on European not Middle Eastern political factors. Again, this study is concerned with a part only of American policy of the period, and it is valueless, though tempting, to make absolute judgments on one policy without knowing the effect the requirements of other policies had on its formulation. Thus Wilson's policy on the Greek occupation of Smyrna cannot be understood without an understanding of his problems with the Italian claims to Fiume, and while it was necessary in this study to take into account the Fiume dispute, it was not possible to pay it full justice. Therefore, no attempt has been made here to come to a conclusion on the correctness of Wilson's decision, notwithstanding its tragic results for Turkey and Greece.

But, taking the limited definition of success, the achievement of a given goal, as more appropriate to this study than the certainly more profound and meaningful analysis of the ends of foreign policy, it is possible to come to certain conclusions. First, Wilson's wartime policy on Turkey was eminently correct. It had two aspects, the determination of the significance of Turkey in the war between Germany and the United States, and the attitude taken by the United States towards Allied policy in the Middle East. In the first case, it is evident that American military force was more effectively applied in France than it could have been in the Middle East, and since the United States had no direct political interests in the area there was no reason why military considerations should not control the decision. As for the second case, the relationship between the national interest and the mutual rivalries of the European powers in the Middle East was far too tenuous at the time to form the basis of a policy, and, moreover, any benefits that might be derived from an attempt to come to terms with the secret treaties were far outweighed by the benefits which accrued to the United States from the maintenance of its freedom of action.

When we come to the period of the Peace Conference, the ground is less firm, but not entirely unstable. Wilson's conduct of his Middle East policy during the Conference was masterly; he not only established the nature of the Eastern settlement without even committing the United States to participate in it, he forced the Conference to what was practically a moratorium on Middle Eastern affairs until the United States was ready to consider them; and he accomplished this in the face of the vigorous opposition not only of the Allies but of his own delegation. But Wilson made one great error. He miscalculated the effect of the signature of the Treaty of Versailles on his diplomatic strength vis-à-vis the Allies, and no sooner had he returned to the United States from Paris than the Italians made their definite rejection of any compromise on the Fiume question; the Italians and Greeks, with the encouragement of France and Britain, came to an understanding on Turkey; France and Britain compromised on the distribution of occupation troops in Syria, and France began to cause trouble about the definition of the Class " A " mandates.

The great unanswerable question is whether this deterioration of the American position could have been repaired by American participation in the treaty of peace with Turkey, or through the League of Nations. There were two major factors involved: The Allies had less to gain from American participation in the Eastern settlement than they had in the case of the German settlement, and the United States could not have afforded to have the Treaty of Peace with Turkey diverge markedly in principle from the principles of the League of Nations. There were also two factors of secondary, but more immediate, importance. These were the direct actions taken by the Allies to further their policies in the East, and the growing revulsion of American officials from the " disgusting scramble " of European international politics. Only Wilson at the height of his powers could have salvaged American interests from such a situation, and under the circumstances it was perhaps better that the United States was not involved in the events in the East after September, 1919. When the Senate rejected the Treaty of Versailles the break was clean, at least.

The withdrawal from the eastern settlement was competent, if one disregards the damage done to other interests and the resentments generated thereby, which were, in any case, according to the Senate, of no significance to the interests of the United States. The American requirements in the former territory of the Ottoman Empire were all met by the Allies, and existing rights were protected. However, in negotiating with the Turkish Nationalists at Lausanne, the United States made an error of judgment. It was realized that the result of American negotiations depended on the success of Allied negotiations, and that the United States could expect no more than the Allies received from Ismet Pasha. But the position taken by the United States during the Allied-Turkish negotiations was such as to weaken Allied negotiating strength. Of course, the American observers were on the horns of a dilemma. If they had supported the Allies, the latter would have gained privileges detrimental to American interests, and American support of the Turks was based on this premise. But the American delegation did not seem to recognize that there was a dilemma, and so no efforts were made to solve the problem. Ismet Pasha made full use of the divergence between the Allies and the United States, not only in his negotiations with the Allies but in his relations with the Americans also. He was aided in this by the short-sighted attitude of the United States.

Two things stand out in the history of American Middle East policy. The first is that the ability of the United States to influence events in the Middle East was exactly proportional to the ability and willingness of the United States to coerce the other powers involved in Middle Eastern affairs. The interests of the United States and the Allies in the Eastern settlement were fundamentally in conflict, though from time to time it happened that one of the Allies found it convenient to co-operate with the United States. The several policies of the Allied Powers were based on the secret treaties, the mandate system notwithstanding, and were an extension of the European balance of power in the Middle East. To the United States this was all irrelevant. American interests required that the eastern settlement reinforce the solution of the European problems that had brought about the World War, not perpetuate them. The coercion applied by the United States did not have to be military—it was in fact almost exclusively political or economic—and it did not have to be direct or overt. It did not often take the form of threat or intimidation; usually the possibility of withholding favors accomplished the American purpose. But every success achieved by the United States in advancing the national interest in the Middle East was due to the fact that the United States could present the other power or powers concerned with a choice of either acceding to American wishes or paying a higher price for refusing to do so than it would cost to agree. Where the United States could not do this, American wishes were ignored.

American diplomatic strength at the Peace Conference was based on the freedom of action of the United States, which had very carefully been preserved by Wilson; this meant that the United States was not bound to a common settlement of the war against Germany and could, unlike the Allies who were bound by treaty not to make a separate peace with the Central Powers, make any agreement it chose with Germany. The value to the Allies of American participation in the settlement, and the willingness of the United States to make full use of this value, was demonstrated unmistakably at the very beginning of peace negotiations, during the pre-armistice talks, when House, by threatening the Allied prime ministers with a separate peace with Germany, made the Fourteen Points an integral part of the peace negotiations. After the United States had signed the Treaty of Versailles and the Treaty of Guarantee with France, and was thus apparently committed to the settlement, much of the weight of the American ability to coerce the Allies was lost, and the latter were not slow to take advantage of this.

One of the striking aspects of the postwar settlement in the Middle East was the difference between the negotiations between the United States and the Allies on American rights in the mandated territories on the one hand, and on the other the negotiations between the United States and the new Turkey. From the Allies the United States obtained all its desiderata, for though much of American coercive power had been lost, enough remained to make it worth the while of the Allies to agree in this instance to what the United States required. (This was the period of the negotiations of the War Debts Settlement and the Washington Conference.) But when one compares what the United States hoped in October, 1922, to get from the Turks with what was actually obtained in the following summer, it is obvious that the Turks gave only what they chose to give, for though Turkey was immeasurably weaker than the Allies this fact did not enter into the situation. The United States was not able to bring pressure on Turkey except at a cost that far outweighed the benefits that would be received.

The second notable characteristic of American Middle East policy is that it was conducted almost entirely at one remove from its object. After the break with Turkey in 1917, the United States had almost no direct political contact with the area; though the Diplomatic Agency in Egypt remained active throughout the war, its contacts were with the British authorities rather than the Sultan's Administration. After the war most of the Ottoman Empire was under Allied control. American efforts to influence events in the Middle East were not directed towards local institutions and individuals but to the governments and leaders of the Allies who had the immediate control of the area. When, therefore, Wilson determined that American interests required that the political organization of the postwar Middle East should follow a certain pattern, he had to persuade, or coerce, the Allied Powers to do this for him. This procedure was effective enough when the United States wanted something done in the Middle East; it was not so successful when American interests required that something not be done—for the United States usually learned of the event after it had occurred, and in this case American policy was always on step behind that of the Allies (or for that matter of the Turks or the Arabs).

A serious disadvantage of this method of indirect implementation of policy was that it was based ultimately on the fundamental nature of the relationship between the United States and the state or states to be influenced along a particular line of action, for the

United States could not trade advantages, as could the Allies among themselves, but had to use coercion. Not only did this mean that the procedure followed was often cumbersome and unwieldy, but also that a quite minor issue always had within it the seeds of a major dispute. When the issue was a major one the problem was, of course, proportionately intensified. Thus Wilson was forced to consider the possibility of renouncing the Treaty of Versailles and the Treaty of Guarantee with France over such relatively insignificant questions, insignificant to direct United States interests at least, as the boundary between the Italian and Greek spheres in Anatolia, Clemenceau's obstinacy on the drawing up of the " A " mandates, and the Anglo-Persian treaty. This state of affairs lasted for forty years, from 1918 to 1958. Throughout this time American Middle East policy, with some exceptions—notably the Truman Doctrine, which, however, was actually an extension of United States European policy rather than a Middle East policy—was conducted by remote control and suffered from the same disabilities that Wilson had to contend with. One is tempted to say that the Suez Crisis of 1956, in its effect on American relations with Britain and France, was implicit in this situation. Certainly there were precedents. It is far from improbable that a similar breakdown in relations might have occurred in 1920 had the United States not withdraw from the Eastern settlement, for it almost came to that in the summer of 1919. The problem that Wilson had to consider—whether American interests were worth taking direct action in Middle East politics—was not finally settled until American marines landed in Beirut in July, 1958.

SELECTED BIBLIOGRAPHY

I. *Primary Sources:*

ADAMOV, E. *Die Europaische Machte Wahrend die Weltkrieges—Die Aufteilung des Asiatischen Turkei.* Dresden, 1932.

BAKER, R. S. *Woodrow Wilson and World Settlement.* Garden City, N. Y., 1922.

CHURCHILL, W. S. *The Aftermath.* New York, 1929.

GARNETT, D. *The Letters of T. E. Lawrence.* New York, 1939.

GEORGE, D. LLOYD. *Memoirs of the Paris Peace Conference.* New Haven, 1939.

GREAT BRITAIN. *Documents on British Foreign Policy, 1919–1939.* First Series (ed. E. L. Woodward and R. Butler), H. M. S. O. Vols. III, IV, VII, XII, and XIII, cited as *British Documents.*

GREW, J. C. *Turbulent Era.* New York, 1952.

LANSING, R. *The Peace Negotiations, a Personal Narrative.* New York, 1921.

LAWRENCE, T. E. *The Seven Pillars of Wisdom.* Garden City, N. Y., 1935.

MANTOUX, P. *Les Délibérations du Conseil des Quatres.* Paris, 1955.

MILLER, D. H. *The Drafting of the Covenant.* New York, 1926.

NEVINS, A. and WHITE, HENRY. *Thirty Years of American Diplomacy.* New York, 1930.

NICHOLSON, H. *Peacemaking, 1919.* New York, 1933.

RIDDELL, G. A. *Lord Riddell's Intimate Diary of the Peace Conference and After, 1918–1923.* New York, 1934.

SEYMOUR, C. *The Intimate Papers of Colonel House.* New York, 1928.

SHOTWELL, J. T. *At the Paris Peace Conference.* New York, 1937.

TARDIEU, A. *The Truth About the Treaty.* Indianapolis, 1921.

TEMPERLEY, H. W. V. (ed.). *A History of the Peace Conference at Paris.* Institute of International Affairs, 1920–1924.

U. S. DEPARTMENT OF STATE. *Papers Relating to the Foreign Relations of the United States,* including the annual selections of documents, the Paris Peace Conference series, and the Lansing Papers; cited as *Foreign Relations.*

WEIZMANN, CHAIM. *Trial and Error.* New York [1949].

WILSON, E. B. *My Memoir.* Indianapolis, 1939.

II. *Secondary Sources:*

ALBRECHT-CARRIÉ, R. "Versailles Twenty Years After," *Political Science Quarterly,* LV, 1–24.

———. "New Light on Italian Problems in 1919," *Journal of Modern History,* XIII, 493–516.

———. *Italy at the Paris Peace Conference.* New York, 1938.

ANTONIUS, G. *The Arab Awakening.* London, 1938.

BAILEY, T. A. *Woodrow Wilson and the Lost Peace.* New York, 1944.

BANDER, I. "Sidney Edward Mezes and the Inquiry," *Journal of Modern History,* XI, 199–202.

418

BEDFORD, A. C. "The World Oil Situation," *Foreign Affairs*, I, No. 3, 96–107.
BEER, G. L. *African Questions at the Peace Conference.* New York, 1923.
BEMIS, S. F. *A Diplomatic History of the United States.* New York, 1945.
BINKLEY, R. C. "Ten Years of Peace Conference History," *Journal of Modern History*, I, 607–29.
BIRDSALL, P. *Versailles Twenty Years After.* New York, 1941.
BUEHRIG, E. H. *Woodraw Wilson and the Balance of Power.* Bloomington, 1955.
CATROUX, GEORGES. *Deux Missions en Moyen-Orient.* Paris [1958].
CHOWDHURI, R. N. *International Mandates and Trusteeship Systems.* The Hague, 1955.
CROLLO, G. *"La Siria e la competizione anglo-francese,"* *Oriente Moderno*, I, 513–23, 577–91.
CUMMINGS, H. H. *Franco-British Rivalry in the Post-war Near-East.* New York, 1938.
DeNovo, JOHN A. *American Interests and Policies in the Middle East, 1900–1939.* Minneapolis [1963].
FLEMING, D. F. *The United States and World Organization.* New York, 1938.
GAUVAIN, A. "Five Years of French Policy in the Near East," *Foreign Affairs*, III, 277–92.
GELFAND, LAWRENCE E. *The Inquiry.* New Haven, 1963.
GIANNINI, A. "La questione Orientale alla Conferenza della Pace," *Oriente Moderno*, I, *passim.*
HALL, H. D. *Mandates, Dependencies, and Trusteeships.* Washington, D. C., 1948.
HOURANI, G. F. "Syria under the French Mandate," *The Contemporary Review*, CXLVIII, 591–98.
HOWARD, H. N. *The Partition of Turkey, 1913–1923.* Oklahoma, 1931.
———. *The King-Crane Commission.* Beirut, 1963.
———. "The United States and the Problem of the Turkish Straits," *The Middle East Journal*, I, 59–72.
———. "The King-Crane Commission, an American Experiment in Peacemaking," *The Moslem World*, XXXII, 122–40.
HUSRI, SATI AL. *Yawm Maisalun.* Beirut, 1947.
KENNAN, G. F. *American Diplomacy, 1900–1950.* Chicago, 1951.
KEYNES, J. M. *The Economic Consequences of the Peace.* New York, 1920.
LIDDEL-HART, B. H. *T. E. Lawrence.* London, 1934.
LINK, ARTHUR S. *Wilson the Diplomatist*, Baltimore, 1957.
LIPPMANN, W. *United States Foreign Policy, Shield of the Republic.* Boston, 1943.
LOGAN, R. W. *The Senate and the Versailles Mandate System.* Washington, 1945.
LONGRIGG, S. H. *Oil in the Middle East.* London, 1954.
MANUEL, F. E. *The Realities of American Palestine Relations.* Washington, 1949.
MILLER, D. H. "Origins of the Mandate System," *Foreign Affairs*, VI, 272–89.
NICHOLSON, HAROLD. *Curzon, the Last Phase, 1919–1925.* New York, 1939.
NOTTER, H. *The Foreign Policy of Woodrow Wilson.* Baltimore, 1937.
OLBERG, P. "France in Syria," *The Contemporary Review*, CLI, 305–12.
POLYZOIDES, A. Th., "Syria's Revolt against France," *Current History*, XVI, 580–83.
RAIHANI, AMIN AL. *Faisal al-Awwal.* Beirut, 1934.
RONALDSHAY, EARL OF. *The Life of Lord Curzon.* London [1928].
SCOTT, J. B. *President Wilson's Foreign Policy.* New York, 1918.
SEYMOUR, C. "Woodrow Wilson in Perspective," *Foreign Affairs*, XXXIV, 175–86.

SHWADRAN, B. *The Middle East, Oil, and the Great Powers.* New York, 1955.

SMUTS, J. C. (the elder). "Woodrow Wilson's Place in History," *Current History*, XIV, 45–48.

SMUTS, J. C. (the younger). *Jan Christian Smuts.* London, 1952.

STEIN, LEONARD. *The Balfour Declaration.* London, 1961.

TOYNBEE, A. J. *The Western Question in Greece and Turkey.* London, 1923.

———. "Great Britain and France in the East," *The Contemporary Review*, CXXI, 23–31.

———. "The Denouement in the Near East," *The Contemporary Review*, CXXII, 409–18.

———. "Angora and the British Empire in the East," *The Contemporary Review*, CXXIII, 681–91.

———. "Islam and the League of Nations," *The Muslim World*, XVII, 116–22.

WAHBAH, HAFIZ. *Jazirat al-Arab fi 'l-Qarn al-Ishrin.* Cairo, 1935.

WOODHOUSE, H. "American Oil Claims in Turkey," *Current History*, XV, 953–59.

WRIGHT, Q. *Mandates under the League of Nations.* Chicago, 1930.

———. "Syrian Grievances against French Rule," *Current History*, XXIII, 687–93.

YALE, W. "Ambassador Henry Morgenthau's Special Mission of 1917," *World Politics*, I, 308–20.

ZEINE, ZEINE N. *The Struggle for Arab Independence: Western Diplomacy and the Rise and Fall of Faisal's Kingdom in Syria.* Beirut, 1960.

INDEX

A

Aidin: Lloyd George and Greek sovereignty, 168; Greek occupation of, 180

Aleppo: Kurdish attack threatened, 25n; conditions in, 252–53

Allenby, Gen. Lord Edmund: on Syrian question, 136–37; on Interallied Commission to Syria, 147; suggested as Supreme Commander in Anatolia, 172; on Arab reaction to French occupation of Syria, 218; Faisal favors as Supreme Commander, 222

Allied Powers: war on Turkey, 26–27; and Ottoman Empire, 29; peace terms of, 30, 31; on U.S. participation in war, 31; missions to U.S., 36; on U.S. declarations of war on Turkey and Bulgaria, 40–42; and U.S. on war aims, 49–51, 59–62; U.S. and Allied policy toward Turkey, 49–85; U.S. public opinion on war aims of, 50, 51; missions to Washington, 51–58; U.S. on peace terms, 51–58; and separate peace with Turkey, 51, 67–68n, 82–85, 84; and U.S. on secret treaties, 52–78 *passim*; conference on Balkan problems, 58–61, 62; conference on conduct of war, 67–71; response to German overtures, 78–80; the landings in Smyrna, 160–89; taxes in Turkey, 324–25; renewal of hostilities with Turkey, 380, 382; propose Greek-Turkish armistice terms, 384–85. *See also* Peace Conference; Peace terms; Lausanne Conference; Mandate system

Anatolia: Greek claims and Allied attitude, 126–27; U.S. mandate for recommended, 154; and Italian share in mandates, 162–63; Italian military movements in, 165; French mandate for, 167; Sultan in, 167; U.S. mandate in, 168, 174, 177, 179, 185, 186, 187–88, 191, 195; extent of Allied influence, 170–71; development of Nationalist movement in, 170–71, 174–78, 185–89, 275, 349–75 *passim*; conditions in, 171–72, 174–75, 176–78, 180, 182–83; Allied conflicts in, 171, 172; Sultan attempts to end strife in, 171–72; Greek occupation of, 173–85; Turkish opposition to Greek occupation, 174–76; elections in, 177–78, 185–86; Greek atrocities and protests, 179–82; Commission of Inquiry, 181–82; rebellion against Turkey in, 182–83; Turkish government unable to control, 183–84, 275; Italian-Greek efforts to reach agreement on, 198, 199, 200; U.S. interest in, 353–57; Turkish-Greek hostilities in, 350–57

Anglo-French Declaration, *Nov. 7, 1918*: promises Arab independence, 111; mentioned, 125

Angora, Turkey: Nationalist government established at, 285, 323

Annexation of conquered territory: Gen. Jan Smuts on, 92–93; Wilson's views on, 93–94; League of Nations as alternative to, 95; claims of British Dominions, 96, 97; claims of France, 97–98, 99

Arabs: plans to overthrow Turkish rule, 24–25n, 24; and the British, 110–11; effect of Fourteen Points on, 111–12n; position on Syria, 117; and Wilsonian principles, 123–25; and Sykes-Picot agreement, 142, 217, 220–21; and French occupation of Syria, 218; oppose French, 245; action against French and British in Syria, 245–46;

421

110–11; instructs Faisal regarding Peace Conference, 117–18n

I

Imbrie, Robert W.: as U.S. delegate to Angora, 338

Indian Muslims: appeal to Council of Four regarding Turkey, 166–67; effect on decision to retain Sultan in Constantinople, 273–74

Inquiry: organized for Peace Conference, 71–72; reports of, 72–74; proposals for peace terms 73, 74–75; on Turkey, 74; in determination of U.S. policy, 74

Interallied Commission to Syria: proposed by Wilson, 137; British-French efforts to block dispatch of Commission to Syria, 137–38, 146, 147, 148, 168, 169–70; and Clemenceau, 137, 138; and Wilson, 138; as delaying tactic of Wilson, 140; Arab reaction, 141; and Faisal, 141–42; discussed by British and French experts, 142; and American experts, 143–44; British oppose visit to Mesopotamia, 144; Zionists oppose, 144

Interallied conference on the Balkans, 58–59, 62

Iraq: Faisal regarding, 123; Arab rebellion in, 248, 249; grants concession to Turkish Petroleum Company, 307; Faisal becomes king of, 316–17, 321; Treaty of Alliance with Britain, 321–22; Anglo-American-Iraqi Convention, 321–22. See also Mesopotamia

Iraq Petroleum Company (Turkish Petroleum Company): negotiates Red Line agreement with British, 307–8

Islam, Shaikh-ul-: call to Jihad, 27; protests Greek atrocities in Anatolia, 180–81

Ismet Pasha: and Turkish-American Treaty of Lausanne, 404–5, 406–8, 414

Italy: welcomes U.S. declaration of war against Turkey and Bulgaria, 41; U.S. willingness to send troops to, 43n; enters war under terms of Treaty of London, 52, 55, 56, 112–13; and St.

Jean de Maurienne agreement, 113, 169; claims to Fiume and Dalmatia, 160–65, 163; Lloyd George and Clemenceau on claims of, 161, 162–63, 164; sends warships to Fiume and Smyrna, 165; returns to Peace Conference, 166; and participation in Turkish mandates, 166, 167; military movements in Anatolia, 166, 169; desires coal and oil concessions in Heraklia and Van, 196; seeks agreement with Greece on occupation of Anatolia, 198, 199, 200; relations with Turkish Nationalists, 353–54; and Paris conference on Near East affairs, 360–61, 364–65; as mediator in Greek-Turkish war, 369; favors conference to settle Turkish questions, 379, 383–84. See also Orlando, Vittorio; Sonnino, Sidney

Izzet Pasha: on Turkish-Greek hostilities, 355–56

J

Japan: question of annexation of former German colonies, 196

Jewish National Home: and Balfour Declaration, 46; Zionists claims to, 128–30; and Commission of Inquiry to Syria, 144; Balfour on, 217; resolution in U.S. Congress supporting, 265; British position on, 316, 319. See also Balfour Declaration; Palestine; Zionists

K

Karabekir, Kazim: organizes Turkish Nationalists, 175; calls Turkish Nationalist Congress at Erzurum, 176; and Bolshevik invasions of Armenia, 289

King-Crane Commission: organization, 145–46; Faisal's attempts to influence, 150–52; returns to Paris, 153; investigations and reports, 153–54; publication of report delayed by Wilson, 154; confidential appendix to report, 154; Faisal's telegrams to Wilson regarding, 155

M

THE JOHNS HOPKINS UNIVERSITY
STUDIES IN
HISTORICAL AND POLITICAL SCIENCE

✶ ✶ ✶

EIGHTY–SECOND SERIES (1964)

1. A Rural Society in Medieval France: The Gâtine of Poitou in the Eleventh and Twelfth Centuries

   BY GEORGE T. BEECH

2. United States Policy and the Partition of Turkey, 1914–1924

   BY LAURENCE EVANS

✶ ✶ ✶

THE JOHNS HOPKINS PRESS
BALTIMORE

THE JOHNS HOPKINS UNIVERSITY STUDIES IN HISTORICAL AND POLITICAL SCIENCE

A subscription for the regular annual series is $8.00. Single numbers may be purchased at special prices. A complete list of the series follows. All paperbound unless otherwise indicated.

vii